A History of the Liberal Party
in the Twentieth Century

A History of the Liberal Party in the Twentieth Century

DAVID DUTTON

With a Preface by
The Rt Hon. Charles Kennedy, MP

palgrave
macmillan

First published 2004 by
PALGRAVE MACMILLAN
Houndmills, Basingstoke, Hampshire RG21 6XS and
175 Fifth Avenue, New York, N.Y. 10010
Companies and representatives throughout the world

PALGRAVE MACMILLAN is the global academic imprint of the Palgrave
Macmillan division of St. Martin's Press, LLC and of Palgrave Macmillan
Ltd. Macmillan® is a registered trademark
in the United States, United Kingdom and other countries.
Palgrave is a registered trademark in the European Union
and other countries.

ISBN 0–333–74655–4 hardback
ISBN 0–333–74656–2 paperback

This book is printed on paper suitable for recycling and made from fully
managed and sustained forest sources.

A catalogue record for this book is available from the
British Library.

Library of Congress Cataloging-in-Publication Data
Dutton, David, 1950–
    A history of the Liberal Party in the twentieth century/David Dutton.
        p. cm.
    Includes bibliographical references and index.
    ISBN 0-333-74655-4 (cloth) – ISBN 0-333-74656-2 (pbk.)
        1. Liberal Party (Great Britain)—History. 2. Liberalism—Great
Britain-History. 3. Great Britain—Politics and government. I. Title
JN1129.L45D88 2004
324.24106'09'04—dc22
                                                            2004046712

10   9   8   7   6   5   4   3   2   1
13   12   11   10   09   08   07   06   05   04

Printed in China

In memory of Paul Hair,
friend and mentor

CONTENTS

Acknowledgements

Though this book makes use of a considerable amount of original archival material, it inevitably owes much to the work of other scholars. Some indication of my debt is given in the notes and the Guide to Further Reading. I also owe a debt of gratitude for the help I have received from the staff of the libraries and archives in which I have worked.

In addition, I should like to thank Jeremy Black for inviting me to write the book; Terka Acton and Sonya Barker at Palgrave for their help and support; the Rt Hon. Charles Kennedy, MP for kindly writing the preface; the Rt Hon. Lord Renton for sharing with me his fascinating memories of the National Liberal Party; the Rt Hon. Lord Owen for discussing with me the troubled history of the Alliance; Philip Bell, Duncan Brack, Mark Egan and Ralph White for subjecting my first draft to critical but sympathetic inspection and thereby saving me from numerous blunders; and Alison Bagnall, Val Fry, Gaynor Johnson, Lucy Mills, Paula Mills, Pauline Oliver and Peggy Rider for invaluable help in producing a final typescript. None of the above, of course, bears any responsibility for remaining errors of commission and omission.

For permission to reproduce material in their possession or in which they hold the copyright I am pleased to thank the Rt Hon. Lord Ashdown, the Earl Baldwin of Bewdley, Mrs Joanna Clement-Davies, the Flintshire Record Office, the Lord Gainford, Sir William Gladstone, Mrs S. G. Graham, Captain J. Headlam and the Durham County Record Office, Sir Charles Hobhouse, the Liverpool Record Office, Miss Ishbel Lockhead, Mr Alexander Murray, the Orion Publishing Group, the Rt Hon. Lord Owen, the Rt Hon. Lord Rodgers of Quarry Bank, Mr Michael Rowntree, Mr John Simon, Mr Matthew Simon, Mr Mike Thomas, the Viscount

Thurso, MP, the trustees of the Trevelyan Family Estate and the Rt Hon. Baroness Williams of Crosby. Permission is also gratefully acknowledged to reproduce material which first appeared in the following articles: 'On the Brink of Oblivion: The Post-War Crisis of British Liberalism', *Canadian Journal of History* 27, 3 (1992), pp. 425–50; '1932: A Neglected Date in the History of the Decline of the British Liberal Party', *Twentieth Century British History* 14, 1 (2003), pp. 43–60, by permission of Oxford University Press. Every effort has been made to trace all copyright-holders, but if any have been inadvertently overlooked the publishers will be pleased to make the necessary arrangement at the first opportunity.

David Dutton
Liverpool, 2004

PREFACE

The Rt Hon. Charles Kennedy, MP,
Leader of the Liberal Democrats

As David Dutton suggests in his introduction to this book, it may surprise some that the story of a party that has not formed a government alone since 1915 has attracted so much academic attention. Part of the explanation, of course, is that the decline of the Liberal party after the First World War sheds so much light on the state of the rest of politics. In seeking to understand why the Labour and Conservative parties came to exert such a stranglehold on British politics for decades, Liberal history is illuminating indeed.

But this book is not just a story of decline. It is also a story of survival, and then of revival. There were chances aplenty for the Liberal party to die. Yet it recovered from the Lloyd George – Asquith feud, so that by 1929 it was once again at the forefront of radical ideas in British politics. It also survived the dark days of the 1950s, when the prospect of being swallowed up by the Conservatives was faced and not resisted in many parts of the country.

The party's survival, and then its revival under the inspired leadership of Jo Grimond, stemmed from the simple fact that there were always enough people who were Liberals. They were not Conservatives, nor Socialists, but Liberals, and no other party offered them Liberalism – a basic commitment to the freedom of the individual, based on a recognition of the importance of social justice in protecting and promoting that freedom, echoing the words of Hobhouse that 'the struggle for liberty . . . is the struggle for equality'.

So, as much as anything else the history of the twentieth-century Liberal party is about the idea of Liberalism itself, and this book plays an important part in documenting that. The challenge for Liberal Democrats now is to ensure that the Liberal flame continues to burn, and that it burns steadily brighter. David Dutton cites Lady Violet Bonham Carter, who said that 'The only purpose of politics is the expression of one's deepest convictions – and their translation into facts.' Any historian who reminds us of that has performed an invaluable task.

INTRODUCTION

The twentieth-century Liberal party has already attracted a wealth of historical attention. Granted that the last purely Liberal government came to an end as long ago as 1915, that attraction might fairly be deemed excessive. In the century as a whole, the Liberals cannot claim anything better than a poor third place in terms of electoral success, significantly behind their Conservative and Labour rivals. Yet the lack of Liberal success at the polls has proved no barrier to continuing historical curiosity. Indeed, it is the party's decline rather than its brief exercise of power that has acted as a magnet to academic investigation.

It cannot be denied that, for a period of at least forty years or, according to some interpretations, considerably longer, the Liberal party was in a process of remorseless and seemingly irreversible decay. This story has all the ingredients of a good whodunnit – a gruesome death, several plausible suspects, a compelling array of character parts, and, in all probability, a generous sprinkling of red herrings. The subject has attracted some of the best and most persuasive of modern British historians. Yet the debate has sometimes been conducted with a predictability of argument and an absolutism of analysis which have not helped historical understanding. 'Labour' historians have preached the inevitability of their party's rise at Liberalism's expense, reluctant to believe that chance and fortune could play any part in the outcome of events. Their 'Liberal' counterparts have sometimes appeared too keen to argue that Liberal decline need never have happened, turning a blind eye to long-term changes in politics and society that were unlikely to help their party's cause. After all, the decline of the British Liberal party was no isolated happening, but was matched by a contemporaneous experience in many other European countries, strong – perhaps compelling – evidence of the existence of underlying forces at work. In the context of European democracy as a whole, the twentieth century saw continental Liberal parties failing to compete successfully with the rival traditions of Social and Christian Democracy. At the same time, both sides in the debate over Liberal decline have tended to claim a monopoly of wisdom, unwilling to concede any strengths in their opponent's case. Yet, whatever the precise truth, it seems improbable that any monocausal explanation will suffice. The notion that Liberalism was already 'doomed' by 1914 is clearly incompatible with the suggestion that it was a perfectly healthy organism until ruined by the impact of total war. Yet it is entirely possible for a political party, like any other organisation, to contain elements of both strength and weakness at the same moment, with the developing balance between the two at the mercy of the unfolding and unpredictable pattern of historical events.

Much of the diversity of this debate is explained by a reluctance to define precisely what it is whose decline is being analysed and explored. A political party is, after all, a multi-dimensional entity. If it is Liberalism as a political philosophy which is under scrutiny, then it is right to pay some attention to those Liberals whose intellectual outlook had difficulty in encompassing the requirements of a state whose government demanded an increasingly collectivist approach. Why, also, were some Liberal intellectuals able to transfer their commitment, apparently without too much difficulty, to the Labour and Conservative causes? Yet Liberalism was always a broad church and some Liberals clearly did adapt their thinking to cope with changing circumstances. It is a striking feature of inter-war British history that the Liberal party still managed to attract impressive and innovative intellectual support long after there was any realistic possibility of the return of a Liberal government. 'If the Liberals met their death during the war', writes Michael Bentley, 'they did not do so at the hands of their thinkers.'[1] Indeed, it is arguably the triumph of the liberal state in our own times, albeit through the medium of Labour and Conservative governments, which justifies the disproportionate attention accorded by historians of the twentieth century to the third party in the political system.

If it is the high politics of the Liberal party – Liberalism at Westminster – which is being examined, then it seems reasonable to accord more importance to the clashes of personality, the accidents of history and the mistakes and miscalculations of a decision-making elite. But the decline of Liberalism in the country, a mass movement made up of activists and voters, may be something subtly different again. At the end of the day, the Liberal party declined, in the sense of diminishing electoral success, because individual Liberal voters decided to change their party allegiance or because the newly enfranchised among them failed to follow the voting patterns of their fathers and grandfathers. Though historians must generalise to make any sense of electoral politics, they should also be humble enough to recognise the individuality of the voter and the impossibility of determining, at this distance in time, precisely why electoral crosses were inscribed in one box on a ballot paper rather than another. In some ways, then, this is an appeal for liberal values – moderation, reasonableness and consideration for the other's point of view – to be applied to the study of the Liberal party's decline. The explanation for what happened is undoubtedly complex; and it may also be more nuanced than has sometimes been allowed.

While the theme of 'decline' figures prominently in this book, it is not allowed to dominate the whole. The passage of time enables the downfall of the Liberal party to be seen in a new perspective. For more than forty years now, the party's fortunes have moved, however tentatively and sometimes uncertainly, in a positive direction. At the time of writing, it stands, in the guise of the Liberal Democrats, reinstated as a significant force in British politics, though the prospect of a Liberal Democrat government remains some distance over the horizon. The very survival of the party, at a time when total extinction appeared its likely fate, and its subsequent substantial recovery offer historical problems equally intriguing as that of its earlier decline. Furthermore, the perspective of the entire twentieth century draws attention to the way in which that century began and ended with evidence of the two left-of-centre parties working in co-operation with one another to the immense disadvantage of the Conservatives and thereby opens up tantalising excursions into the counterfactual realm of 'what might have been' if this co-operation had been maintained during the intervening years. These perspectives, in which the story of 'decline' is given an important but not all-encompassing place in the history of the Liberal party over the past hundred years, dictate the policy of this book to treat the whole century as evenly as possible, irrespective of the party's inherent strength at any particular moment.

'The only purpose of politics', declared Lady Violet Bonham Carter, daughter of the Liberal Prime Minister Herbert Henry Asquith, 'is the expression of one's deepest convictions – and their translation into facts.'[2] Naturally enough, those convictions are likely to predate the establishment of a political party or movement designed to promote and enact them. Thus, in the British context, the philosophy of 'liberalism' has been traced back at least as far as the seventeenth century and the writings of John Locke (1632–1704). Locke claimed that individuals are born equal and free, that legitimate governments can only be created through a process of consent and that, even when they have been created, the individual retains certain fundamental rights, such as freedom of conscience and belief. A 'liberal' political tradition may be discerned, independent of the embryonic political structure of Whigs and Tories that grew up in the late seventeenth and early eighteenth centuries, running through the English Civil War and the Glorious Revolution to a belief in the values which underlay the American and French Revolutions in the later eighteenth century. It was associated with a defence of civil and religious liberties, a steadfast opposition to arbitrary government, the advocacy of a limited state, a belief in the rights of dissenting individuals and a faith in a man's conscience as the most appropriate determinant of his actions. Taking a fundamentally optimistic view of the human condition, the Liberal approach was to preach moderation, reason and restraint, and to abhor extremism and bigotry. The struggle for liberty would enable men to live their lives to the full, maximising the talents with which the Creator had endowed them.

The term 'Liberal' began to be used in the politics of post-Napoleonic Britain and was first officially adopted by a political party in the course of the General Election of 1847. Over the following decade a recognisable Liberal party began to coalesce around a number of groupings of which the Whigs, the Radicals and the Peelite free-trade Tories were the most important. History, in the quest for a precise beginning, has tended to endow a meeting in Willis's Rooms in 1859, when these groups agreed to serve in a government under Lord Palmerston, as the moment when the party formally came into being. By this time, Liberalism had taken on board the theories of economic liberalism propounded by Adam Smith, whose seminal work, *The Wealth of Nations*, had been published in 1776. Liberalism thus became synonymous with the doctrines of free trade and laissez-faire, and tended to attract support from the new industrial and commercial interests in opposition to the Tory landowners. Free trade, by facilitating economic relations between states, would help foster harmonious diplomatic relations and build an international community in which war would be excluded as an inherently unreasonable activity. Laissez-faire implied a more active role for the state than has sometimes been implied, not least because only the rule of law could prevent liberty degenerating into licence. Indeed, it was the function of the state to intervene to protect the free market, enforce competition and remove barriers. Looking back from the vantage point of the 1930s, the historian and Liberal intellectual, Ramsay Muir, insisted:

> It is often said that the Liberal party has stood for the policy of laissez-faire, or leaving things alone. This was never true; on the contrary the intervention of the modern State in industrial questions began with the first Liberal Government in 1832, and most of the functions which the State has assumed in this field have been due to Liberal legislation. There have always been a few Liberals who have been bitterly critical of any enlargement of the functions of the State. But there have always been others, more numerous, who were prepared for great enlargements.[3]

Under W. E. Gladstone, who led the party for most of the period between 1868 and 1894, Liberalism reached its zenith as a political movement. The party championed the causes of free trade, sound finance, religious toleration and a pacific foreign policy. Gladstone's first two governments of 1868–74 and 1880–85 boasted substantial records of progressive reform. Yet even at this stage historians have discerned some worrying features, prompting some to suggest that, at the very time of its political pre-eminence, the party already contained the seeds of later decay. More helpfully, it may be argued that the Liberal party never displayed all the characteristics deemed to be necessary for success in the modern era. In particular, as Sir William Harcourt put it in 1891, 'like the Kingdom of Heaven, the Liberal party is a house of many mansions'.[4] Activists were attracted into Liberalism, not necessarily because they agreed with all its ideas, but in order to promote, and hopefully achieve, specific objectives such as temperance, franchise extension or church disestablishment. As a result, the party developed into 'a composite of [sometimes] mutually exclusive pressure groups',[5] prone to internal dissension and schism, and never attained any genuine internal coherence. Thus 'the danger of division was always inherent in Liberal politics by the very nature of the party'.[6] In a revealing diary entry of May 1885, Gladstone recorded:

> Very fair cabinet today – only three resignations. Members of the cabinet who within the last month have, on one ground or other, appeared to consider resignation: Lord Chancellor, Lord Northbrook Lord Hartington, Mr Chamberlain, Sir Charles Dilke, Mr Lefevre, Lord Spencer, Sir William Harcourt, Chancellor of the Exchequer. A majority.[7]

Notwithstanding the tendency of Liberal factions to go their own way, it was Gladstone's particular achievement to maintain an essential party unity by focusing Liberal attention on a succession of single great issues which needed to be tackled before further progress could be made on the often-disputed agenda of reform. Only in elevating the cause of Irish Home Rule to this status did his strategy unravel, prompting the split of 1886 with the defection of the Liberal Unionists. Even this development was not entirely negative, since the majority of the defecting Whigs had been unlikely bedfellows of Liberal radicals and now found a more comfortable home in the ranks of Conservatism. But it was also Gladstone's achievement that a party born in the restricted electorate of the mid-nineteenth century had, by the 1880s, become in most parts of the country the principal party of the urban working class, enfranchised for the first time in substantial numbers following the passage of the Second Reform Act of 1867. Many trade unions appeared content to seek their political representation through Liberal channels, leading from the 1870s to the emergence of a group of Lib–Lab working-class MPs, particularly in coal-mining constituencies.

By this time the Liberals had taken on most of the characteristics of a modern political party. These included an important organisational structure operating beyond the confines of the Westminster village. The National Liberal Federation was founded in 1877 as a body independent of the parliamentary party and represented the mass party in the country. From its beginning it sought to influence party policy and, despite efforts, particularly after the split of 1886, to curb its pretensions in this direction, the potential for conflict with the party leadership remained. As late as July 1923 the *Liberal Magazine* described the NLF as an organisation 'through which party opinion may be brought to bear on Members of Parliament'. The structure created in 1877 would remain fundamentally unchanged until 1936 when the party's annual assembly agreed to replace the NLF with a new Liberal Party Organisation.

After the split of 1886 the party remained in opposition for almost two decades, except for three years of unhappy minority government between 1892 and 1895. Gladstone's final retirement in 1894 removed the controlling influence of his masterful personality and allowed the inherent divisions within the party to become ever more apparent. Liberal leaders turned their attention to personal rivalries and, in a mood of bitter recrimination, the party itself degenerated into a period of 'faddism', in which its members seemed concerned only to promote their own, often unrelated, single-issue causes. The danger existed that what had been until recently a successful party of government would become no more than an impotent party of protest. 'The overwhelming sense conveyed by Liberal history after 1895', writes Michael Bentley, 'is one of shrinking horizons and a feeling of involution. What Liberals want to discuss is themselves: their leaders and their limitations, the poverty of their organization, the trouble caused by their own imperialists.'[8] Insiders predicted a further lengthy period on the opposition benches. 'The disease of the Party is deep-seated', warned the Chief Whip. 'Time alone can eradicate it, and Time will take ten good years of its own self to do the job.'[9]   By the end of the decade the evolving crisis in South Africa had opened up new cleavages. After Gladstone's departure, Liberals such as Lord Rosebery demanded a reappraisal of the anti-imperialism with which the party was traditionally, though not always accurately, associated. Dubbing their opponents 'Little Englanders', the Liberal Imperialists insisted that the party must show that it, equally with the Conservatives, was able to champion and administer the great empire which Britain now headed. The outbreak of the Boer War in 1899 inevitably emphasised this latest line of division, with the radical wing of the party blaming the Unionist government for engineering an unnecessary conflict. In the absence of any other viable candidate, Sir Henry Campbell-Bannerman was chosen as leader in the same year. While both sides welcomed the appointment of a man of the centre, the task of holding the warring factions together looked daunting. Indeed, the formation of the Liberal Imperial Council in 1900 and of Rosebery's Liberal League in 1902 seemed to presage a complete split. In all the circumstances, the party's performance in the 1900 'Khaki' General Election in reducing the Unionist government's parliamentary majority was a creditable and surprising one.

Also worrying, though, was the geographical pattern of the party's parliamentary representation. By the end of the nineteenth century Liberalism was looking increasingly like a party of the Celtic fringe, or at least of the non-metropolitan periphery. It remained well represented in Wales, Scotland and the North of

England, where the nonconformist vote was strongest, but it seemed incapable of winning a majority of English seats. In 1895 Liberals were successful in less than a quarter of English constituencies. This did not imply the imminent demise of the British Liberal party, but it did perhaps suggest that a Liberal government at Westminster was not necessarily the natural order of things.

But the factor which, above all others, would determine the party's future prospects was its relationship with the working-class voter, especially in the context of a now irreversibly advancing democracy following a further extension of the franchise in 1884. It was, as Herbert Samuel argued, 'the abiding problem of Liberal statesmanship to raise the enthusiasm of the working class without frightening the middle classes'.[10] By the 1890s there was clear evidence of the beginnings of an institutional separation between the Liberal party and an increasingly organised Labour movement. The Social Democratic Federation had been founded in 1881 and William Morris's Socialist League in 1884, but neither developed into a mass movement. More importantly, the formation of the Independent Labour Party (ILP) in 1893 and the Labour Representation Committee (LRC) in 1900 bore witness to the limitations of Lib–Lab politics as practised hitherto and the partial failure of the Liberal party to contain the forces of Labour radicalism within the existing party structure. In areas such as Manchester, ILP candidates quickly started to make gains at Liberal expense in municipal elections. This is not to suggest that the working class was as a unified entity waiting to be represented by a new political party, but insofar as an organisational separation between the Labour movement and the Liberal party did take place, the potential for competition for the working-class vote was bound to increase.

Yet in most instances the working man was not being pulled away from Liberalism by the attractions of a new creed. Ideology was much less important in the formation of a new political party than the desire of working men to secure representation in parliament by members of their own class. Despite the existence of the group of Lib–Lab MPs, in most working-class constituencies the

Liberal candidate was not a working man. The typical Liberal MP of this era was a middle-aged and middle-class businessman or lawyer with a public school or university education. Despite encouragement from the party leadership, most local Liberal Associations proved extremely reluctant to adopt working-class candidates, and it was this lack of response, rather than any conversion to 'socialism', however defined, which drove working men towards independent political action to further their own sectional interests. By contrast, where Liberals were accommodating, the demand for separate Labour representation was reduced. The experience of some of the key figures of the early Labour movement is instructive. Keir Hardie, Arthur Henderson and Ramsay MacDonald all sought adoption as Liberal candidates before deciding that only a new political party could secure their goals. Turned down for the Liberal candidature at Dover, MacDonald was driven to 'the conclusion that there is no sympathy at headquarters with candidates who respond to Labour desires'. His 'greatest regret is that I am now driven to the conclusion of my friends of the ILP. I have stuck to the opinion that Liberalism was a sufficient gospel for the above politicians until but a few days ago.'[11] Yet, 'had MacDonald been able to say "I have a thousand pounds at my back and I am not in favour of the entire labour programme", the rascals would have gone for him. His enemies admit even now that he is far and away the best man. But he is tainted with Labour!!'[12] MacDonald joined the ILP in 1894 and stood as its candidate at Southampton the following year.

The Trade Union Congress of 1899 was dominated by complaints about the failure of the working class to secure their objectives through the vehicle of the Liberal party and provided the impetus behind the formation of the LRC the following year. The Taff Vale ruling of the House of Lords in 1902, which seemed to throw into question a trade union's basic right to strike, added greatly to the pressure for independent parliamentary representation, since only through a change in the statute law could this decision be reversed. That said, the LRC was not committed to a different programme from the Liberal party. Indeed, it had no programme. Its task was limited to the election of MPs who would serve the interests of the working man. Historians have identified a considerable degree of overlap between the aims and aspirations of the Liberal and Labour traditions at this time, seeing them as but two wings of the same 'progressive' movement. Furthermore, many LRC activists did not wish to see the LRC develop into a separate party. Their aspiration was for a pressure group, voting together on labour issues, but generally supporting the Liberal party. On the other hand, there were those, particularly in the ILP, who did want an independent party ready to fight the Liberals as vigorously as it would the Conservatives. When the Liberal, Herbert Samuel, stood as the 'Liberal and Labour Candidate' at a by-election in Cleveland in 1902, a leading figure on the ILP's national administrative council, J Bruce Glasier, was appalled:

> I cordially hope Samuel will be defeated. His insolence in using the title 'Labour' candidate proves the unscrupulous character of the fellow. My idea is that we should issue a manifesto and get it into the press, reciting what was done by the Liberals to prevent a genuine Labour man being adopted and strongly repudiating alike the Imperialism and pseudo Labour pretensions of Samuel.[13]

So while, as the new century opened, the working-class vote had in no sense been lost by the Liberal party, there were certainly those for whom this development had become a key objective.

The denigration of Samuel's efforts to bridge the gap between Liberalism and the Labour movement is striking, for Samuel was among the Liberal thinkers of this period who were engaged in what many historians have judged to be the most promising attempt to prepare the party to be a viable player in the electoral politics of the modern era. Although in the 1890s Liberals at Westminster seemed determined to pull their party apart, an important rethinking of Liberal ideology was also taking place. An impressive group of academics and journalists, influenced by the Oxford philosopher T. H. Green, had taken on the task of reinterpreting Liberalism for a new age. The starting point of the so-called 'New Liberals' was their belief that until now the central concept of 'liberty' had been too narrowly defined, being largely restricted to legal, political and religious issues. Now, not least because so many of the original objectives in these areas had been achieved – 'the old Liberalism had done its work'[14] – the quest for liberty should be extended to the social and economic sphere. The material condition of much of the population acted, in practice, as a restraint upon the liberty of the individual. It was therefore the duty of the state – a state which Liberals had themselves reformed and in which they could now place greater confidence – to create the conditions which would permit each individual to develop his talents to the full. This implied the need for social reform carried out by a much more interventionist state than Liberals had envisaged hitherto. Because of the cost involved, it also suggested a new attitude towards taxation and the use of the government's annual budget as an instrument of redistributive justice. As was argued in the first issue of the *Progressive Review*, published in October 1896, 'if Liberals still cleave to their honourable name they must be willing and desirous to assign a new meaning to liberty; it must no longer signify the absence of restraint, but the presence of opportunity'.[15]

While most of this reappraisal was carried out away from the coalface of party political conflict, it nonetheless had clear implications for the position of Liberalism *vis-à-vis* the evolving Labour movement. For Samuel the purpose of the *Progressive Review* was to prevent a Lib–Lab split which could only work to the advantage of the Conservatives and 'to forestall such a disruption of the progressive forces in British politics'.[16] For the journalist and academic, L. T. Hobhouse, 'the breach of principle' between Liberalism and Socialism was 'much smaller than might appear on the surface'.[17] Similarly, when in 1896 C. P. Scott of the *Manchester Guardian*, a leading organ of the new ideas, invited Hobhouse to join the newspaper, he stressed that

> the relations of Liberalism and Labour must govern the future of politics, and that the problem was to find the lines on which Liberals could be brought to see that the old tradition must be

expanded to yield a fuller measure of social justice, a more real equality, an industrial as well as a political liberty.[18]

New Liberals moved easily towards the concept of an interdependent society in which individual citizens would freely contribute to the general good of the organic whole. This implied co-operation rather than confrontation between classes and was particularly important within a climate of mounting industrial militancy at the end of the nineteenth century. It suggested that the Liberal party should seek to bring the forces of capital and labour together, to settle industrial disputes harmoniously in the interests of society as a whole. Liberals therefore needed to counteract the arguments of those who sought to convince the working classes that their interests were fundamentally incompatible with those of the classes above them, whose unfailing inclination was to exploit the working man for their own selfish financial advantage. The more, therefore, the members of the British working class developed a sense of their own distinct and corporate identity, the less purchase the ideas of the New Liberalism were likely to enjoy. But New Liberals themselves ran some risk that their own plans for social reform based on redistributive taxation would create social tensions and divisions rather than the unity and harmony which they proclaimed. While the New Liberalism, therefore, offered tantalising possibilities for the regeneration of the Liberal party at the start of the twentieth century, it by no means represented a straight and uncomplicated path to political salvation. Furthermore, as the next chapter will consider, there was also the question of how far the work of writers and publicists would succeed in permeating the thinking and then determining the conduct of those who carried the Liberal standard in local and national politics.

1

STRANGE DEATH OR EDWARDIAN SUMMER, 1902–1916

The period between the end of the Boer War in 1902 and the General Election of January 1906 saw a transformation in the fortunes of the Liberal party. As a general rule it is governments which lose elections rather than oppositions which win them, but on this occasion the actions of the Unionists not only weakened them but also contributed directly to the strengthening of the Liberals by providing the latter with that factor which they had patently lacked, at least since the retirement of Gladstone – unity. The 1902 Education Act, with its marked bias towards Anglican schools, rode roughshod over the sensibilities of nonconformist opinion and greatly assisted the process of Liberal reunification. The Licensing Act of 1904, an apparent sop to the Unionists' supporters in the brewing trade, had very much the same effect. Organised Labour was alienated by the government's failure to introduce legislation to reverse the Taff Vale judgement of 1902 and by the scandal surrounding the exploitation of Chinese workers in the mines of the South African Rand. Even more important was Joseph Chamberlain's celebrated speech in Birmingham on 15 May 1903, in which the Colonial Secretary called for the ending of the prevailing system of free trade and the substitution of a regime of imperial preference. Chamberlain's initiative started a debate which would dominate the last two and a half years of Balfour's government, in the process doing damage to the Unionist cause. Divided now between tariff reformers, free traders and Balfourite retaliationists, who would only impose tariffs in response to comparable action by foreign states, the government never again possessed the internal unity and cohesion necessary for an effective administration. Unionism was starkly revealed as an uneasy coalition of forces whose unity was overly dependent upon the single issue of Ireland and opposition to Home Rule. But Chamberlain's move also exercised a decisive influence over the Liberal party, by calling into question the sacred creed of free trade, one of the few issues upon which Liberals were fully united. Chamberlain was unequivocal about the advantages which he believed the introduction of tariff reform would bring about: 'You have an opportunity,' he told his Unionist supporters, 'you will never have it again.'[1] But his words might just as well have been directed to the Liberal opposition. Campbell-Bannerman commented: 'This reckless – criminal – escapade of Joe's is the great event of our time. It is playing old Harry with all party relations . . . All the old war-horses about me . . . are snorting with excitement. We are in for a great time.'[2]

The change in the political climate was soon apparent. Public opinion had begun to move strongly against the Unionists by 1904. Seven seats were lost in by-elections that year and a further seven in 1905. As early as October 1904 Henry Lucy noted 'a rare consensus of opinion' that the next general election would result in a victory for the Liberal party.[3] Seldom in British electoral history can a governing party have been more pessimistic about its prospects at a forthcoming poll. St John Brodrick, the Secretary of State for India, feared that 'we shall get hideously beaten', while Chamberlain himself privately predicted a combined Liberal–Irish majority in the order of 120 seats.[4] Finally, with his government visibly breaking up around him, Balfour resigned on 4 December 1905 and the King invited Campbell-Bannerman to form a minority Liberal administration. This task was successfully accomplished, in itself no small achievement as the new Prime Minister had to overcome an attempt by three leading Liberal Imperialists to determine by themselves some of the key appointments to the cabinet. Asquith, Grey and Haldane had earlier concluded the so-called Relugas Compact by which they had agreed not to serve under Campbell-Bannerman unless the latter agreed to go to the

House of Lords, leaving Asquith as Leader of the Commons and Chancellor of the Exchequer. In addition, Grey was to be Foreign Secretary and Haldane Lord Chancellor. Campbell-Bannerman stood his ground and formed a cabinet on his own terms which left him in the Commons and firmly in control of the situation. It was an important moment, revealing that the new Prime Minister was made of sterner stuff than many of his colleagues believed. Then, on 16 December, Campbell-Bannerman announced the dissolution of parliament for an election to be held in January. Though Chamberlain's policies had never become official Unionist policy, everyone recognised that the election would amount to a national referendum on the competing merits of tariff reform and free trade.

Given the seminal importance, particularly in terms of welfare legislation, of the Liberal government which would be endorsed by this General Election, it is necessary to determine the basis upon which it was elected. The Liberal party's campaign focused above all else on the defence of free trade. Ninety-eight per cent of Liberal candidates included this issue in their election addresses. Liberals argued that, although Chamberlain's proposals might assist a few specialist producers, they would in general damage the economy and in particular lead to an increase in the price of food. To this extent the party waged an essentially reactive campaign. Free trade was 'the great umbrella; fighting negatively, the Liberals got every disaffected element underneath it'.[5] Much of the Liberal campaign looked back to the nineteenth century, rather than forward into the twentieth, with Campbell-Bannerman standing for 'a policy covered by the oldest and best of political watchwords, "Peace, Retrenchment and Reform" '.[6] But it was also striking that more than two-thirds of Liberal candidates included social reform among their priorities. As the historian of the election notes, 'although the need to repeal or amend the Education and Licensing Acts of 1902 and 1904 came first in many Liberal minds, pledges made to other social reforms amounted to a recognisable and extensive commitment'.[7] Poor-law reform and pensions were particularly prominent. Quite how such reforms might be financed was, however, another matter.

The fact that Campbell-Bannerman also promised a massive reduction in public expenditure did not suggest that the new government had thought through a clear programme, let alone costed it.

The outcome of the election exceeded all Liberal expectations. The party's strength in the new House of Commons stood at 400 MPs, while the Unionists were reduced to just 157. It was the biggest anti-Conservative majority for more than eighty years and very few areas of the kingdom could now be described as Unionist strongholds. The Liberal tally included 224 gains and just eight losses, giving the party a majority of 130 over all other parties combined. In practice, because the Labour contingent of 30 MPs and the 83 Irish Nationalists were hardly likely to vote with the Unionists, the government's effective majority over the opposition stood at an impregnable 356 seats. Surveying the picture in Lancashire, where the Liberals had done particularly well, the *Manchester Guardian* only slightly exaggerated what had happened:

> A candidate had only to be a Free-trader to get in, whether he was known or unknown, semi-Unionist or thorough Home Ruler, Protestant or Catholic, entertaining or dull. He had only to be a Protectionist to lose all chance of getting in, though he spoke with the tongues of men and of angels, though he was a good employer to many electors, or had led the House of Commons, or fought in the Crimea.[8]

Yet the dimensions of the Liberal triumph must be subjected to closer analysis. The sheer scale of the victory in terms of Commons seats, way beyond what the party had achieved in its Gladstonian heyday, has only added to the mystery of what now followed. Within two decades of this unprecedented triumph, Liberalism had been confined to the sidelines of British politics. But it is clear that the electoral system, which in future years would consistently work to the party's disadvantage, had exaggerated the Liberals' performance in 1906. In terms of the popular vote, the gap between the two leading parties remained relatively narrow: 49.5 per cent for the Liberals against 43 per cent for the Unionists. On a simple system of proportional representation the Liberals would have secured 285 seats and the Unionists 236. Put another way, it took almost two and a half times as many votes to return a Unionist to Westminster as it did a Liberal. The actual margin of the Liberal victory reflected the fact that Liberal votes had been distributed to the party's greatest advantage, with a marked swing in those constituencies where Unionist seats could be captured. Against this background it becomes easier to see some merit in Alan Sykes's judgement that 'The 1906 success was not the continuation of Victorian supremacy but the aberration from the emerging pattern of Liberal weakness, caused primarily by the renewal of Conservative divisions and their adoption of deeply unpopular policies which reignited old Liberal passions for one last time.'[9]

For all that, the Liberal party had, statistically at least, secured a stunning triumph. Most of this book chronicles the party's (generally forlorn) attempts to secure political power. But in 1906 the Liberal government held the reality of power in its hands. The question now was the use to which that power would be put. It was by any criterion an able administration. Campbell-Bannerman could deploy the talents of three future Prime Ministers, Asquith, Lloyd George and Churchill, as well as those of such accomplished political practitioners as Edward Grey, R. B. Haldane and John Morley. By its end in 1915, the government could look back upon a distinguished legislative record, the main components of which would gain in lustre as the twentieth century progressed. But ultimate achievement should not be confused with original intent. 'With its connotations of social justice, state intervention and alliance with Labour,' writes Peter Clarke, '[progressivism] aptly describes the basis of Liberal policy after 1906.'[10] This is surely a misreading of the evidence. The government arrived in office without having worked out a clear or defined programme of legislation which it wished to enact. Its members had been more successful over the preceding three years in identifying what they opposed than in delineating what it was that they stood for. The government's first burst of legislative energy thus gave a misleading impression. The Trades Disputes Act of 1906 overturned the Taff Vale judgement and restored to trade unions those legal immunities in relation to strike action which they had presumed they enjoyed prior to the ruling of the House of Lords. Significantly, the government in this instance dropped its own more cautious bill and accepted an alternative drawn up by the parliamentary Labour party. A new Workmen's Compensation Act, a School Meals Act, based upon a private member's bill introduced by a Labour MP, and a Medical Inspection Act quickly followed.

All of this gave a somewhat exaggerated view of the closeness of the Liberal–Labour alliance and of the extent to which the progressive spirit had permeated government thinking. In the last days of the Unionist government, Lord Crewe had warned Campbell-Bannerman that 'more than ever before the Liberal party was . . . [on trial] as an engine for securing social reforms'.[11] But the Prime Minister's attitude and that of most of his leading ministers was more cautious. They recognised that measures to improve the condition of the working classes might well serve to alienate middle-class support which the Liberals could ill afford to lose. Campbell-Bannerman was therefore resolved to strike a balance, and placed the unity of his party before dynamic policies of reform. 'If we have two sops for Labour', he told Asquith, 'we ought to have some other Bills of general interest to balance them.'[12] It was these 'other Bills', and in particular Education and Licensing measures to satisfy the traditional Liberal noncon-formist vote, that were at the forefront of the government's prior-ities. The other key measure of its first year in office, a bill designed to end the anomaly of 'plural voting', also seemed to hark back to an earlier, albeit unfinished, agenda of constitutional reform.

There was, then, a certain 'confusion of aims' in the govern-ment's strategy.[13] But this was compounded by a seemingly intractable constitutional obstacle which had confronted earlier Liberal governments, the obstructive powers of the Unionist-dominated House of Lords. In the immediate wake of electoral defeat in January 1906, the Unionist leader, Arthur Balfour,

conscious of his party's continuing strength in the upper chamber, had made the cavalier statement that his party 'should still
control, whether in power or opposition, the destinies of this
great Empire'. In practice, the Unionist leadership behaved somewhat more circumspectly than these words might have implied,
weighing up the likely popular reaction to each individual piece
of proposed legislation before deciding what to do. As a result,
while the Liberals' Education and Plural Voting Bills were
wrecked, the Trades Disputes Act was allowed to pass on to the
statute book with little resistance. In June 1907 Campbell-
Bannerman moved a resolution that the Lords' powers to reject or
amend bills coming up from the Commons 'should be so
restricted by law as to secure that within the limits of a single
Parliament the final decision of the Commons shall prevail'. But
granted that any legislative changes to the constitution would
themselves need to get through the upper house, it was by no
means clear how this aspiration could be achieved.

The Liberals found little from which to draw comfort in 1907.
The Irish Councils Bill, a measure designed to devolve power to
Irish local government, was badly mishandled and had to be withdrawn. With the ministry 'apparently drifting into a period of
futile and aimless endeavour',[14] the economic climate now began
to show a marked deterioration. Unemployment started to climb
alarmingly. For Chamberlainites these developments seemed to
presage the imminent collapse of the government's free-trade
finances and gave an enormous boost to the cause of tariff reform
within the Unionist ranks. Protective measures, it was argued,
could safeguard British jobs. Election results suggested that the
political tide was already moving against the government. As early
as November 1906 the municipal elections had witnessed heavy
Unionist gains. Then in 1907 the government lost three by-
elections (one to Labour – 'the most deadly blow the Liberal party
has ever received at our hands'[15] – one to the Unionists and one
to an independent socialist candidate), followed by three more (all
to Unionists) in the first three months of 1908. By that time it was
clear that Campbell-Bannerman's premiership was nearing its
end. His first year in office had been marred by his wife's illness

and death; during the second his own health began to collapse. In April 1908 he was obliged to resign and, too ill to leave 10 Downing Street, he died there before the month was over. During its brief lifetime his government had shown some creditable signs of reforming zeal, without suggesting any significant developments in the general scope of public policy. The one exception perhaps was Asquith's 1907 budget, which asserted the important principle of differential rates of taxation in raising that on unearned income to one shilling in the pound.

The governmental reorganisation which followed Campbell-Bannerman's resignation marked a distinct change in the balance of forces at the top of the Liberal party. No one seriously questioned Asquith's claim to the succession. But the new Prime Minister himself was not the key to the change. 'His concept of progress was limited,' writes Cameron Hazlehurst. 'He gave intellectual assent to much of the new Liberalism; he gave it no passion or inspiration.'[16] Lord Riddell offered a comparable contemporary assessment. Asquith, he believed, was 'really an old-fashioned Radical of the Manchester school, who [was] leading a heterogeneous band of followers'.[17] Of greater significance was the promotion of David Lloyd George to the Treasury from the Board of Trade to fill the vacancy created by Asquith's elevation and the appointment to Lloyd George's old place of Winston Churchill, who now joined the cabinet for the first time. These ministerial changes initiated the most constructive era in the history of the Liberal government and the period which provides the most telling evidence of the influence of New Liberal thinking within the upper reaches of the party. Lloyd George, in particular, seemed to recognise that, if his party was to thrive in the era of mass politics, it needed to respond to the problems generated by an industrial society. 'L. G. is the only leading man who has the courage to attack the rich and powerful,' declared Lord Riddell. 'All other leading politicians deal with the stock political commodities, such as Home Rule, Disestablishment, Tariff Reform . . . L. G. says what the mass of the people feel but cannot express.'[18] Over a period of four years the government introduced old-age pensions (long promised by both leading parties), established labour exchanges and trade boards, created a National Insurance scheme to cover sickness, invalidity and unemployment, and passed a Miners' Minimum Wages Act. Each of these measures combined caution in its specific immediate provisions with far greater long-term significance as regards assumptions about the role of the state and its duties towards its citizens. But we should be hesitant to suggest that all of this Liberal legislation necessarily led to a strengthening of the electoral relationship between the party and the working-class voter. Old-age pensions seem to have been well received. The rewards (5s. a week) were relatively small and the qualifying age (70) high, but the take-up was bigger than expected and by 1914 nearly a million people were receiving state pensions at a cost to the Exchequer of more than £12 million per annum. Some other Liberal reforms were, however, less welcome, either because they smacked of paternalistic interventionism or because they came at a price. National Insurance benefits, unlike old-age pensions, were dependent upon direct contributions and, even if the benefit was greater than the contribution – '9d. for 4d.' – for large numbers of working people on low incomes it nonetheless involved their first and unwelcome experience of taxation by central government.

Accompanying changes to the taxation system, particularly those embodied in the 1909 budget, were equally, if not more, significant. This established the principle that the annual Finance Bill could be used to finance new areas of spending by the state and that it was a proper function of the government to redistribute wealth from the better-off to the poorer members of society.

After extensive debate inside the cabinet, Lloyd George introduced what was his first budget – Asquith having taken responsibility for that of 1908 despite his elevation to the premiership – on 29 April 1909. It was, he declared, 'a war budget . . . for raising money to wage implacable war against poverty and squalidness'. The Chancellor sought to raise an additional £13.6 million in taxation. He proposed to increase income tax and to subject annual incomes of over £5000 to a supertax. Additional death duties would raise £4.8 million and stamp duty £1.25 million. There would also be additional duties of £1.8 million from spirits and £2 million from tobacco, together with a £2.25 million rise in the cost of liquor licences paid by publicans and brewers. The proposed land taxes represented a fundamental departure, even though the estimated revenue to be generated was modest. Lloyd George proposed a 20 per cent tax on the increments of land value, a halfpenny in the pound tax on the value of undeveloped land and a tax of ten per cent on the value of leasehold reversions. Even so, this was more a case of Lloyd George attacking his traditional enemy, the landlord, rather than a significant move in redistributive taxation.

Accurately predicting many of the Chancellor's proposals, his junior minister, Charles Hobhouse, had foreseen that 'such proposals, if propounded to the country, ought to insure the rejection of the budget by the Lords [and] enforce a dissolution'.[19] Nonetheless, the general consensus of recent historiography is that Lloyd George, in introducing his budget, had no devious plan to goad the Unionist peers into rejection and thus towards constitutional and electoral suicide.[20] The government's need for extra revenue was genuine enough, not least to finance pensions and to carry out its naval building programme to counter a perceived German threat. With an anticipated budget deficit of £16–17 million, the Chancellor had no alternative but to introduce some startling measures. But Lloyd George may well have foreseen that, by going so far to undermine the revenue motive for tariffs, his budget was likely to provoke Unionist tariff reformers into some strenuous form of resistance. If he was able to raise the necessary income by means of ordinary taxation, then one of the most powerful arguments in favour of tariff reform would have been decisively refuted. Asquith had himself conceded that 'if it could not be proved that Social reform . . . can be financed on Free Trade lines, a return to Protection is a moral certainty'.[21] The budget also confirmed the Liberals' long-standing argument that, by requiring a tax on the food of ordinary people, protection was an essentially unfair device which now compared unfavourably with Lloyd George's more 'democratic' proposals. Many tariff reformers rapidly concluded that attack was the best form of defence and, goaded by some inflammatory pronouncements by the Chancellor, began to argue for the outright rejection of the bill. Indeed, since the case for tariff reform, now dominant in the Unionist ranks, could only be given its chance if the Finance Bill was stopped in its tracks, the party leaders moved inexorably towards rejection by the House of Lords as the summer of 1909 progressed. Finally, on 16 November, Lord Lansdowne as leader of the Unionist peers gave notice of the fateful amendment which would destroy the Finance Bill. Thus was the well-established principle, that financial measures fell outside the remit of the upper chamber, defied and a first-class constitutional crisis created. With the budget rejected, the business of government became impossible and a general election a constitutional necessity. And, though the Liberals had been forced to the polls much earlier than they might, in the context of seven-year parliaments, have planned, it was a contest which the government had some reason to welcome. Lloyd George's Finance Bill had, it seemed, succeeded in forcing the Unionists into a morally indefensible position as the defenders of a reactionary alliance between food-taxers and hereditary peers, opposed to the people of the country and their budget.

No party could draw total satisfaction from the election results of January 1910. The most striking feature was the complete erosion of the Liberals' independent Commons majority secured just four years before. Although the Unionists had failed to maintain their by-election momentum of 1907–09, losing gains made in the three previous years, they did regain 116 seats lost in 1906, thereby recovering their traditional status as the majority party in England. Overall, the Unionists now held 273 seats compared with the government's 275. In terms of percentages of the popular vote, the figures were 46.9 and 43.5 respectively. Unionist gains appear to have owed more to the renewed support of voters who had abstained in 1906 than to Liberal defections. Crucially, despite the narrow gap between the two main parties, the Liberals could expect to rely on the 40 Labour and 82 Irish Nationalist members in the new House to safeguard their parliamentary majority and the continued existence of their government. As will be seen, however, the support of the minority parties, especially the Irish, would come at a price.

There was a widespread feeling that the cry of 'Peers versus People' had saved the situation for the government. The fact that Unionists had gained seats, particularly in the South of England, owed more to a general recovery of support for the party in its traditional strongholds after the altogether exceptional results of 1906 than it did to any great appeal exercised by tariff reform or the party's stance in the constitutional crisis. But not all the novel features of 1906 had been reversed. A number of working-class constituencies, particularly in London and Lancashire, which had been Unionist before 1906, did not return to the fold. This, taken with the effective containment of any significant further advance on the part of the Labour party, suggested that the Liberals had been markedly successful in attracting the working-class vote. One Unionist candidate suggested that working-class constituencies in Lancashire, Yorkshire and Cheshire had been lost by his party because 'masses of the extremely poor have been attracted by the Lloyd Georgian programme of vague suggestions that something is to be given to them, which at present belongs to somebody else. They do not know what it is, but want to take their chance of getting it whatever it may be.'[22]

'The big thing', wrote Beatrice Webb at the end of November 1910, 'that has happened in the last two years is that Lloyd George and Winston Churchill have practically taken the *limelight*, not merely from their own colleagues, but from the Labour Party.'[23] The practical effect was that, after January 1910, the electoral map was drawn more clearly on class lines than ever before. Though the average swing to the Unionists across the country from 1906 was 4.3 per cent, this figure marked a wide range whose effect was to leave Britain broadly divided between a Liberal-dominated North of England, Scotland and Wales and a Unionist-controlled South. Mrs Webb well captured what had happened: 'What is remarkable is the dividing of England into two distinct halves, each having its own large majority for its own cause: the South Country – the suburban, agricultural, residential England – going Tory and tariff reform, and the north Country and dense industrial populations (excluding Birmingham area) going radical socialist.'[24]

Though confirmed in office, the Liberal government had, to a large extent, lost control over the political agenda. The Irish Nationalists, by contrast, were quick to appreciate the strength of their position. The parliamentary arithmetic now made possible – or, from an Irish point of view, inevitable – the introduction of a third Home Rule bill, something which the government had deliberately excluded when it had been in possession of an independent Commons majority and therefore in no need of Irish support. But the prerequisite would be action to curtail the powers of the House of Lords; otherwise any Home Rule measure would be likely to suffer the fate of its predecessor of 1893. Not therefore until April 1910, when the government made clear its intention to introduce a Parliament Bill, did the Irish help the government to get the Finance Bill through the Commons. Having lost the vote in the country, the Lords now withdrew their opposition and the budget of 1909 belatedly became law. But a further impediment to progress on Lords reform, not to mention Home Rule, lay in the King's insistence that the government should hold a second general election before he would agree to create enough new Liberal peers to ensure that the upper chamber agreed to its own emasculation. It was in this situation that Edward VII died suddenly on 6 May and, in an attempt to effect a compromise which would spare his inexperienced successor a number of difficult decisions, four senior representatives of each of the two main parties met in a constitutional conference over the summer and early autumn.

Much mystery and speculation once surrounded the course of the ensuing inter-party discussions, largely because, though negotiations proceeded over several weeks, no record was published either at the time or subsequently, and perhaps also because of the intrusion of Lloyd George's dramatic and unexpected proposal for a coalition government. But it would appear that, without compromising on fundamental principles, each side genuinely sought to reach a settlement. Soon after the conference resumed in October after the summer recess, negotiations reached an impasse. Basic agreement seemed to have been reached on the submission of deadlocked legislation to a joint sitting of the two

Houses of Parliament, but the sticking point was whether, as the Unionists insisted, constitutional changes including Home Rule, should be excluded from such a provision and submitted instead to a referendum. At this point, however, consideration of such constitutional niceties was pushed temporarily to the periphery by Lloyd George's bold suggestion that the outstanding issues of the day could best be resolved by the formation of a coalition government. The Unionists showed some interest before finally drawing back. The Chancellor's motives for putting forward this proposal remain a matter of debate. He may have been thinking of how to ease the passage of the National Insurance legislation to which his fertile brain had now turned, but it also seems likely that he shared the irritation which had frequently been voiced over the preceding decade by radical politicians in all parties at the sterility of the party political struggle. His attitude at other times in his long political career supports the view that, though he lived and died a Liberal, he was never as wedded to the notion of party for its own sake as were most of his political contemporaries. Lloyd George had political goals and his party was never more than a vehicle to achieve them.

When the government compromised to the extent of suggesting that a general election should intervene on the next occasion that a Home Rule bill was rejected by the Lords, but on this occasion only, and that subsequent Home Rule measures should be treated like ordinary legislation, it was clear that the Liberals had gone as far as they could. But it was also clear that the Unionists would not accept a settlement on such terms. Not surprisingly, the conference was finally wound up at its twenty-second session on 10 November. A further General Election was now inevitable, though the King insisted on waiting for the Lords to reject the Parliament Bill before granting a dissolution. Jesse Herbert, the Treasurer of the Liberal Central Association, the body charged with maintaining communication throughout the party, suggested that the Liberal and Labour parties stood to gain about thirty seats in England and Wales, while the Unionists were clearly apprehensive about the country's verdict. Under pressure from moderates in his own ranks, Balfour was obliged to water down his party's commitment to tariff reform. On 29 November, and only days before voting began, he announced at the Albert Hall that if the Unionists were to win the election, no taxes would be imposed upon food until the electorate had had the opportunity to express its views on this single issue in a referendum.

In the event, the outcome of the election was something of an anticlimax. The December poll saw only marginal overall changes from that in January. The Liberals and Unionists now both held 272 seats; Labour's tally went up slightly to 42. In fact more seats had changed hands than these figures suggested. The Liberals had won 23 seats from the Unionists, but suffered 25 losses, including one to Labour. Even so, the transfer of votes was on a relatively small scale. The government would remain in power, dependent still upon the support of Labour and the Irish Nationalists. In the short term it could now proceed with the Parliament Bill. Under its terms the Lords would not in future be able to amend or reject a money bill; any other legislation rejected by the Lords would become law automatically providing not less than two years had elapsed between its introduction and third reading in the Commons; and the maximum life of a parliament would be reduced from seven years to five. Asquith's trump card was the promise, extracted in secret from a reluctant monarch shortly before the December election, that the latter would, if needed, be ready to create the requisite number of peers to ensure the bill's passage. Even so, a substantial number of Unionists preferred to 'die in the last ditch' rather than voluntarily surrender their powers. In the event, enough Unionist peers went into the government lobby on the crucial vote on 10 August 1911 to cancel out the 'ditchers', while the majority of their number followed the lead of Lord Lansdowne and abstained.

The curtailment of the powers of the House of Lords seemed to open up the prospect of a further tranche of reforming legislation from the government, of a kind that might have had little chance of success hitherto. Yet it is hard not to conclude that, after the passage of the National Insurance Act later that year, the government lost some of its momentum. At the level of personnel, the departure of Churchill to the Admiralty in October 1911 was a significant loss from the forces of progressivism on the domestic front. As First Lord, Churchill had different priorities. He had 'become quite a Tory,' noted Lloyd George in 1912. 'He has changed immensely.'[25] But more generally the change was in large part the inevitable consequence of a renewed fixation upon the problems of Ireland. Between 1906 and 1910 Ireland had occupied a lowly position among the government's priorities. Previous Liberal governments having badly burnt their fingers on this issue, this was scarcely surprising. The limit of the government's ambitions had been to try to satisfy the Irish with minor reforms, while preparing the electorate for the possibility of Home Rule some time in the future. In November 1905 Campbell-Bannerman had revealed his cautious step-by-step approach to the Irish Nationalist leadership. While he would not pledge his party to full Home Rule in the new parliament, he did intend to enact 'some serious measure which would be consistent with and lead up to the other'.[26] In the event, the ill-fated Irish Councils Bill of 1907 had represented the sum total of the government's endeavours. While there were still Liberals who regarded the quest for Home Rule as something of a crusade, the majority had come to agree with Joseph Chamberlain that it was 'death and damnation' for their party as a whole.

After 1910, however, Home Rule was the issue which dominated the government's thinking and latterly its parliamentary agenda, right up to the outbreak of the First World War. The two general elections of 1910 had recreated the parliamentary situation of 1886 and 1892 in the sense of leaving the Liberal government dependent for its continued survival upon the support of the contingent of Irish Nationalist MPs, who were insistent upon seeing their aspiration for Home Rule satisfied. The electoral results of 1910 were, in the words of George Dangerfield, 'like historical graffiti, the naughty calligraphy of Fate itself'.[27] But the key difference in the post-1910 situation was that the passage of a third Home Rule Bill would not, thanks to the Parliament Act, fall victim to the immovable Unionist majority in the upper house. Indeed, the destruction of the Lords' veto added an element of precision and predictability to the bill's parliamentary progress.

Contemporaries could now calculate, accurately enough, the cumbersome yet inevitable timetable by which Home Rule would wend its way on to the statute book. Even allowing for the full exercise of the Lords' remaining powers of delay in 1912 and 1913, Ireland would become self-governing by the summer of 1914. In the intervening period the government could expect to be fully occupied. Unionists would respond to the challenge of Home Rule with every bit of the passion and determination with which a Liberal might defend free trade.

Home Rule thus became an obsession for government and opposition alike, with genuine conviction on both sides of the argument rather than the stylised rhetoric which so often accompanies political debate. Mounting tension in Ireland was characterised by the growth of armed volunteer forces on both sides of the argument, carrying with them at least the threat of civil war. At the height of the crisis one cabinet minister recorded: 'History if it concerns itself with us at all will write us down as either the most patient, wise, foreseeing Govt. this or any country ever had, or else as the inept, blind and cowardly crew that ever disgraced Downing Street. No middle judgement will be possible.'[28] Yet it is doubtful whether the Liberals, any more than their Unionist opponents, derived any significant electoral advantage, at least on the British mainland, from the stance which they adopted. Rather the Irish problem appears as an enormous distraction, a throwback to the constitutional struggles of the nineteenth century, even though its resolution would continue to elude successive British governments for the remainder of the twentieth century. Meanwhile, Asquith's government missed possible opportunities to advance its own cause. In November 1911 the Prime Minister announced that the government would bring in a Franchise and Registration Bill designed to grant full manhood suffrage and at the same time remove the anomaly of plural voting. Significantly, and despite the fact that the cabinet was deeply divided on the issue, the bill was so drawn up as to permit the introduction of an amendment which would enfranchise women on the same basis as men. This duly happened. In January 1913, however, the Speaker ruled that the amendment would so transform the nature of the bill as to render it invalid. This ruling was of questionable merit, but there was no obvious way in which it could be challenged, and the government decided to drop the whole measure.

As the Home Rule Bill progressed, both sides became anxious to secure a compromise settlement, based probably upon the exclusion of Protestant Ulster from the bill's provisions. Both sides, however, had to be wary of the potential reaction of extremists in their own ranks. For the Liberals, this meant ensuring that they could carry the Irish Nationalists with them. In the event, agreement on the details of a compromise – which counties might be excluded and for how long – proved elusive and historians can only speculate as to what would have happened if the enactment of Home Rule had come up against the steely determination of Protestant Orangemen to resist government from Catholic Dublin. As it was, only the coming of European war in August 1914 forced the Irish issue on to the legislative back burner. On 24 July, as a last-minute conference at Buckingham Palace to try to break the Irish deadlock collapsed, the Foreign Secretary informed his colleagues of the text of an ultimatum sent to Serbia by Austria–Hungary. As Churchill memorably recalled:

> [Edward Grey] had been reading or speaking for several minutes before I could disengage my mind from the tedious and bewildering debate which had just closed. We were all very tired, but gradually as the phrases and sentences followed one another, impressions of a wholly different character began to form in my mind . . . The parishes of Fermanagh and Tyrone faded back into the mists and squalls of Ireland, and a strange light began immediately, but by perceptible gradations, to fall and glow upon the map of Europe.[29]

Nor was Ireland the government's only worry in the last years of peace. The campaign of the militant suffragettes provided ministers with a considerable distraction. Then the period after 1911 saw an unprecedented wave of industrial unrest with strikes and lockouts hitting large parts of British industry. More than 40 million working days were lost in 1912 alone. Some of these strikes carried a syndicalist undertone, threatening the overthrow of capitalism and the setting up of a workers' republic, although economic factors were the more usual cause. By 1913, moves had been made to co-ordinate the activities of the railwaymen, the miners and the transport workers in a so-called Triple Alliance. The control of these unions over the country's transport gave them the capacity to call something approaching a general strike. In 1913 the cabinet itself was badly shaken by the Marconi Scandal, which threatened the careers of three government ministers, Lloyd George, Herbert Samuel and Rufus Isaacs, and the former Chief Whip, the Master of Elibank. Accused of what would today be called 'insider trading', the four men had probably been unwise and lacking in candour rather than genuinely corrupt. 'There was no corruption,' judged the new Tory leader, Bonar Law, 'but they acted imprudently and improperly.'[30] More generally, both the cabinet and the parliamentary party seem to have been more divided than in earlier years. Issues of defence policy were often the cause. Thirty-seven Liberal MPs voted to reduce military and naval expenditure in March 1911. The following July 23 members opposed the supplementary naval estimates and, in March 1913, 14 Liberals again defied their government over increased naval expenditure. Churchill's appointment as First Lord only exacerbated the problem for he now 'embraced the cause of naval might as eagerly as he had [once championed] retrenchment'.[31] In his new post, Churchill clearly intended to secure peace by preparing for war. Added to this was a growing personal opposition from many of his cabinet colleagues who objected to his overbearing manner and his tendency to intervene in each and every cabinet discussion, no matter how far removed it was from the First Lord's departmental concerns. Though Churchill's estimates for 1913–14 got through the cabinet without difficulty, trouble erupted when, at the end of 1913, he proposed an additional increase of £3 million. At one point half a dozen cabinet ministers, including Lloyd George, seemed likely to resign unless Churchill backed down or himself resigned. 'The Government may break up on the question of the Navy estimates,' judged Reginald McKenna in January 1914.[32] In the event,

by the middle of February the crisis had passed and no resignations had been tendered. Churchill promised to effect substantial
reductions in expenditure the following year. The resolution of
disputes such as this was perhaps Asquith's greatest skill as Prime
Minister. His readiness to skirt around awkward issues and postpone difficult decisions, and his ability to charm, to cajole and to
conciliate his colleagues all helped to hold an exceptionally
talented but often potentially divergent cabinet together. In the
context of war there would be a downside to this style. For the
time being, however, it worked well.

The troubled history of the last years before the outbreak of the
First World War, compounded by a knowledge of the fate which
awaited British Liberalism in the years to come, makes it all too easy
to take a very gloomy view of the party's likely prospects. But in
recent years historians have drawn attention to clear signs that,
Ireland and other problems notwithstanding, the government and
in particular Lloyd George were beginning to embark upon a second
wave of radical reforms. Despite opposition from fellow Liberals,
Lloyd George was determined to push ahead. As C. P. Scott recorded:

> There were of course people in the party who in their hearts
> hated all reforms and he constantly came across nominal Liberals
> whose one cry was 'Why not let it alone?' They did not realise
> that for Liberalism stagnation was death. The worst kind of Tory
> was the nominal Liberal.[33]

The new focus of the Chancellor's attention was the land, and his
proposals included establishing security of tenure for tenant farmers and creating Wage Boards to set minimum wages for agricultural workers. There were plans too for the towns, involving rating
reform to facilitate improvements in urban housing. Like so much
else, these schemes, launched in the autumn of 1913, fell victim
to the changed priorities of the war years. But 'most of the signs
that are available suggest that the land campaign had every
chance of success when war intervened to transform the political
landscape'.[34] More generally, the land campaign offers clear
evidence that the government had by no means run out of steam

in 1914 and indeed that it was succeeding in placing the opposition on the back foot as far as the forthcoming General Election
was concerned. This was particularly the case as regards English
rural constituencies, two-thirds of which were in Unionist hands.
The Unionists' response to Lloyd George's initiatives was slow and
uninspiring. Their difficulty was that to adopt a counter-policy to
alleviate the lot of the rural working class would be to run the risk
of alienating their traditional support among the land-owning
community. By June 1914 Sir Arthur Steel-Maitland, the Unionist
Chairman, privately conceded that his party had completely lost
the initiative on the land question and that Unionist prospects for
the coming autumn looked extremely unfavourable.[35]

The renaissance of Liberal radicalism was also evident in Lloyd
George's 1914 budget, the first £200 million budget in British
history. This provided for grants of more than £4 million to local
authorities for subsidising the rates, to be paid for by a rise of 2d.
in income tax (to 1s. 4d.) and increased supertax and death duties.
As such it represented a significant extension of the principle of
graduated taxation and a further step in wealth redistribution,
and has been described as marking 'the climax of the fiscal strategy of the New Liberalism'.[36] But the budget provoked strong
opposition within the ranks of the parliamentary Liberal party. A
group of around forty MPs organised themselves under the leadership of the wealthy Liverpool ship-owner and MP for Hexham,
Richard Holt. Historians have disputed the importance of the so-
called 'Holt Cave'. It has been suggested that the actions of Holt
and his colleagues represented a significant body of opposition to
the general progressive direction of government policy, including
Lloyd George's land campaign. Contemporaries were struck by the
wealth of the members of the Cave, with *Punch* making fun of the
Adullamite activities of 'Holt's Cave for Plutocrats'. These were the
men with most to lose from the Chancellor's policies, which were
directed even more markedly at the rich than had been the provisions of the People's Budget of 1909. One former cabinet minister
judged the group to be 'a clique of rich men determined to read a
lesson to L. George by resisting a budget which taxes them'.[37] Holt
led a deputation of between forty and fifty MPs which met

Asquith on 15 June. The Prime Minister's failure to satisfy the rebels resulted in a letter to *The Times* on 18 June, which even Asquith found 'a very able document'.[38] The Cave's efforts ended with the government withdrawing some of its proposals and agreeing to halve the projected increase in income tax. This, it has been argued, 'clearly defined the limits of [the Liberal] Party's tolerance for social and economic change'. Possibly, indeed, 'the budget debacle of 1914 marked the end of the New Liberalism'.[39]

This is an exaggeration. Recent research has stressed the fluid composition of the Holt Cave, whose numbers fluctuated during the brief weeks of its existence between fifteen and sixty members. According to Ian Packer, it was 'by no means a straightforward expression of anti-progressive sentiments' but rather 'a disparate group of MPs whose membership and grievances varied enormously'.[40] Furthermore, Packer has shown that the government's concessions had more to do with procedural difficulties of its own creation than with pressure applied by Holt and his associates. So the Cave may have been less significant for the long-term evolution of the Liberal party than was once thought. That said, it is difficult to ignore Holt's own analysis. The Cave, he said, was 'a combined remonstrance by business men and some survivors of the Cobden-Bright school of thought against the ill-considered and socialistic tendencies of the Government finance'. The government had 'certainly travelled a long way from the old Liberal principle of "retrenchment" and I deeply regret it'.[41] Holt himself, and presumably at least some of those who acted with him at this time, represented a continuing strand of non-interventionist, laissez-faire Liberalism which was out of sympathy with the New Liberalism and with much that the government had been doing since 1908. Even one of Lloyd George's cabinet colleagues had earlier found it difficult to accept a Chancellor of the Exchequer who urged expenditure rather than economy and who seemed 'to have no idea that he is the guardian of the public purse'.[42]

By the outbreak of war the Liberal party had – albeit with some support from its allies – emerged victorious from three successive general elections. The next contest would have to be held before the end of 1915 and not all Liberals looked forward to it confident of a fourth victory. But neither for that matter did the Unionist opposition, some of whose leaders were privately anticipating a fourth successive defeat. Though the outcome of a general election which was never held must necessarily remain uncertain, what can be said is that the Liberals were trying to create the most favourable conditions for their next appeal to the country by pushing through a bill to abolish plural voting. This anomaly, it was believed, had added as many as thirty seats to the Unionist tally in December 1910. The government's measure awaited its third and final reading in the House of Commons when the coming of war disrupted the whole pattern of its planned legislative programme. At the same time Liberals believed that Lloyd George's land campaign would lead to gains rather than losses in English rural seats at the forthcoming contest. And, even if the General Election of 1915 had resulted in a Liberal defeat, this is the nature of the democratic process and such an outcome should not be equated with the party's total disintegration and the end of its claims to be a party of government.

In such a situation it might seem bizarre, absurd indeed, to suggest that the historic Liberal party was in any sense 'doomed' to oblivion by the time that Gavrilo Princip fired his fateful shots in the Balkan town of Sarajevo. Hindsight, however, imposes a heavy burden. The short timescale of the party's decline in the decade after the First World War, and its replacement by Labour as the leading opponent of the Conservatives, has encouraged the belief that Liberalism must already have been fatally wounded before the coming of European war. Ever since the mid-1930s, therefore, when the young Oxford-educated historian, George Dangerfield, penned his celebrated *Strange Death of Liberal England*, historians have been engaged in 'the scholarly pursuit of listening to the heartbeat of the Edwardian Liberal party in order to record its formal death'.[43] Dangerfield's analysis, expressed in compelling if somewhat melodramatic prose, contains two essential elements. Most famously, he suggested that Liberal England died 'strangely' in the period 1911–14, the victim of a pattern of violence made up of the intransigence of the House of Lords, the militancy of the trade unions, the excesses of the suffragettes and the fanaticism of the Protestants of Ulster. To this pattern of internal violence the coming of external war provided but a fitting climax. In the face of this concerted onslaught, Liberalism – moderate, rational, tolerant – collapsed and died, an anachronistic relic of an age that had now passed.

No serious scholar would now subscribe to anything like this thesis. Fundamentally, no 'pattern' of violence ever existed, merely an 'accidental convergence of unrelated events', [44] the sorts of problems which it is the business of elected governments to confront and resolve. By 1914 some of these problems had indeed been resolved; others, though serious, were fully capable of resolution. In particular, the supposed link between international and domestic violence is an illusion. But Dangerfield also made a more challenging suggestion. Writing from a perspective when not only was the decline of Liberalism an issue of contemporary politics, but also, notwithstanding the setback of 1931, the Labour party appeared to be engaged in an inexorable rise from its foundation in 1900, he pointed to a causal link between the two phenomena. Indeed, for the Liberal party the writing was already on the wall in the hour of its greatest electoral triumph in 1906:

> The Liberal Party which came back to Westminster with an overwhelming majority was already doomed. It was like an army protected at all points except for one vital position on its flank. With the election of fifty-three Labour representatives, [a total which Dangerfield can only reach by adding those Lib–Lab MPs who took the Liberal whip to the representatives of the newly formed Labour party] the death of Liberalism was pronounced; it was no longer the Left.[45]

Expressed in more measured, but still forceful, terms, the relationship between the prewar Liberal and Labour parties has become one of the central components of the historiographical debate over Liberalism's decline. Put simply, argument has raged and continues to rage over whether the Liberals were in the process of being overtaken by Labour even before European war distorted the pattern of domestic political development, or whether they remained in 1914 the undisputed party of the British working class, with the pretensions of the Labour upstart held firmly in check.

The idea that there was something 'inevitable' about the rise of Labour and its consequent destruction of the Liberal party has exercised a strong appeal for Marxist and quasi-Marxist historians in particular and Labour historians in general. In their vision, a growing understanding that the interests of employer and employee, of capital and labour, were ultimately incompatible (something which Victorian Liberalism had always denied), was bound to find expression in new political organisations based upon the specific interests of the working class. Thus the establishment of the Labour Representation Committee in 1900, and its rapid transformation after the 1906 General Election into the Labour party, signalled the eventual destruction of the Liberals, even if that process was partially concealed before 1914 by the restricted nature of the Edwardian franchise.[46] The pattern of prewar Liberal electoral success was therefore nothing more than a deceptive Indian summer, quickly revealed as such when the Representation of the People Act of 1918 signalled a significant move towards full democracy. According to Henry Pelling, Liberalism's demise was not the consequence of wartime quarrels or the erosion of Liberal values: 'Rather it was the result of long-term social and economic changes which were simultaneously uniting Britain geographically and dividing her inhabitants in terms of class.'[47] The period before 1914 saw the growth of 'a sort of undogmatic "Labourism"' – a feeling that 'the Labour Party, and not the Liberal, was the party for working men to belong to'.[48] If this transformation did not immediately translate into electoral success for Labour, this did not matter. That party's greatest strength lay in its extra-parliamentary organisation in the trade union movement where the period 1906–14 saw a growth in the number of affiliated members from 900,000 to more than one and a half million. More recently, Ross McKibbin has confirmed the rise of 'an acutely developed working-class consciousness', reflected above all in a flourishing trade union movement:

The eclipse of the Liberal party was not due to 'the war', or a wrong-headed pursuit of lassez-faire, or the split between Asquith and Lloyd George, or the conversion of the workers to socialism, but to a slow change in the way popular affiliations were decided. As political allegiance became more and more determined by class self-awareness, the Liberal Party found it could make no claim on the loyalties of any class.[49]

In such a scenario the impact of war may have accelerated the pattern of change, but it did not initiate it. The triumph of Labour and the collapse of Liberalism were already well advanced by 1914.

These 'Labour' interpretations have inevitably been challenged by historians with a more sympathetic disposition towards the Liberal party. Writing in the mid-1960s and early-1970s respectively, Trevor Wilson and Peter Clarke[50] pointed to the fundamental strength of prewar Liberalism. Whatever caused the party's eventual replacement by Labour, it was not to be found in the Edwardian era. Wilson, explicitly, and Clarke, largely implicitly, sought to divert attention to the 'accidents' of the war years as the source of Liberal decline. Clarke's analysis provided a particularly telling response to the 'inevitabilists'. Basing his study on the electoral politics of the county of Lancashire, he did not attempt to deny that political allegiance by 1914 had come to be determined largely by the question of class. Rather, he confirmed that by 1910 the 'change to class politics was substantially complete', and clearly reflected in the electoral map of that year when the prosperous south returned, by and large, to the Conservative fold after the aberration of 1906. There were, however, no signs that such a transformation would be accompanied by the supersession of one party by another. Instead, it appeared that 'both Labour and Liberalism would be subsumed in progressivism'.[51] In other words, enough common ground existed between Edwardian Liberalism and the preponderant Social Democratic wing of the Labour party to produce eventual fusion – if the First World War had not intervened. By adopting the ideas of the New Liberalism, as exemplified in the legislation enacted by Lloyd George and

Churchill and publicised through the circle surrounding C. P. Scott, editor of the *Manchester Guardian*, the Liberal party had successfully adapted to the new era of class politics and, in so doing, had entrenched itself as the party of social reform and of the British working class. Nothing, according to Clarke, suggests that the party was in serious difficulties before the coming of European war. Indeed, the evidence indicates that Liberal success would have continued, 'if not to the degree of 1906, at least at a level markedly above that of the Gladstonian party'.[52]

Such starkly differing interpretations are not easily reconciled. Their incompatibility demands that the history of Liberal–Labour relations in the decade before the First World War be reviewed. As is well known, in September 1903 the Liberal and Labour parties had entered into a secret electoral pact signed in the names of Herbert Gladstone, the Liberal Chief Whip, and Ramsay MacDonald, Secretary of the Labour Representation Committee. From a Liberal point of view, the need for such a pact might seem unclear. But that is to see the question through the perspective of the party's great electoral triumph of 1906. At the time of the pact's signature over two years before, the Liberal party had been out of power for eight years, during much of which time it had not even managed to appear as a viable alternative government. For the best part of two decades, with the exception of three unhappy years in office between 1892 and 1895, the party had been permanently confined to the opposition benches. In 1903, however, Gladstone and MacDonald identified a common purpose in defeating a Unionist government whose fortunes had begun to wane but which might still emerge victorious at the next general election if the progressive vote were to be split by Labour and Liberal candidates competing against one another. The dangers to Liberalism of three-cornered contests had been highlighted by Labour's victory in July in a by-election in Barnard Castle at which the Liberal candidate had come bottom of the poll. The pact also offered Liberalism the chance to confirm its working-class appeal by aligning itself with an avowedly working-class organisation, while at the same time affording the opportunity to limit the financial demands on hard-pressed party funds.

Yet, as some contemporaries recognised and as later historians have not been slow to point out, the pact was not necessarily an unmixed blessing. Liberals faced a dilemma which had some parallels with that which confronted their successors nearly eighty years later at the formation of the Social Democratic party. By admitting Labour's organisational independence, the pact created the possibility that the new party, now virtually guaranteed a significant bridgehead in the next House of Commons, might become a Trojan horse threatening the Liberal party's supremacy on the left-wing of British politics. In short, Liberal benevolence might have the effect of 'nursing into life a serpent which will sting their Party into death'.[53] Jesse Herbert, Gladstone's secretary, who played a leading role in the negotiations leading to the pact, set out the potential hazards with commendable fairness:

> Are the principles and objects of the LRC such as to justify such a benevolent attitude? Will the success of the Liberal party at the polls be too dearly purchased at the price? Ought the Liberal party to prefer defeat rather than assist in any way to foster the growing power of the Labour Party?

On balance, however, he had no doubt of the compelling electoral advantages:

> The gain to the party through a working arrangement would be great, and can be measured best by a comparison of the results of 'no arrangement' with those of 'an arrangement'. Should [LRC supporters] be advised to vote against Liberal candidates, and (as they probably would) should they act as advised, the Liberal party would suffer defeat not only in those constituencies where LRC candidates fought, but also in almost every borough, and in many of the Divisions of Lancashire and Yorkshire. This would be the inevitable result of unfriendly action towards the LRC candidates. They would be defeated, but so also should we be defeated.[54]

Fundamental to the willingness of the Liberal party leadership to enter the pact of 1903 was the perception that Labour still represented a kindred spirit rather than an ideological challenge. Gladstone, who had for long encouraged Liberal constituency parties to look favourably upon the claims of working-class candidates, readily accepted MacDonald's assurance that 'the candidates of the LRC will be found to be in almost every instance earnest Liberals, who will support a Liberal Government'.[55] The Chief Whip could find 'no material point of difference' between the two parties in terms of policy.[56] MacDonald himself predicted the evolution of 'a united democratic party appealing to the people on behalf of a simple, comprehensive belief in social reconstruction'.[57] Such hopes seemed to be confirmed by the sort of Labour men who were successful at the General Election of 1906. Though many professed themselves to be 'socialists' they were in practice 'really no more than advanced Liberals'.[58]

At all events, few could question the effective working of the pact at that election. The results seemed to vindicate the strategy of avoiding a division in the anti-Unionist vote, while at the same time confirming Labour's continuing electoral dependence on the Liberal party. Gladstone judged that the pact was 'the chief factor' in his party's unprecedented triumph.[59] Thirty-one of the LRC's 50 candidates stood without Liberal opposition. Of these, 24 were successful. But only five LRC candidates prevailed in the face of Liberal opponents. Strikingly, in Scotland, where the pact did not apply, there were ten three-cornered contests and the Liberals were defeated in six seats which they might otherwise have won. Jesse Herbert celebrated the Liberals' achievement:

> The sum of the matter is that in England and Wales Liberals and Labour-men held 367 seats out of 495, i.e. a majority of 239, and there are only 2 cases in which we have any ground for complaint against the Labour people, and one case in which they have just ground of complaint against us. Was there ever such a justification of a policy by results?[60]

It is thus possible to argue that a relatively small concession on the part of the Liberal party had enabled it to contain the challenge of Labour and ensure continuing Liberal leadership of the progressive left in British politics. For all that, the election for the first time of a substantial body of Labour MPs could not be ignored. Symbolically, the LRC now formally rechristened itself as the Labour party. The Unionist leader, Arthur Balfour, seemed to anticipate Dangerfield when he drew dark parallels between Labour's gains and recent revolutionary events in St Petersburg. More cautiously, it may be noted that the British electoral system makes it extremely difficult for new parties to establish a parliamentary presence. For Labour this hurdle had now been overcome, courtesy of their Liberal partners. But did the new party's band of MPs pose, as Dangerfield suggested, a long-term if not immediate threat to the Liberal party? David Powell has suggested that 'once the Labour party had come into existence, it rapidly acquired an identity and momentum of its own and was able to present itself as a credible alternative focus for working-class loyalties'.[61] Such an analysis is certainly logical. Whether it is what actually happened over the following eight years is more open to question.

The parliament of 1906 saw no real change in the relationship between the two parties, at least at the level of national politics. Labour and socialist candidates secured spectacular by-election gains at Jarrow and Colne Valley in 1907 and at Sheffield, Attercliffe in May 1909, but these were more representative of a predictable slump in the government's mid-term fortunes, against the background of a trade recession, than of any fundamental change in voting patterns. For the most part the pact of 1903 was maintained, although MacDonald had one eye open to the chances of extending Labour representation in order to conduct future negotiations from a position of greater strength. The most significant event of the period was the ballot conducted by the Miners' Federation of Great Britain in 1908 which resulted in a clear but far from overwhelming majority in favour of affiliation to the Labour party. As a result the latter's nominal strength in the House of Commons rose to 45, though most of the mining MPs who now joined Labour continued to co-operate with the Liberals in their own constituencies and three chose to stand again under their old Lib–Lab colours in the General Election of January 1910.

Against this background, Labour's performance at that election – three gains and five losses producing a total of forty MPs – was scarcely a stunning advance. Though the extent of the Unionist recovery left Labour (along with the Irish Nationalists) in a strong position, the dynamics of the Liberal–Labour relationship still seemed to be weighted heavily in the Liberals' favour. In essence the Liberals had allowed the pact to continue on the basis of what had happened in 1906 but with no new concessions. J. A. Pease, the party's new Chief Whip, argued that Liberals should 'respect the seats which at the last General Election returned Labour Representation candidates and that the LRC organisation should respect other progressive candidates standing for seats held by other Labour representatives or Liberals in 1906'.[62] Labour and Liberal candidates opposed one another in 24 constituencies, none of which returned Labour MPs and in 20 of which Labour came bottom of the poll. In December 1910 Labour's overall tally went up to 42 seats, but once again victory in triangular contests proved beyond them. Overall, the results of the two general elections 'appeared to confirm what Liberals had emphasised for some years; that Labour's success in elections was directly related to the extent to which they were willing to co-operate'.[63] Labour seemed to be dependent on Liberal support to win seats; but there were seats which the Liberals could hold in the face of Labour opposition.

In the absence of evidence from a 1915 General Election, the by-election statistics of the years 1911–14 have been subjected to more than usually detailed scrutiny without, it has to be said, any definitive conclusion being reached about what this information tells us of the health of the Liberal party or the condition of Liberal–Labour relations at the coming of war. What is clear is that the Liberal government experienced a disappointing run of by-election losses. The beneficiaries, however, were not Labour but the Unionists, to whom the Liberals lost 15 seats, leaving the Unionists the largest party in the House of Commons by a clear margin. Some of these seats were lost in straight fights, but Labour intervened in 11 formerly safe Liberal constituencies, causing five seats to be lost to the Unionists. 'As a result of three-cornered contests,' warned C. P. Scott in July 1912 from the pages of the *Manchester Guardian*, 'it is quite possible that while Liberalism and Labour are snapping and snarling at each other the Conservative dog may run away with the bone.'[64] By 1914 this alarm had spread to the heart of the Liberal government. In a speech at Ladybank in April, Asquith pointed out that all but one of the Liberals' losses over the previous two years had been due to a 'split in the forces of progress'. Indeed, when Unionist candidates took seats on a minority vote, Liberals were still inclined to stress that the combined Progressive vote showed that, while the government's candidate might have been defeated, its policies had not.

What deductions may safely be drawn from these figures? Many believe that the most important feature of the electoral history of the immediate pre-war period is the weakness of the Labour party. Both Roy Douglas, writing even of Labour's 'decline', and Peter Clarke have emphasised that Labour came third in 14 three-cornered contests in industrial constituencies between 1911 and 1914. 'With two or three possible exceptions', writes Douglas, 'there was not a constituency in the land which Labour could be tolerably certain of holding if both the Liberals and the Unionists chose to field candidates; and there were not many where, in such circumstances, Labour could even expect a second place.'[65] Labour seemed unable to offer a distinctive alternative to Liberalism and was only able to muster the support of those trade unionists who felt obliged to back a candidate of their own class. In general, Liberals could still attract the bulk of the working-class vote. 'The reason why the Labor [*sic*] Party has been able to make so little of a fight against Liberalism', declared *The Nation*, 'has been that Liberalism has gone so far in the direction of the Labor Party.'[66] As a result, few leading Labour figures seemed to be anticipating a significant Labour breakthrough. Indeed, in 1913 Philip Snowden even declared that 'the present Labour representation in parliament is there mainly by the goodwill of the Liberals, and it will disappear when that goodwill is turned into active resentment'.[67]

Yet this same evidence has been used to produce a very different interpretation. According to Ross McKibbin, though Labour was not yet winning by-elections, its vote was often impressive, especially in constituencies which it had not hitherto contested. Where Labour had already stood at the General Election, it often improved on its earlier performance. In Holmfirth in June 1912, Labour took 28.2 per cent of the vote compared with 14.9 per cent in January 1910. What was happening amounted to a steady erosion of Liberal support which would have profound long-term implications. He accepts that Labour's challenge was not ideological, but points to a growing feeling that the Liberal party had ceased to be the party of the working class, while 'in some perceived if indefinable way the Labour party was'.[68] But for McKibbin the level of Labour support was less significant than the very fact that Labour was now far more ready to compete with the Liberals for the same vote. In short, he points to the breakdown of the Progressive Alliance and the damage this was likely to do to the Liberals' position at the forthcoming General Election. Had that election taken place in 1915, McKibbin believes that Labour would have contested up to 170 seats. Sensing the danger, the *Liberal Magazine* called, in the summer of 1914, for 'a policy of accommodation between Liberal and Labour, which will reproduce in the constituencies the co-operation which obtains at Westminster'. But such was the growing spirit of Labour independence in the country that, even if it had been proposed by the party leadership, the Labour movement as a whole would not have accepted a renewal of the sort of electoral arrangement which had protected the progressive vote at the last three national contests.

Regional studies have confirmed the complexity of the overall picture. Both the viability of the Progressive Alliance and the electoral fortunes of the Liberal party itself varied considerably from region to region. Martin Petter notes a 'curious contrast' in Liberal–Labour relations 'between harmony in Parliament and friction in the constituencies', a conclusion endorsed by George Bernstein's examination of the situation in Norwich, Leicester and Leeds. In municipal politics, Labour candidates seemed more prepared than nationally to stand as 'socialists', thereby differentiating themselves from Liberalism and undermining the viability of a progressive alliance between the two parties. Liberals were 'unable to come to terms with a movement which insisted upon espousing an ideology so hostile to their own'.[69] Electoral contests between the two parties were frequent in the West Riding and, according to Keith Laybourn and Jack Reynolds, revealed considerable Labour progress at the municipal level as early as 1906 and possibly irreversible Liberal decline before 1914. 'By any yardstick', they conclude, 'Labour had made substantial political gains in West Yorkshire between 1906 and 1914. Whilst Liberalism remained the preponderant force at the parliamentary level, the roots of its parliamentary success were being rapidly eroded by Labour at the local level.[70] In the North-East, Liberals seem to have made a considered decision as to whether to oppose LRC candidates on the basis of the latter's views and whether they were compatible with Liberalism. But here the Liberal position was much stronger than in the West Riding. The period after 1906 witnessed a successful Liberal counter-attack in the North-East which held Labour firmly in check.[71] London was, predictably, *sui generis*. Paul Thompson sees the Liberal recovery which took place in the first decade of the new century being based on a 'temporary revival of Nonconformist and trade union support and of old radical political issues', which could not disguise an otherwise 'disastrous decay' dating from the late nineteenth century. The Liberal party lacked a firm basis of electoral support among London's working classes, even though the Labour challenge came relatively late upon the scene.[72] Many of these local findings have been confirmed by Chris Cook's wide-ranging study of pre-war municipal elections. He draws a picture of serious Liberal decline in many areas, together with a failure to define a clear electoral strategy in relation to the Labour party. In some areas Liberals were already starting to join forces with the Conservatives in an anti-Labour front. But Cook stresses that the main beneficiaries of this Liberal retreat were the Conservatives and that, apart from a few heavily industrialised areas in the large cities, Labour's advance remained negligible or non-existent.[73]

Duncan Tanner provides one further twist to this historiographical plot. The strength of his argument derives from the wide-ranging nature of his research and his unwillingness to make unsustainable generalisations. Tanner has discovered enormous regional variations in the strength of the Progressive Alliance and in Labour's capacity for independent action. Overall, Labour was 'comparatively strong where the Liberal party was weak [but] unable to seriously rival it in most Liberal areas'.[74] He shows that Labour–Liberal by-election contests in the years 1911–14 were no more numerous than they had been in the corresponding period of the 1906 parliament and suggests that these contests should be viewed less as evidence of the collapse of the Progressive Alliance than as skirmishes in an on-going tactical battle. 'Threatened campaigns were part of the process of public negotiation which characterised the Progressive Alliance' and suggestions that Labour would field around a hundred and fifty candidates had also been current prior to the General Elections of 1910.[75] Tanner argues that, but for the war, there was every likelihood that the two parties would have brokered some new electoral arrangement. National Executive Committee lists prepared for a meeting in June 1914 indicate that in many parts of the country the electoral pact of 1903 was continuing to hold. Nationally, Labour had not so far developed the sort of political strength which could have sustained an expansionist strategy. As a result, a general election in 1914 or 1915 would probably have witnessed a Labour campaign which was a 'little larger' than in 1910 and Labour–Liberal conflict 'a fraction more pronounced', but in general 'history was about to repeat itself'.[76] Tanner concludes that there is no real evidence that the Labour party in 1914 was in any sense on the verge of replacing the Liberals as the leading party of the left.

The viability of the pre-war Liberal party was not solely dependent upon the strength of Labour's challenge. Its own intrinsic vitality must also be considered. After all, it was central to Peter Clarke's thesis that the Liberals had made a successful adaptation to the changing electoral conditions of the twentieth century in a way that undermined the very need for a specifically working-class party. But there was always a suspicion that Lancashire, the focus of Clarke's analysis, was untypical of the country as a whole, even though contemporaries certainly recognised its importance in determining the outcome of national contests. As a result, much detailed work has been done to assess the extent to which the doctrines of the 'New Liberalism' had genuinely gone beyond the realm of journalists and intellectuals to penetrate both the party at Westminster and the country at large.

The evidence suggests that the process was far from complete. Lloyd George, at least, seemed to recognise the importance for the Liberal party of policies which dealt with the 'condition of the people'. 'Liberalism', he declared in October 1906, 'will never be ousted from its supremacy in the realm of political progress until it thoroughly deserves to be deposed for its neglect or betrayal of the principles it professes.'[77] As has been seen, however, the election of 1906 was largely a victory for traditional Liberal values and the Campbell-Bannerman government was very much in the mould of typical Liberal cabinets of the nineteenth century with only the Trades Disputes Act of 1906 fully reflecting the impact of Progressive politics. The advent of Asquith's administration provided a fresh impetus and by 1914 the government had an impressive record of social legislation, involving state intervention on an unprecedented scale. Old-age pensions, insurance against sickness and unemployment, labour exchanges, school meals and the tentative introduction of progressive, redistributive taxation all indicated a willingness to intervene in the actions of the free market to the benefit of the working man and his family, which stood in marked contrast to the presumptions of the Gladstonian era. Nineteenth-century notions of the minimal state had finally been abandoned. But it would be unwise to suggest that the New Liberalism had come completely to dominate the party or the government. It is striking how much of the progressive legislation passed after 1908 was the work of just two cabinet ministers, Lloyd George and Churchill, assisted by a few like-minded junior ministers, most notably C. F. G. Masterman. 'I don't know exactly what I am', confessed Masterman in 1912, 'but I am sure I am not a Liberal. They have no sympathy with the people.'[78] 'Rival Liberal strands', argues Duncan Tanner, 'were still strongly represented' in the government. The diary of Charles

Hobhouse represents an on-going critique, written from the perspective of traditional Liberalism, of what he considered to be the socialistic excesses of his cabinet colleagues, Lloyd George and Churchill. Traditional Liberal concerns – temperance, free trade and religion – remained firmly on the party's agenda. One estimate suggests that only about a tenth of the parliamentary party were 'advanced radicals' and perhaps a fifth strongly committed to interventionist policies.[79] Edwardian Liberalism, concludes Geoffrey Searle, was 'Janus-faced', looking back to the traditional doctrines of Cobden and Bright as much as it projected forward to the social democracy of the later decades of the twentieth century.[80] Michael Bentley notes in the papers of the leading party figures of this time an absence of evidence of progressive motivation. He is struck by the fact that

> A pragmatic imperialist with a revulsion from philosophy of all kinds [Asquith] held the premiership during just the period when progressivism is meant to have flowered; and that his closest collaborators . . . injected prominent offices of state with the Oldest of Liberalism and treated progressivism with a mixture of suspicion and contempt.[81]

Similarly, David Powell believes that those same leaders were hamstrung by their social background in fully understanding and thus responding appropriately to the needs of the working class, leaving them insufficiently committed to the sort of changes demanded by the trade union movement.[82] George Bernstein develops the same point. Even when the impact of the New Liberalism was at its height, Liberals still recognised limits beyond which they would not go on issues of fundamental concern to the working class, such as the right to work, strike action and a national minimum wage. 'If the emergence of class politics meant that working people wanted a party whose first priority was the concerns of the poor and the working class then they would have to look elsewhere.'[83] The motivation behind the government's social reform legislation was complex and varied. Genuine philanthropy was accompanied by a keen awareness of the benefits

which would accrue to the country as a whole through the elimination of poverty and distress. But it is striking that those Liberals
who expressed sympathy for working-class aspirations often did
so primarily in terms of the possible electoral advantages for
themselves. With a measure to deal with unemployment,
suggested J. A. Pease in 1908, 'we shall be able to resist Tory reaction and Socialism and drive a wedge between the practical and
impractical Labour politicians'.[84] Though his words were no
doubt coloured by his dismay that the government had taken the
country to war, C. P. Scott's comments in August 1914 are instructive: 'We have I think no longer a Liberal Government – had we
really one before?' He felt able to contrast what existed with what
he wanted – 'a real Liberal Government resting on Radicalism and
Labour'.[85]

Regional studies have also done much to qualify the conclusions drawn from Clarke's analysis of Lancashire. Generalisation
remains dangerous, but overall the impression is that in most of
the country the New Liberalism had not by 1914 transformed an
older pattern of political debate. In areas such as the North-East,
West Yorkshire, London and Wales, it was still the traditional
Liberal issues of individualism, free trade, nonconformity,
retrenchment and temperance which dominated the party's
agenda. In an important study of the politics of Norwich, Leeds
and Leicester, George Bernstein showed that such questions were
far more important for provincial Liberals than was the new
programme of social reform.[86] In West Yorkshire Liberalism
remained 'dominated by the factory master and Nonconformity'
and, 'unbending in its support for self-help and charity', showed
few signs of trying to capture the working-class vote by way of
progressive social policies.[87] This survival of an older Liberalism
did not necessarily indicate that the party was in electoral difficulties. Walter Runciman's victories in Dewsbury 'sprang from the
unexhausted seam of nineteenth-century Liberalism'.[88]
Liberalism's hold in the North-East had hardly been affected by
Labour's challenge before the outbreak of war, while Wales, where
the prewar Liberal ascendancy was complete, 'remained sunk in
the politics of nostalgia and its Gladstonian past . . . The new

liberalism barely existed.'[89] But the absence, or at least the relative weakness, of the New Liberalism in these areas does surely place a searching question mark over the party's long-term capacity to withstand the advance of an avowedly working-class political movement.

Conflicting theories and evidence, marked regional variations and a series of unanswerable 'what if' questions posed by the coming of European war do not lead easily towards confident conclusions. But the attempt must at least be made. For if Labour in 1914 was indeed on the verge of replacing the Liberals as the main non-Conservative force in British politics, then the debate on the decline of the Liberal party may effectively stop at this point. If, on the other hand, Liberalism remained a viable, indeed a vibrant, political force at the outbreak of war, then attention must inevitably shift to what happened during the war itself and possibly to the postwar era as well. The most optimistic case sees the Liberal party fully grounded in working-class support on the basis of an interventionist ideology of social reform, capable of absorbing the non-socialist wing of the Labour party and of developing in the years ahead into something like the Democratic party in the United States. At the opposite end of the scale, Liberalism had already surrendered the advantage to Labour in a new era of class-based politics and was only maintaining a tenuous hold on power by virtue of a series of passing advantages – the restricted franchise, Labour's financial difficulties and a crumbling electoral alliance.

Neither of these absolutist interpretations seems tenable. Labour was not on the verge of triumph in 1914, but neither was the Liberal party without its problems. The Liberals still attracted the allegiance of large swathes of working-class support; they had not surrendered control of industrial Britain. The party was certainly weaker in 1914 than in 1906. But whether this 'decline' was merely the natural fate of a party that had been in government for eight years and whose level of support was reverting to what it had tended to enjoy in the late nineteenth century, after the aberration of 1906, or whether it was part of underlying trends which boded ill for Liberalism in the long term is almost impossible to determine.

Much of the electoral support which the party had lost since 1906 had transferred to the Unionists rather than to Labour. Profound social and economic changes were taking place, but no clear *national* pattern is discernible and no general statement seems applicable to the country as a whole. Such changes would have continued whether or not the war had intervened, though the timescale of change in the absence of a war, and the scope this would have afforded for Liberal adaptation, is entirely problematic. The argument that Liberalism had been saved by its intellectual vitality, by 'the medicinal powers' of the New Liberalism which had sufficient purchase on the working-class vote to counteract the growth of socialism, is unconvincing.[90] The new ideas seem to have exercised less influence on the party at Westminster and in the country at large than was once claimed. Significantly, Liberals won three successive general elections primarily on issues determined by their Unionist opponents – free trade and the House of Lords. There is also evidence to suggest that issues such as wage rates and job security loomed larger among working-class priorities than did the sorts of social reform introduced by the Liberal government, however significant these may have been in the long-term history of welfare provision. This was by no means fatal for the Liberal party. The ideas of an older Liberalism could still deliver electoral success as the experience of Wales and elsewhere showed, but in the longer term the party surely needed to recognise that issues of class were coming to replace religious rivalries as the key determinant of voting behaviour.

All this suggests that the future of the Progressive Alliance was of fundamental importance. In the three general elections of 1906 and 1910 the Unionists' share of the vote ranged from 43.6 per cent to 46.9 per cent, but Labour and the Liberals so managed their relationship as to keep the Unionists out of power. In 1922 the Conservatives would secure a comfortable Commons majority on the basis of just 38.2 per cent. Almost certainly then, the outcome of the General Election of 1915 would have been decided by the development of relations between the Liberal and Labour parties, rather than by the performance of the Unionists. The larger the number of Liberal–Labour contests the greater the probability of a

Unionist victory. Some sort of renewed electoral deal might well have been stitched together in time for the coming general election, but it is well to remember that there had always been a strand of Labour thought, particularly within the ILP, which was inherently suspicious of pacts with the Liberals and anxious to raise the banner of socialism 'out of the slough of [Liberal] individualism'.[91] The potential clearly existed for Labour, assisted from 1911 by the introduction of payment for MPs, to become a stronger element within the British political system. And, even assuming some new arrangement had been reached for 1915, a question remains over how long it would have been content to exist as the junior partner of the Liberal party. Once freed from the dominant Liberal agenda of constitutional reform, Irish Home Rule and the disestablishment of the Welsh Church, Labour would have the chance to outbid the Liberals on specific working-class issues.

In the longer term it is reasonable to question the viability of a party whose candidates and organisation remained overwhelmingly middle-class presenting itself as the, or even a, party of the working class. With hindsight, the Liberals' failure to adopt more working-class men as parliamentary candidates seems to have been a fundamental error. Many working men had been driven to Labour not in the quest for socialism but simply to secure representation of their own class interests. The intense industrial unrest of the years immediately preceding the First World War indicated some measure of working-class disenchantment with the Liberal government, a sign perhaps that belief in the identity of interest between the forces of labour and those of capital was losing its appeal. The loss of the institutional support of the trade unions, whatever the voting behaviour of individual trade unionists, was a further matter of concern. Chris Wrigley has pointed to the significance of the Trade Union Act of 1913, which partially reversed the Osborne Judgement of 1909 and allowed unions to hold ballots to authorise the setting up of political funds. By the beginning of 1914 trade unions with a membership of more than 1.2 million had voted in this sense. 'These votes', writes Wrigley, 'ensured Labour's post-First World War electoral finances, and in themselves reflect an element of the explanation for the rise of the Labour party and the decline of the Liberal party in the early twentieth century.'[92] As this account moves to a consideration of the impact of the war years, its cautious judgement must be that Liberalism in 1914 was a varied, but generally robust, political force – but one that was beset by more than its fair share of problems.

'Liberalism tore its heart out between 1914 and 1918 in a private agony about true and false Liberals, right and wrong Liberalism.'[93] At one level it is difficult to dispute Michael Bentley's verdict. The Liberal party, which entered the First World War in August 1914 under the leadership of Herbert Asquith with more than eight continuous and largely distinguished years in government to its credit, left the conflict badly divided, about to be humiliated in the Coupon Election of December 1918, held just weeks after the armistice came into force, and destined never again to form a government in its own right. That election saw the independent party, the governing party of 1914, still headed by Asquith, reduced to a rump of fewer than thirty MPs. Few would fail to include the impact of war in any list of the factors which contributed to the party's demise. Indeed, the more evidence that has been accumulated to show that the Liberal party was in no imminent danger of collapse in 1914, the more significance must be attached to the war as the key explanation of what subsequently occurred. Even so, the precise effect of four years of unprecedentedly intense conflict, the first total war in British experience, remains a matter of considerable controversy. Geoffrey Searle has identified three broad explanations of what happened. Some historians have focused on the accidents of history whereby key individuals – Lloyd George, Asquith and their followers, although the precise division of responsibility has been a further matter of vigorous debate – contributed by their mistakes and misjudgements to their party's decline. Others attach the greatest importance to the processes of social change, begun or perhaps only accelerated by the war, which created a system of class-based politics in which Liberalism, having coped perfectly well before 1914, found itself outflanked by an advancing Labour party. Finally, and most seductively, there are those who stress the inability of Liberalism as a political creed to cope with the demands of modern warfare.[94] 'It was their principles', asserts Kenneth Morgan, 'which the very fact of total war with the unbridled collectivism and the "jingo" passions which it unleashed, appeared to undermine.'[95] In the memorable image of Trevor Wilson, the war was like a 'rampant omnibus' which, out of control, mounted the pavement and ran over an unsuspecting pedestrian. That pedestrian, the British Liberal party, may have had its pre-war problems but it was perfectly capable of survival – until confronted by the unequal odds of the First World War.[96]

Each of these ideas may have some validity, but none on its own provides a complete explanation for the transformation which, whenever it began, had clearly overtaken British politics by the end of 1918. It is easy to suggest that the very coming of European war represented a contradiction of basic Liberal principles of internationalism and the primacy of reason over force. When Percy Illingworth, the party's Chief Whip, learnt of the outbreak of hostilities, he was heard to mutter, 'liberalism is dead'.[97] Yet the first point to note is not the damage which the coming of war did to the Liberal party but the fact that both party and government escaped from this potentially traumatic event largely unscathed. Indeed, it is worth stressing that, at this stage at least, the war seemed likely to inflict more damage on the Labour movement than on the Liberal party. ILP Socialists, including Ramsay MacDonald himself, opposed the war from the outset, whereas the majority of the parliamentary party followed the lead of the patriotic and non-ideological working man in backing the government. Despite the long-term ascendancy of Sir Edward Grey on matters of foreign policy, there had always been more potential within the Asquith cabinet for a major split in this area than on any other issue. For much of the crisis of August 1914, moreover, Asquith could not rely on a numerical majority of his cabinet colleagues to endorse a declaration of support for France. This is not to argue that a large and committed antiwar group of fixed resolve ever existed inside the cabinet. Rather there were as many as ten or twelve waverers who felt varying degrees of disquiet at the prospect of intervention. But these men lacked genuine agreement among themselves and they produced no leader. Lloyd George, whose past history perhaps cast him as the likely leader of a radical protest, was among the first to be won over to the Asquith–Grey camp. As the crisis developed, moreover, it became clear that Britain would intervene. The only question left was the political complexion of the government that did so. Asquith handled the situation with consummate skill, making sure that waverers understood that any substantial number of resignations would lead to a coalition government, a development which, as one of them argued, 'would assuredly be the grave of Liberalism'.[98] As a result, only the veteran Morley, by now a quaint survivor of Gladstonian days, and the working man, John Burns, withdrew from the cabinet, this pair creating scarcely a ripple in the government's equanimity.

This situation was matched inside the House of Commons where the vast majority of the parliamentary Liberal party had little difficulty in accepting the British declaration of war on 4 August. The crucial factor for most Liberal MPs was the German violation of Belgian neutrality which enabled the government to present British participation as a moral issue rather than as a question of *realpolitik*. Before the Belgian issue arose, it was another matter. As Richard Holt wrote on 2 August, 'it is impossible to believe that a Liberal government can be guilty of the crime of dragging us into this conflict in which we are in no way interested'.[99] Yet a week later his mood had dramatically changed: 'I had thought we might and should have kept out of the war but when Germany decided on an unprovoked attack upon Belgium, whose neutrality Germany equally with ourselves had guaranteed, it seemed impossible for us to stand by.'[100] Many Liberal politicians who had been ready as late as 3 August to join peace rallies were reconciled to, if not enthusiastic about, the fact of war only a day later. By insisting, prior to the violation of Belgian neutrality, that Britain was not bound to any particular course of action, Asquith could carry the vast majority of the parliamentary party with him. The public justification of Britain's involvement may not have matched the motivation which actually guided the key figures inside Asquith's cabinet, but it all amounted to a remarkably successful example of the government's skills of policy presentation.

At the same time, a significant minority of Liberals did refuse to endorse the government's line. C. P. Trevelyan, who resigned from his post as Parliamentary Secretary to the Board of Education, soon found himself co-ordinating the activities of around two dozen Liberals who wanted to work with Labour opponents of the war. The numbers involved were less significant than the coming together of radicals from differing political traditions and the scope this opened up for a transference of political allegiance. Trevelyan invited Ramsay MacDonald to a dinner of Liberal dissidents 'for the purpose of considering joint action and the creation of a new Parliamentary Party which will take action immediately, more particularly after the war has spent itself a little and which may be a permanent combination. They ask me to lead it both in the House and the country.' As MacDonald later noted, 'clearly wartime conditions raised prospects of political realignment'.[101] Another dissident Liberal recorded the outcome of the dinner:

> MacDonald, E. D. Morel, Angell, Ponsonby, Trevelyan – we talked until late last night about the organisation that will be required in future to advocate a safe foreign policy and the way in which this will probably effect [sic] parties in the future. It's early days to speak yet but it looks to me as if this war will probably result in the creation of a new party composed of men from both the Radical and Labour parties.[102]

Outright opposition to the war was difficult in the prevailing atmosphere of patriotic enthusiasm which greeted the outbreak of hostilities, but many doubters found it easier, now that war was a reality, to focus their concerns on the means by which it was conducted. They argued that Britain must fight on the basis of 'liberal' principles and avoid at all costs adopting the tactics of 'Prussianism' against which, after all, the war was being waged. This sort of thinking was behind the formation of the Union of

Democratic Control (UDC) which held its first meeting in September. Here radical Liberals encountered and exchanged ideas with like-minded men from other parties. The meeting was attended by a number of prominent Liberals including Morel, Ponsonby, Trevelyan, F. S. Cocks and C. Roden Buxton, but also by well-known figures from the ILP. Gradually the UDC developed into an important conduit which eased the passage of many Liberals into Labour's ranks. Such movements did not reflect ideological conversion but rather the closeness of existing views compounded by a shared hatred of secret diplomacy and wartime jingoism, and a mounting suspicion that the Liberal leadership could no longer be trusted to uphold Liberal values. Their new party, deserting Liberals hoped, would prove to be more 'liberal' than the one they had left. It was the beginning of a process by which 'the Labour Party via the ILP was able to sap the intellectual strength of the Liberal Party'.[103] By the early 1920s Trevelyan, Ponsonby and Morel were all Labour MPs under MacDonald's leadership. Trevelyan, who served as President of the Board of Education in both of the first two Labour governments, reflected, shortly before his appointment to a Labour cabinet, on the formative importance of the war years to the political journey travelled by men such as himself: 'Nothing could shake our feeling which grew during the war years that there is no one except you [MacDonald] who is big enough to give Europe the necessary lead.'[104]

The waging of the war undoubtedly contributed to the erosion of Liberal principles and values. As one Liberal MP warned, 'it would be a tragedy worse than war if, in order to win the War, England ceased to be the beacon of freedom and liberty which she has been in the past'.[105] Some Liberals clearly feared the slippery slope. 'Do you imagine', warned Trevelyan, 'that, if you start with this [seizure of UDC pamphlets] you are going to be able to stop? The outcome before long must be that you will have to begin imprisoning men for their opinions.'[106] But compromise was inevitable. The Defence of the Realm Act, 'which wipes out Magna Carta, the Bill of Rights, etc, in a few lines',[107] curtailed traditional liberties; the restrictions placed upon the freedom of the press and the internment of enemy aliens flew in the face of conventional Liberal presumptions; the National Registration Bill of July 1915 was widely interpreted as preparing the way for full-scale conscription; and McKenna's budget of October 1915, which imposed heavy duties on a wide range of luxury goods, represented a renunciation of the sacred Liberal creed of free trade. The clear temptation is to interpret the later split between Asquith, Lloyd George and their respective followers as but the visible manifestation of a more fundamental divide based upon a parting of the Liberal ways along ideological lines. But to suggest that Liberalism, as a laissez-faire philosophy, proved to be intellectually defenceless in the face of the necessary wartime encroachments of a collectivist state would be to impose an all too simple if convenient explanatory straitjacket on a complex set of events. In the first place it does scant justice to the way in which Liberalism had already abandoned much of its nineteenth-century outlook long before war broke out. It fails in short to allow for the impact of the New Liberalism on the party's outlook and ideas. Indeed, it has been suggested that, by 1914, the Liberal party was more committed to the notion of state intervention than were the Conservatives.[108] Secondly, it is striking that most of these measures were successfully enacted by a Liberal government, or at least by Liberal ministers within a Liberal-dominated coalition, prior to the crisis of December 1916, and without apparently doing any irreparable damage to the coherence of the party at Westminster. Furthermore, once the focus is shifted from the parliamentary arena to Liberalism as a national movement, it appears that such measures were accepted with little difficulty.[109] The Liberal party, in fact, proved to be a more flexible and pragmatic body than has often been allowed or than is indicated in the surviving documentation of articulate but not necessarily typical individuals. Thirdly, the divisions of December 1916 did not, at a personal level, accurately reflect the attitudes struck before that date. Committed Asquithians, supported by the impeccably 'liberal' *Westminster Gazette*, proved as ready as the followers of Lloyd George to swallow apparently illiberal measures. Ministers cannot be slotted neatly into opposing camps labelled 'laissez-faire' and 'control'. Rather, opinions varied depending on the particular issue at stake. McKenna, Runciman and Haldane backed the idea of government intervention to ensure the country's self-sufficiency in the production of aniline dye – whose importance extended beyond the colouring of cloth to the manufacture of high explosives and poison gas – and did so against the combined opposition of Asquith and Lloyd George.

The issues of the formation of a coalition and the introduction of conscription were of a different order. The two were linked in the sense that it was widely recognised that the presence of Conservatives inside the government made the abandonment of the voluntary principle markedly more likely. Historians have long picked over every available piece of evidence without reaching a definitive conclusion about the pressures which persuaded Asquith to take the opposition parties into his administration in May 1915. As one has written, 'unless the papers not so far available to researchers happen to contain an unusually convincing letter in the hand of one of the three men responsible for the decision, this question seems well placed to defy solution indefinitely'.[110] For long the debate alternated between the contending theories of a dispute at the Admiralty between the First Lord and the First Sea Lord over the conduct of the Dardanelles operations and an impending crisis over the supply of munitions to the Western Front as the primary factor forcing Asquith into the embrace of his Conservative opponents. More recently, it has been suggested that Asquith, unwilling to face the uncertain prospect of a wartime general election, was a more proactive architect of the First Coalition than these explanations tend to allow, an analysis which fits more comfortably with the continuing Liberal domination of the coalition cabinet and, particularly, of the great offices of state. Though Conservative pressure did oblige the Prime Minister to drop Haldane from the government and remove Churchill from the Admiralty, the paucity of Conservative representation in the reorganised government must remain striking, with the Tory leader, Bonar Law, securing no more than the Colonial Office. In the present context, however, the motivation behind Asquith's actions is less important than their consequences, although uncertainty about that motivation did contribute greatly to the feeling of unease which now pervaded the parliamentary Liberal party.

The ending of what proved to be the last purely Liberal government in the country's history provoked intense opposition among the rank and file. Asquith announced the formation of a coalition without warning or preparation and, 'told that all the "cream" of our party . . . were in open revolt . . ., wouldn't stand it at any price and were passing hot resolutions against it', had to act decisively to fend off a party revolt.[111] On this occasion at least, Richard Holt expressed the feelings of a broad spectrum of Liberal opinion:

> Why this has happened is not clear to anyone. There has been a campaign in Lord Northcliffe's press, but that could not have produced the result, and a quarrel between Winston Churchill and Lord Fisher at the Admiralty. Liberal opinion is dissatisfied and many Liberal members . . . are vexed and suspicious. The PM attended an impromptu meeting of Liberal members on Wednesday 19th [May] and alleged foreign affairs of an unrevealable character as his reason in a speech impressive but not ultimately convincing.[112]

Those who had felt misgivings about the actions of their own government had fewer qualms about giving voice to their concerns now that a 'mongrel coalition' was in power. But what did the new government portend? 'Nothing will persuade me', wrote Charles Hobhouse, 'that this is not the end of the Liberal party as we have known it.' Those Liberals who prostituted themselves by sharing power with Conservatives would become 'responsible for measures you disapprove, but cannot in the supposed "national" interest reject'.[113] C. P. Trevelyan concurred: 'This is the end of the Liberal Party. Now all Liberalism will be abandoned and we shall live under conscription and martial law.'[114] As the bonds linking the party leadership to its nominal followers became strained, groups of dissidents started to organise. Sir Charles Nicholson, MP for Doncaster, was the head of a small group known originally as the 'seven wise men'. 'We are meeting regularly', recorded Holt in June 1915, 'and discussing the situation with a view to giving the Government a Liberal pull whenever possible.'[115] One of their first concerns was the growing campaign for conscription.

Conscription was, wrote H. W. Massingham, an 'all-dominating anxiety', whose introduction would mean the end of national unity, leaving the Liberal party 'not merely suspended but broken for ever'.[116] For many Liberals, even among those ready to make compromises in the interests of military victory, conscription represented a step too far which would violate the most sacred principle of individual liberty, the right of a man to decide for himself whether he fought and quite possibly died for his country. Asquith himself was far from enthusiastic. In August he recorded the warnings of his own Chief Whip:

> Gulland . . . tells me that he gets letters from Liberal chairmen etc., all over the country denouncing Lloyd George as a lost soul, and some of them predicting that conscription would bring us to the verge, or over the verge of revolution. I have had several interviews with colleagues – Harcourt, Simon etc. – all strong in the same sense.[117]

By the end of the year this issue threatened to cause a serious rupture inside the cabinet as well as the parliamentary party. McKenna, Runciman and Simon all indicated that they would have to consider their positions if the government went ahead. Asquith responded by appealing to his colleagues not to deliver 'a shattering blow to the Government and I believe to the National Cause'.[118] Worse, however, was to follow when Edward Grey, the Foreign Secretary, indicated that, should McKenna and Runciman resign, he would feel obliged to follow them. Though Grey was no longer the force within the government that he had been until the outbreak of war, his departure might still have had fatal consequences for Asquith's continued premiership. For perhaps the last time, the Prime Minister displayed those skills of man-management which had kept his talented but sometimes wilful cabinet together for the last seven and a half years. While he worked upon Grey, Maurice Hankey, the Secretary to the War Committee, sought the possible basis of a compromise. In the event, only Simon, the Home Secretary, resigned, immovable on the basic proposition that it was wrong to compel a man to be a soldier against his will. In the House of Commons 35 Liberals voted against the government in a division on the conscription of single men on 6 January 1916. But unease went much deeper than this figure suggests. Many more abstained while others were cajoled into supporting the government in the knowledge that defeat would lead to the fall of the government and a probable Conservative victory in the subsequent general election. A few months later 41 Liberals recorded their votes against the conscription of married men. 'With this wanton breach with historic Liberalism', recorded *The Nation*, 'that great movement practically comes to an end, and a new alignment of parties must gradually take place, with new leaders to conduct it.'[119] The fact that Lloyd George appeared to have helped force Asquith's hand on this issue, and that personal relations between the two men were never quite restored thereafter to their former cordiality, made these words prophetic. 'None of the Radicals in the Cabinet is working with [Lloyd George],' recorded Lord Riddell as early as November 1915. 'He finds his supporters amongst the Conservatives.'[120]

Over the months that followed, Asquith failed to mould the coalition government into an effective instrument for waging war. In the allocation of ministerial portfolios he had tried to strike a balance between those who still sought to protect Liberal values and those who called for ever more far-reaching intervention on the part of the state. It was not an easy position to maintain. 'During 1916', writes Peter Clarke, 'the Liberal dilemma became sharper. Liberal methods could only be vindicated by military victory; yet victory seemed unattainable without abandoning Liberal methods. It sometimes seemed as though Asquith's Liberal credentials were only being confirmed by his apparent readiness to lose the war.'[121] Asquith himself satisfied neither side in the debate. To the interventionists his approach was too lackadaisical and his commitment to victory at whatever cost open to doubt. A group of about forty Liberal MPs constituted the so-called Liberal War Committee and did not seek to conceal their dissatisfaction with Asquith's leadership. They called for further measures of national mobilisation and for action against shirkers and unpatriotic dissidents. To the guardians of true Liberalism, Asquith's record was already tarnished by what he had done or allowed to be done since the outbreak of war. Almost certainly his own powers were beginning to wane. As early as November 1915 one of the Prime Minister's own backbenchers described him as 'a tired, almost broken man'. 'I have my doubts whether he is really strong enough in nerve and will power to go through.'[122] The balance between the virtues and faults of his peacetime leadership did not significantly change. But in a wartime context it was the latter which became increasingly apparent. Ministers commented upon his indecisive and excessively indulgent chairmanship of the cabinet. Stories abounded of his ability to find the time to play bridge while affairs of state were left in abeyance. Asquith seems to have been badly shaken when his youthful confidante, Venetia Stanley, announced her engagement to one of his own ministers, Edwin Montagu, in May 1915. The death in action of his eldest son, Raymond, in September 1916 left him deeply depressed. That autumn he became increasingly withdrawn and difficult to approach, absenting himself from several meetings of the cabinet. 'It is difficult to avoid the conclusion', judges Cameron Hazlehurst, 'that the strain of the war premiership, augmented by ill health and private grief, had rendered him unfit to continue at the head of the nation's affairs.'[123]

Above all, however, Asquith's fate was tied to the British war effort and dissatisfaction with his leadership was primarily a function of the country's inability to secure the often-promised victory. The year 1916 saw British pride badly shaken at Jutland and British manpower drained on the Somme, and still there was no prospect of an end to the war in sight. Against the background of the coalition, new political alignments began to take shape around the issues of the day, particularly the question of grand strategy. These alignments were not constant and there was much regrouping in the face of a changing political agenda. Nothing predetermined the eventual split between Asquith and Lloyd George, and indeed the two men came together again over the issue of a possible Irish settlement in the spring of 1916. Gradually, however, the debate at the heart of the administration came to crystallise around Asquith's failure to streamline the machinery of government to provide an effective decision-making body which could respond quickly to the developing war situation. Particularly after he succeeded Kitchener as War Minister in July, Lloyd George emerged as the leader of those determined to secure fundamental reforms. By this date he was of the view that the Liberal party had, 'so far as the war was concerned, become the Conservative Party. Any criticism of the War Office or the Admiralty . . . was regarded by the Liberals in Parliament as an indirect attack on the Prime Minister and they had become a positive hindrance to any reform.'[124] Furthermore, with Bonar Law's position at the head of the Unionist party by no means secure, the two men came to see the possibilities of a mutually advantageous partnership. Strikingly, Margot Asquith reacted to Lloyd George's appointment to the War Office with deep foreboding for her husband's future: 'We are out,' she insisted, 'it can only be a question of time now when we shall have to leave Downing Street.'[125]

The outcome of the final crisis of December 1916 was determined as much by chance and miscalculation as it was by intrigue and ambition. The issue at stake was the creation of a small war cabinet and, more particularly, the membership of it. Lloyd George later declared that he 'neither sought nor desired the Premiership'.[126] The first proposition is probably wholly true; the second partially so. What Lloyd George was determined to secure was executive control over the country's war effort. If this could be done while Asquith remained as Prime Minister, so be it. In the event, however, Asquith was persuaded that such an arrangement would have involved an unacceptable affront to his own standing and self-respect. In this situation the first wartime coalition came to an end. More importantly, Asquith and Lloyd George, for more than eight years the indispensable axis of the British government, went their separate ways. As a former Liberal Chief Whip put it, 'theirs has been the most formidable political combination that this country has ever known. Look what has been achieved within the last ten years.'[127] The new government still had a Liberal at its head but, noted Charles Hobhouse, 'if [Asquith] yields to George, taking Grey with him, the last remnant of liberalism and moderation vanishes from the Government'.[128] As Lloyd George formed a new coalition, in its heavy dependence on Conservative support different in kind from that of his predecessor, the question now was whether the Liberal party itself had been dealt a mortal blow.

2

THE LIBERAL CIVIL WAR, 1916–1935

So much has been written of the Lloyd George–Asquith split of December 1916, identifying it as a seminal moment in the fortunes of the Liberal party, that it is tempting to assume that the formation of the second wartime coalition marked a point of fundamental and irreversible division, after which little could be done to halt the processes of political decline. Arguably, however, it was less the fact of the split than its duration which did the party most damage. What is beyond dispute is that between 1916 and 1923 – and even in 1923 reunion and reconciliation were at best only partially secured – the Liberal party moved from being the leading party of government to the position of third force in British politics. In the same seven-year period, the Labour party moved from the periphery of the political spectrum, first to the status of official opposition and then to the verge of forming its first, albeit minority, government. As the third party the Liberals would be obliged to operate within an electoral system which fails to convert a minority party's share of the popular vote into a commensurate share of seats in the House of Commons. This fact in turn has the further long-term effect of discouraging the electorate from backing such a party, out of a desire to use their votes in support of a realistic contender for government. Once a party is consigned to the 'third party trap', therefore, it becomes increasingly difficult to escape from it, because of the self-perpetuating nature of its predicament. But was the Liberal party's descent to this status inevitable? There are, of course, strong arguments that it was destroyed by long-term structural changes in British society and politics. But a study of the decade and a half following the events of December 1916, during which period the Liberals remained a significant political force, lends weight to the view that the party was as much the victim of avoidable events as of ineluctable forces.

For some Liberals the war had certainly created a crisis of ideals and values with which they found it difficult to cope. For such men the Lloyd George–Asquith split afforded the opportunity to reassert true Liberalism, rescuing it from the contaminating constraints of association with an alien political philosophy. Richard Holt epitomised such a point of view: 'L. G. has behaved scandalously', he declared, 'and the section of the Liberals he takes with him are certainly not men conspicuous for their character.'[1] But to recognise such individuals is not the same as suggesting that the split of 1916 symbolised a fundamental ideological division in Liberal ranks between those capable of adapting to the demands of total war and those doomed to perish as they sought to uphold an outdated political philosophy which had no place in the increasingly collectivist twentieth century. A. J. P. Taylor once speculated that the split of 1916 reflected 'a division long a-growing' along class lines. But detailed analysis has failed to reveal any clear differentiation along generational, occupational, ideological or class lines. Nor were pre-war divisions accurately reflected in the new alignments.[2] In broad terms it is possible to suggest that the right wing of the party now looked to Lloyd George while the left turned to Asquith, but the critical consideration was an assessment of the abilities of the two Liberal leaders to manage and win the war. Such a judgement cut across all other patterns of division, placing Liberals of every hue in each camp. But what really confused the picture was the stance of the two leading protagonists. According to their pre-war pedigrees, it was by any analysis Asquith, the old Liberal Imperialist, who should have headed the right and been a more natural ally of the Conservatives, leaving the radical Lloyd George to champion the voice of pure Liberalism. The false position in which both men, especially Asquith, now found themselves did much to determine relations between the two factions for the remainder of the war and beyond.

Though he no longer headed the government, Asquith retained most of the apparatus of power in the Liberal party within his own hands. Party headquarters, funds and officials remained under his control and he enjoyed the support of the National Liberal Federation. The party's chief whip, John Gulland, also committed himself to Asquith. Most of the Liberals who agreed to join the Lloyd George government were figures of the second rank. The appointment of Churchill was for the time being blocked by opposition from the Conservatives. Even the number of rank-and-file MPs ready to support the new Prime Minister appears to have been exaggerated by the overenthusiastic Dr Addison, who was now promoted to the post of Minister of Munitions. Many of those whom Lloyd George was encouraged to regard as fully committed supporters actually voted against him in key parliamentary divisions in the second half of the war. In practice, nothing that could be described as a Coalition Liberal party existed before the autumn of 1918. Lloyd George relied heavily on Conservative support to supplement a shifting band of Liberal backers, the consistent core of which comprised no more than fifty MPs. But if Asquith held most of Liberalism's trump cards, his was not an easy hand to play. Barry McGill has defined his predicament as 'how to use his political prestige and his power as a party leader to support the war effort, without identifying himself and his followers with the government'.[3] This was never going to be an easy task, but it would be difficult to suggest that Asquith successfully carried it out. In particular, he proved an immense disappointment to those Liberals who, *faute de mieux*, had rallied to his standard in December 1916, many of whom had been uncertain from the outset about British participation in the war and critical of many of the actions of the wartime government of which he had been the head. One practical result of Asquith's stance was that a precarious party unity was maintained. Liberal whips continued to canvass the whole of the parliamentary party. Each side drew back from any step which would formalise existing cracks into a permanent division. On several occasions between the spring of 1917 and the end of the war Lloyd George put out feelers to see if Asquith could be persuaded to rejoin the government. But the former Prime Minister held aloof, revealing that, although the breach in the Liberal ranks had yet to be institutionalised, much ill-feeling would have to be overcome, before unity could be restored. 'Under no conditions', Asquith insisted in May 1917, 'wd. I serve in a Govt. of wh. LlG was the head. I had learned by long and close association to mistrust him profoundly. I knew him to be incapable of loyalty or lasting gratitude.'[4] Asquith, in fact, nurtured a sense of grievance about the way in which he had been treated in December 1916 which he never lost and which was shared by many of his closest associates. Liberal politics would continue to be scarred by such bitterness until his death and beyond.

But the policy of offering general support to the government from outside its ranks also had the practical effect of condemning the Asquithian wing of the party to political impotence at a time when it was in urgent need of revitalisation. 'My old party, the Liberals, are not fertile at present', noted the former Lord Chancellor, Lord Haldane, in November 1917. 'The feeling is that their work is over for the present.'[5] In particular, Asquith proved incapable of reclaiming for Liberalism the leadership of the radical left in British politics, leaving this position to be appropriated by Labour. Not surprisingly, after 1916 'Labour became a more serious positive political force, the Liberals a less serious opposition'.[6] Equally predictably, the tendency for radical Liberals to transfer to the Labour party, which had begun earlier in the war, continued apace. R. L. Outhwaite, R. C. Lambert, H. B. Lees-Smith and Joseph King were among Asquithian MPs who, by the end of the war or soon afterwards, had cut themselves adrift from Liberalism and joined the Labour ranks. This steady draining away of the radical content of the Liberal party – one estimate suggests that between 1917 and 1919 as many as 2000 Liberal activists joined the ILP alone – would have important consequences for the character of the post-war party and its ability to compete in the new political environment which emerged after 1918.

In so far as a coherent Liberal opposition to the Lloyd George government emerged between December 1916 and the armistice of November 1918, it did so despite rather than because of

Asquith. Listing those who were prepared to negotiate with the German government, Lloyd George's whip, Frederick Guest, included in the summer of 1918 'the Asquithians (except Mr Asquith)'.[7] Assiduous attendance at the Commons and purposeful leadership of his followers would, according to Holt, enable Asquith to recapture the initiative and put a rapid end to 'the L. G. villainy'.[8] But Asquith would not play the role for which Asquithians hoped. Nonetheless, a group of Liberals gradually developed the habit of opposing the government. In March 1917, 46 Liberals voted against the government's Cotton Duties Bill while 59 supported it. An analysis of 11 key wartime divisions shows that 24 Liberal MPs went into the opposition lobbies on at least seven occasions.[9] By the end of the year another unlikely alignment came into being as radical Liberals responded enthusiastically to the suggestion of Lord Lansdowne, the former Unionist Foreign Secretary, that the war should be brought to a compromise conclusion before civilisation itself was destroyed in the futile attempt to achieve outright victory. What was different about the celebrated Maurice Debate of 9 May 1918, which resulted from the publication of a letter from the recently removed Director of Military Operations charging that Lloyd George had misled parliament about the strength of British forces on the Western Front, was that this was the only occasion on which Asquith and the Asquithian whips gave their backing to a division against the government. With the support of the Conservatives Lloyd George easily survived but it was striking that as many as 98 Liberals backed Asquith and only 72 Lloyd George. Yet it is doubtful whether Asquith derived much benefit from his change of approach. Having demoralised his followers for so long, he now forfeited his claims to patriotic self-restraint. At the same time, he mishandled the parliamentary occasion by choosing to focus on the technical question of setting up a select committee rather than calling Lloyd George to account. *The Times*, drawing attention to the 'debut of an organized Opposition', believed that the first step had been taken 'towards what may become a permanent cleavage', and certainly steps were now taken to turn the Coalition Liberals into a separate party organisation. At the same time negotiations began for an electoral pact with the Conservatives.

That election was planned in the first instance as a wartime contest but, because of the sudden collapse of German resistance from the late summer onwards, took place just a month after the armistice. Lloyd George had no fixed view of the political basis upon which the election should be fought. He expected the Labour party to remain within the coalition and had not ruled out the possibility of Liberal reunion. Gradually, however, the logic of his close partnership with the Conservatives and their numerical dominance within his government became compelling. Lord Derby, the British ambassador in Paris, recorded a revealing conversation with the Prime Minister at the beginning of November:

> Lloyd George then said that the Liberal Party had been trying to get him very hard to go back to them. They told him that they quite understood if he went back he would be the Prime Minister and they would get rid of Asquith, but he told them 'No', that that would not be playing the game by our [Conservative] Party.[10]

Even so, Lloyd George sought almost to the end to bring Asquith back into the fold. In early October Lord Murray of Elibank, acting as intermediary between the two men, was authorised to offer Asquith a deal which included the latter's appointment to the Woolsack in a reconstructed government. Asquith's refusal seemed to Murray to be of more than passing importance: 'Unless I am very much mistaken, in these two conversations I have been present at the obsequies of the Liberal Party as I know it.'[11]

As many contemporaries recognised, the General Election of 1918 was of far greater significance than the split of two years before in determining the fortunes of the Liberal party. According to Asquith, writing in 1926, 'the disintegration of the Liberal Party began with the Coupon Election. . . . It then received a blow from which it has never since recovered.'[12] Herbert Gladstone concurred: 'The result of 1918 broke the party, not only in the

House of Commons but in the country. Local associations perished or maintained a nominal existence.'[13] As late as 1928 Lord Crewe still felt able to describe on-going party squabbles as 'perhaps the inevitable result of the infamous 1918 Election'.[14] But such judgements did not reflect a clear ideological or even policy division between the two Liberal factions which contested the election. The campaigns of coalition and independent Liberals revealed no great differences. In his first major speech of the campaign Asquith concentrated his attack on the Conservative element in the government, while defining himself as a Liberal 'without prefix and suffix, without label and hallmark of any sort and description'. Lloyd George assured a delegation of Manchester Liberals that he himself remained a Liberal, that he would never call on anyone to sacrifice Liberal principles and that, while continuing coalition was the condition for successful reconstruction, his government would put forward 'a great Liberal programme'.[15] Indeed, most Liberals could applaud the recognisably Liberal content of the coalition manifesto. Though limited measures of protection were proposed to safeguard key industries from foreign dumping, the essentials of free trade were maintained. In addition Lloyd George promised Home Rule for Ireland (with safeguards for Ulster) and church disestablishment for Wales.

The problem lay not in policy but in Lloyd George's ready acceptance of the bargain struck by Guest with the Conservatives that only 150 Liberal candidates would receive the letter of endorsement, or 'coupon', signed by Bonar Law and himself. In the circumstances of 1918, amid the euphoria surrounding the recent military victory, this imprimatur represented a virtual passport to Westminster for its fortunate recipients. Until the issuing of the coupon to his Conservative opponent, recalled Percy Harris, the sitting MP for Harborough, 'all had been going well, but now my friends melted away like snow in the night'.[16] But the paucity of favoured Liberals meant that Lloyd George was obliged to endorse large numbers of Conservatives against the representatives of his own party. By this act he created lines of division which were altogether more rigid than any drawn up in 1916, while putting himself permanently beyond the political pale as far as most Asquithian Liberals were concerned. In Yorkshire, for example, where the party's parliamentary representation had been largely Asquithian, it was Lloyd George's supporters who were now elected. Yet rank-and-file Liberals retained their earlier loyalties, thereby undermining the party's unity within the local constituencies.[17]

Finding themselves in opposition to 'couponed' candidates, Asquithian Liberals had little with which to tempt the voter. Asquith's own election address reiterated the classic doctrines of Gladstonian individualism, but seemed to have abandoned those social priorities of the New Liberalism with which his pre-war government had been so closely associated. It was all very disappointing for the dwindling band of Liberal radicals who were keen to take up again the progressive themes which the war had inevitably sidelined. Campaigning in Manchester, E. D. Simon began by welcoming the challenge of producing a party programme to 'put against the excellent programme prepared by [Sidney] Webb for Labour'. He had made a clear decision that 'the Liberal Party is the right place for me notwithstanding the attractiveness of the Labour programme'. By polling day, however, he was bemoaning 'the utter lack on the part of the Liberal Party, and the [Manchester] candidates in particular, of any knowledge of or interest in industrial problems and the great question of equality between the two nations of England'.[18] Matters became no easier for uncouponed Liberals as the campaign progressed and government spokesmen responded to the increasingly shrill demands in the popular press for the draconian treatment of the defeated German enemy. Simon was horrified by the way in which Lloyd George, 'following the irresponsible levity and the lust for blood of the yellow press', had 'reduced the election to the lowest level of demagoguery'.[19]

Overall it is hard to resist the conclusion that the Liberal party of 1918 was no longer, as it had been at the outbreak of war, the major party of the British working class. Its own problems and divisions were compounded by the way in which the war had helped to develop a unified class-consciousness in which earlier distinctions between skilled and unskilled workers were less sharp and which now translated into a belief that the Labour party represented the natural vehicle for working-class aspirations. As only 258 Asquithian candidates, compared with 358 Labour ones, stood for more than seven hundred seats, many erstwhile Liberal voters looking to oppose the government were forced to choose between voting Labour and abstention.[20] With the pre-war progressive alliance consigned to history, existing patterns of party allegiance may well have been broken. But any analysis of electoral behaviour in 1918 has to encompass the impact of the Representation of the People Act, or Fourth Reform Act, passed earlier in the year, as a result of which the electorate was almost three times as large (21.4 million) as it had been at the previous contest in December 1910 (7.7 million). Allowing for deaths in the intervening period and for those too young to vote in 1910, only about a quarter of the electorate of 1918 had entered a polling booth before. Much interest and considerable controversy has attached to the way in which these newly enfranchised voters exercised their political voice.

An important article published in the mid-1970s seemed for a time to have discovered the elusive explanatory factor in the replacement of the Liberals by Labour as the main force of the progressive left.[21] Historians had become increasingly aware that the Second and Third Reform Acts of 1867 and 1884 had fallen some way short of creating universal manhood suffrage. The franchise was significantly limited by difficult residence qualifications which meant that only about 60 per cent of adult males were on the electoral register at any one time. Though only about 12 per cent were formally excluded, the remainder changed residence too regularly or merely failed to register. Thus, it was now argued, a restricted pre-war franchise which left about half the working class without the vote had inevitably limited Labour's ability to tap into its natural constituency of support. When full male suffrage was achieved in 1918, the effect was entirely predictable. A working-class electorate turned to Labour, as it would probably have done before 1914 had the opportunity been open to it. Thus a genuinely democratic pre-war franchise would have enabled

Labour to challenge the Conservative–Liberal duopoly far more effectively than it did and, although 'we cannot say how many votes the introduction of universal franchise was worth to Labour . . . we can say that it was a critical element in the emergence of the party as a major political force'.[22] The post-war electorate, moreover, swamped by less sophisticated voters from the lower social classes, was one to which the Liberals with their demanding political ideas would find it increasingly difficult to appeal. In this analysis the significance of the war in determining the changing fortunes of the parties of the left was clearly diminished. What happened after 1918 would largely have happened before 1914 had the advent of full democracy not been delayed.

This seductive theory has been attacked at many levels and is now largely discredited. In the first place it tends to overlook the fact that the greatest single addition to the electorate in 1918 came from the newly enfranchised female vote rather than from additions to the ranks of the male franchise. Then, as Duncan Tanner has shown, it is misleading to suggest that all the voteless men of the pre-1918 era were working-class and therefore natural, but frustrated, Labour supporters. The existing bias of the constitution was in favour of householders and against lodgers, irrespective of class or income. Many middle-class men were prevented from voting either because their work made them too mobile or because of the complexities of the voting qualifications relating to lodgers in the pre-1918 period. Tanner concludes that the difference between the pre-war electorate and its much larger post-war equivalent was not substantial when measured in class terms and insufficient to explain a significant change in the electoral performance of the Liberal and Labour parties, a line of argument which tends to reinstate the importance of the war in transforming voting behaviour.[23] Three-quarters of the newly enfranchised male voters could not vote in municipal elections, yet the Labour party flourished in such contests after 1918. By contrast, in areas such as the East End of London, which had a particularly low parliamentary franchise before the war, the post-war Liberal performance remained relatively strong. Furthermore, the advocates of the 'franchise factor' have too readily assumed that what did happen after 1918 would necessarily have happened before 1914, had a more democratic electorate existed at that time. By underestimating the size of the pre-war working-class vote, they tend to ignore the success of Edwardian Liberalism in presenting itself as the natural and legitimate party of the British working class. The real question to be asked is why the Liberals were unable to maintain that image in the post-war era.

Recent research suggests that the bias of the pre-war franchise was more apparent in terms of age than of class. Thus it may be that the mounting problems of the Liberal party in the decade after 1918 had less to do with a transfer of allegiance to the Labour party on the part of existing working-class voters than with the Liberals' failure to attract a sufficient proportion of successive cohorts of new working-class voters as they qualified, by age, to vote. The generation which came of age in the second and third decades of the century underwent 'increasingly similar educa-tional experiences, increasingly similar leisure pursuits, and increasingly similar working conditions' which inclined them towards a 'more inclusive and less hierarchical identification of their class and its particular needs', in other words, a growing propensity to vote Labour.[24] As a result, existing Liberal voters died off and were not, despite the usual tendency of children to copy the voting patterns of their parents, replaced in sufficient numbers from the next generation. Such an interpretation is consistent with the steady progress made by the Labour party, largely at Liberal expense, *throughout* the 1920s, whereas the 'fran-chise factor' explanation in its crudest form would be more compatible with a 'big bang' of Labour advance as soon as the franchise was widened in 1918. As it was, Labour improved its share of the poll at *every* election between December 1910 and May 1929, a fact easily lost sight of because of the vagaries of the electoral system which produced a Labour government in January 1924 but consigned the party to opposition again in the following October.

Whatever the forces at work, nothing could conceal the enormity, at least in statistical terms, of the catastrophe inflicted on British

Liberalism by the General Election of 1918. One hundred and thirty-three Liberal Coalitionists were returned, though these were easily outnumbered by 335 Conservatives. But only 28 Asquithians – and the term has to be used loosely for these were men who were opposed to or not supported by Lloyd George rather than followers of the party leader – took their seats in the new House of Commons. At the same time, Labour's representation went up to 63 with a further 10 MPs elected as Labour supporters of the government. Though the results were delayed in order to count the service votes, many Liberals seem to have sensed their fate before it was announced. 'It seems pretty clear that the poll yesterday was disastrous,' recorded Richard Holt. 'I saw some politicians and found the same impression everywhere – complete defeat of the Liberal party.'[25] E. D. Simon 'drove round the Committee Rooms and Polling Stations of Manchester and had 'no doubt that we are badly beaten'.[26] All the Liberal ex-ministers who had gone into qualified opposition in December 1916 now went down to defeat. Asquith himself was ousted in East Fife, a constituency he had represented for 32 years. In Frome in Somerset, the Liberal candidate and, except for a short break, its sitting member since 1892, now lost his deposit. According to *The Times* only three non-coalition Liberals with any front-bench experience survived the slaughter, George Lambert, F. D. Acland and William Wedgwood Benn. When a journalist asked John Simon, defeated at Walthamstow, to comment on this rout, he responded bravely: 'We have been snowed under, but snow melts.' Thirty years later he added an apparently appropriate postscript. 'But while snow melts, it may in the meantime crush the life out of that which it has buried.'[27]

That said, the party's plight, at this stage at least, can easily be overdrawn. The salient feature of the Coupon Election was the overwhelming personal triumph of Lloyd George. 'There has never been an election like this one in its one-man nature,' wrote Edwin Montagu in a comment which managed to combine flattery of his political master with objective observation. 'Somebody said to me the other day that the only speeches in the papers were your speeches, that the only thing the country listened to was what you said.'[28] So great in fact was the personal endorsement registered by the electorate that it seems reasonable to suppose that Lloyd George would have been victorious in 1918 whatever the political organisation he had headed, including a united Liberal party. Even in defeat, such a party would have had much greater prospects of recovery, while Lloyd George himself would have been well placed to inherit its formal leadership whenever Asquith chose to stand down.

The reality in 1918, however, was that the Liberal party was divided, that it would stay divided, and that its divisions would become deeper during the remaining years of the coalition government. Between the elections of 1910 and 1918 independent Liberalism had gone from governing to third-party status without alighting at an intermediate position. Now, with Asquith, whatever his failings, out of parliament, the party scarcely cut an impressive figure. From what was admittedly a limited pool of parliamentary talent, the somewhat dull figure of Sir Donald Maclean was chosen as sessional chairman pending Asquith's assumed return to the House of Commons. Meanwhile, the party seemed shrouded in gloom, as if completely overpowered by the magnitude of the disaster which had befallen it. Its preoccupation with the divisions in its own ranks impeded any remaining hope of building upon pre-1914 foundations to develop policies to respond to the mass working-class electorate. Ramsay Muir later recalled the condition of the party in the immediate post-war period:

> What was left of the Liberal party was a merely negative and querulous faction, mumbling the shibboleths of the xix cent. and not even capable of understanding the change of orientation implicit in the pre-war legislation and demanded by the postwar situation. Liberalism stood for nothing but complaints of LG, and therefore it sank to futility . . . It had to be given a 'constructive programme', not as a bait to catch the electorate, but as a means of keeping its soul alive.[29]

Defeat at East Fife gave Asquith, now in his sixty-seventh year, the opportunity to retire gracefully from the scene. Instead, he clung on for eight more years to the reins of leadership, motivated as much as anything else by a negative determination to deny Lloyd George the chance of the succession. He appears to have believed that a revival was just around the corner and that he was destined to lead the party back to the promised land of Liberal government. These years formed a sad postscript to a distinguished career and, as even his most sympathetic biographer concedes, did nothing to enhance his historical reputation.[30] Indeed, it is impossible to escape the conclusion that the post-war Asquith was but a shadow of his former self, using, as Edward Grey put it, 'the machine of a great political brain to rearrange old ideas'.[31] Asquith did return to parliament following a by-election in Paisley in 1920, but the position scarcely improved thereafter. He had little to offer in terms of energetic new ideas and seemed curiously incapable of taking an effective stand against the government, despite or perhaps because of his intense hatred of its leader. The Asquithian court resembled 'an extra-parliamentary conclave of the elder venerated, meeting in spacious drawing-rooms to await the second coming'.[32]

Asquith's uninspiring leadership and his inability to exercise any great impact on national politics had an inevitably debilitating effect upon his party. 'The leadership is an immense drawback in the eyes of many people', complained Henry Gladstone, 'because it leads them to the conclusion that there is no alternative Govt. to LG's.'[33] Yet the establishment of an active leadership was a fundamental prerequisite for the party's rehabilitation: 'The party is not in a position to run itself.'[34] Such thinking gave rise to a half-hearted attempt to bring Edward Grey, despite his failing eyesight, back into the centre of Liberal politics, either to lend some backbone to Asquith or ultimately to replace him. If the latter option could be arranged, thought the Liberally-minded Conservative, Lord Robert Cecil, 'the Liberal Party has a great future before it'.[35] Some believed that a political realignment, which included the recreation of something like the pre-war progressive alliance, offered the best chance of salvation. 'A Grey Cecil Asquith Government is the best hope,' argued Herbert Gladstone. 'They would get much support from Thomas, Clynes and the moderate Labour men.'[36] In what was in many cases an act of self-delusion Liberals continued to believe that the two parties of the left represented complementary wings of the same movement. Yet most of those for whom this was the case had already made the transition to Labour or were contemplating doing so. Radical Liberals could make this transition without themselves undergoing any dramatic conversion. They moved to Labour not because they were changing their own views but because Labour now had a stronger claim to traditional Liberal values and aspirations than did the Liberal party itself. E. D. Simon pondered the possibilities of a parliamentary career:

> the question of Liberal and Labour parties seems likely to become acute. A modified radical party would suit me best, or a new combination of radical Labour if only that could be brought about . . . But about four fifths of the people whose political views I admire are in the Labour Party! Of course if I do go for Parliament it would be rather nice to stand for Withington; and if I made up my mind and worked for it I could probably be Liberal (or for that matter Labour!) candidate next time.

But few Asquithian stalwarts would have accepted Simon's contention that 'economic equality (at least of opportunity) is probably the acid test as to whether the Liberal party still represents a Liberal spirit'.[37]

What is most striking about the post-war Liberal party is the picture of a backward-looking movement which had cut itself adrift from the New Liberalism of the pre-war period. The party failed to develop relevant social and economic policies to confront the problems of industrial Britain. The outdated slogans of the nineteenth century were not likely to entrench the party in a solid base of working-class support, yet this is precisely what most leading Liberals proceeded to offer. 'The party leaders', recalled Simon, 'still lived in the old idea of laissez-faire; their only industrial policy was free trade.'[38] The unrelated John Simon offered confirmation. His major preoccupations remained free trade and 'economy', a crusade to reduce wasteful government expenditure. Traditional laissez-faire would, he believed, open the way for social progress, industrial prosperity, security of employment and a high standard of living. In similar mode Maclean had 'nothing heroic to offer. I believe we will only get things adjusted naturally by . . . simple commonsense and homely wisdom . . . the only way to get back to national health is by way of economy.'[39] Henry Gladstone sought refuge in the familiar platitudes of his father's generation: 'Peace, Retrenchment and Reform, the fine old watchwords are again the necessity of the moment.'[40] 'All too plainly', concludes Michael Bentley, 'liberalism was out of date.'[41] The traditional issues which had dominated the Liberal agenda of the nineteenth century – political and religious emancipation, disestablishment, the Lords veto, licensing reform, home rule – had now either been resolved or else were incapable of exciting the enthusiasm of earlier years. In their place the party failed to develop a new agenda of social and economic reform, despite the promising start made in the two decades before the First World War.

So while many Liberals in the early 1920s still looked wistfully to a partnership with Labour, these same men often also voiced an unqualified opposition to Labour's commitment to state regulation and public expenditure. 'The weak point in the situation apart from Libs and Labour opposing each other', suggested Henry Gladstone, 'is the extravagant policy of Labour. They don't seem to mind how much money is spent on Home Depts.' If only Labour would postpone the nationalisation of minerals, including mining royalties, he would 'not be so much afraid'.[42] Yet even a more imaginative Liberal approach than this would have been unlikely to prompt a favourable response from Labour. While welcoming individual defections, Labour now opposed any realignment with the Liberals on strategic rather than specific policy grounds. Its leaders, particularly Ramsay MacDonald, saw that it was in Labour's long-term interests to maintain the lead it had established over the independent Liberals in 1918 and to drive them into a permanent third-party position, thus leaving Labour as the only viable alternative to Conservative government. 'By the 1920s', concludes Peter Clarke, 'the ideological convergence of Liberals and social democrats was matched by a tactical divergence . . . much to the frustration of those of a progressive outlook.'[43]

Whatever may be said of the Liberal party, Liberalism was not wholly moribund in this period. During the winter of 1918–19 a group of Manchester businessmen began meeting on a regular basis at the home of E. D. Simon, a local manufacturer and expert on housing, to discuss industrial questions. To begin with, the reaction of the party leadership was discouraging, but in June 1920 Simon recorded: 'we sent a resolution to the Leamington meeting of the NLF demanding an industrial policy. To our surprise, instead of hostility, we were received with open arms, given seats on the platform, and our resolution accepted by the official gang.'[44]

At a meeting at Simon's Herefordshire farm in the spring of 1921, attended by Ramsay Muir, Professor of History at the University of Manchester, and Edward Scott, son of the proprietor of the *Manchester Guardian*, the notion of the Liberal Summer School was devised. The idea was to provide a forum in which a range of social and economic issues could be discussed, from a Liberal point of view but separate from any formal party structure. The Summer School, which met for the first time in Grasmere in September 1921, would bring together the Manchester group and a number of Cambridge intellectuals including J. M. Keynes, Walter Layton and Hubert Henderson. 'I am really hopeful', recorded Simon, 'that it will be the beginning of a genuine awakening of thought and study in Liberal circles.'[45] Over the decade the movement sought to build upon the foundations of the New Liberalism of the pre-war era in the direction of greater state intervention without going down the path of doctrinaire socialism. It was hoped that it would have the sort of impact upon the Liberal party that the Fabian Society had exercised over the Labour movement.[46]

The influence of the Summer Schools was most marked in the second half of the decade, once Lloyd George had assumed the party leadership. For the time being, however, the immediate problem was the reunion of the party's severed wings. In the early days of the post-war coalition, the lines of Liberal divisions were far from clear. There was some movement between the two groups, generally in the direction of the Independent Liberals, or 'Wee Frees' as they came to be called, while, in the House of Lords, Liberals continued to behave very much as a single party under the leadership of Lord Crewe. The selection of George Lambert, who had not received the coupon at the election, as parliamentary chairman of the coalition Liberal group, suggested a conciliatory attitude towards the Asquithians. A joint committee to promote unity met on several occasions early in 1919 before negotiations broke down in March. Most Liberals could find something to applaud in the government's programme. At least until the economies effected by the 'Geddes Axe' from August 1921, Liberal influence was fully apparent in the coalition's policies of social reform and reconstruction. Despite the passage of the Safeguarding of Industries Act in 1920, Britain remained in essence a free-trade country. Individual measures could still prompt the reassertion of an essential Liberal unity. Seventeen Coalition Liberals supported a motion moved by the Asquithian, Wedgwood Benn, to delete moves towards Imperial Preference from Austen Chamberlain's budget of April 1919, while many more abstained. Only perhaps the government's repressive policies in Ireland, and in particular the excesses of the notorious 'Black and Tans', suggested that Lloyd George had lost touch with his Liberal roots. In a letter to *The Times* in April 1921 John Simon condemned the government's Irish tactics as 'politically disastrous and morally wrong . . . exposing us to the scorn of the world'.

But what really stood in the way of reunion was the intransigent opposition of the Asquithian leadership, which was in no mood to forgive Lloyd George for what he had done. 'I would not trust him,' confessed Henry Gladstone. 'I am not sure I would not prefer to vote for a Tory rather than a man who would support Lloyd George and his Coalition for another five years.'[47] Matters came to a head at the meeting of the National Liberal Federation General Committee at Leamington in May 1920. Here the Coalition Liberal delegation, led by the Attorney General, Sir Gordon Hewart, walked out in protest against the patent hostility of the Wee Frees. In the months which followed, area federations and constituency parties found themselves having to choose between the two factions. Only in Wales did the Lloyd Georgeites retain the upper hand. In many local associations the result of bitter in-fighting between the two groups was an almost complete collapse of organisation and activity. Even then, most Coalitionists continued to hanker after reunion, but Lloyd George was always aware of the danger of alienating his Conservative partners, upon whose parliamentary backing his premiership ultimately depended. Concerned, as throughout his career, with policies rather than parties, he saw little future for Liberalism in the post-war era and seemed more interested in the possibilities of a wide-ranging political realignment. 'The so-called Liberal party', he told Lord Riddell in 1919, 'consists mostly of plutocrats who have no sympathy whatever with the aspirations of the mass of the people.'[48] 'Liberal labels', he warned his ministers, 'lead nowhere: we must be prepared to burn them.'[49] But Lloyd George failed to carry his Liberal supporters with him in the quest for a new centre party and, by the spring of 1920, had few options left other than to try to convert the Coalition Liberals into a permanent organisation. Guest set himself the aim of creating a local Coalition Liberal party in every parliamentary constituency, but the task proved much more difficult than had been expected.

With division ever more firmly entrenched, it was scarcely surprising that Liberalism failed to benefit from the government's mounting unpopularity. Three early by-election victories in March and April 1919, at which substantial government majorities were overturned, proved deceptive. During the parliament as a whole Independent Liberals came third in 15 out of 24 three-cornered contests. Only two further by-election gains were recorded before the General Election of 1922 and both of these were in rural seats with a strong Liberal tradition. In industrial, working-class constituencies it was Labour, with 13 gains in the course of the parliament, which profited from the government's misfortunes. What was particularly worrying was the evidence of what could happen if the party remained divided. When, at the end of 1919, a vacancy arose in the Spen Valley division of

Yorkshire following the death of the sitting Coalition Liberal member, the local Liberal association, anxious now to run an Independent Liberal candidate, selected the former Home Secretary, Sir John Simon. Until this point Lloyd George had happily supported Coalition Conservatives against Asquithians, but had stopped short of engineering a direct contest between competing Liberals. At Spen Valley he took a different line, putting forward a Coalition Liberal candidate. As the Liberal vote was clearly going to be split, it is evident that the desire to exclude Simon was more important to the Prime Minister than the election of a government supporter: 'I don't care who wins if that blighter is last.'[50] The outcome of the by-election was entirely predictable. The Coalition candidate siphoned off enough Liberal votes from Simon to deliver the seat to Labour. The Spen Valley result would come to be seen as a signal moment in Labour's transition to the status of a party of government.

The fall of Lloyd George's government in October 1922, following the decision of rank-and-file Conservative MPs to reject the advice of their leader, Austen Chamberlain, that they should fight the next election still bound to the coalition, offered an obvious opportunity to repair the breach in the ranks of the Liberal party. But the decision of the new Prime Minister, Andrew Bonar Law, to call an immediate General Election offered no time for such a development to take place, even had the will existed on the part of the two principals, Asquith and Lloyd George. As a result, and with the Conservatives also divided between the adherents of the new government and those, led by Chamberlain, who still hankered after a renewed coalition, the General Election of 1922 represented 'a state of confusion unknown in any former election. The old party lines [were] gone.'[51] Some Liberal candidates stood as unequivocal adherents of one or other Liberal leader, others tried to paper over the party's divisions, and some campaigned specifically for reunion. As Lloyd George recalled:

the Liberals spent a great part of their strength in fighting each other. It was the hardest job I ever had and I hope never to have such another . . . You never knew from what quarter the attack would come and the conditions varied from constituency to constituency. The people who were helping each other in one constituency would be fighting in the next.[52]

The Asquithians, in particular, seemed ill-prepared. A few weeks before the election, Maclean had found Asquith 'devoted to bridge and small talk, doing no real work and leaving the party leaderless'.[53] With only 328 candidates for a parliament of over six hundred seats, the Independent Liberals could not realistically expect to control the outcome of the election without the co-operation of Lloyd George and his followers.

But this was an important contest. The unique circumstances of 1918 and the very existence of a coalition had not provided the easiest background against which to assess the standing of the parties in the newly unfolding post-war political environment. Despite the new lines of division, the election of 1922 at least represented a return to something like the normal pattern of domestic politics. Perhaps the most striking feature was the extent to which, with the Liberals still focusing on an essentially pre-war agenda, Labour had now taken over from them as the party of the industrial working class. Campaigning for her father in Paisley, Asquith's daughter, Violet Bonham Carter, sensed the change of mood resulting from high levels of unemployment: 'In places where there was no distress or unemployment – Huddersfield for instance – one felt quite different straightaway. There Liberalism had the democratic wind – or a gust of it – and there was no bitterness in the fight.'[54] But Liberals were also in danger of being outflanked on the right. Bonar Law's Conservatives had taken over the fight for retrenchment and decontrol upon which many Asquithians had campaigned since the end of the war.

In the event, neither Liberal faction had much cause for satisfaction. The Independent Liberals gained 43 seats and ended up with a total of 54, a considerable improvement over their performance in 1918. But 14 seats had been lost, 9 of them to Labour, and their showing in mining seats, where they had done well before 1914, was especially disappointing. Their best results came in straight fights with the Conservatives in those traditionally

Liberal rural constituencies which had been lost in the peculiar circumstances of 1918. The performance of the Lloyd Georgeites was, if anything, even worse. They won just 62 seats as against 133 in 1918 and went down badly in industrial areas. But the Liberal performance also needs to be seen in the overall party political context. Contests among themselves may have cost Liberals up to fourteen seats, mostly to the advantage of Labour. Had these stayed in Liberal hands, the combined Liberal total might have been enough to deprive Labour of the psychologically important status of 'official opposition' to which it now rightfully laid claim. Also striking was the fact that, taken together, Labour and the Liberals, the partners in the old Progressive Alliance, captured 58.6 per cent of the popular vote. The Conservatives with just 38.2 per cent won 483 Westminster seats and a Commons majority of 75. In the Liberal landslide of 1906 the Progressive parties had won 54.9 per cent of the vote against the Unionists' 43.6. However it was analysed, the 1922 result offered Liberals little solace. 'People have either gone back to Conservatism or have swung right over to Labour,' suggested John Simon. He sensed a 'very grave danger' that Liberalism could be 'crushed out between the upper and nether millstone', but took comfort in the belief that there was a great deal of sympathy for the party in the country which had not been expressed at the polls.[55] C. P. Scott of the *Manchester Guardian* was altogether more brutal; the result, he believed, was even worse than in 1918 'because there was less excuse for it'.[56]

In fact the General Election of 1922 showed how difficult it would be for the Liberals to re-emerge as serious contenders for power in the new three-party system which had, for the time being, been superimposed on a political structure best suited to just two competitors. The combination of the first-past-the-post electoral system and a preponderance of three-cornered contests in the elections of the 1920s produced a succession of unrepresentative results in which a marginal shift in votes could lead to a significant change in parliamentary representation. Sometimes this worked to the advantage of the Conservatives; sometimes Labour benefited. But Liberalism almost invariably lost out. By 1922 the disadvantages of third-party status were already becoming apparent. In rough terms the combined party had secured nearly 30 per cent of the popular vote but less than 20 per cent of the seats in the new House of Commons. The Conservative election campaign had been focused on the Labour challenge in a way that was designed to polarise the debate and at the same time squeeze out the Liberal party as a largely irrelevant factor. If Liberalism was to have any chance of recovery, it needed to define its specific position in the changed political spectrum with far greater clarity than it had so far achieved.

A further prerequisite of Liberal revival was reunion of the party's warring factions, if for no other reason than that the party needed access to Lloyd George's political fund, derived largely from the sale of honours during his premiership, to sustain its electoral viability. The auguries, however, were not good. 'While my opinion is all for reunion,' wrote Lord Cowdray, 'I consider, if reunion involved in any way our acceptance of Lloyd George, that we cannot afford to pay such a price.'[57] An early approach from Lloyd George was coolly rebuffed. The question of leadership was obviously a potential stumbling block, especially as the Asquithians moved quickly to block the Welshman's claims to the succession. Asquith and John Simon decided that Simon should become deputy leader of the party and the latter agreed to give up all his legal work which might interfere with his new parliamentary duties. With Asquith now 70 years of age, Simon clearly anticipated that he rather than the ageing leader would be the driving force in the party's parliamentary activities. But merger with the former coalitionists would throw Simon's eventual claim to the succession into question. 'The whole problem of Liberal reunion', reported the *Evening Standard*, 'will soon resolve itself into the single question of Liberal leadership. Asquith, Lloyd George or Simon.' A short session of the new parliament began on 20 November and ended less than a month later. George Lambert tried to summon a joint meeting of MPs from both groups, but neither leadership responded positively. 'Because . . . I have tried to avoid the peril of Liberal disunion,' he complained to Herbert Gladstone, 'the rival Popes of Liberalism have placed me on the index of the politically damned.'[58]

Lloyd George, however, became increasingly convinced of the need for reunion and, in the spring of 1923, made a series of public speeches urging this cause as the precondition of Liberal revival. 'If we do not reunite,' he insisted, 'Liberalism is done as a national driving force.'[59] A motion in favour of reunion was signed by 73 Liberal MPs in March, but the annual meeting of the National Liberal Federation at Buxton ignored insistent demands from the constituencies. None the less, two by-elections in Anglesey and Ludlow saw Coalition Liberals and Asquithians coming spontaneously together, efforts towards reunion began in other constituencies and by September more than fifty local Liberal and National (Lloyd Georgeite) Liberal associations had merged. But what no one could have anticipated was that it would be Stanley Baldwin, the new Conservative Prime Minister, who would succeed, where Lloyd George and other Liberals had failed, in giving the final push towards bringing the two factions together. Baldwin had taken over from the ailing Bonar Law in May, with the parliamentary majority secured by the latter the previous November still intact. In a speech in Plymouth on 25 October, however, he declared his wish to secure a fresh mandate to introduce tariffs. He was impeded in doing this by a pledge given by Law not to impose them without the nation's express approval.

The effect upon Liberalism was dramatic. Still at this date no single issue was as likely to cement the disparate strands of Liberalism into a single whole as the defence of free trade. This issue had the potential to give Liberals a tactical advantage over Labour, perhaps the only question that could still do so. Once Lloyd George had returned from a visit to the Unites States, a combined committee of Liberals which included Asquith, Simon, Lloyd George and Sir Alfred Mond managed to hammer out a joint election manifesto and it was agreed that Liberals would fight as a united party across the country. It was also announced that Liberal candidates would take the field in sufficient numbers to make the party a practical alternative to the Conservative government. For this to happen, of course, Lloyd George's finan-cial support was imperative. Asquith had no alternative but to bite the bullet, but he evidently felt uncomfortable when he and Lloyd George appeared together on the same platform in Paisley. 'I have rarely felt less exhilaration than when we got to the platform amid wild plaudits and a flash-light film was taken, "featuring" me and Ll.G separated only by the chairman.'[60]

The Liberals' campaign rested overwhelmingly on a negative defence of free trade. Lloyd George was almost alone in making a few more radical and constructive statements. While this approach enabled the party to pick up the votes of free-trade Conservatives and retain its traditional support in rural areas, it also helped take the party's eye off its real enemy, Labour, which on the question of tariffs found itself in the same camp as the Liberals. The latter thus adopted an essentially backward-looking stance which did little to put down new roots for the electoral contests of the future. 'Every speech delivered in the course of this electoral campaign', declared the *Western Mail*, 'lends emphasis to the fact that Liberalism is living in the dead past.' Yet, in purely statistical terms, the results represented a distinct revival in Liberal fortunes. With 30 per cent of the popular vote, 158 MPs were elected. But not all features of the election outcome contained cause for satisfaction. The Liberal revival was largely at the expense of the Conservatives and was concentrated in rural and middle-class urban areas. The party found itself winning seats which had returned Conservatives even in 1906, scarcely evidence that it was retaining an image of left-of-centre progressivism. More than sixty seats had been won in straight fights and might be vulnerable in the event of future Labour intervention. Most disturbing was the party's failure to make significant inroads into the Labour vote. Indeed, the flag of Liberalism was still retreating in industrial Britain as the party suffered a net loss of ten seats to Labour.

But the most significant feature of the election result was the failure of any one party to secure an absolute majority. Though the Conservatives with 258 seats remained the largest single party, the combined Labour and Liberal contingents represented a clear majority for free trade after an election fought specifically on the question of tariffs. Holding the balance of parliamentary power, a contingency to which the leadership appears to have given little prior consideration, Liberalism now faced a tactical dilemma – the creation of its own relative success at the polls. The party's long-term future might well depend on the correct decisions now being taken. The unenviable choice lay between sustaining a Conservative government which had just been defeated on a central plank of its programme and installing a minority Labour administration in its place. This fundamental issue found the party leadership badly divided. Their indecision reflected the party's failure since 1918 to get to grips with the 'impact of Labour' and its implications for Liberalism's survival as a potential party of government. Should Labour be regarded as an ally, a rival or a mortal foe? It also stood as testimony to the continuing mutual distrust of the Lloyd George and Asquith factions, despite the shotgun reconciliation which had recently taken place.

The option of keeping the Conservatives in power was soon ruled out. As E. D. Simon, elected for the Withington division of Manchester, explained:

> if we now support the Conservatives Labour will represent it as a capitalist combination to keep them out of power and will undoubtedly gain hundreds of thousands of votes by it. The one way of ensuring a Socialist Government in full power in the course of the next few years would be for us to come to an agreement to keep the Conservatives in power now.[61]

Thereafter, agreement was harder to secure. When Liberal leaders met soon after the election to settle their immediate policy, Asquith urged that the party should vote with Labour to turn Baldwin out when the new parliament met and then, assuming Labour succeeded in forming a government, the Liberals should combine with the Conservatives to oust that as well. Thereafter, with no one ready to force yet another general election, the King would be obliged to invite Asquith to form a government. Such a sequence of events would at least succeed in maintaining the distinctive identity of the Liberal party in the eyes of the electorate. Lloyd George, however, was unconvinced and the meeting adjourned without a final decision being reached. By the time that it reconvened, Asquith had modified his stance and was not now prepared to go beyond voting out the existing Baldwin government. The Liberal attitude towards any subsequent Labour administration would be non-committal. Though Asquith's new approach smacked of the fatal 'wait and see' style which had discredited his wartime premiership, Lloyd George, who clearly envisaged sustaining a Labour government in office, accepted it as a step in the right direction. This, in essence, is what happened when parliament reassembled in January 1924.

But the dangers from a Liberal point of view were obvious. The Liberals were voting Labour into office without really considering what they would do thereafter and without trying to extract any policy commitments, such as electoral reform, of benefit to themselves. An appropriate line might have been a fixed-term arrangement on the basis of an agreed legislative programme. The parliamentary arithmetic, was, moreover, against them. As there were more Conservative MPs than Labour, it would not be enough for the Liberal party to abstain if Labour was going to survive for any length of time. The Liberals did not have the option of acquiescing in Labour government; they had positively to support it. When Asquith told the parliamentary party that a Labour government could hardly be tried out under safer conditions, he was probably fully justified. But his further remarks were totally unfounded: 'It is we, if we understand our business, who really control the situation.'[62]

Those Liberals who still spoke the language of the Progressive Alliance saw enormous possibilities opening up. As Labour unfolded its legislative programme, E. D. Simon enthused about the 'immense field of constructive work in which we could fruitfully co-operate . . . Foreign Affairs, Unemployment, Education and Housing are the most important.'[63] In the early months of the government he remained optimistic:

> Up to now the Labour Government has shown a real desire to avoid impracticable and Socialistic legislation, and to concentrate on practical social reforms on Liberal lines as for instance the

removal of the unemployment gap, the extension of the Trade Facilities Act, and more generous administrative provision for the needs of education and public health. In other words they are acting almost exactly on the lines of a Liberal government. By far the best chance for the continuation of such legislation is for the Liberals to maintain Labour in power.[64]

But by the end of Labour's first brief term in office, Simon's mood had completely changed. 'The session as a whole', he confessed, 'was a tragedy.' The two parties could, he believed, have stayed together 'for years' and enacted a far-reaching programme of radical legislation. What had gone wrong? Simon enumerated his points of explanation:

1 A considerable section of Liberals didn't want radical legislation.
2 A section of Labour – Wheatley and Co. didn't want radical legislation. MacDonald joined them and Sidney Webb in having as their first object to kill the Liberal Party – as the only means of an ultimate Labour majority.
3 Liberal leadership was lazy and aloof. Not only did they not consult one another, but they made no real attempt to consult Labour.
4 The vacuity and self righteousness of R[amsay] M[acDonald] and his unfortunate habit of telling lies in the House made co-operation very difficult. No Labour leader ever thanked a Liberal for support or help, though for 6 months the Liberals as a whole gave them really good support.[65]

Both in his focus on Labour's attitude and his disappointment at the performance of the Liberals themselves, Simon got to the heart of the matter.

Labour would not play the part that Liberals had mapped out for them. The Labour leadership was clear in its view that the destruction of the Liberal party was a necessary precondition of their own party's further advance. In taking office MacDonald saw it as his primary task to establish Labour's credentials as a respectable and moderate party of government rather than to embark upon some far-reaching radical agenda in conjunction with the Liberals. 'The only kind of cooperation which is possible', insisted MacDonald, 'is the cooperation of men and women who come over and join us.'[66] Indeed, in the broader context of the electoral history of the 1920s as a whole, it is evident that Labour was determined to pursue this strategy, involving as it did abandoning the possibilities of a short-term Liberal–Labour preponderance, even at the cost of allowing the Conservatives a stranglehold on government. Even those like Lloyd George, who were keen to sustain Labour in office, soon became disillusioned by the response given to the Liberal hand of friendship. 'Liberals are to be the oxen', he complained in April 1924, 'to drag the Labour wain over the rough roads of Parliament for two to three years, goaded along, and at the end of the journey, when there is no further use for them, they are to be slaughtered. That is the Labour idea of cooperation.'[67] But many Liberals voiced their indignation in a way that suggested ignorance of the game Labour was clearly playing. Vivian Phillipps, the party's chief whip, found MacDonald's behaviour particularly disappointing: 'Not only does he appear not to seek our goodwill and cooperation, but on several occasions it has seemed as if he went out of his way to make it as difficult as possible for us to back him.'[68] In this situation Liberals were unlikely to derive much benefit from having put Labour into office. Those who had voted Liberal to resist the dangers of socialism realised either that the Conservative party represented a more effective bulwark or else that Labour was not as dangerous as they had supposed and might even serve as the vehicle for those radical aspirations which had previously attracted them to Liberalism.

Irrespective of Labour's long-term strategy, the parliamentary Liberal party remained deeply divided in its attitude towards the government. Even on the initial vote, which brought down the Baldwin government and opened the way to a Labour administration, ten Liberals had voted in the Conservative lobby. Thereafter, the shallowness of the reconciliation effected by Baldwin's pronouncement on tariffs was soon revealed. Lloyd

George's point-blank refusal to amalgamate his Political Fund with the diminished financial resources of the Asquithian party was indicative of an on-going absence of confidence and goodwill. On major issues of policy the party could still not present a united front. Percy Harris, MP for Bethnal Green, South West, recalled 'a distinct cleavage of thought' that was apparent at every party meeting: 'The old Coalitionists were always looking for excuses to vote with the Tories, while the Independent Liberals were pressing for radical reforms and were only too glad to support legislation of a kind they had been advocating for years.'[69] On questions such as Labour's decision to discontinue development of the Singapore naval base and the Eviction Bill in April the whips could exert little discipline. E. D. Simon, perturbed at the party's 'utter failure of leadership', and holding Asquith particularly responsible, vividly described the way in which Liberal policy was determined in the latter case:

> There were about a dozen present and we were unanimously and strongly of the opinion that [the government's bill] was grossly unfair to the particular landlord whose tenant happened to be unemployed, and utterly indefensible . . . Mr. Asquith said nothing, but after fifteen minutes discussion . . . the matter was practically settled, the only question being who was to speak and how the case should be put. At that moment in came Lloyd George. He had not looked at the bill: it was explained to him, and he immediately said 'This will never do. There are millions of tenants who may be unemployed and if we oppose this they will say we are against them and goodbye to their votes.' . . . He went on like this for ten minutes . . . but I assumed that he would be tactfully suppressed by Mr Asquith. To my absolute horror, all Asquith said was 'Very well, in view of what you say, perhaps you will put the case for us in debate'. And immediately broke up the meeting, without giving any opportunity for further discussion![70]

In similar vein Wedgwood Benn recorded the frustration which would ultimately help propel him into Labour's ranks:

> Policy at the present moment is very difficult. Mr A of course works in the background with Conferences with the Mausoleum. LLG will appear from time to time to force the Party into stunts. Party meetings are difficult to hold, but without them, trouble will ensue. Brilliant nagging at the Government is all very well but seems to me to lead nowhere.[71]

It was perhaps not surprising that there was talk of holding a regular 'Gladstone dinner' at the National Liberal Club, 'something to collect all Liberals, none of whom feel too enthusiastic about their leaders at the present moment'.[72]

Liberals in fact were now facing the problem inherent in their third-party status of defining their position in relation to two larger parties. Caught inevitably somewhere in the middle of the Labour–Conservative electoral contest, they struggled throughout the decade to determine whether their basic inclination was to lean to the left or to the right. Their inability to give a single, coherent answer to this question would lead ultimately to a further and catastrophic breach in the party's ranks. Yet just as Labour would no longer play the role of pliant partner, so too the attitude of many Conservatives had also undergone a fundamental change, with the Liberals' decision to allow Labour to form a government often proving the turning-point. Austen Chamberlain was among those who, since 1918, had consistently sought a partnership with Liberalism as the only reliable means of preventing the advent of socialist government. But he was appalled by Asquith's decision to let Labour take office. The change in his attitude was evident in the no-confidence debate on 21 January which finally bought down Baldwin's government:

> [Asquith] has taken his choice and he has by that choice constituted his own immortality. He will go down to history as the last Prime Minister of a Liberal Administration. He has sung the swan song of the Liberal Party. When next the country is called upon for a decision, if it wants a Socialist Government it will vote for a Socialist; if it does not want a Socialist Government it will vote for

a Unionist. It will not vote again for those who denatured its mandate and betrayed its trust.[73]

A week later Chamberlain wrote to his Conservative colleague Samuel Hoare, explaining that the Conservatives' task was now 'to smash the Liberal party'. Two-thirds of it, he claimed, was already Labour in all but name and the task of Conservativism was to draw over and eventually absorb the other third – rather as the Liberal Unionists had been absorbed into the Unionist party.[74] Leopold Amery was of the same mind. As he explained to Baldwin, the real division in politics now lay between constructive conservatism and Labour Socialism. It was in the interests of both to clear the ground of the Liberal party which stood for nothing except 'an organized hypocrisy'. The two leading parties could each hope to pick up the larger share of the Liberal carcass, but the 'great thing is to get the beast killed and on that we can be agreed'.[75] While, then, there are good reasons for dwelling upon the damage which Liberalism did to itself in the decade and a half after the Lloyd George–Asquith split of 1916, it is also plausible to argue, as did many contemporary Liberals, that the party was the victim of a two-pronged pincer assault launched by its political opponents.

Liberalism was 'rescued' from its dilemmas when the Labour government decided to turn a Liberal proposal to set up a Select Committee into its handling of the so-called Campbell Case (designed in fact to offer the government a means of escape from a crisis created by its own ineptitude) into a vote of confidence. There was no need for the government to take the Liberal amendment, as opposed to the original Conservative motion of censure, as an issue of confidence and John Simon declared that to do so would be like a man asked to produce a document from his drawer preferring to burn down his own house. But the Liberals could not stop the Conservatives supporting their amendment and Labour probably preferred to face defeat on this matter rather than on a proposed trade treaty with the Soviet Union, where Liberals and Tories were also expected to vote together. By 364 votes to 198 the government fell. But the act of 'rescue' was only nominal. While the end of the Labour government did free Liberals from the intolerable burden of sustaining an opposing party which offered nothing in return, it also made inevitable another general election. This the party could scarcely afford to fight in purely financial terms and its outcome would reveal the extent of the Liberal collapse that had been predictable since the party's decision to install Labour in power. On the day Labour fell, Wedgwood Benn wrote in his diary of the 'suicide of the Liberal party'.[76]

. In late April Herbert Gladstone had advised Asquith of the imperative need to secure enough financial support to guarantee a sufficient number of candidates at the next general election. In practice this meant courting Lloyd George and difficult negotiations proceeded throughout the year. Lloyd George, however, was disinclined to relinquish control over what was his chief negotiating counter in the party's internal power struggle, at least without the guarantee of a degree of control over Liberal policy and strategy such as the Asquithians were reluctant to concede. Sir Robert Hudson found one 40-minute session with Lloyd George so 'poisonous' that he 'took to [his] bed with a temperature the next afternoon'.[77] In the event Lloyd George agreed to contribute just £50,000 for the campaign of October 1924, only about a quarter of the sum needed to meet the party's anticipated costs. As a result the Liberals were able to field no more than 340 candidates, effectively disqualifying themselves at the outset as serious contenders for power. 'We could not make candidates without straw', recalled Herbert Gladstone, 'and straw was denied us.'[78] At one point the figure looked likely to be even lower. As the Chief Whip put it: 'This was the death-blow. We had assumed that reunion meant reunion of resources . . . We had striven at every stage to meet Ll. G's views in the long-drawn-out negotiations and we now found ourselves left without the means to put more than 300 candidates in the field.'[79] But financial worries merely compounded the problems of a party which, at constituency level, was both divided and demoralised. Even Lloyd George conceded that the party went into action looking like a 'disorganized rabble'.[80] In the emotionally charged atmosphere in which the campaign was conducted, with the Conservatives playing upon the red scare of the Zinoviev Letter, Liberals found it difficult to project a distinctive identity. The party's manifesto was an uninspiring document, highly critical of Labour's performance in government but with little to offer as an alternative, especially in terms of economic policy. Calls for temperance and free trade were beginning to look curiously dated. Post-war electoral history had suggested that the party's best hope lay in an appeal to the largely non-unionised working class of the countryside, but there is no evidence that the leadership tried to turn the party in this direction.

After an uninspiring campaign in which not even Lloyd George seemed able to raise much enthusiasm for his party's prospects, the Liberals confronted a predictable disaster. The Conservative party secured a landslide victory with more than four hundred seats in the new House. Though Labour lost nearly forty seats, its percentage of the overall vote actually increased. It could look back on its first experience of government with some satisfaction. Its day would come again. But for the Liberals the result was, in Sidney Webb's words, 'the funeral of a great party'.[81] With just 42 MPs returned, three-quarters of the parliamentary party had gone down to defeat including Asquith at Paisley. The progress made in 1923 at the expense of the Conservatives in rural and middle-class constituencies was emphatically reversed. Throughout the land only seven Liberals were successful in three-cornered contests. As many as 31 candidates defending Liberal seats finished third behind Labour and the Conservatives. Though eight gains were recorded against Labour, compared with sixteen losses, seven of the eight were in constituencies where no Conservative took the field. The fall in the Liberal vote from 4.3 million in 1923 to 2.9 million were less dramatic, especially in view of the reduced number of Liberal candidates. But even this served to emphasise the extent to which the third-party trap was now beginning to bite. Liberals were still polling respectably enough, but an average 30.9 per cent of the vote per opposed candidate was insufficient to win many seats in the existing electoral system. At least the party's manifesto appeal for 'a real correspondence between Parliamentary representation and electoral strength' had been well timed.

The 1924 results need to be set in a somewhat broader chronological context. Three general elections had taken place in just two years and, despite some passing signs of encouragement for Liberals, the overall effect had been to set in place the two-party pattern which would dominate British politics for the next half century, with the Conservatives and Labour the only serious contenders for power. The Liberals had been firmly relegated to third place in a system which operates to the advantage of just two players. The political objectives of both Labour and the Conservatives involved squeezing out the Liberal party from the electoral front-line and this had now largely been achieved. Labour had mounted a successful challenge to the Liberals in industrial Britain; the Conservatives were well advanced in a similar campaign in suburban and rural areas. For the foreseeable future Liberal prospects looked bleak, not least because the party no longer enjoyed an easily identifiable constituency in the electorate. This placed it at a grave disadvantage in the increasingly class-based politics of the time, as becomes clear when the electoral history of the decade is considered as a whole. 'The Liberals in the 1920s', writes Geoffrey Searle, 'were quite successful in winning seats . . . their problem was rather one of holding on to their gains.'[82] With few constituencies that could now be regarded as safely, or even characteristically, Liberal, the party lacked the solid base from which to launch a successful revival.

Nor did the picture look significantly better at the level of municipal politics. The period since 1918 had witnessed an intensive Labour challenge in local elections which the Liberals had been unable to resist. Indeed, the latter suffered a net loss of seats every year during the 1920s except for 1922. This Liberal decline was matched by a steady fall in the number of their municipal candidatures, even at times when the national party was showing signs of renewal, so that by 1929 less than one in eight of those standing in provincial borough elections was a Liberal. In many towns a Liberal presence was only maintained as a result of the establishment of anti-socialist municipal alliances with the Conservatives. But while such pacts tended to delay the final extinction of Liberal representation, they ran the parallel danger of the progressive loss of a distinct Liberal identity which encouraged the transfer of allegiances to one or other of the two main parties.[83]

As the dispirited band of MPs gathered at Westminster after the 1924 General election, Liberalism seemed in danger of total disintegration. A gathering of Liberal leaders organised by Lord Beauchamp was 'knee-deep in condolences and tears'.[84] The shallowness of the reconciliation effected by the defence of free trade was only too apparent. Unlike the election of 1923, that of 1924 had swung the party's internal balance of power in Lloyd George's favour. Over half the surviving parliamentary party were former coalitionists. But hatred of Lloyd George himself had not abated. 'I could very well stand LG's defeat,' confessed Henry Gladstone, 'for Asquith's disappearance from the House must otherwise promote him to a position which he is not worthy to hold. I fancy distrust of LG has a good deal to do with the Liberal smash.'[85] Walter Runciman judged that personal difficulties were more acute than ever and could never be resolved as long as Lloyd George 'insists on pushing himself as leader or deputy leader'.[86] In fact no one sought to deprive Asquith of the nominal party leadership. At the same time, it was unlikely that he would ever again secure a seat in the House of Commons and, indeed, early in the new year he accepted a peerage, going to the Lords as the Earl of Oxford and Asquith. In Asquith's absence attention shifted to the position of sessional chairman. John Simon urged that the post should remain vacant with Godfrey Collins, the new chief whip, taking the chair at party meetings. This idea was put forward when Liberal MPs met on 2 December to decide the matter. It was rejected by 26 votes to 9 after which an amendment was carried to appoint Lloyd George. After the latter had taken the chair, Simon swallowed his pride and appealed for unity and comradeship. Though Asquith would retain the formal leadership until October 1926, the era of Lloyd George's ascendancy had begun. Nonetheless, on the day after the party meeting, 11 Liberal MPs, with Runciman as their chairman, formed a 'Radical Group', pledged to work with the rest of the parliamentary party but effectively disowning Lloyd George's authority. The designation of a Gladstonian businessman such as Runciman as 'radical', especially in contrast to Lloyd George, epitomised the kaleidoscopic confusion which had come to characterise Liberal politics. Personality rather than doctrine, and specifically a hatred of Lloyd George, seemed to be the new group's primary motivation. Its members secured their own room in the Commons and began to issue their own whip. Liberalism's internecine conflict showed no sign of coming to an end.

With a comfortable parliamentary majority, Baldwin's Conservative party was likely to be in office for four or five years. Labour was equally firmly established as the alternative government. It was now apparent that the Liberals had been the least successful participants in the post-war political contest. Their image remained largely negative. They were against excessive state power, against militant trade unionism, against waste, socialism and jingoistic imperialism, but in favour, it seemed, of very little apart from prudent economy and free trade. Their position in the political spectrum was somewhere inside the comfortable middle ground, between the supposed extremes of their Labour and Conservative rivals, within which space their leaders could mouth reassuring platitudes which failed to inspire. 'Look neither to the right nor to the left', Asquith told his audience in October 1926 at the time of his final retirement, 'but keep straight on.' In this situation it was inevitable that many Liberals, activists and voters alike, would be pulled towards the positive qualities of the other two parties, each of which, without being as extreme as Liberal spokesmen claimed, could better achieve Liberal aspirations, whether these were to oppose socialism or to promote radical change. Indeed, some seemed curiously satisfied with the idea that Liberalism's remaining function would be to infuse Liberal values into the other two parties. E. D. Simon drew a distinction between the survival of the party and that of its philosophy, while Maynard Keynes suggested that possibly the party could best serve the state 'by supplying Conservative Governments with Cabinets and Labour Governments with ideas'.[87] Meanwhile, those Liberals who had sought to inject a new vigour into the party and interest it in a social and industrial agenda tailored to the 1920s had received scant support from the party leadership, the Asquithian 'mausoleum' as Wedgwood Benn styled it. The leadership, aware that its past was more glorious than its present (and in all probability than its future), was all too inclined to live in that past 'and regard it as the whole duty of a Liberal to cheer lustily when Gladstone, or Free Trade, or Home Rule are mentioned'.[88] Appropriately, it was Gladstone's son Herbert, a still influential figure in the party's inner councils throughout the decade, who best articulated this deeply engrained strain of reaction. In 1927, by which time Lloyd George was trying to do something about the situation, he wrote:

> The programme, I confess, does not attract me. Land comes from the stockpot in a new dress but carries no inspiration. Coal and Power is not a political question at all. In my view, apart from Free Trade and the League of Nations, there are two questions which in sheer Liberalism stand out first and foremost, drastic retrenchment founded on policy and licensing not founded on fanaticism.[89]

By the middle of the decade those genuine radicals who had not already deserted the Liberal ranks faced a clear dilemma. As E. D. Simon explained soon after the 1924 General Election:

> The big decision I have to make as regards my individual political work is whether I should
>
> 1 do all in my power to help to revive the Liberal Party at the next election . . .
> 2 do the same kind of thing, but half-heartedly, giving only limited time to it.
> 3 withdraw from national politics altogether for the present.
> 4 join the Labour party.
>
> My political aim is to give the best chance to every child, and to remove the excessive inequalities of today. That is practically the

aim of Labour. At Dundee I agreed with my extreme Labour audiences as regards political aims far more than with my Liberal chairman. All the enthusiasm and driving force is in the Labour Party, except for a few fanatics on land, or temperance or Free Trade.[90]

To his credit Lloyd George now began to address this problem. Finally abandoning his earlier flirtation with the Conservatives, he set about taking the party to the left, not towards doctrinaire socialism, but adopting a clearly radical agenda which would win public support and offer some hope of returning himself to power. He now realised that Asquithian Liberalism would lead, as arguably it did in 1931, to Conservatism. Negative anti-socialism was the proper stance of a Conservative. But Liberals needed not so much to oppose the socialists as to compete with them on an alternative platform. The country was gripped not by political extremism but by the moderation of the centre-left and centre-right against which Liberalism could offer a radical alternative. He was not, he stressed, a socialist but a Liberal who believed that the elimination of private enterprise and individual incentive would be a disaster for the wellbeing of the country. At the same time, it was not enough for Liberals to take satisfaction from belonging to a party of noble principles and a glorious record. Much work and sacrifice would be needed before the party could apply those principles to the needs of the day and thereby make that record even more glorious.[91] The ultimate aim, according to Frances Stevenson, was a new political alignment: 'D[avid]'s idea is to go definitely towards the *Left*, and gradually to co-ordinate and consolidate all the progressive forces in the country, against the Conservative and reactionary forces. Thus he will eventually get all sane Labour as well as Liberalism behind him.'[92] But the task would not be easy, not least because most of Lloyd George's existing supporters, a legacy of the Coalition, were men of the right, while Asquith 'who is really a Whig is accepted as a better Liberal than he'.[93]

Lloyd George's first initiative was to take up again the question of the land with which his fertile brain had been engaged in 1914 before international developments compelled a reordering of everyone's priorities including his own. The report of the Land Inquiry Committee was published as *Land and the Nation* in October 1925 and soon became known as the Green Book. Radicals were excited and enthused but the proposal to end the private ownership of agricultural land by making farmers into 'cultivating tenants', supervised by county committees, aroused considerable opposition. But beyond specific policy difficulties lay the fact that Lloyd George was still not in a position to direct the Liberal party. Asquith held on to the shadow and in some ways the substance of power from his base in the House of Lords, for no other reason it seemed than to deny Lloyd George his inheritance. More and more Liberals recognised that it was time for the old man to go but, as Lady Kennet noted, 'few cared to be rude to Mr. Asquith. Oh dear!' she continued, 'how I wish he could have died when he should in 1916. What a great name my beautiful friend would then have left.'[94] Lloyd George now regarded his nominal chief as a 'silly old man drunk with hidden conceit', but seemed prepared to bide his time.[95] Time, after all, was on his side, at least in terms of the internal politics of the Liberal party, and so was money which remained the younger man's whip hand. 'There was nothing for it', conceded Herbert Gladstone, 'but to maintain amicable relations or keep on endeavouring to bring [Lloyd George] over to our views.'[96] In practice, neither strategy proved possible. Relations between the two factions continued to deteriorate throughout 1925 before coming to breaking point in May of the following year.

The event which brought matters to a head was the General Strike. The Liberal shadow cabinet declared that society was obliged to secure victory over the strikers, but from the outset Lloyd George blamed the government for the crisis and called for a negotiated settlement. In a significant if controversial intervention on 6 May, John Simon, with the authority he derived as one of the country's leading barristers, declared the strike illegal. Every trade union leader was guilty of incitement to breach of contract and liable therefore to damages 'to the uttermost farthing of his personal possessions'. When the shadow cabinet met again on 10 May Lloyd George pointedly absented himself, writing instead to the chief whip to express his unwillingness to be associated with any declaration against the strike which failed also to condemn the government's handling of the situation. Lord Oxford's initial response was one of no more than mild displeasure, but his colleagues saw in this latest divergence the chance of a final break with Lloyd George. As had often been the case since 1916, the leader's followers were ready to be more Asquithian than Asquith himself. An increasingly acrimonious exchange of correspondence now ensued, most of it published in the press, which seemed to indicate a readiness on both sides to push matters to an open rupture. The climax came when twelve members of the shadow cabinet sent Oxford a public letter of support, amounting to an indictment of Lloyd George's actions since the reunion of 1923 and, in particular, denouncing his manipulation of his private political fund. His actions during the General Strike had to be 'regarded in the light of this general position'. The letter concluded:

> We have done our best in the highest interests of the cause of Liberalism to work with Mr Lloyd George in the consultations of the party and we regret to say that we cannot any longer continue to work with a colleague who, in our judgement, is not worthy of the trust.[97]

But the Asquithians had miscalculated. The party at large was sick of the perpetual infighting and regarded the latest attack on Lloyd George as little more than victimisation. The latter, moreover, could still command majority support inside the parliamentary party. The annual meeting of the National Liberal Federation at Weston-super-Mare on 17 June offered Oxford a last chance to regain control over the situation. Less than a week before the meeting, however, he suffered a serious stroke which removed him from the political stage. With Oxford out of action, most Liberals saw that they needed Lloyd George. The mood was for reconciliation. To be leaderless was one thing; to be penniless quite another. John Simon's private secretary summed up the situation:

Undoubtedly the preponderating desire of the delegates [at Weston] was that the recent published correspondence should not split the Party. While reaffirming its confidence in Lord Oxford as Leader, the Conference was equally emphatic that Lloyd George must be associated with the Party. How that was to be achieved I am afraid the delegates did not trouble to think about. All they were concerned with was that the Party should not be torn asunder.[98]

In October Oxford finally resigned the leadership. Though he had attached his colours firmly to Oxford's mast ever since 1916, Richard Holt now passed a harsh but valid judgement. He was 'in some ways a great figure, yet he succeeded to the leadership when the party was in overwhelming strength and he left it a ruin, sunk lower than any great party ever sank. It is impossible to acquit him of the major responsibility for this event.'[99] While some hoped that Simon would emerge as the champion of an Asquithian succession, most realised that, if the Liberal party was to have any future at all, it had to capitulate to Lloyd George or at least to readmit him fully into the Liberal fold. In the words of the *Manchester Guardian*: 'Many people in the party, not specifically associated with one side or the other are hoping that in the entirely different situation caused by Lord Oxford's resignation the leading signatories [to the letter to Oxford of 31 May] may find it possible to make a gesture of reconciliation.'[100] Asquith's daughter put the matter more bluntly. The choice was whether 'to starve or be bought'.[101] In November the Million Fund Administration Committee, set up after the last general election, narrowly agreed to accept Lloyd George's terms for a massive grant from his political fund. It was, thought Holt, an 'iniquitous transaction', but for all that it was inescapable.[102] Without Lloyd George the Liberal party faced imminent bankruptcy. Having captured the party organisation, he began to remove entrenched Asquithians from its bureaucracy. The Liberal party was now effectively his. The only question was whether the takeover had come too late, both for himself and for the party.

Many regretted what had happened. '*If* Grey were younger and had his eye-sight,' bemoaned Violet Bonham Carter, 'if Simon were even ¾ of a man and had an ounce of courage and a few strong ounces of blood and a heart that beat. But these are all fairy-tale dreams.'[103] In fact, while Simon drifted away from domestic politics, taking on the chairmanship of the Indian Statutory Commission, Grey took the lead in organising the dissidents into the so-called Liberal Council. Runciman became the new group's chairman and effectively its parliamentary leader. Almost a party within the party, the Liberal Council claimed to represent a pure and uncorrupted form of Liberalism. It hoped to field candidates in opposition to Lloyd Georgeites at the next general election. For the Asquithian old guard, the winning of power for the Liberal party was evidently less important than thwarting Lloyd George's hopes in the same direction. So the Liberal civil war continued. The respected former cabinet minister, Herbert Samuel, was made chairman of the Liberal Party organisation in 1927 to try to effect a bridge between the contending factions, but the appointment was only a partial success. Runciman's wife, Hilda, refused to let Lloyd George speak on her behalf in a by-election at St Ives in March 1928, while a year earlier Runciman had declared that what was needed was a Gladstonian policy, which 'the average non-political citizen . . . does not feel he can get . . . from the Liberal party'.[104]

But most Liberals were content to see what Lloyd George could do and it seems clear that the Welshman's ascendancy provided the party with a sense of purpose which had been lacking for many years. Building upon the foundations laid earlier in the decade by the Liberal Summer School movement and bringing that body now to the forefront of the party's activity, Lloyd George proceeded to endow Liberalism with a distinctive set of policies, relevant to the times, such as had been largely lacking since before the war. It represented a belated correction of the anomalous situation which had existed since 1916 when, *faute de mieux*, Asquith had become the nominal leader of progressive Liberals. For a brief interlude the party displayed at its heart an intellectual liveliness which belied its gravely weakened political standing. In a post-Keynesian age the policies put forward in these years appear somewhat less compelling than was once the case, yet it is hard to deny that out of Liberalism's intellectual renaissance emerged those ideas which revolutionised British society in the post-Second World War era. The Liberal Industrial Inquiry, set up in 1925, brought together an impressive array of politicians and economists, including E. D. Simon, Walter Layton, Maynard Keynes, Herbert Samuel, Ramsay Muir and Lloyd George himself. Their report was published in February 1928 as the 'Yellow Book', *Britain's Industrial Future*. It argued that, in modern conditions, the traditional antipathy of individualism and socialism had become unreal and put forward far-reaching proposals for government planning of and intervention in the economy. Then, a committee headed by Lloyd George, his former secretary Lord Lothian and the sociologist Seebohm Rowntree set about drawing up plans for schemes of national development. The report, *We Can Conquer Unemployment*, published in March 1929, envisaged a vast programme of public works, with an emphasis on road-building and housing and formed the basis of the party's manifesto for the General Election later that year. Looking back at the end of the decade, E. D. Simon reflected upon the achievements of the Summer School movement:

> A great success – I knew exactly what I wanted. I learnt from Webb and Tawney the necessity of an industrial policy – the Liberal leaders ignored it. Through the Summer School we both [Simon and Ramsay Muir] worked out the policy and in just under 10 years effectively imposed it on the party. Biggest achievement the Yellow Book . . . I think it is a model of what political parties ought to do in an ideal democracy!

With more prescience than he could have known, Simon added 'whether it is of any use to the Liberal party politically is another and less important matter'.[105]

For a while, however, Lloyd George's imagination and energy seemed able to inject new life into Liberalism both as a political force and as an intellectual movement. In March 1927 the party captured Southwark North from Labour. Further by-election gains followed at Bosworth (May 1927), Lancaster (February 1928), St Ives (March 1928), Eddisbury (March 1929) and Holland with Boston (March 1929). After such a run of successes, few contemporaries could have guessed that Holland with Boston would be the Liberals' last by-election gain for almost thirty years. But more perceptive observers did sense the limits to this latest Liberal revival. The party's victories were almost entirely confined to agricultural constituencies. After Southwark all the gains were from the Conservatives and, over the parliament as a whole, it was the Labour party which made most progress at the expense of an increasingly unpopular Conservative government, with no fewer than twelve gains overall. Lloyd George himself was worried that Labour would still not co-operate with the Liberals, even if the consequence of a continuing split in the progressive vote was to be further Conservative victories. 'If Tavistock goes the same way [as Cheltenham]', he wrote in September 1928, 'then it means that Labour in their blind jealousy of Liberalism are more intent on doing us in than in putting the Conservatives out.'[106]

The leader's mood at the beginning of 1929 was far from sanguine. 'I am fighting with an army paralysed by divided generalship', he confided to his secretary and mistress. 'It is cankered with jealousy and suspicion.'[107] None the less, when Baldwin called a general election for 30 May, many Liberals believed that their party once again had a realistic prospect of seizing power. Donald Maclean declared that it was well within the bounds of possibility that Liberals would be forming the next government, while some activists even spoke of repeating the performance of 1906. Almost all seemed ready to put past differences aside to make the most of the opportunity offered. 'Of course you and I can never trust the man', admitted Henry Gladstone to his brother, 'but there he is the only possible leader for the time being.' A few months later he was ready to admit that 'new life' had been put into the party by Lloyd George's campaign and that 'no Liberal of any colour will have a chance of getting into Parliament without making unemployment a first plank in the policy of the Liberal party'.[108] Richard Holt, standing in North

Cumberland and making a sixth and final attempt to return to the Commons, found a 'strong feeling that Ll G. has touched the popular imagination and that we ought not to throw cold water on his schemes'.[109] John Simon also managed to pose as a loyal acolyte of Lloyd George. Back in September 1928, between two visits to India, he had warned that the Liberal party should not go into the next election 'like a cheap-jack in the fair' offering a 'patent remedy' to cure unemployment. Coming shortly after the publication of the Yellow Book, his words had been understandably interpreted as a stricture upon his own party's proposals. Now, however, he explained, although without total conviction, that he had been referring only to protection and socialism as spurious cures for the problem of unemployment, and he expressed his unqualified support for 'the remarkable man who now leads the Liberal party'.[110] Even Runciman modified his campaign to maintain an appearance of unity, though his ultimate aim remained to get enough like-minded Liberals elected to be able to snatch control of the party away from Lloyd George after the General Election.

That election was the most competitive of the decade and as such provides the best guide to the underlying strength of the three main parties. More than three-quarters of all constituencies witnessed three-cornered fights and the Liberals themselves put 513 candidates into the field. For the Liberal party the most important feature of the results was confirmation of its third-party status. Its representation went up to 59 MPs, compared with 40 in 1924. But these figures concealed more complex trends. Instead of building upon the base-line of 1924, Liberals contrived to lose 19 of the seats won that year while gaining 35 new ones. The party had made a net gain of 28 seats from the Conservatives but suffered a net loss of 15 seats to Labour. Thus, in the contest that really mattered, Liberalism was still losing ground. Indeed, the most depressing feature was the continuing erosion of the party's position in the industrial areas of London, Lancashire, Yorkshire and the North-East. Labour, which now emerged as the largest single party in the new House of Commons, had confirmed its status as the natural party of the British working class. Despite their stress upon the issue of unemployment, the Liberals had done worst in the largest cities. Arguably, they would have been better advised to focus their campaign on the needs of rural voters, that section of the electorate where the Liberal appeal remained strongest, than on the urban unemployed, most of whom were already firmly in the Labour camp.

In terms of votes the picture was somewhat more encouraging. More than five million electors (because of a further extension of the franchise in 1928, a higher figure than Liberals had ever secured before), 23.4 per cent of the total, had supported the party. But these figures only underlined Liberalism's dilemma. Its support was now spread too thinly to be effective within the existing electoral system. There were very few solidly Liberal constituencies, let alone areas, and only 15 candidates had secured an absolute majority of votes cast. The party's compelling need for electoral reform was starkly revealed. On average, there was one Liberal MP for every 91,000 votes; one Conservative for every 34,000; and one Labour member for every 28,000. 'You can imagine', John Simon told the Indian viceroy, 'that our Liberals feel rather sore about this.'[111]

Once again, then, the Liberal party had to decide how it would respond to a minority Labour government. It had at least the advantage compared with 1924 that, with Labour now the largest single party, the government could survive a Liberal abstention and beat off Conservative opposition in the House of Commons with its own votes. In the wake of the election Liberals suffered what had now almost become the ritual of further defections. W. A. Jowitt, elected in the party's colours, found his way into the Labour government as Attorney-General, while Freddie Guest, having lost his seat in Bristol, defected to the Tories. For the time being, however, most Liberals seemed agreed on the need for united action to safeguard their party's existence. At the first party meeting after the election, John Simon 'smote his breast and declared that except on matters which could only be fitly decided in the sacred court of conscience – or words to that effect – no matter of opinion would induce him to do other than follow the crack of the whip'.[112] Seeming to have learnt from the experience of 1924, Lloyd George voiced his determination to secure a reform of the electoral system, 'a speedy redress of this glaring wrong'. But E. D. Simon found the general tone of his leader's speech 'threatening', instead of 'looking forward to legislation on the fruitful field which is common to both parties'.[113]

Gradually, however, two distinct points of view emerged, or rather two extremes between which the by no means numerous members of the parliamentary Liberal party placed themselves at assorted points. E. D. Simon, looking benignly upon early evidence of Labour's plans for social reform, believed that 'in the national interest . . . it is quite clearly up to us to keep them in power and do all we can to help them to carry out an effective progressive policy'.[114] At the same time, he recognised that, from a party point of view, the position was more complex. If Liberals enabled Labour to complete a two-year programme of constructive reform it would be the government which would get the credit. If, on the other hand, the Liberals turned out Labour prematurely, the country would resent it and punish the Liberals accordingly. But another group of Liberals, not interested like Simon in 'economic equality', viewed Labour's proposals without enthusiasm. The parliamentary progress of the government's coal bill, published in December 1929, revealed the extent of Liberal divisions. On second reading the official Liberal stance was to oppose the bill, but two Liberals went into the government lobby while a further six abstained. At the committee stage, four Liberal MPs voted against a Liberal amendment and eight abstained. Any hope of consistency was doomed by marked changes in Lloyd George's own position. After a year of Labour government Simon sensed that there had already been three distinct changes in the leader's outlook: 'We have . . . had three periods during the year; a first one of peace, followed by one of war; then again a peaceful period. Now, judging by the last meeting, Mr Lloyd George intends another period of war.'[115]

By the second half of 1930 John Simon had emerged as the leading critic of Lloyd George's strategy. In the face of rapidly mounting unemployment the Labour government seemed to have few ideas and even fewer solutions. It was striking that when

Oswald Mosley, one of the few ministers with a strategy to tackle the problem, resigned from the government, Simon wrote to express his 'great admiration'.[116] Then, in late October 1930, just before the opening of the new parliamentary session, Simon wrote to Lloyd George to give him advance notice of his present feelings on relations with the Labour government. He argued that, after 17 months in power, Labour had proved a complete failure in almost all departments. As a result, Liberals were deriving no benefit from the present situation, but they were exposing themselves to the reproach that they were trying to save their own skins by avoiding another election. Simon announced that, should the government attempt to reverse the Baldwin government's trade union legislation, then he would not be able to support them and on a vote of confidence would go into the Conservative lobby: 'We are in danger of carrying offers of assistance to the point of subservience and I do not believe that this is the way in which Liberalism is likely to become a more effective force in national and Imperial affairs.'[117]

At the heart of this dispute lay an issue which had become central for all Liberals in the era of three-party politics but which had not needed a response when the Liberal party itself had been one of the two contenders for power. Where exactly did it stand in relation to Labour and the Conservatives? 'The fundamental question for the Liberal Party,' wrote E. D. Simon,

> which has never been properly discussed at a party meeting, is whether, broadly, in the present circumstances, we prefer a Labour Government, with ourselves holding the balance, or whether, on the other hand, we should prefer to force a General Election, which would almost inevitably result in a Conservative Government with a large majority over both the other parties combined.[118]

Liberalism's inability to answer this question with a single voice signalled the outbreak of yet another and potentially fatal phase of its self-destructive civil war. While John Simon now wished to bring the government down at the earliest opportunity, Lloyd

George was moving towards the idea of a formal pact with Labour. The stances taken by the two men involved a curious piece of symmetry. Lloyd George, who had worked in coalition with the Conservatives until 1922, now seemed ready to co-operate with Labour. Simon, who began the decade expressing sympathy with the objectives if not the means of the Labour party, was about to open negotiations with the Conservatives which would eventually propel him into high office in the Conservative-dominated National Government. The personal political odysseys of the two men serve to emphasise the impossibility of subjecting the kaleidoscopic pattern of post-war Liberal politics to neat patterns of ideological division and interpretation. The very diversity of Liberal thinking, once seen to be one of the party's strengths, was now contributing to its undoing. Nothing revealed this more clearly than the issue of free trade, the ark of the Cobdenite covenant which had remained for so long an article of faith for all who professed to be true believers in the gospel of Liberalism. Rather like Home Rule after 1886, free trade had become the indispensable cement holding the party's disparate strands together. By the late 1920s, however, as the British economy faced new and apparently intractable problems, particularly the ever mounting levels of unemployment, even this most sacred of doctrines came under review. As Keynes told the Summer School in 1925, 'we have to invent new wisdom for a new age'.[119]

Keynes and E. D. Simon were in fact among the first Liberal intellectuals to challenge the doctrine of free trade. Keynes became committed to the idea of tariffs during the course of 1930, while Simon found himself asking whether traditional free trade, appropriate to the time when Britain had been the undisputed workshop of the world, was still relevant in the changed circumstances of the twentieth century. At the Summer School of 1930 he called for a free and open enquiry into the whole subject and suggested the advisability of a 10 per cent tax on all imports except raw materials. By the following March John Simon too stressed that he was 'not going to shut out of [his] mind the consideration of fiscal measures which may be found to be necessary, even though they involve steps which in times of prosperity and abounding trade Liberals would never contemplate'.[120] For many it was simply the case that, while theoretically desirable, free trade made no sense in a world where other nations were imposing tariffs.

The extent of the party's disarray became apparent when parliament reassembled in the autumn of 1930. When the Conservatives put down a motion on the King's speech, the official Liberal line was to abstain, but five Liberals including John Simon and the chief whip, Sir Robert Hutchison (who promptly resigned), voted with the Tories, while four others went into the government lobby. Hutchison 'created a record by issuing a whip . . . and then voting against it himself'.[121] Yet, at the meeting called to choose the chief whip's successor, only 30 Liberal MPs bothered to attend. Leading members of the party assembled on 20 November to hear Lloyd George propose a formal pact with Labour for two years. Simon spoke forcefully against this plan. The Labour government was already discredited and nothing would be gained by putting Liberal assets into a bankrupt concern. Indeed, at a subsequent general election Liberal candidates could scarcely criticise a party which they had helped to sustain in power. The meeting broke up having established little except the extent of the party's divisions. At a further meeting a week later, Lloyd George suggested a pact for a shorter period than two years in return for the introduction of the Alternative Vote which, some Liberal strategists believed – probably erroneously – would double Liberal representation in the House of Commons. Simon, backed by Lord Reading, the Liberal leader in the Lords, opposed the whole notion of a bargain with the government. An arrangement for one year would turn into a bargain for two, since after twelve months it would be said that more time was needed to secure concessions from the government. Confusion again prevailed:

> Something was said at the end by Lloyd George about the differ-
> ence between an agreement and an understanding and the
> conference ended . . . without any clear information either as to
> what Lloyd George . . . intended to say to the Cabinet Ministers,

or as to what account might hereafter be given of the result of their further conversation.[122]

In the first months of 1931 the Liberal party visibly collapsed as a unified political force. The parliamentary party was reduced to little more than a disorganised rabble. 'I am all for the party being independent and having a mind of its own', conceded Archibald Sinclair, the new chief whip, 'but if individual members claim the same right, it is impossible for us to work effectively in the House of Commons.'[123] While Simon negotiated with the Conservatives about the possibility of their support at the next general election for himself and those Liberal MPs prepared to follow him, Lloyd George moved closer to Labour, assuring George Lansbury that 'the great majority of our party are in accord with yours in the general line of advance for the next ten years'.[124] By the summer he seems to have been in talks with the government about a formal coalition which would have seen him become Leader of the House and Foreign Secretary or Chancellor. In the meantime Simon, accompanied by Hutchison and Ernest Brown, formally resigned the Liberal whip on 26 June. The occasion was the Liberals' confused parliamentary response to the government's land tax proposals, a cause to which Lloyd George had first attached himself before the First World War. The specific issue scarcely merited Simon's withering indictment that the parliamentary party had reached a 'lower depth of humiliation than any into which it had yet been led'.[125] But in truth Simon's actual departure only symbolised a breach that had been growing ever since the Labour government took office.

'The effect on the party is serious,' judged one Lloyd George supporter. This was a considerable understatement. Beatrice Webb was nearer the truth when she predicted the dissolution of the historic Liberal party.[126] Had events been allowed to run their course, it seems probable that the Conservatives and the Simonite Liberals would have tried to eject the government once the House reassembled after the summer recess. As it was, such plans were overtaken by the dramatic internal collapse of the Labour cabinet. With the pound under severe pressure and the government unable to agree on a package of economy measures, the cabinet tendered its resignation on 23 August. On the following day, however, MacDonald re-emerged with the King's commission to form an all-party administration, charged with tackling the country's growing economic crisis. Lloyd George had been taken seriously ill in late July and it was his deputy, Herbert Samuel, who handled negotiations on behalf of the Liberal party. In an atmosphere in which the King urged all the party leaders to put the national interest first, Samuel had little alternative but to agree to Liberal participation. He and Reading now took office as Home and Foreign Secretary respectively in a new ten-man cabinet, while Donald Maclean, as President of the Board of Education, Sinclair as Scottish Secretary, and Crewe as Secretary for War, also took senior offices. The decision was warmly endorsed by the party as a whole, with even Lloyd George giving guarded support from his sickbed. The new government pushed though a package of economies, but failed to 'save' the pound which was forced off the Gold Standard on 21 September.

Though Simon had not received office in the National Government he was ready to offer his wholehearted support. On 23 September, 29 Liberals joined Simon, Runciman and Leslie Hore-Belisha in a memorial to the Prime Minister, supporting any measures the cabinet thought necessary to deal with the deficit in the balance of trade. As free-trade Liberals fully understood, this was meant to imply tariffs. Simon now accepted the invitation of more than two dozen Liberal MPs to lead the so-called Liberal National party and on 5 October his group formed a separate organisation for the specific purpose of contesting the next election in alliance with the Conservatives and with MacDonald's tiny band of National Labour supporters. The holding of that election was bitterly opposed by the still ailing Lloyd George and somewhat less strenuously by Samuel and Reading. Their reasons were clear enough. On the one hand the Conservatives were now looking to the electorate to offer a mandate for the introduction of tariffs. At the same time Liberals had good reason to fear the consequences of an election from a purely party point of view. Lloyd George's financial support had been ended in June 1930 with immediate consequences for the grass-roots organisation of the party. As a result, Liberals had contested only a small percentage of the by-elections held during the lifetime of the Labour government, passing up several opportunities where Liberals had performed respectably in 1929. In those contests where Liberals did take part, they performed disastrously.

But against Liberal opposition a general election was called for 27 October, with the government seeking a 'doctor's mandate' to continue its economic policies. Internal cabinet difficulties were papered over with the suggestion that each party should put forward its own programme under a blanket of anodyne words supplied by the Prime Minister. But Lloyd George denounced the election as 'an incredible act of reckless and criminal folly', while the growing separation of the Samuelite and Simonite factions was underlined by the differing situations their candidates faced in the constituencies.[127] While Conservatives opposed Samuelite Liberals in 81 seats, only four constituencies witnessed a clash between Conservatives and Liberal Nationals. Thus, while the Samuelites fielded 112 candidates, itself a somewhat pathetic total, their individual chances of victory were generally lower than those of the 41 Simonites. Liberal morale was low; the enthusiasm of 1929 had passed. The Samuelites had little to offer beyond an appeal for sacrifice at a time of national emergency and an increasingly hollow faith in free trade. Maclean, wary of any perception of an alliance with the Conservatives, had little to contribute:

> the only thing left to us was to make it clear to the country that we had not supported the decision to have the election and that we had been prepared to continue the necessary effort to stabilize financial credit, and that we were facing the issue as free traders. That, at any rate, would be a clear, understandable position whatever the result . . . . We should maintain the existence of the party and avoid any responsibility for what was coming, namely another coupon Election.[128]

The outcome of the election was a major setback, only partially concealed by the peculiar circumstances in which it had been held. The Conservatives returned no fewer than 473 MPs; Labour was reduced to just 52, the first real setback in its apparently inexorable rise over the previous 30 years. On the surface, the Liberals had done better; there were 33 Samuelites, 35 Liberal Nationals and four followers of Lloyd George. But the Liberal 'advance' compared with 1929 reflected only the electorate's temporary alienation from a Labour party which the National Government had successfully presented as running away from its responsibilities in the face of a national emergency. Only ten Liberals had been successful in the face of Conservative opposition. Thirteen seats won in 1929 were now lost, all to Conservatives, while 26 new gains were made, all at Labour's expense. Overall, the Liberal vote had fallen by more than three million, largely because of the reduction in the number of candidates. But it was striking that in 51 constituencies fought by all three parties in both 1929 and 1931 the Liberal share of the poll dropped by 7.5 per cent, suggesting a measurable move to the Conservatives. Despite the latter's overwhelming strength in the new House of Commons, MacDonald was keen to emphasise the continuing 'National' character of his government. Though both Reading and Crewe now retired, John Simon was rewarded for his loyalty by appointment to the Foreign Office, while Runciman became President of the Board of Trade. But was this, as Lloyd George had predicted, 'the death warrant of the Liberal Party as a separate Party'? 'You may have Ministers who are nominally Liberal in the so-called National Government', he warned, 'but they will only be a miserable row of plucked boobies.'[129]

There has in fact been widespread agreement among historians that the 1931 General Election marked the end of the road for the historic party of Gladstone and Asquith, at least in terms of its aspirations to be a party of government, and that there now began Liberalism's 'long diminuendo'.[130] Optimists, of course, were ready in 1931 to twist statistics to their own satisfaction. If the various Liberal factions were added together, a combined total of 72 MPs was reached. This enabled Walter Rea, soon to become the Samuelites' Chief Whip, to argue that Liberals were now once more the second largest party in the House of Commons, with 20 seats more than Labour. Such a claim was disingenuous. Whatever had happened to its strength in the House of Commons, Labour's vote had held up quite well in 1931 – 30.6 per cent of the total compared with 37.1 per cent in 1929 – and was in any case nearly three times as large as the combined total of the assorted Liberal groupings. That said, it is at least arguable that the body of the Liberal party was not yet a corpse and that the possibility of a partial recovery still existed, not least because of the huge setback which the electoral system had administered to Labour. That party had suffered a considerable blow, not least in terms of its credibility as a party of government because of the circumstances in which MacDonald's administration had collapsed. The apparently irreversible advance of the previous decade, achieved largely at Liberal expense, had for the time being at least been arrested.

The key factor in the Liberal performance in 1931 was that, largely because of individual constituency arrangements reached by the various components of the National Government, the number of Liberal candidates fell from 513 in 1929 to just 160 in 1931. Thus, if many Liberal MPs now owed their presence in the House of Commons to the forbearance of the Conservatives, it was also the case that many Conservative votes and probably some Conservative MPs were equally the consequence of the absence of Liberal candidates. Indeed, the 1931 election was held in such peculiar circumstances that it was unlikely to offer a reliable barometer of underlying Liberal support. It seems unrealistic to think that the potential reservoir of Liberalism in the country had dried up as dramatically or as quickly as the 1931 results suggested. After all, a little over two years earlier almost a quarter of the electorate had registered its support for Lloyd George's party. Furthermore, even in the parliament of 1931, a united Liberal party, outside the National Government, might have re-emerged as a significant challenger to the dominant Conservatives, especially in the context of Labour's disarray. Lloyd George certainly sensed an opportunity. 'If the Liberal Federation were to raise the standard', he insisted, 'and bring out a resounding policy [at the annual meeting of the National Liberal

Federation] at Clacton, millions of those who formerly looked to the Labour Party with hope, would rally to that standard.'[131] Early by-elections gave evidence of the Liberals' opportunities. Labour's financial embarrassment was the main reason why no Labour candidate entered the field in as many as five by-elections in 1932. Meanwhile, there were some signs of a Liberal resurgence. In the absence of a Labour candidate, the Liberals performed respectably at Henley on 25 February, cutting the Conservative majority by almost 50 per cent. At Dulwich in early June they moved up to second place from their third position at the General Election. Then, on 22 July and against most expectations, the Liberals held on to North Cornwall, notwithstanding the decision of the Conservatives, with whom they were still in nominal partnership inside the National Government, to field a candidate against them. Again, the Liberal performance was boosted by the absence of a Labour opponent. Sinclair enthused that this was the first time since the General Election that a government supporter had managed to increase his majority.

Yet if the Liberals were going to stage a comeback, perhaps not to power but at least to the status of a significant parliamentary force, their basic requirement was unity. The formation of the National Government in August had served partially to conceal the reality of a divided party. That government was one which both the Samuelites and Simonites supported; both factions were now represented inside the cabinet. As long as the two groups remained within the same government, or both moved into opposition, there was always the possibility that they would eventually reunite. Certainly, the rank and file of both groups do not seem to have believed that there had yet been an irrevocable parting of the ways. In the autumn of 1931 it did not seem inconsistent to be a member of the Liberal National group and also to belong to the Liberal party itself. One Liberal National MP recorded attending a Liberal party meeting on 2 October, after which he moved on to a gathering of the Simonite group.[132] But the following months would reveal that key figures in the Liberal National ranks, particularly Simon himself, stood very self-consciously in the way of reunion. The Liberal civil war, which had begun a decade and a half before, was ready to inflict one final and almost fatal body blow.

Once the election was over, Samuel moved rapidly to mend broken Liberal fences, only to meet with an unequivocal rebuff from both Lloyd George and Simon. The former, who had of course objected to holding an election, now insisted that he was not prepared to hold office again inside the parliamentary party, preferring instead to plough a lonely political furrow at the head of his tiny family grouping of MPs. Before long his inclination was no longer 'in the direction of regaining the Liberal Party with its cranks and hypocrites at the top who all hate me and have always done so'.[133] Simon offered feeble excuses to avoid attending a meeting of Liberal leaders and then gathered the courage to suggest that such a meeting should be postponed for the time being. The Samuelites issued a Liberal whip to all those MPs whose candidatures had been endorsed by local Liberal associations, but Simon's supporters chose instead to accept the government whip. Simon himself seemed more concerned about his relationship with the Prime Minister than that with his erstwhile Liberal colleagues. At a dinner of his followers he insisted that 'the great thing was to assure Ramsay that he had a solid block behind him, irrespective of the Tories'.[134]

But at least both groups insisted that they remained 'Liberals'. If major divisions over policy could be avoided, the two factions might gradually coalesce, despite Simon's unhelpful attitude. Ironically, therefore, it was the issue of free trade, the issue which had brought Asquithians and Lloyd Georgeites to a qualified reconciliation in 1923 and which remained for many Liberals the acid test of any potential adherent's credentials, which now ensured that there would be no coming together of the disparate strands of Liberalism. But if some Liberals continued to regard free trade as part of the party's holy grail – 'I will vote regularly and persistently against this deadly tariff danger,' insisted Maclean[135] – for others it had lost its supreme significance in a rapidly changing world. Many now saw tariffs as a temporary tactical expedient which could be negotiated away when international circumstances changed. As Clement Davies later explained, the imposition of measures of protection by foreign countries meant that 'we had to take some counter-measure in order to bring these other countries to a sense of reality'.[136] Early in 1932 the government's Import Duties Bill nearly provoked a major crisis inside the cabinet. Superficial unity was only maintained when ministers agreed to follow Lord Hailsham's novel suggestion that, on this one issue, the traditional doctrine of collective cabinet responsibility should be suspended, allowing members the luxury of agreeing to differ. The agreement to differ did not prompt any significant movement inside the Liberal party. But it did contribute to a growing mood of bewildered confusion about what Liberals were doing within the National Government. Divisions became publicly apparent when on 24 February an amendment was moved in the Commons to exclude food from the list of commodities which would be subject to duties. The Samuelites voted as a group in support of this amendment but the Simonites were divided – ten following their Liberal colleagues, but nine voting with the government. This might have been the occasion for compromise but such thoughts appear not to have entered Simon's mind, convinced as he now was of the need for protectionist measures. In the current state of the national economy, it was 'no good prescribing a long sea voyage as a cure for persistent haemorrhage; you must try to stop the bleeding'.[137] Simon's vision of the future appeared not to encompass Liberal reunion:

> I have a feeling that, after the experience through which we have passed, both in peace and in war, it may very well be that there will emerge an outlook on current political questions which will not be confined to any one of the old political parties and in which we shall be able really to influence one another.[138]

A further important step towards the formalisation of divisions within the Liberal ranks was taken in July 1932 with the setting up of the Liberal National Council. Designed as a rallying point for those Liberals who wanted to give wholehearted support to the National Government, it was also part of a concerted effort by the

Liberal National leadership to present their group rather than the Samuelites as the true standard-bearers of Liberalism in the country.

Matters came to a head later in 1932 when the government succeeded in negotiating the Ottawa Agreements to establish a scheme of Imperial Preference. For most Free Trade Liberals this was the last straw. But the Prime Minister was keen to keep the Samuelites inside the government in order to maintain the pretence that this was an all-party administration and thus to justify his own position at its head. 'If you go,' he pleaded with Samuel, 'I am no longer the head of a combination . . . I should be regarded as a limpet in office.'[139] As MacDonald had only managed to bring a small number of Labour MPs into the National Government, the Liberals enjoyed an importance beyond their numerical strength. Their presence helped to conceal the essentially conservative nature of the programme upon which the cabinet had embarked. Simon, however, urged that the presence of the Liberal Nationals alone would be enough to sustain the government's 'national' credentials, while the Liberal National President of the Board of Trade, Walter Runciman, pressed for the immediate filling by Liberal Nationals of any governmental vacancies caused by the resignation of free traders in response to Ottawa: 'This is partly for the look of the thing – preserving the broad base – and partly to keep alive loyalty to the government in circles which had Liberal antecedents.'[140] Senior Liberal Nationals were fully aware of the enormous importance of what might now happen. 'Assuming we continue our support of the Government,' wrote the Group's Chief Whip, Geoffrey Shakespeare, 'our lines of communication with the Liberal party will be cut for ever. Ottawa will be our Rubicon. There can be no re-crossing.' Such a price was only worth paying if the Liberal Nationals could secure assurances from the Conservatives regarding the content of the government's future programme, the allocation of government posts vacated by the Samuelites and the withdrawal of Conservative opposition at constituency level at the next general election.[141]

By the early autumn Simon had succeeded in striking as good a bargain as he could have hoped for from the Conservatives. He met Baldwin on 27 September and followed up his interview with a letter the following day. His chief concern was with 'the prospective electoral position' of his Liberal National group 'who represent a large body of Liberal opinion'. Once Samuel and his followers had left the government, 'the position of these friends of mine in the constituencies will be much more difficult and they will very soon be exposed to every sort of attack and pressure from the organisations who approve Samuel's démarche'. Simon argued that the Commons division on the second reading of the bill implementing the Ottawa Agreements should be seen as the acid test. He hoped that those Liberal Nationals who supported the government on this occasion could be assured that they would not face a Conservative opponent at the next general election.[142] In the circumstances there was more than a trace of hypocrisy in Simon's scribbled note of pained regret passed to Samuel at the cabinet meeting held on 28 September at which the latter and his colleagues finally announced their resignations. A private letter to Lady Hilton Young came closer to expressing Simon's true feelings: 'Samuel has chosen an amazing moment to go, for the whole world is now rocking and in the middle of an earthquake it will not be much good to howl "Ottawa".'[143]

While Baldwin pondered Simon's proposals, the Liberal Nationals had good reason to be pleased with the outcome of the governmental reshuffle necessitated by the Samuelites' resignations. The appointment of Godfrey Collins to the vacant Scottish Office meant that there were now three Liberal Nationals in the cabinet. At the same time, several others, including Leslie Hore-Belisha and Leslie Burgin, were promoted within the junior ranks of the government. It was said that rank-and-file Conservatives were dismayed by the allocation of posts which had given the Liberal Nationals an influence within the administration out of proportion to their numerical strength. Baldwin then sent Simon a 'letter of reassurance' about the position of sitting Liberal National MPs and gave public expression to his message in a speech at Blackpool on 7 October. His statement that those who backed the Ottawa Bill 'right through' should not suffer was, he informed Simon, received enthusiastically. Though Baldwin had to remind him that local Conservative constituency parties were not under the direct control of Conservative Central Office, he felt that he was 'entitled to assume that support will be forthcoming for those Liberal Members of Parliament who are prepared to give consistent support to the Government'.[144] The position of the Liberal Nationals was thus secured. But how long they would be able to maintain any genuine independence of the Conservatives was another issue. One suggested that Ottawa might lead to a new alignment of political parties: 'It may mean the creation of a Centre or National Party to face the country when next the opinion of the electors is sought.'[145] Just as likely, however, the Liberal Nationals would soon be subsumed within the ranks of the Tory party.

By contrast, the position of Samuel's independent Liberals was becoming anomalous in the extreme. Though they had left the administration, they continued to occupy government benches in the House of Commons. Samuel was concerned that in crossing the floor he might well suffer the loss of further MPs. For another year, therefore, the Liberals stayed on the government's side of the House amid mounting protest from the party's rank and file, an eloquent commentary on their ill-defined identity. 'The longer we remain in our present position,' warned Sinclair,

> the more inglorious, embarrassing and insignificant it becomes. Our speeches of criticism of the government and manifestos of Liberal policy will make no impression so long as it lasts; and while it is true that it would be disastrous to go into opposition at a time and manner that commanded no public interest or support, I doubt if we can remain where we are for long without witnessing the complete disintegration of the party.[146]

By the autumn of 1933 even Samuel recognised that this state of affairs could go on no longer: 'the party would fade away'.[147] But when the move did take place, the party suffered further damage. As Samuel had feared, several MPs remained on the government's side of the House and eventually joined the Liberal Nationals.

The events of 1931–33 were of crucial long-term importance for the Liberal party. It may be argued that, by his withdrawal from the National Government on a point of principle and his eventual resumption of opposition status, Samuel ensured that the Liberal party would survive as an independent entity in British politics. But the circumstances in which these events occurred meant that the party was now a less effective force than it had ever been. British politics would now be re-established on a two-party basis and, despite its performance in the General Election of 1931, the path was clear for the Labour party to re-emerge as the only viable alternative to the Conservatives. Although Lloyd George rejoined the Liberal party in November 1935, the Samuelite–Simonite split of 1932 proved to be permanent. For some time the Samuelites behaved as if this latest breach could be healed. In late November 1932 Henry Morris-Jones found them making 'desperate efforts to win over Simonites'.[148] A year later Samuel was still proclaiming that his aim was to gather together all Liberals. In 1934 the *Liberal Magazine* suggested that the Liberal Nationals were bound in the course of time to reunite with the Liberal party. But the Liberal National leadership had made its choice and that choice precluded reunion. The years ahead would witness several attempts to restore Liberal unity but to no avail, though many individuals did continue to cross over from one group to the other. Drawing ever closer to their Tory allies, the Liberal Nationals (restyled the National Liberals in 1948) maintained a theoretically independent identity into the 1960s before finally fusing with the Conservative party.

The continued existence of the Liberal Nationals prevented Liberalism from maximising its potential vote at a time when the mainstream party continued to decline remorselessly. Liberal Nationals were in place and tended to remain in place in constituencies where a significant Liberal tradition persisted. One option was for the Liberals themselves to try to reassert their claim to that tradition. But, after burning their fingers in a by-election in East Fife in February 1933, the Liberals drew back from challenging Liberal Nationals in their constituencies. As a result, only in Oldham and Denbigh did the two factions confront one another in the 1935 General Election. Some confusion thus persisted through the 1930s and into the post-war era as to who really represented true Liberalism. In 1937 a former Liberal party treasurer used the argument of reclaiming sole ownership of the Liberal name in order to justify his suggested strategy of destroying the Liberal National party.[149] More importantly, the close association of the Liberal Nationals and the Conservatives enabled the latter to broaden their appeal to the electorate to attract the residue of the Liberal vote, especially in constituencies where no Liberal candidate came forward. Philip Snowden, Labour's former Chancellor who left the National Government at the same time as Samuel, summed up the situation as early as January 1933: 'the Simonite Tories keep up the pretence of being Liberals in order to secure the support of innocent Liberals for the Tory Party'.[150] This strategy was consciously employed by Baldwin in the 1930s and by an array of post-war Conservative leaders including Churchill. It contributed to the telling argument that there was no longer any need for a Liberal party *per se* as the Conservatives had been liberalised from within. The Tories thus managed to keep a firm grip on that spectrum of political opinion which was vital to the Liberals if they were ever to revive, even as a third force in British politics.

This situation left the independent Liberals, even after they crossed over to the opposition benches, with a crisis of identity. Two years of struggling to come to terms with a minority Labour government had been followed by a similar period of disarray over the issue of participation in the National Government. Even now, however, the Samuelites experienced some difficulty in differentiating themselves from the government. The National Government had taken over the traditional Liberal rallying cries of retrenchment and sound finance, but without managing to appear unduly reactionary or illiberal. 'So long as Baldwin presses so far to the middle and is at war with his Diehards,' commented Sir William Sutherland, Lloyd George's former Press Secretary, 'it is not clear where Samuel is going to crash in with a separate identity and policy.'[151] There was still a reluctance to oppose a government which had been set up to deal with a national emergency:

> Therefore in the opposition which it will be the duty of the Liberal Parliamentary Party to offer in the House of Commons . . . there will be no resort to those traditional tactics of Parliamentary warfare which are aimed at the indiscriminate obstruction of Government business and are animated by a desire to thwart, embarrass and trip up the Government by every legitimate Parliamentary resource.[152]

One Liberal activist complained that while the man in the street knew roughly what a Socialist state and a Conservative one would mean, 'he has precious little notion of the Liberal state'.[153]

An attempt to hammer out a coherent set of Liberal policies began under Lord Lothian's auspices in the autumn of 1932 and continued throughout the following year. But agreement on issues other than free trade proved elusive. Even on this question the commitment of some Liberals was weakening, not least because improvements in the balance of payments suggested that the introduction of tariffs was having a beneficial effect. One leading Samuelite was ready to admit that 'the possibility of a world system of complete free trade has gone and probably will never return'.[154] At this time Liberals needed the fertility of a mind like Lloyd George's, but it was not available to them. Samuel was an able parliamentarian but he lacked the qualities of inspirational leadership of which his party was in desperate need. Lloyd George's interventionist philosophy was progressively abandoned. According to one Liberal newspaper, many in the party were 'not in love with the proposals which emanate from some of their leaders for borrowing and spending huge sums of money'.[155] Sinclair's biographer has well captured the increasingly conservative image projected by the party in the early 1930s: 'When it came to policy the party would henceforth follow the path of caution, returning like wounded animals to the safe lairs of the past, espousing free trade, justice and equality, none of which was directly relevant to Britain's immediate problems. The Yellow Book gathered dust on Liberal shelves.'[156] The radicalism that had characterised the Summer School movement of the early twenties and the Lloyd George revival later in the decade retreated once more to the periphery of the Liberal party. It was still there. Ramsay Muir, for example, published *The Liberal Way* in 1934. He suggested, *inter alia*, that the Bank of England 'ought to be freed from any suspicion that its powers might be used for party ends' – an idea not acted upon until the late 1990s.[157] But Muir's was no longer the public face of British Liberalism.

It is difficult to escape the conclusion that many leading Liberals were losing faith in themselves, with inevitable and disastrous consequences for the party in the country. Ramsay Muir, a man who had done much to keep alive the flame of independent Liberalism, now took 'a most gloomy, almost a despairing view of our prospects. We are beaten in advance by the public idea that we are done for, and this affects our own people.'[158] Sinclair warned of a 'real danger' that the party would 'cease to be regarded as an effective fighting force'. A shortage of both money and personnel in the constituencies made it hard to 'maintain . . . activities at a level of intensity over a prolonged period'.[159] The decline of Liberalism as a force in local government continued apace. Apart from 1931 the party suffered a net loss of council seats each year as the decade progressed. The process of decay was particularly marked in the industrial towns of the North and Midlands. A few scattered gains at Conservative expense in middle-class seaside resorts afforded scant compensation. Symbolically, even in Manchester with its long radical tradition, Liberals effectively gave up their independence when, in 1931, they joined the Conservatives in an anti-Labour pact.[160] By 1933, with Labour showing signs of moving back to the political centre ground, Lothian concluded that the position of the Liberal party was 'almost hopeless'.[161]

The loss of Lloyd George had inevitable financial implications. By 1931 revenue from the subscription list of the Liberal Central Association had fallen to about £500 per annum. Party headquarters was in effect being maintained by Lloyd George who had earlier promised a sum of £30,000 for the next general election. When, however, that election was held in circumstances of which he disapproved, Lloyd George withdrew his offer and the election was fought by means of a hastily raised fund of just £17,000. From the Whips Office, Harcourt Johnstone bemoaned the 'worry and strain of trying to carry on the organisation of a political party without knowing for two months in advance whether the inevitable liabilities can be met or not'. He doubted whether he had 'ever in these 10 miserable, discouraging years . . . been so sorely tempted to chuck the whole thing and be a free man again'.[162] In brief, the Liberal party now lacked the capacity to pose as a credible party of national government. Its resources were insufficient and its local base too attenuated to play the role it had just about sustained throughout the 1920s. The logical option may have been to focus on a clearly targeted narrow front in those areas of the country such as the South-West where Liberalism remained a viable political force. An alternative would have been to seek an alliance with Labour in the face of the Conservatives' overwhelming strength in the House of Commons. But most of the party's leading figures 'still regarded politics purely in terms of major international and domestic issues, which meant that they were unable to adopt an alternative role based on low politics'.[163] As a result, the party tried hard to convince itself that revival was at hand and that a Liberal government remained a realistic proposition rather than a self-deluding pipe-dream.

Liberals thus had no reason to face the General Election of 1935 with anything other than apprehension. There was little sign of a clear and viable political identity emerging. On some social issues the party seemed indistinguishable from Labour. On other matters differentiation from the National Government was not easy. By May 1935 the Liberals were ready to support the government's policy of increased expenditure on defence. By-election performances since going into opposition had been distinctly poorer than before this move. At Cambridge in February 1934 the Liberal share of the vote fell from 25 per cent in 1929 to just 7 per cent. A week later at Lowestoft the corresponding fall was from 31 per cent to 10 per cent. Largely for lack of money, the party failed to contest seven of the twelve by-elections held between April and December of that year. The fiction was maintained that the party would contest the General Election on a broad front, thus offering voters the realisable prospect of a Liberal government. To declare otherwise would be to invite 'a scream of rage from all the Party Organizations and an immediate collapse of the Associations which had been told that it was not intended that they should contest the election'. 'We must try to keep up the bluff until the last moment', declared Harcourt Johnstone, 'or decide here and now to disband the Liberal Party as an organized political entity.'[164] Attempts to restore Lloyd George to the party's inner councils appear to have broken down over the Welshman's efforts to radicalise the Liberals' programme for the forthcoming contest. Thereafter he showed a growing readiness to endorse selected Labour candidates and, early in 1935, launched his New Deal campaign with the aim of bringing together all those of progressive views who were critical of the National Government's performance.

In the event, Baldwin, Prime Minister since June, called the election for 14 November. As late as June fewer than a hundred Liberal candidates were in place. Last-minute funding for those willing to subscribe to Lloyd George's Council of Action helped bring the total up to 161. But the resulting narrow front campaign was not one for which the party had carefully planned. It represented no more than the tactics of necessity and, in any case, many constituencies were fought where the Liberals entertained no hope of success. The brief Liberal manifesto contained no surprises and aroused little interest. Several national newspapers ignored its publication. Its stirring title, *A Call to Arms*, seemed curiously ill-chosen. The *News Chronicle*, the only mass-circulation national newspaper to offer the party its support, still noted that the Liberals would 'be lucky to hold what they have'.[165] It was somewhat strange that two of the three Liberal radio broadcasts were delivered by Lloyd George, whose connection with the party was now tenuous, and Lord Snowden who, despite a close association with Samuel since 1932, was still best remembered as a Labour Chancellor of the Exchequer. Samuel's own broadcast on 6 November conceded that the government had made some progress since 1932, but argued that issues such as the Means Test, high unemployment and the Ottawa Agreements remained to be tackled. Where no Liberal candidate was standing, he urged support for candidates who had satisfied the scrutiny of Lloyd George's Council of Action questionnaire. But that still left about 300 seats where Liberal voters were offered no guidance. Perhaps it was not needed. Much of the National Government campaign, not least its apparently firm commitment to the Covenant of the League of Nations, was geared towards that band of centre opinion which Conservative Central Office believed held the key to its return to office. In his broadcast on behalf of the government, Simon stressed that Liberalism was distinct from the Liberal party and assured Liberal voters that they could confidently place their trust in Baldwin.

After what most observers judged a feeble campaign, Liberals should have been prepared for a result of unmitigated disaster. With only 6.4 per cent of the total vote, the party saw just 21 MPs returned to the new House of Commons. Except for Archibald Sinclair, the party's entire front bench including Samuel, narrowly ousted by the Conservatives in Darwen, went down to defeat. Meanwhile, despite a net gain of 94 seats for Labour, the National Government remained firmly entrenched with an overall majority in excess of 250 seats. It was rewarded for seeing the country through the worst phases of the international depression, its reputation reinforced by the expectation of still better times to come. Perhaps as many as 150 of the Conservatives elected in 1931 had owed their success to their 'National' credentials. The fact that many of them held on to their seats in 1935, by which time the Liberal party was once more in opposition, was indicative of Baldwin's success in convincing the electorate that his version of Liberal Toryism had now captured the vital centre ground of British politics. The government had retained the support of a substantial proportion of the country's 'Liberal' vote. As a result, and for the first time in the century, the Liberal party itself appeared entirely irrelevant to the country's political fortunes. Its small band of MPs could exert no influence in the face of the parliamentary arithmetic of the day. Whether the victim of suicide or murder, the body itself seemed indubitably dead.

3

SO FEW AND SO FUTILE, 1935–1955

In the 20 years after the General Election of 1935 the Liberal party showed few if any signs of genuine revival. All the statistics and indices of decline, which had already become so established, continued to move in an unfavourable direction. The debilitating haemorrhage of Liberal votes seemed to have no end. Both in parliament and local government the reduction of Liberal representation went on apace. The parliamentary party of 21, bequeathed by Herbert Samuel to his successor, went down progressively at succeeding general elections before reaching an all-time low of just five MPs following the loss of the Carmarthen by-election in February 1957. Ironically, the victor in this contest was Lloyd George's daughter, Megan, newly welcomed like so many radical Liberals before her into the ranks of the Labour party. Five months earlier Gallup had put the party's national support at a derisory one per cent of the electorate. Municipal elections continued to witness a fall in both the overall number of Liberal candidates and in the percentage of those who were successful at the polls. The proportion of council seats won by Liberals dropped from 14 per cent in 1931 to just 7.2 per cent in 1938.[1] The existing tendency of Liberal councillors to form local pacts with their more numerous Conservative counterparts intensified. Bristol was among the important cities where Liberals in the 1930s submerged their identity within an anti-Socialist alliance. This trend may have saved individual Liberals from exclusion from their councils, but it did nothing to preserve a separate and recognisable Liberal identity and it stored up problems for any future attempt to redefine independent Liberalism. In many ways the logical conclusion to this spiral of decline was the complete elimination of the Liberal party, at least as a national political force. Many saw its survival as no more than 'the obstinate refusal of a dying party to accept [its] fate'.[2] Yet survive it did, even though this survival owed less to rational calculation than to the unshakeable conviction of a small band of dedicated followers that better days would eventually return.

Archibald Sinclair, newly chosen to lead the parliamentary rump following the electoral debacle of 1935, faced a disheartening future. Demoralised by the loss of key colleagues and with benefactors and supporters continuing to leave an apparently sinking ship, he personally doubted whether the Liberals could possibly sustain their credentials as a nationwide organisation for much longer.[3] With the periodic subventions from Lloyd George's political fund now consigned to history, finance remained the party's most obvious headache. Despite hopes that their basis of financial support could be broadened, the Liberals continued to rely on the generosity of a small number of wealthy benefactors. But the available cash was seldom adequate. Over the next decade the party's annual income never reached £15,000 and sometimes struggled to attain half that figure, a slim foundation indeed for a supposedly national party.

The state of the party's organisation was the easiest cat to kick. The Meston Committee was set up with a broad remit to propose changes. Its major recommendation led to the replacement in 1936 of the National Liberal Federation by the Liberal Party Organisation, with the aim of creating a single policy-making body, though in practice authority over policy remained divided. Nonetheless, some improvements did result and the party was certainly in better heart in the late 1930s than during the years of Samuel's leadership. More fundamental issues witnessed less progress. Perhaps the most basic were the party's identity and place within the political spectrum, and its resulting best strategy for the future.

It was not obvious by the mid-1930s what made independent Liberalism distinctive. Sinclair would mouth platitudes about a non-socialist alternative to the Conservative-dominated National Government, but convincing the electorate of the viability of this image was another matter. Lothian had identified the problem as early as 1933:

> From a party point of view Liberalism is in an almost hopeless position, so long as Baldwin is leader of the Conservative Party and Arthur Henderson the leading figure in the Labour Party. [The point was equally valid once Attlee became Labour leader in 1935.] Both are democrats, liberally minded, supporters of disarmament and the League of Nations, and constitutionalists. Both, too, are moderate tariffists, even friendly, in theory, to free trade.[4]

For all its subsequent bad press, the National Government was in no sense an administration of the far right. Its leading Conservative members, men such as Baldwin, Neville Chamberlain and Samuel Hoare, had well-established moderate, even liberal, pedigrees, while right-wingers such as Churchill were kept firmly on the political sidelines. In part this was a matter of conviction. But Conservative strategists also believed that, by shifting the party's centre of gravity leftwards, Conservatism could appeal to a far broader electorate, including the supposedly still large 'Liberal vote', than would otherwise be the case. The National Government's continued electoral supremacy throughout the decade lends a measure of credibility to this analysis. As Lothian reflected in the wake of the 1935 General Election, though a distinctive Liberal attitude to public affairs appeared to persist, the voters seemed to identify it with Baldwin.[5]

Not the least of the Conservative leader's advantages in the development of this strategy was his on-going partnership with the Liberal Nationals. As the Conservative leader once commented of his block of 'Liberal' supporters, 'they are my body guard'.[6] The continuing existence of the Liberal Nationals had the effect of sowing seeds of confusion in the minds of some electors about who in fact now represented the authentic voice of British Liberalism. In policy terms little seemed to divide the two Liberal factions by the middle of the decade, other than their attitudes to the existing administration. But, spared Tory opposition at the recent general election, the Liberal Nationals had become the numerically stronger parliamentary body.

The Liberals' quest to establish a distinctive identity was not helped by their own continuingly equivocal attitude towards the Liberal Nationals. After the experience of the East Fife by-election in February 1933, the mainstream party was extremely reluctant to confront Liberal Nationals in their own constituencies or even to set up rival local Liberal Associations. As a result, only two isolated contests took place between the competing groups at the 1935 General Election. Liberal Nationals were thus allowed to hold the field in many constituencies where there was a signifi-cant Liberal tradition. As Sinclair wrote as late as 1937: 'We at Headquarters cannot – at any rate yet – countenance attacks upon seats held by Liberal National members of Parliament. They have not yet done it to us openly, and we should have to consider very carefully before we took the initiative against them.'[7] The position did change somewhat after the St Ives by-election that June, when Isaac Foot came close to defeating the Liberal National candidate. Even so, a tendency remained to look upon the Liberal Nationals as errant sheep who would one day return to the fold, and it was striking that the Liberal Year Books continued to list Liberal National organisations amongst those of the Liberal party itself until the end of the decade.

The period before the outbreak of war saw few new develop-ments in party policy. In 1939 J. L. Hammond commended Lord Crewe for his consistency to 'Mr Gladstone's principles' without apparently seeing that Crewe's on-going commitment to the Liberalism of the nineteenth century was part of the party's prob-lems.[8] Ironically, while the radical ideas which had been worked out in *Britain's Industrial Future* and *We Can Conquer Unemployment* began to find their way into the thinking of such bodies as Political and Economic Planning and the Next Five Years Group, becoming by the mid-1940s part of a new orthodox consensus, their importance within Liberal circles declined. With Baldwin's Conservatism espousing the more traditional Liberal virtues of fiscal prudence and retrenchment, Liberals had little beyond the increasingly weather-worn slogan of 'free trade' to call their own. But free trade had lost much of its electoral appeal in the face of mounting unemployment and a stagnant economy. It also hindered attempts to carve out an electorally appealing agricultural policy for those rural areas where a residual inclination towards Liberalism was probably strongest. No single Liberal ideology prevailed at this time and the party embraced both planners and free marketeers. On balance, however, 'the Liberal Party was consistently libertarian rather than collectivist. It placed the greatest stress upon the basic importance of the individual, saw the government's role as sustaining his rights [and] was aware of the dangers of the concentration of economic and political power.'[9]

It was foreign policy which offered Liberals the clearest opportunity to strike out on their own and, in particular, to differentiate themselves from the Conservative-dominated National Government. The turning point was the Hoare–Laval crisis of December 1935. Coming only months after a general election in which all parties had competed with one another to convince the electorate of their commitment to the principles of the League of Nations, this attempt to buy off Mussolini's aggression at the territorial expense of the African kingdom of Abyssinia suggested a lack of good faith on the government's part. Donald Johnson, who had contested Bury for the Liberals at the election, later recalled that while 'the Hoare–Laval Plan did not save Abyssinia or even a portion of it, it did . . . save the Liberal Party for a further lease of life'.[10] A plausible case has recently been made out for a viable Liberal alternative to the government's policy of appeasing the European dictators. Until 1938 this involved 'making it clear that the League was capable of and willing to remedy, grievances through formal procedures which would lead to economic disarmament'.[11] By 1938, recognising that the League was all but dead, Liberals moved towards a stance of ensuring that all concessions had behind them the threat of force from a powerful alignment of states ready to act if Germany or Italy broke their agreements. The Liberals' position was similar to

Labour's but free of the latter's reluctance to accept the need for rearmament.

Sinclair himself certainly deserves credit for his honourable stance during a decade which ruined the reputations of so many of his political contemporaries. He retained, for perhaps too long, an idealistic faith that the League could still play an effective role in international affairs. In 1938, however, he urged a strong stand over Czechoslovakia and after Munich condemned the government's successive retreats in the face of aggressive dictatorships. But the divisions which had plagued Liberalism when it was a much larger force in the House of Commons had not gone away now that it was reduced to a parliamentary rump. In the key Commons debate on the Munich settlement in early October 1938, fourteen Liberals voted against the government, but four voted in support and two did not vote at all. Over the introduction of conscription early in 1939, Liberal divisions were even more apparent with six MPs voting in favour and seven against. The Liberal alternative to the government's policy may have been articulated by Archibald Sinclair, but it was not espoused by his predecessor, Herbert Samuel, whose support for Munich was such as to prompt Neville Chamberlain to offer him a seat in the cabinet. Arguably, of course, 'appeasement' was the authentic and tragically mistaken view of liberalism (if not of Liberalism) in the inter-war years – the unshakeable belief in man's rationality and a refusal to contemplate his complete corruption by the forces of evil.

At all events it seems unlikely that the party's approach to international affairs did much to enhance its electoral prospects. Sinclair recovered his optimism, buoyed up by a mini-revival in the party's electoral fortunes in 1937 when, in addition to near misses at St Ives and North Dorset, Donald Johnson polled respectably at Bewdley, vacated when Baldwin moved to the calmer political waters of the House of Lords. Confident that Liberal revival lay on a tantalisingly near horizon, Sinclair resisted the alternative strategies of electoral pacts and co-operation urged upon him by other senior Liberals. Lothian, for example, had contemplated the need for Liberals to join either the Conservative or Labour party and 'liberalise from within'.[12] By 1938 there were calls for Liberal participation in a Popular Front to oppose the National Government at home and fascism abroad, but Sinclair refused to compromise the party's independence. In the event, the promising performances of 1937 proved to be no more than a typical mid-term reaction against the incumbent government. In 1938 the party contested just two of the eighteen by-elections which took place. T. L. Horabin held on to North Cornwall in a by-election in July 1939, but there seems little reason to question his opinion that there was no prospect of any substantial Liberal gains in the General Election widely anticipated for the autumn of that year.[13] In the view of the admittedly not impartial Hugh Dalton, the party had become 'a living corpse'.[14]

Over the 1935 parliament as a whole the parliamentary party cut a poor image, notwithstanding some impressive personal performances by Sinclair. One MP of this era recalled that, while Liberal MPs met on a weekly basis to decide their voting intentions, in the event each tended to vote as he wished.[15] Too much work fell on to the shoulders of a small if willing band. As Percy Harris, the party's Chief Whip, ruefully remembered:

> 'Speaking on behalf of my honourable friends', I would say, to the jeers of the honourable members opposite, looking to the left of me, only to find I was alone on the bench. It was a great experience: I learnt every move in the game and I hope it was worth while, though I sometimes doubt it. Certainly Liberals outside knew little of the work I was putting in to save their heritage for them.[16]

The coming of European war in September 1939 disrupted the normal patterns of political development in Britain, not least because it postponed for the duration of hostilities the by then imminent general election. Prime Minister Neville Chamberlain invited the Liberals, along with Labour, to join his government, but both opposition parties declined. With no position in the War Cabinet on offer, Liberals decided that they would be obliged to accept joint responsibility for government policy without sharing control over its creation. In May 1940, however, Churchill succeeded in forming a genuinely all-party coalition in which Sinclair became Secretary of State for Air, while Harcourt Johnstone and Dingle Foot were appointed to junior positions at the Board of Trade and the Ministry of Economic Warfare respectively. For the first time, therefore, since the resignation of the Samuelites in 1932, Liberals returned to the seats of power. Though not a member of the War Cabinet, Sinclair took part in the crucial discussions of late May 1940 over whether to open peace talks. Yet it is doubtful whether the party derived any long-term advantage from its occupation of office, with Sinclair incurring criticism for his failure to exert influence over the general tone of the government. If anything, the circumstances of wartime served to exacerbate those internal divisions which had plagued it for at least a generation. Sinclair's understandable absorption with the Air Ministry deprived the party of a sense of leadership and direction, while encouraging the suspicion that he might ultimately follow the example of so many Liberals before him and defect to the political enemy. 'I feel sure', noted Violet Bonham Carter in June 1944, 'that Archie's one desire is to remain with W[inston] and continue to work in much the present set-up.'[17] Sinclair had served as second-in-command to Churchill with the 6th Royal Scots Fusiliers in the First World War and there were those who believed that he continued, metaphorically at least, to stand to attention when in the Prime Minister's presence.Those Liberals for whom no government office was found grouped themselves, almost as a party within the party, under the leadership of Percy Harris. But even here divisions persisted over the extent to which the government could legitimately direct and manage the wartime state, divisions which were bound to become acute once attention turned to the problems of reconstruction and the sort of society Liberals wanted to see emerge when peace returned

As in the First World War the politicians of the three main parties responded to the grave external threat from Hitler's Germany by declaring a moratorium on domestic politics with the suspension of by-election contests, allowing the incumbent party to nominate an unopposed successor in the event of a parliamentary vacancy. It was not long, however, before this self-denying ordinance began to create frustration among the Liberal rank and file. When attempts to move a resolution against the Party Truce were thwarted at the 1941 Assembly, the Liberal Action Group, later renamed Radical Action, was formed that November. The founders included Lancelot Spicer, Honor Balfour, Everett Jones and Donald Johnson, and they were later joined by more prominent Liberals including Clement Davies, Megan Lloyd George and Tom Horabin. Over the following three years, several known Liberals stood at by-elections as 'independents' and often achieved respectable polls, benefiting like the short-lived Common Wealth party from the national wartime swing against the Conservatives. Johnson came close to victory at Chippenham in August 1943, while Miss Balfour all but regained Samuel's old seat of Darwen that December. The following February Mrs Corbett Ashby secured 44 per cent of the vote at Bury St Edmunds.

These performances encouraged many Liberal activists to believe that their party was on the brink of a great resurgence, held back only by the constraints of the wartime truce and the delay in holding a general election. Such thinking received apparent endorsement from the increasingly 'liberal' ethos which came to permeate the war years. John Maynard Keynes and William Beveridge, the two men whose ideas seemed set to dominate the post-war world, were, after all, both Liberals and the latter entered parliament as a beneficiary of the by-election truce as member for Berwick-upon-Tweed in October 1944. Beveridge himself 'believe[d] genuinely in the Liberal Revival of which [he] spoke'.[18] But he probably overestimated the party's readiness to move towards the sort of state-regulated economy which he espoused. It was striking that when two veteran Liberal peers discussed their party's approach to the parliamentary debate on the Beveridge Plan, Lord Crewe merely informed Lord Samuel that 'he might say something very briefly in general support of the proposals though not making any direct attack on the Government' – scarcely a ringing endorsement of the most significant blueprint for social progress since before the First World War.[19] Nine Liberal MPs including T. L. Horabin went into the opposition lobby as a protest against the government's lukewarm reception of the Beveridge Report. The party proved incapable of taking any real advantage of Beveridge's sudden and spectacular prominence. Two revealing Mass Observation reports summed up its problems. That of March 1942 noted: 'Over and over again we come back to the widespread feeling, among pro-Liberals, anti-Liberals and apathetics, that the Liberals are essentially *something of the past* rather than *of the future*'. Three years later Mass Observation found a basic feeling of goodwill towards the Liberals but also a sense that a vote for the party would be a wasted one.[20] Thus, while the mood of the times 'may technically have been more liberal than socialist . . . this was a technicality which the party could not exploit'.[21] The fruits of wartime hopes and aspirations for a better world were preparing to fall into the lap of Clement Attlee, and not that of Sinclair or any other Liberal.

As in 1931, the existence of a coalition government brought Liberals and Liberal Nationals into the same administration and it was almost inevitable that there should be renewed talk of reunion. On this occasion the initiative came from Ernest Brown, who had taken over the leadership of the Liberal National group in December 1940. From the outset, however, there was a suggestion that Brown's approach was largely tactical – 'to put ourselves right with our Liberal supporters in the country who might accuse us of maintaining divisions against Liberals' – and even that it had been 'decreed' by Churchill, who saw the fusion of the sundered wings of Liberalism as the first stage in the development of a broad anti-socialist alliance to confront the Labour party in the post-war era.[22] At all events Sinclair was willing to explore the possibility of reunion, not least because it seemed, in the face of the advance of Radical Action, to offer the chance to strengthen Liberalism's right wing.

Talks began in the summer of 1943. But Sinclair was careful to stress that his primary concern was to ensure the survival of the Liberal party as an independent political force. In practice, this meant that the Liberal Nationals would have to sever their Conservative associations if the negotiations were to have any chance of a successful outcome. As Sinclair told his fellow Liberals: 'I want to see the Liberal Party strong, united and reinforced by all men and women who subscribe to its principles, will support its policy and will resolutely maintain its identity and independence. On that basis I shall be very glad to talk things over with Mr Brown.'[23] When, therefore, at the end of October 1943 Brown made explicit his opinion that a National Government should continue even after the end of the war, any possibility of formal Liberal reunion was effectively at an end, even though desultory talks continued into the following year. Dingle Foot, dismissing the Liberal Nationals as 'Vichy Liberals', was able to reassure Megan Lloyd George that 'nothing remotely resembling a basis of agreement ever looked like emerging'.[24] But Clement Davies, only recently returned to the Liberal fold, offered a more interesting interpretation of the 1943 negotiations:

> One set of people, namely so-called leaders, desire amalgamation so that they would join with Winston Churchill in forming a Centre Party; the others, like myself, feel that for a considerable time men have borne wrong labels. And that there are, in both branches, Radical elements which should join together with the object of carrying out a true Liberal or Radical policy which would certainly be opposed by Winston Churchill and the Tory Party.[25]

A feeling that the political tide was running their way caused many Liberals to rejoice at the breakdown of the negotiations with the Liberal Nationals. But their optimism was misplaced. Though the Liberals had been the first of the three main parties in setting up a reconstruction committee as early as the autumn of 1940, this was not generally indicative of their preparation for the return of normal party politics. The party's organisation atrophied during the war years at all levels. As Percy Harris later recalled:

> Up to 1944 it was almost impossible to persuade Liberals to take any active interest in party politics or even to consider adopting candidates. It was not until early 1945 there was any

real awakening of activity among the Liberals in the constituencies, and the same applied to possible candidates.[26]

Violet Bonham Carter noted going through a list of English seats and candidates and being 'depressed by the tracts of Liberal wasteland'.[27] The chief whip pressed the need for the party to embark upon a major publicity campaign in 1944, but Sinclair, constrained by his loyalty to Churchill's government, refused his consent. In October 1944 the parliamentary party accepted a resolution to 'put forward, without any commitments to any other parties, the largest possible number of candidates in complete independence, presenting the party's independent programme'.[28] Sinclair himself had wanted the wartime coalition to continue until the Japanese were defeated, a task which, it was widely believed, would require an additional eighteen months or two years of attritional fighting. In February 1945, however, the party conference voted to leave the coalition as soon as the European war was over, a decision which scarcely gave Liberals the time to recover from their wartime inertia or to arrive at a coherent picture of what the party now represented. A last minute upsurge of enthusiasm could not make up for several years of organisational neglect.

In the circumstances it was perhaps not surprising that Liberalism gave out different and sometimes confusing messages during the 1945 election campaign. The election addresses of Liberal candidates showed a greater diversity and inconsistency than was revealed by their political opponents. That said, the party's manifesto was probably the most left-wing on which it campaigned in the whole of the twentieth century. While stressing a belief in private enterprise and the value of individual effort, the manifesto said that Liberals would demand nationalisation 'without hesitation' where this was the most economical option: 'Where there is no further expansion or useful competition in an industry or where an industry or group of industries has become a private monopoly, Liberals say it should become a public utility.' In addition, there were calls for extensive state control over the use of land and a statement that Liberals would not be satisfied until a separate dwelling had been provided for each family at a reasonable rent. The tone of the manifesto owed much to the Liberals' expectation of a Conservative victory and their need to differentiate themselves from that party rather than from Labour.

Against this, Sinclair, certain that the relevance of traditional Liberalism had not diminished, tended to conduct the party's campaign very much as he might have done in the 1930s. But the themes which had given the party strength and vitality in earlier decades no longer had the same appeal in post-war Britain. After the sacrifices of the struggle against Hitler, the electorate wanted something more tangible than a high-minded reassertion of abstract values: 'its ideals of freedom and tolerance; its assertion of the principle that every human being, and not merely the specially privileged, is a personality with a right to a reasonable share in the moral, intellectual and material progress of the world'.[29]

In general, the Liberal campaign never captured the popular imagination, not least because the other two parties, recognising that the real contest lay between themselves, paid it scant attention. In his celebrated 'Gestapo' broadcast, Churchill contented himself with the assertion, which would become a Conservative commonplace over the next decade, that 'there is scarcely a Liberal sentiment which animated the great Liberal leaders of the past which we do not inherit and defend'.[30] Even after listening to a speech by Beveridge in Edinburgh, an observer of the election concluded that 'the old fire of Liberalism . . . was now almost extinct'.[31] Beveridge and his ideas naturally figured prominently in the Liberals' campaign, but without redounding significantly to the party's advantage. Despite his Liberal credentials, Beveridge's ideas were not a Liberal monopoly. With varying degrees of emphasis, most of his plans had found their way into the electoral programmes of the Labour and Conservative parties, and the growing 'liberal' consensus in the country did not necessarily presage Liberal success at the polls.

The Liberal party's other basic difficulty was to convince the electorate that it was a serious aspirant for power. In the end, despite more ambitious predictions, only 306 candidates were nominated, a figure which would not have been sufficient to constitute a Commons majority even had every one been elected. Of this number as many as 87 per cent were fighting an election for the first time. Some were so inexperienced as to do the party little credit on the hustings. In any event, Gallup polls since 1943 had seen Liberal support stuck at around 10 per cent, rising to a peak of just 15 per cent in June 1945. Though such statistics enjoyed less credibility than has since become the norm, the best that the party could realistically hope to achieve was to hold the balance of power in a hung parliament. In such a situation potential Liberal voters would wish to know where the party's support might go. But when asked this question Sinclair could only reply that 'it would be unwise and impractical to try to decide now what form of government should be constructed in a parliamentary situation which none of us can accurately foresee'.[32] The party's manifesto clearly implied a leaning towards Labour; but the ever present Liberal emphasis upon 'freedom' ultimately suggested a stronger affinity with the Conservatives.

In all the circumstances, the electoral outcome was entirely predictable. The party secured just 2.2 million votes, about 9 per cent of those cast. Liberal support per opposed candidate had fallen from 23.9 per cent in 1935 to 18.6 per cent a decade later. But in parliamentary terms the position was far worse. Liberalism's pre-dissolution strength of 18 MPs was reduced to 12. As had become the norm at pre-war elections, there were a number of high-profile casualties. Sinclair lost by 62 votes in Caithness, while Percy Harris and William Beveridge were also defeated. This left Gwilym Lloyd-George, who had been Minister of Fuel and Power since 1942 but whose commitment to Liberalism was now a matter of speculation, as the only surviving MP who had ever held government office. Liberalism now seemed to be a party of the Celtic fringe, emphasising its remoteness from the seats of power. Six of the surviving MPs sat for rural Wales. Four MPs were returned in the absence of Conservative opponents and four without Labour opposition. Only perhaps the outposts of Cardiganshire and Montgomery now looked secure in Liberal hands.[33] Nor was the party strategically well placed to stage an effective comeback at the next election. Only 8.8 per cent of Liberal candidates secured second place, while 84.9 per cent came third.[34]

Officially the party put a brave face upon what had happened: 'Though this figure [of 2.25 million votes] fell considerably short of what was expected, it demonstrates quite clearly that there exists a substantial body of voters who are not prepared to compromise their Liberal principles and whose views are not adequately represented by either of the larger parties.'[35] Even in a private letter Samuel reacted with a blind optimism which may have been a necessary ingredient in the party's survival but which flew in the face of all logical calculations: 'The result of the election here was a reversal of all our hopes for the Liberal Party. But a change might come as suddenly in the opposite direction, and we regard it as our duty to maintain the Party in being for any future eventuality that might arise.'[36] In fact, it was difficult to conceal the enormity of the catastrophe that had been sustained. Six months later the November municipal elections provided a sad but apparently inevitable reaffirmation of this verdict. The party lost 111 of the 245 council seats it attempted to defend and now controlled not one of the 80 county boroughs. Only in a handful of textile towns in Lancashire and Yorkshire did it remain the strongest party. There seemed no way of stopping, let alone reversing, the downward and inexorable spiral of decline.

The reaction of the *Manchester Guardian* was symbolic of the party's problems. This once steadfast bastion of Liberal support commented that, while the adoption of proportional representation might offer the party a viable future, 'under the present system its hopes must be slender'. Under the editorship of A. P. Wadsworth, the newspaper had moved towards increasing support for Labour as the only realistic vehicle of radical progress and the General Election of 1945 effectively ended the formal links between the *Guardian* and the Liberal party.

Once the dust of electoral battle had settled, the parliamentary party's first task was to choose a new leader. From a rather bizarre process in which the MPs – many of whom did not know one another well – discussed the qualities and credentials of each of themselves in turn, Clement Davies, MP for Montgomeryshire since 1929, emerged as the parliamentary party's choice. Even so, he was not formally appointed to the wider position of party leader, not least because of an expectation that Sinclair might soon return to the House of Commons. The latter's victorious Conservative opponent in Caithness had earlier pledged to stand down in Sinclair's favour, but in the event never did so.

The somewhat erratic course of Davies's political career to date is important in trying to make sense of the direction in which he might now try to steer the Liberal party. Davies had joined the Liberal National ranks in 1931, but insisted, as did most Liberal Nationals, on his continuing personal commitment to Liberalism. 'I stood as a Liberal. I was nominated by the Liberals as a Liberal. I remain a Liberal,' he told his electors in 1935. But he had left the Simonite faction in 1939 and organised an all-party ginger group opposing the continuation of Chamberlain's premiership in the winter of the phoney war before playing a crucial if little appreciated role in bringing down the government in May 1940. Unrewarded by the new Prime Minister, he became for a time an independent critic of Churchill before rejoining the mainstream Liberal party in 1942 and becoming prominent inside Radical Action. In June 1945 he offered a clear statement of his position within the political spectrum: 'I stand on the side of the progressive. If two parties such as Labour and Conservative were equally balanced then I would vote Labour. Members of the Labour Party and myself can walk side by side for a long way. There are many things on which we agree.'[37] His own election address advocated the nationalisation of coal, transport, electricity and even the land. This clear leftward inclination was still evident when Davies made his first Commons speech as parliamentary leader, when he gave the new Attlee government a warm welcome, wishing it well and rejoicing at the end of the Tory regime with its 'reaction and chaos'. A more traditional Liberal such as Sinclair, still optimistic that his own political career had been interrupted rather than ended, was worried that Davies might even try to outflank Labour from the left, instead of concentrating on such time-honoured Liberal virtues as individualism, freedom and free trade.

Broadly speaking, Clement Davies's Liberal party continued in this vein for the first two years of the Labour government. Davies looked forward to promised Labour initiatives in health and social insurance as the implementation of Liberal policies going back to the great reforming government of 1905–15. 'It would be ignoble to hinder that work', he insisted in July 1946, 'merely because it happens to be in the hands of other people to promote.'[38] Yet any overall assessment of Davies' 11-year leadership of the party must conclude that the period as a whole witnessed Liberalism moving distinctly to the right. This about-turn is not wholly easy to explain. Davies's own thinking clearly underwent a transformation. Before the end of 1947, by which time the Labour administration had experienced its first major crisis, he had become critical of the government's centralising and illiberal tendencies. 'Everything is being organised from the centre', he complained, 'and the centre is a small oligarchy. Freedom is threatened by conscription for the Army in peacetime and now by the direction of labour in industry. Hitler and Mussolini began their appeal to the people as Socialists.'[39] But notwithstanding any change in Davies's own thinking, it would have been an almost impossible task to lead Liberalism, or at least the rump of it which survived as a parliamentary force, in the direction upon which he had apparently embarked in 1945. No matter how far the party's strength in the House of Commons diminished, it never succeeded in speaking with a single voice. Indeed, the divisions of earlier years, which could sometimes be passed off as the dissent of the party's periphery, seemed to indicate a more fundamental cleavage now that the number of Liberal MPs only just exceeded single figures. The same group which encompassed the radical Megan Lloyd George, who tended to retain the attitude with which Davies had begun in 1945 of broad sympathy for the Labour government, also contained a laissez-faire purist such as Rhys Hopkin Morris, MP for Carmarthenshire, who remained immovably hostile to all signs of government direction – 'subsidies, restrictions, planning, everything in fact that the Labour

Government stood for'.[40] In broad terms the party was divided between those who wanted a basic anti-Tory orientation and those whose primary political concern was resistance to the spread of socialism. But this crude division masked a kaleidoscope of views extending across the full spectrum of historic Liberalism. As Davies put it in 1950, 'there is no Party but a number of individuals who, because of their adherence to the Party, come together only to express completely divergent views'.[41]

Increasingly, Davies despaired of giving *any* sort of lead to the parliamentary party. His priority, something like that of Harold Wilson in the Labour movement 20 years later, was progressively reduced to trying to hold it together. 'My own position', he bemoaned in 1950, 'is one of almost supine weakness, for if I give full expression to a definite course of action that at once leads to trouble and a definite split. It is that split that I am so anxious to avoid. We have suffered so much in the past from these quarrels . . . Any further division now would, I fear, just give the final death blow.'[42] Perhaps more than any of his predecessors, Davies also had to take account of the attitude of the party outside parliament. Reduced by electoral vagaries to a largely rural and Celtic rump, there had never been a parliamentary party which was 'less representative of the Party as a whole. Its ten members', argued Violet Bonham Carter in 1949, 'are constantly at variance with one another, with the Liberal Party Organisation and with their colleagues in the House of Lords.'[43] Figures like Lady Violet, who never succeeded in getting elected to the Commons, enjoyed at least as much influence as the majority of her parliamentary colleagues. In any case, by 1948 those colleagues had begun to go their separate ways. The debate over the government's plans to nationalise the iron and steel industry saw the first significant divisions within the parliamentary party. 'I was elected to the House as a Liberal', noted W. J. Gruffudd, member for the University of Wales, 'which means, as things are at present, that I can be eclectic in my politics.'[44] At the 1948 party assembly, radical Liberals could only look on askance as the right called for a drastic reduction in government expenditure and, in an early anticipation of

Thatcherite Conservatism, argued that council tenants should be given the right to buy their homes.

While most commentators have adopted a broadly sympathetic attitude towards Davies's leadership, pointing in particular to his successful resistance of a deadly Tory embrace in 1951, it is difficult to resist the conclusion that the party was left to drift with little sense of purpose or direction while he remained at the helm. He claimed to define a distinct niche for the Liberal party of the late 1940s. 'Do not run away with the idea that Liberalism provides the middle way between the other two,' he insisted in 1949. 'Still less that it is a compromise between them. Liberalism is a distinct creed – a distinct philosophy; distinct from Socialism, from Communism and from Conservatism.'[45] But it is doubtful whether many of his followers fully understood what the creed was, or at least whether a consensus existed upon it. Instead, Liberals 'have teetered between the other two parties like a drunken referee who despite his size is constantly trying to separate the heavyweights and fell each of them with a blow which is neither a left nor a right'.[46] Jo Grimond, first elected to parliament in 1950, recalled that loyalty, gratitude and admiration bound him to Davies, 'but I was never quite sure on what branch he could finally settle'.[47] More significantly, the ordinary Liberal voter was often left confused, especially in constituencies where no Liberal candidate was standing.

Yet it is at least open to question whether any alternative leader would have been more successful than Davies in carving out a distinctive Liberal identity in the decade after the end of the Second World War. The debate over the existence or otherwise of a post-war political consensus lies outside the scope of this study. But it seems incontrovertible that the gap between Britain's two major parties did narrow substantially after 1945. On the one hand the Conservatives reacted to the shock of electoral defeat by committing themselves to a moderate programme of pragmatic policies firmly grounded within the political parameters established by Attlee's Labour government. On the other, that same government had by 1947 abandoned most of its pretensions to genuine socialism, preferring instead the techniques of Keynesian demand management to finance the emerging Welfare State. Ironically, therefore, while Labour and the Conservatives competed with one another in terms of their espousal of the ideas of two outstanding Liberals, Keynes and Beveridge, little scope was left in which a separate Liberal party could flourish. In an 'era of centrist politics, there was no room for a centre party'.[48]

Ironically, too, while little seemed to divide the two political giants, at least in terms of their immediate party programmes, the partisans of the two sides were ready to stick with their chosen course with unquestioning loyalty and zeal, apparently believing that an unbridgeable divide separated them from their political opponents. Labour was remarkably successful in holding on to its electoral support through the vicissitudes of government. Even in its defeat of 1951 the party managed to poll 48.8 per cent of the popular vote. In that election as much as 96.8 per cent of the total vote was shared between Labour and the Conservatives; in 1955 the comparable figure was 96.1 per cent. Class-based voting was now at its height and few electors seemed uncertain where their allegiance lay. It was not surprising that surviving pockets of Liberalism were to be found in those relatively remote areas – rural Wales, the Highlands and Islands, and South-West England – where the politics of class had found it most difficult to penetrate. In what most viewed, however inaccurately, as a clear choice between the political heavyweights, many erstwhile Liberals determined either that Labour had become the modern vehicle of their progressive instincts or else that the liberalised Conservative party of Butler, Eden and Macmillan was their best chance of resisting the encroachments of the 'socialist' state. Donald Johnson was among the latter group. Concluding that 'the main political objective of any liberal-minded person in the present day world must inevitably be the defeat of socialism', he joined the Conservative party in 1947.[49]

Nor did the problems of Liberalism disappear when the Conservatives returned to power in October 1951. Notwithstanding dire Labour predictions about the consequences of a Tory victory, Churchill's government made few radical deviations from the path already charted by its Labour predecessor. The term 'Butskellism' may miss some of the nuances of subtle difference between the strategies of economic management pursued by the two administrations, but it remains a revealing contemporary observation on a broad pattern of continuity. Liberalism was not well placed to break out of, or even to challenge, this prevailing consensus. Davies was not a particularly original thinker in terms of new policy initiatives, though he encouraged the idea of co-ownership in industry and he did commit his party to support British participation in the early moves towards greater European integration. Davies praised the Schuman Plan of 1950 for a Coal and Steel Community as the greatest step towards peace in the annals of European history. In part this enthusiasm could be traced back to Gladstonian idealism about the concert of Europe; in part it suggested that Liberals were readier than their political rivals to come to terms with Britain's diminished status in the era of the Superpowers. To their credit, moreover, postwar Liberals confronted the political dimension of the European movement head-on, in a way that their Labour and Conservative opponents did not. But Europe was not at the forefront of the political agenda until at least the 1960s. In this situation only the themes of free trade and proportional representation really served to set Liberalism apart, and the former now looked increasingly anachronistic. It sat uneasily alongside prevailing assumptions about a planned and tightly controlled economy, while causing embarrassment over protection and farm subsidies for a party which was largely confined to agricultural constituencies.

In this situation the danger clearly existed that Liberalism might be swallowed up by one of the other two parties. In the event, it was relations with the Conservatives which dominated the party's strategic thinking throughout the post-war decade. Even in the 1945 campaign Churchill had reminded Liberal voters of his own Liberal past and urged them to support the Conservatives as the only viable means of thwarting socialism. The Liberals tried to use their election broadcasts to fend off Churchill's unwanted advances, while the *Manchester Guardian* poured scorn on the idea that Conservatism now embraced the central tenets of Liberal belief.[50] As the Conservatives of the late 1940s adopted an increasingly progressive stance, however, the

Guardian's conclusion looked more open to challenge. Furthermore, such was Labour's margin of victory in 1945 that many Conservatives concluded that their chances of reversing the result next time would be negligible unless a majority of the more than two million Liberal voters could be persuaded to join the Conservative camp.

In September 1945 a letter appeared in the *Spectator* from Quintin Hogg, MP for Oxford and a leading light in the Tory Reform Group, a body which for some time had been pressing the Conservative leadership to adopt a positive attitude towards the Beveridge-inspired social reforms which Labour was now enacting. Claiming to speak for thirty or forty Tory MPs whose views 'showed no striking difference from the Liberals', Hogg suggested that 'if only the Liberals would come and help ... we could, together, capture the Conservative Party'.[51] By early 1946 informal discussions were taking place inside a small committee of Conservatives and Liberals chaired by the future Chancellor of the Exchequer, Peter Thorneycroft. It was decided to draw up a joint policy statement entitled *Design for Freedom*. Progress was such that by November a rather alarmed Liberal party headquarters was obliged to issue a statement denying rumours of a Liberal–Conservative pact.[52] By the following January a draft document had been drawn up and only when Davies spoke out against it at Colwyn Bay in February 1947 did this particular initiative collapse. Liberal headquarters now called upon Liberals to dissociate themselves from the *Design for Freedom* movement and reaffirmed the party's independence.[53]

In the meantime a somewhat different approach had been adopted by Harold Macmillan, who had lost his Stockton-on-Tees seat to Labour at the General Election. From his personal experience Macmillan understood how important Liberal votes might be for the future salvation of the Conservative party. Returning to parliament in the Bromley by-election of November 1945, he noted that while the Labour vote had remained 'uncomfortably high', that of the Liberal candidate had slumped disastrously, falling by more than half from the figure secured at the general election.[54] Macmillan even toyed with the idea of dropping the name 'Conservative' since it failed to reflect the sort of moderate and progressive ideas which he was keen to advocate and which alone could woo further Liberal voters. He aired these themes at Conservative rallies in the summer of 1946 and elaborated his views in an article in the *Daily Telegraph* that October under the heading 'Anti-Socialist Parties' Task: the Case for Alliance or Fusion'. This article, intended to coincide with the opening of the Conservative Party conference, urged Liberals and Conservatives to come together to promote a policy 'not of passive anti-Socialism, but of an active and dynamic character'.[55] But the mood of the Conference was not with Macmillan and, for the time being, his ideas were allowed to lapse.

If merger with the Conservatives threatened to result in the extinction of British Liberalism as an independent political force, reunion with the Liberal Nationals offered a more constructive and less suffocating prospect. In particular, it would at least make it harder for the Conservatives to lay claim to be the true inheritors of Liberal traditions because of their close association with the Liberal Nationals. In the summer of 1946 the Liberals and Liberal Nationals of London quietly came together and there was some optimism that this merger would be repeated elsewhere. But the leadership of neither wing showed total commitment to the further healing of old wounds. Davies, still espousing the left-wing views which had characterised his recent election campaign, was wary that reunion might undermine his hope of turning the Liberal party into a radical, but non-socialist, third force in British politics. By contrast, the Liberal National leadership, aware that its parliamentary strength – down to 13 seats after the 1945 General Election – was largely a function of Conservative acquiescence at constituency level, was keen not to break its relationship with the Conservatives altogether. None the less, tentative discussions took place between Ernest Brown and the Liberal peer, the Duke of Montrose, in the course of 1946. Here it became clear that it was the independence of any fused party rather than detailed issues of policy which posed the most significant stumbling block to agreement. Faced with a Liberal National insistence on a definite arrangement for Liberal representation in a future Conservative government, the negotiations had stalled by the end of the year.[56] In the wake of the failure of this final effort at Liberal reunion, the Liberal National and Conservative parties rapidly formalised their association. Under the Woolton–Teviot accords of May 1947, the two parties were effectively fused at constituency level. It was agreed that, in constituencies where each party had an existing organisation, a combined association would be formed under a mutually agreed title. In constituencies where only one of the parties had an organisation, that body would consider enlarging its membership to include all who supported joint action against socialism. The result was that in the General Election of 1950, 53 candidates stood under such assorted labels as National Liberal and Conservative, Conservative and National Liberal, Conservative and Liberal, and Liberal and Conservative.

Davies's fears for Liberal independence were well founded. The success of the Woolton–Teviot agreement encouraged renewed Conservative efforts to swallow the bigger fish of the Liberal party itself. In April 1947 Woolton, as Conservative chairman, proclaimed that the great need was for those who understood the threat of socialism to unite. In practice, this meant supporting the Conservative party as the only party capable of forming a non-socialist government. Macmillan, too, re-entered the fray, taking his message to a rally at the Gladstonian shrine of Hawarden Castle. Here he asked: 'What divides – at this moment – the Liberal and Conservative parties? What separates them? Nothing – except the memories of the past . . . . Each condemns with equal vigour the grave mishandling by the present socialist Government of our internal and external economy.'[57] As a consequence of the Woolton–Teviot agreement 1947 saw the setting up, in constituencies such as Dunstable, Bideford and North Angus, of so-called 'Liberal and Conservative Associations'. These derived from meetings at which actual Liberals were either greatly outnumbered or actively excluded. Liberal headquarters felt obliged to issue a 'Declaration of Independence' and warned that Conservative Central Office was pursuing a deliberate and care-fully conceived campaign to destroy the Liberal party's constituency organisations. Valiantly, the call went out to 'all

Liberals throughout the country to stand firm against Conservative overtures and to concentrate their energies upon preparing for the coming fight'.[58]

The problem was that many on the Liberal party's right wing were increasingly ready to respond positively to Conservative advances. Optimism about Liberal prospects, which was widespread in 1946, had soon begun to evaporate. As so often in the past, the party had put its faith in structural reorganisation as the panacea for future recovery. After the electoral disaster of 1945 many remained convinced that a revivified party organisation was the way in which to translate the millions of potential Liberal voters – the 'Liberals-but' who had been uncovered in surveys of public opinion – into actual crosses on ballot papers. An eight-member Committee on Reconstruction was set up in the autumn of 1945 to produce a prescription for revival. Its report, 'Coats off for the Future!', was presented to the spring assembly in 1946 amid scenes of renewed energy, enthusiasm and confidence. But the picture on the ground was less encouraging. By-elections continued to indicate a falling Liberal percentage of the popular vote. In the second half of 1947 Liberal candidates contested five seats, but lost their deposits in four of them. Discussions with the Chief Whip, Frank Byers, convinced Lady Violet Bonham Carter of the possibility of the party as a parliamentary force being completely wiped out at the next general election. She and Byers calculated that, even if every Liberal candidate took 15 per cent of the Labour vote and 10 per cent of the Tory, the net result would be a gain of only six seats nationally. More probably, there would be substantial losses among the party's ten existing MPs if they were faced with three-cornered contests. The alternative, Lady Violet concluded, 'would be a deal over seats with the Tories with PR as a condition and an agreed programme. I shldn't like it and it might split the Party in half and give the Left Wing to Labour. I see all the rocks and shoals very clearly but I *fear* complete Parliamentary extinction.'[59]

In a rare letter to Megan Lloyd George, Lady Violet spelt out her anxiety. She confessed that she no longer believed that the Liberals could stage an effective comeback, certainly not by 1950.

The only condition which would ensure the ultimate survival of any third party was electoral reform.[60] It was difficult to say more than this to Megan Lloyd George, but a month earlier Harold Nicolson had gained a clearer picture of Lady Violet's thinking:

> She abuses the Government for abandoning all moral principle. Until now she had believed that the Liberal Party were closer to the Socialists than to any other party. Now she doubts it . . . No, she feels closer to the left-wing Tories today. All of which suggests that the Liberal Party are about to create a common anti-communist front.[61]

In fact, the daughter of Asquith had already begun to sound out her friend and her father's one-time colleague, Winston Churchill. The latter's response was vague but not entirely discouraging:

> stressed the need for Lib. Independence – no alliances etc. – but 'Lay off a little against us. We might help each other – make some arrangement which would be mutually convenient etc.' I said that only *an issue* cld determine such an alignment – not a cold-blooded arrangement. *I* cldn't deliver the goods. Could *he do so*? Cld he for instance 'deliver' Electoral Reform?[62]

Liberal disunity became increasingly apparent during 1948. The year began with rumours that Megan Lloyd George was about to join Labour, but in February she told the Cambridge University Liberal Club that the Liberal party was moving not to the right but to the left. It was a claim which reflected little more than her own wishful thinking. At the beginning of the following year Davies made a vain attempt to impose unity on the party by appointing Lady Megan as deputy leader. But, despite her new status, she made few efforts to moderate her views, calling upon the party to adopt a truly radical programme and adding, rather provocatively, 'of course, that means shedding our Right Wing'. The *Western Morning News* responded: 'There have been hurried consultations between some of the other leaders of the party, who interpret this statement as a declaration of war against, perhaps, a substantial majority of its members . . . Lady Megan's attitude, far from bringing unity, might split the party.'[63] Along with such colleagues as Dingle Foot, she continued to urge the party to align itself unambiguously on the left and frequently found herself at odds with the majority of her colleagues on policy issues. Discussions on the state of the economy highlighted the differences of approach. The left was fearful of being seen to accept too much of the Conservative critique of government policy. As Foot put it:

> It looks to me as if the Tories . . . are girding themselves up for an attack on the social services . . . and a rise in unemployment figures. To my mind it would be fatal for us to lend ourselves, even by inference, to this campaign . . . Even if we have to preach a form of austerity . . . we should do it as *defenders* of the social services and full employment and not as an alternative gang of destroyers.[64]

In the meantime Davies's own efforts to boost his party's self-confidence met with rebuke from his colleagues. His claim, reported in the *Economist*, that the party had doubled its membership appeared to have been based on nothing more concrete than the findings of a Gallup Poll about the numbers of those who said they would vote Liberal and on the large and enthusiastic audiences attending Liberal rallies. Yet, warned Violet Bonham Carter, such facts could scarcely justify the conclusions which Davies had drawn and his assertions would prove embarrassing if challenged.[65] As the 1945 parliament drew towards its close, such internal dissensions scarcely augured well for the party's electoral prospects.

By contrast, the Conservative party went into the General Election of 1950 in a mood of optimism. The ageing Labour government appeared to have run out of steam, while the Liberals seemed to pose few threats. The Tories again strove to present themselves as the true heirs of the great Liberal tradition, even if this meant sowing confusion in the mind of the electorate. Liberals could only respond by insisting that the differences between Liberalism and Conservatism were fundamental and that the intimacy between Conservatives and National Liberals was an entirely different matter.[66] As the election approached, Lord Moynihan, chairman of the Liberal Party Organisation, tried to clear up any confusion, suggesting to Woolton that Conservative candidates and those who supported the Conservative party should be prepared to fight the contest as Conservatives and that 'the name "Liberal" should not be used by them in order to confuse the issue'. Woolton replied, with some justification, that the National Liberals had as much right as anyone else to use the word 'Liberal' in their title.[67] At this point the party leaders entered the dispute. At his adoption meeting in Woodford, Churchill spoke scathingly of 'the very small and select group of Liberal leaders who conceived themselves the sole heirs of the principles and traditions of Liberalism and believed themselves to have the exclusive copyright of the word "Liberal" '.[68] Two days later Churchill and Lord Rosebery, President of the National Liberal Council, issued a joint statement in which they made a rather half-hearted call to 'Liberal–Conservative' candidates to use the prefix 'National' whenever a candidate from the mainstream Liberal party was also standing. Clement Davies felt bound to protest and there was even talk of the Liberals taking legal action. But Davies was wide open to Churchill's rejoinder that he himself had been happy enough to carry the label 'Liberal National' for the best part of a decade.[69]

From the Liberal point of view this wrangling over nomenclature was an unwanted distraction, but one which showed how unsuccessful they had been since 1945 in staking out a viable political identity of their own. Furthermore, internal party disputes remained just beneath the surface. It was against Davies's wishes that the party's annual assembly went ahead immediately prior to the election. The leader's private comments are instructive: 'My one prayer now is that there will not be much discussion, debate or disputing. Now is the time when we should agree upon the spirit, and not debate the finer points. We must have unity and also show that we are a Party of action, and not a debating society.'[70] As at all General Elections during their years in the political wilderness, Liberals had a difficult decision to take as to whether to fight on a broad or narrow front. The argument was finely balanced. Those who favoured the former line saw it as the best means of giving national credibility to the small number of candidates who had a realistic chance of success, by encouraging potential Liberal voters to believe that the party was still a national political force. Those who supported the narrow front wished to concentrate the party's limited resources and avoid a large number of humiliating results in individual constituencies. In the event, 475 candidates were nominated, 169 more than in 1945. Even this decision did not command unanimous support. Two Liberal peers, Lords Reading and Rennell, who for some time had been showing signs of dissatisfaction with party policy, argued that the party was in danger of spreading its resources too thinly. 'Of course what they really mean', complained Davies, 'is that there should be some kind of pact with the Tories.'[71] Only tactful handling by the party's veteran leader in the upper house, Lord Samuel, prevented another damaging row.

At a national level no formal pact was made between Liberals and Conservatives, despite the claims of many observers that, without it, the anti-socialist vote would be split. Churchill wrote to Davies shortly before the dissolution, suggesting an arrangement between their parties: 'There is a real measure of agreement', he claimed, 'between modern Tory democracy and the mass of Liberals who see in Socialism all that their most famous thinkers and leaders have fought against in the past.'[72] In Huddersfield a local arrangement was arrived at whereby the Conservatives agreed not to contest the town's west division, while the Liberals stood down in the east. In Dundee the local parties seemed near to agreement, but were thwarted when Liberal headquarters in London put up their own candidate independently of the Dundee Liberal Association. Elsewhere Liberal headquarters tried to turn the Tory argument on its head by suggesting that in constituencies such as Bethnal Green it was the Conservative candidate who should stand down, since only the Liberal could possibly defeat Labour. The Conservatives refused further concessions, though in three other constituencies – Carmarthen, Greenock and the

Western Isles – no Conservative stood and local support was given to the Liberal candidate.

For the most part, Conservatives were left with the telling argument, 'robustly declared in hoardings, speeches, and election addresses', that a vote for the Liberal party was a vote wasted.[73] The claim carried credibility. Opinion polls and general perception suggested that the gap between the two leading parties was narrow, while few believed that the Liberals by themselves could achieve very much. This theme was taken up in the press with the *Daily Telegraph* emphasising the futility of running so many candidates, while the *Sunday Times* stressed the need for a common stand against socialism and criticized the vanity of Liberals for refusing to recognise reality. Churchill conducted a skilful campaign, blaming the Liberals for their refusal to co-operate, while emphasising his own liberalism and the lack of substantial differences between the two parties by offering Violet Bonham Carter one of the broadcasts that had been allocated to the Conservatives.

The Liberal manifesto, *No Easy Way*, failed to make much of an impression. Many of its proposals appeared insufficiently distinctive, while no single theme or concept seemed to run through the whole document. It tried to strike a balance between Liberalism's warring factions by putting forward a right-leaning approach in economic policy and a leftward incline in the social sphere. Conservatives drew attention to a considerable measure of overlap with their own statement, *This Is the Road*; the Labour party tended to ignore it.

By comparison with the major parties, the Liberals' national campaign of 1950 looked amateurish. Five years of supposed preparation since the last general election bore few fruits. Shortage of money limited the number of paid agents and workers, while on the hustings the party suffered from a lack of big names. Recognising that their individual success was by no means assured, figures such as Davies, Sinclair, Byers and Megan Lloyd George concentrated their electioneering in their own constituencies. As the campaign progressed, the Liberals' argument that they were now fielding enough candidates to secure a Commons majority began to appear a sham. Many of those standing had been adopted very late in the day, lacked credibility as aspiring politicians and were not even well-versed in the policies of their party. As one veteran Liberal commented: 'I felt in listening to a good number of speeches that our candidates made a poor impression, rather as if they thought it was fun to stand if their expenses were paid, but they had very little to say except rather out-of-date appeals to party feeling'.[74]

The historian of the 1950 election has commented on the Liberal performance that 'to win 9 seats with 475 candidates, and to lose 319 deposits . . . was a defeat on a scale which it would be hard to parallel'.[75] Jeremy Thorpe, then at Oxford, likened the result to a replay of the charge of the Light Brigade.[76] Frank Byers narrowly lost his seat in North Dorset; Sinclair failed to regain Caithness; only the success of Jo Grimond in Orkney and Shetland offered a crumb of comfort. Violet Bonham Carter captured the mood of despair as the results came in: 'Two of our dear supporters slunk in with a N[ews] C[hronicle] looking shattered. One hardly dared look at them. It was like meeting after a death.'[77] It is true that the party's total vote increased to 2.6 million, but as the Liberals were fielding 50 per cent more candidates than in 1945, this was scarcely a noteworthy achievement, especially as the overall turnout was up by nearly four million. As few as 3.8 per cent of Liberal candidates even managed to finish second, whereas 93.2 per cent were in third place. The Liberal vote was evenly distributed by class, age and sex, and, while this might imply that Liberalism still had a universal appeal, it also suggested that there was no likelihood of a future electoral breakthrough under a first-past-the-post voting system.

As in 1945, party headquarters responded to disaster with defiance. 'The Liberal Party carries on. Let there be no doubt about that.' But much of the press was highly critical. *The Times* highlighted the 'national disservice' which Liberal intervention had occasioned and suggested that the party could best serve the interests of Liberalism in the future by allowing its supporters to judge for themselves which of the two larger parties could do more to put the Liberal spirit into practice. The *Daily Mail* agreed. The

Liberal effort had 'chiefly served a wrecking purpose', but now 'the game [was] up'. Even the still generally sympathetic *Manchester Guardian* wondered whether the Liberals' thinly scattered vote could really form the future basis of a national political party. Clement Davies, while maintaining a brave public face, privately admitted that the party now faced a more difficult situation than at any time since the parliament of 1929. He took refuge in the iniquities of the electoral system and was soon writing to Prime Minister Attlee to press the case for electoral reform. But it was perhaps Harold Nicolson, a Liberal at heart though the Liberals were the one party he never formally supported, who expressed the most common sentiment. 'I am sorry, of course, for the Liberals', he admitted, 'but they asked for it.'[78]

From a Conservative point of view, the problem was clear enough. During the campaign the veteran Tory MP, Cuthbert Headlam, had expressed his 'great fear' that 'the infernal Liberals are going to queer our pitch all over the country'. He found the division in the anti-socialist ranks 'really amazing' and failed to understand why people who appreciated the menace of socialism insisted on fighting one another simply 'because in the past their parents and grandparents fought each other as Tories v. Whigs or as Conservatives v. Liberals'.[79] Arguably, Headlam's fears had been proved correct. It was widely assumed that the Conservative and Labour parties had polled at something like their full strength. The outcome was a Labour Commons majority of five over all other parties combined. Yet between them the Tories and the Liberals had captured about 1.85 million more votes than the victorious Labour government. The conclusion was not difficult to draw. The problem was how best to get those who had voted Liberal on this occasion to vote Conservative at the next – and probably not long delayed – election. In March, Churchill proposed the setting up of a shadow cabinet committee to 'go into all the questions open between Conservatives and Liberals and to see what can be done to secure greater unity among the forces opposed to Socialism'.[80] Attlee made fun of the Conservatives' courtship of the Liberal party. Were the intentions of the Leader of the Opposition honourable or not?

> He has been a very ardent lover of this elderly spinster, the Liberal Party. The elder sister – the National Liberals – was married long ago; she is now deceased. This now is the younger sister, but she is getting on. I can never make out whether the Rt. Hon. Member for Woodford is going to play Petruchio or Romeo. He has given her a slap in the face, then offers her a bunch of flowers.[81]

Attlee's sarcastic tone may well have been designed to strengthen Liberal resolve to resist the Conservative embrace, since by-elections afforded some evidence that former Liberal voters were more likely to go to the Tories than to Labour.

Undeterred by Attlee's wit, Churchill continued on his chosen course. To the backbench 1922 Committee he declared on 16 May that Conservatives had to obtain Liberal support both as individuals and if possible as a party, not by any political deal but by proclaiming the fundamental principles on which those who voted against socialism were agreed. On 29 April, Woolton insisted that he did not know 'of any practical issue on which Liberals and Conservatives are not agreed', a claim which prompted Clement Davies to reiterate that there was no intention of compromising the independence of the Liberal party.[82] The Conservative Chairman's statement followed the formal defection of Lords Reading and Rennell to the Conservative camp, a move which seemed, in Lord Salisbury's words, 'to underline the broad measure of agreement which exists between those who believe in the free way of life, to whatever party they have hitherto belonged'.[83] When Lords Willingdon and Cowdray also left the Liberal party in early May, it seemed that the process of defection might escalate out of control.

Davies suggested that what was needed was a short statement of Liberal principles, which defined what was distinctive about Liberalism and belief in which was fundamental to being a Liberal. Yet it was striking, and perhaps indicative of the difficulties faced by the party at this time, that the leader should make this suggestion without stating what that distinctive Liberal creed actually was. His predecessor, on the other hand, was thinking in rather more practical terms. According to Sinclair, the electorate had lost faith in the capacity of Liberal candidates to win seats and were now tending to vote against the candidate they liked least, rather than for the candidate they liked best. He judged, therefore, that all other considerations must be subordinated to the attainment of electoral reform. It was the duty of those with responsibility for the party's future 'not to indulge in the luxury of expressing heroic sentiments', but to ensure that the party survived. The way forward was an arrangement with the Conservatives on the lines of the Huddersfield pact, limited to the next general election and based on a concrete Conservative pledge to introduce a measure of electoral reform in the next parliament if they were returned to power.[84] Violet Bonham Carter's mind was moving along the same lines. The party leadership, she believed, had been irresponsible. Their attempts to convince the public at the last election that the Liberal party could form a government had been either fraudulent or so out of touch with reality 'as to disqualify those who made them from any claim to political *sense*'.[85]

The possibility that the Conservatives might espouse a system of Proportional Representation was less remote in 1950 than it has since become. Harold Macmillan, more than ever convinced of the need for an alliance with the Liberals, saw 'a great deal to be said, in principle, for an experiment in Proportional Representation, limited to the big cities. It could do no harm and might do good.'[86] Even Churchill was favourably disposed and, according to Nigel Fisher, made a moving but unsuccessful appeal to the 1922 Committee to be allowed to pursue an agreement along these lines.[87] 'On Electoral Reform,' R. A. Butler confirmed, 'the battle is only too seriously engaged.'[88]   During the summer Churchill entrusted to Butler, in conditions of great secrecy, the task of negotiating with the Liberals in the person of Lady Violet. Butler's position on the liberal wing of the Conservative party had been assured by his part in remodelling party policy in the late 1940s. The aim was a pact for the next election and in June Butler drew up a document entitled 'Overlap Prospectus of Principles'. The two negotiators were agreed that there should be no joint endorsement of a common programme but merely a statement of those general principles upon which both parties were agreed. Though Lady Violet regarded it as the key issue, Butler urged her not to press electoral reform for the time being lest it damage the whole negotiating process. In any case, Conservative Central Office seemed less enthusiastic about the whole enterprise and Woolton delayed making a firm approach to Davies on seats. In the event, the talks had ground to a halt by the end of the summer, partly because of the outbreak of the Korean War and partly because of the differing priorities of the two sides.[89]

Whether Davies wholeheartedly went along with these negotiations, whether in fact he accepted Sinclair's arguments in favour of an electoral arrangement, is unclear. When he stated the Liberal position to Churchill and Woolton, Davies was at pains to emphasise not only that the Liberals must remain an independent party, but also that there could be no national agreement on the allocation of constituencies whereby one party would undertake to withdraw its own candidate in favour of the candidate of the other party. Such an agreement, he insisted, would never be accepted by the Liberal rank and file.[90] Despite this hesitation, the Liberals were evidently moving closer to the Conservatives than at any time since the end of the war. Yet it was not a direction in which a substantial minority of the divided parliamentary party wished to travel. By the autumn of 1950 three MPs, Lady Megan Lloyd George, Emrys Roberts and Edgar Granville, supported by figures such as Dingle Foot and Philip Hopkins, had begun to organise a rearguard action against Davies's drift to the right. At a series of party meetings the left protested against the possibility of an electoral arrangement with the Conservatives. Davies claimed that the dissidents were 'concerned about themselves only and think that their best chance lies in help from Socialists'.[91] In reality, however, his position was a difficult one, especially as he had issued a statement in the May issue of *Liberal News* to the effect that 'the Liberal leaders have no knowledge of Conservative intentions or of Conservative proposals and no negotiations are taking place'.

This renewed division made the parliamentary party something of a laughing stock. Its nine members – nicknamed by

Labour the 'Nimble Nine' – might have been expected to exercise an influence out of proportion to their numerical strength in a Commons which was finely balanced between the two leading parties. Instead, as in 1924 and 1929–31, the proximity to power seemed to have a counterproductive effect. Despite protesting his own impotence and even considering resignation, Davies was partly responsible for this confusion, failing to provide the strong lead which the situation demanded. A cartoon in the *Sunday Graphic*, captioned *Spring Double*, pictured Davies riding two horses, one named 'Labour' and the other 'Tory'. In practice the Liberal party was reluctant to help the Conservatives bring down Attlee's government. It was in no position, especially financially, to fight another early election. Davies even sought an agreement with Churchill to limit the number of parliamentary divisions. Yet the regularity of these was part of the Conservative strategy to wear the government down and bring it to its knees.[92]

By the autumn of 1950 a mood of widespread depression seemed to have gripped the party's senior figures. Davies tried hard to rally the Liberal Assembly at Scarborough, but his claim that the party was united and free of jealousies and envy was a hollow one. At the same gathering, Megan Lloyd George avoided accusing the leadership of dealing with the Conservative enemy – this might have necessitated revealing her own discussions with Labour's Herbert Morrison about how to stop the Tories regaining power – but still complained about the party's slippage towards the right. Privately, Violet Bonham Carter warned Davies of the possibility of electoral extinction. By-election results seemed to give weight to her fears. The Conservatives were enjoying a series of promising results partly, contemporaries noted, because of a collapse in the Liberal vote. Granted that the Liberals were unlikely to be in a position to fight many seats at the next general election, a pact with the Conservatives made even more compelling sense from Lady Violet's point of view.

After a meeting of Liberal leaders in October, at which majority opinion was clearly in favour of seeking regional arrangements on the Huddersfield model, Lady Violet tried once more to stir Davies into action. It was no longer possible to dodge the central issue – 'whether on balance we desire the return of a Socialist or a Conservative Government next time'. For the Liberals, survival was the problem. If the party was reduced to only four or five MPs, as seemed entirely possible, then 'we can no longer pretend to be a National Party with rooms in the House of Commons, a Chief Whip, a Party Broadcast etc'. A decisive declaration of intent might well split the party, 'but better even a split with survival than a united death'. Lady Violet felt that the party was drifting without purpose, that an election might find it unprepared and that the time had come to renew contact with Lord Woolton.[93] Davies replied that he personally was prepared to help bring down the Labour government, but that such a proposal would immediately prompt a party split. With another election likely within a matter of months, the Liberal party again seemed to be on the verge of disintegration.

In the event the election was delayed until October 1951. At the opening of the campaign, it was reported that the Liberals had 174 candidates provisionally adopted. Soon, however, many withdrew, while some constituency associations found that they lacked sufficient funds to support a contest. With the number of confirmed candidates dropping alarmingly, the party announced on 26 September that it had decided to fight on a narrow front. Just 109 candidates were put into the field. But this was less a matter of considered tactics than of necessity. The party 'appears, in fact, to have fought on as wide a front as was practicable'.[94] It was not even as if Liberal efforts were concentrated in the most promising locations. Seats such as Rochdale, Torrington, Caernarvon and Salisbury, where the party had performed respectably in 1950, were now left uncontested. By contrast, a number of hopeless battles were fought once again, including 29 where deposits had been lost at the previous general election. Davies's claim that the Liberals had deliberately planned to contest selected seats does not stand up to scrutiny. At best, therefore, Liberals could only hope to hold the balance of power in a hung parliament. The cry of the 'wasted vote' was likely to be more potent than ever, unless Liberals gave a clear indication of the way in which they would employ their parliamentary strength. In the words of a Conservative election leaflet, 'the Independent Liberal Party has no hope of power and to support a party without hope is itself a hopeless action'. Davies, however, refused to give any advance commitment of support to either of the two major parties, though it was widely noted that his broadcast on 28 September attacked only the Labour party and contained little which would have caused exception for a Conservative. In practice, many ex-Liberal candidates in areas where no Liberal was standing showed their preference by throwing their weight behind other candidates, in most cases Conservatives. Among the minority of constituencies was Bristol North-East. Here the secretary of the local Liberal association came out in favour of Labour shortly before polling day. In response several Liberals, accused by the secretary of being National Liberals, wrote to urge support for the Conservatives.

Party organisation was even weaker than in 1950. The number of full-time agents, which had stood at 140 in October 1949, was now down to 44. In only a few seats were Liberals able to mount a full-scale campaign. Elsewhere, issuing an election address and holding a few poorly attended meetings was all that was attempted. The party faced 'an impossible task in trying with very limited resources to make the electorate aware of the party's continued existence and of the justification for it'.[95] Some Liberals seemed ready to forsake the traditional goal of electoral success for the more ethereal ambition of permeating the political thought of the other parties. The seeds of Liberalism, declared Jo Grimond during the course of the campaign, 'blow far and wide. We welcome it when they take root in the Conservative or Labour parties, but we must tend and water the plant from which they come.'[96] The Liberal Manifesto, *The Nation's Task*, stressed the importance of securing strong Liberal representation in the new parliament in order to check the extremism of the other parties. But it failed to give a clear picture of Liberal policies. Apart from a commitment to Scottish and Welsh parliaments and a vague call for European unity, the manifesto contained little that was distinctively Liberal. Lord Teviot of the National Liberals seized the opportunity to argue that, as there was no fundamental difference in policy between Liberals and Conservatives, Liberals in constituencies where no Liberal candidate was standing should be urged to vote Tory.[97] It was an invitation which Davies continued to resist.

Some limited efforts were made to extend the 'Huddersfield formula'. A comparable pact was reached in Bolton where Conservatives did not oppose the Liberal candidate in Bolton West, while the Liberals stood down in Bolton East. In three seats in rural Wales, Liberals were not opposed by Tories and in Dundee too the Conservatives did not stand. Most strikingly, Violet Bonham Carter was not opposed in Colne Valley and Churchill made a point of speaking on her behalf. His theme was entirely predictable: 'I find comfort in the broad harmony of thought which prevails between the modern Tory democracy and the doctrines of the famous Liberal leaders of the past.'[98] For Labour Clement Attlee tried to counter this argument by suggesting that Liberals who accepted Conservative support ceased to be Liberals. One Conservative leaflet, which appealed to the memory of David Lloyd George, urging Liberals to make their votes effective and preserve Liberalism by voting Conservative, stirred up controversy. His daughter Megan, insisting upon her lifelong radicalism, pointed out that she had been faithful to the traditions of her father in supporting every measure which the Labour government had brought before parliament which would have the effect of improving the lot of the working man. In general, the Conservatives were more restrained in their quest for Liberal votes than in 1950, recognising perhaps that the effect of too overt a courtship might be counterproductive.

Probably no Liberal seriously expected anything but another electoral disaster. The party's vote slumped to under three-quarters of a million – less than 2.6 per cent of the total; its representation in the Commons fell from nine to six, while 66 candidates had forfeited their deposits. Only a few pockets of genuine strength now remained, concentrated in Wales, Scotland and the West Country. Elsewhere the Liberal vote was distributed fairly evenly, though it was strongest in agricultural areas. The modest figure of 20 per cent support was secured in just three urban seats.

Only Jo Grimond was returned in the face of Conservative opposition and it was a reasonable proposition that the party would have retained three seats at most if Conservatives had stood against all its candidates. *The Times* commented that the 'party, which for thirty years has fought to survive with almost incredible tenacity, has received a fresh blow'.[99] The *Manchester Guardian*, which had recommended a full term for Churchill as the country's best option, offered an even gloomier message:

> It is hard to see in this depressing picture much ground for building up a country-wide political party on the old model. Unless there is some change in the Conservative Party or some break-up in the Labour Party, the Liberal Party can look forward only to further attrition and further losses to the two major parties.[100]

Liberal votes certainly seem to have been decisive, but only in the sense of helping the Conservatives to secure a narrow, but still comfortable, majority of 17 over all other parties. The statistics suggest that few Liberals, deprived of a Liberal candidate in 1951, felt unable to register a vote and that the majority of them transferred their support to the Tories. In constituencies where Liberals stood in 1950 but not in 1951, the swing to the Conservatives was greater than in the country as a whole. Something like 60 or 70 per cent of those who had supported Liberal candidates in 1950 seem to have transferred their allegiance to the Conservatives when the possibility of a Liberal vote was no longer an option. This factor may have accounted for more than half the seats which the Conservatives won from Labour.[101] Harold Macmillan's contemporary assessment was that Liberal votes had been decisive in securing Conservative successes north of the River Trent, areas 'which have suffered under the Socialist tyranny'.[102]

If the result of the election were not bad enough, one further pitfall awaited the depleted party – albeit one dressed in an appealing disguise. Churchill's parliamentary majority was adequate enough and he had no real need to seek Liberal support. But the election had seen the defeat of those left-wing Liberals – Granville, Roberts and Megan Lloyd George – whose presence in the party's ranks had been the most serious impediment to closer relations with the Tories. Perhaps also Churchill was keen to re-create the sort of 'National' rather than party political authority which he had enjoyed during the war, or he may simply have seen a golden opportunity to extinguish the party of which he had once been a member. At all events, Churchill decided to offer Clement Davies a post in his cabinet as Minister of Education.[103] Davies, who had never held government office, was keen to accept, but felt obliged to consult senior colleagues including Lord Samuel before giving his decision. On 28 October, party head-quarters announced that Davies felt unable to accept Churchill's offer, but that, in view of the government's narrow Commons majority, Liberals would be willing to give it support for measures 'clearly conceived in the interest of the country as a whole'.[104] The decision was a crucial one as even those such as Violet Bonham Carter, who urged Davies to accept, came to realise. So low were Liberal fortunes at this time that, had Davies accepted, the remaining party could easily have disintegrated. His refusal was probably the greatest act of service rendered to his party during 11 years as leader.

Defiance in adversity had become a Liberal trade mark. After 1951 it seemed particularly hollow. 'Our beachhead is not enlarged,' the party conceded, 'but it remains.' 'We refuse to be stamped out,' Davies told the Liberal Assembly the following year. 'In spite of all temptations we still prefer our own doctrine and we are determined to maintain our independence.'[105] Privately, he took some comfort from the strength of Liberalism among the under-graduate population. He was, he insisted, less down-hearted than he had been in 1945 or 1950: 'I cannot give a reason for this. It is just a state of mind and may be quite illogical.'[106] At least the danger of assimilation within Conservatism had largely passed. Having achieved a majority government on the basis of their own efforts, the electoral imperative of the late 1940s appeared less acute in Conservative minds. In any case, it seemed logical to assume that the steady attritional erosion of the Liberal vote would continue and that the party would eventually fade away without the need for further pacts or negotiations at a national level, and in particular without the concession of Proportional Representation. In this sense the Liberal party's very weakness in the early 1950s may well have proved its salvation – an ironical conclusion from the vantage point of the new century, when Liberal Democrats have set themselves the goal of replacing the Conservative party as the main opposition to New Labour.

But the party's problems were far from over. 'I truly believe, and, of course, I sincerely hope', wrote Davies in the wake of the election, 'we have now reached the nadir and that from now on we shall begin to climb steadily the hill of prosperity.'[107] In fact, the situation continued to deteriorate. Liberals did badly in by-elections, contesting only eight of the forty-five which were held during the 1951–55 parliament and saving their deposit just once. Only a respectable second place in December 1954 on 36 per cent of the vote on a low turnout at Inverness, not even contested in 1951, provided a crumb of comfort. The position in local elections was no better. In 1950 only 2.2 per cent of borough councillors were Liberals; by 1955 the figure stood at 1.5 per cent. After 1953 Liberals were the largest party in just two borough councils in the country, Huddersfield and Mossley. The last geographical strong-holds of Liberal support seemed to be vanishing, with Labour steadily mopping up the nonconformist vote in rural Wales as the decade progressed. By 1955 the number of affiliated local associa-tions fell below 300. As individual membership declined, the party's financial worries increased and its fragile dependence upon the generosity of a few wealthy benefactors became ever more apparent.

In the House of Commons the parliamentary rump under the ageing Clement Davies presented an unimpressive picture. Most of those Liberals who enjoyed national recognition stood among the defeated. Violet Bonham Carter saw no future chance of secur-ing election, except perhaps as a Conservative. Megan Lloyd George, concluding that she was 'too left for the modern Liberal taste',[108] announced in 1952 that she would not fight her old Anglesey constituency again and declined re-election as a party vice-president. Egged on by Philip Noel-Baker, her clandestine lover on the Labour front bench, Lady Megan now stood aloof from such efforts as were made to sustain the radical tradition in Liberal politics and prepared the ground for her eventual move to the Labour ranks. Frank Byers had failed to regain his seat and now reconciled himself to an important but non-parliamentary role in the party's affairs. Donald Wade and Arthur Holt, the respective beneficiaries of the local pacts in Huddersfield and Bolton, were welcome additions to Liberalism's depleted ranks in the House of Commons, but they remained vulnerable to any future change of heart on the part of the Conservative party.

The position in the House of Lords was little better. Sinclair had given up hope of returning to the Commons and, enthused 'by the prospect of leaving his cold hermitage in Caithness for the rhetorical delights of Westminster', was created a viscount in the New Year Honours of 1952.[109] But plans that he should become the party leader in the upper house were thwarted by his own ill health. Sinclair did not take his seat until 1954, nor make his maiden speech until 1956. As a result, Samuel stayed on as leader in the Lords until 1955 by which date he was 85 years of age. A survey carried out at around this time revealed that, notwithstanding a nominal contingent of 46 Liberal peers, only 16 were deemed to be 'valuable attenders'. The average age of the party's 'first-line' in the upper chamber was 77.[110] The depths of the party's roots in history had been a major factor in keeping it going when so many other factors had pointed towards extinction. Samuel's ministerial career went back to 1905 and his final retirement cut a last tie binding Liberals to an earlier, happier age. Violet Bonham Carter now admitted that it was 'hard for those who remember the great men of our Party to continue to serve its shadow among the lesser ones'.[111]

Inside parliament, the Liberal party proceeded to give general support to Churchill's government. Many took comfort in the belief that the Conservatives now embodied most of what was best in Liberal thinking. 'I am really inclined to think that it is the Tory party that is extinct, not the Liberal,' insisted Gilbert Murray. 'They have had to accept a more than half Liberal leader, and on the main lines of policy people like Winston and Eden scarcely differ from us.'[112] Four years later this lifelong Liberal expressed satisfaction at a further Conservative general election victory: 'Nearly all the educated people I meet are Liberal, but vote Conservative' – a course he had taken himself.[113] Such complacent thinking did not go unchallenged. The Radical Action group of the war years flickered back to life in the guise of the Radical Reform Group, with the predictable backing of figures such as Dingle Foot. The 1953 and 1954 Party Assemblies witnessed heated debates between individualists, who continued to preach the time-honoured Liberal virtues of free trade, personal liberty and minimum government intervention, and radicals who traced their political pedigrees back via the interventionist policies of Beveridge and Keynes to the New Liberalism of the turn of the century. But to most observers such disputes seemed largely irrelevant. The public found little in Liberalism to give it a distinctive appeal. As one despairing Liberal candidate put it, 'our words cut no ice, for the single reason that we have nothing new, original or constructive to say. If we had something to say on these lines, the probability is that we should be branded as non-Liberals.'[114] In short, Liberals had become, as Churchill was reported as saying, 'so few and so futile'.

Against this background, the General Election of 1955 offered little cause for optimism. From a Liberal point of view it looked very much a re-run of 1951. Liberals fielded 110 candidates, just one more than at the previous election. The choice of seats seemed marginally more appropriate than four years earlier and their campaigns were somewhat more efficiently run. Even so, a number of forlorn candidates were sent forth to face inevitable slaughter and compared with the better-resourced Labour and Conservative parties, the Liberals still looked amateurish. Bristol North was a constituency which the party decided to fight as early as July 1954. Not until the following April, however, was a prospective candidate in place. But the local party still fought the election without a full-time agent, being unable to afford the £12 a week salary which this would have required. Even a sufficiency of envelopes appeared to pose problems. The candidate himself 'was not able to give all his time to the campaign, and was handicapped in the early stages because he had no one to drive him round the constituency. He was not completely mobile until a supporter, able to drive a car, came back from holiday.'[115]

The Liberal manifesto accepted that the country had moved into somewhat calmer waters than had existed four years earlier, but insisted that the party still stood as security against two class-based parties seeking to use their power in the interests of 'their particular clients'. It criticised Labour and the Conservatives for the timidity of their approaches to European integration, warned about the dangers of inflation, stressed the need to scrutinise government expenditure and reiterated earlier calls for Scottish and Welsh devolution and electoral reform. Its most distinctive features, suggested the *Manchester Guardian*, were 'an appeal to the middle-class vote and an attack, in the name of liberty, on the tendency of trade unions to limit the freedom of individuals within the unions'. It was perhaps not surprising that, a month before polling day, Megan Lloyd George announced her entry to the Labour party, concluding that the Liberal party had lost all touch with the radical tradition that had once inspired it. Talks with Conservative officials to see if the Huddersfield and Bolton arrangements could be extended soon broke down in the face of unrealistic Liberal demands. Though the party gave no formal advice to Liberal supporters in constituencies where no Liberal candidate was standing, it was striking that the Tory lists included thirteen candidates who had previously stood as Liberals, seven of whom were elected. Churchill, standing as a humble back-bencher, restated his familiar refrain that a broad harmony now existed between the aims of the modern Conservative party and those of the great Liberal leaders of earlier times.

In all the circumstances the outcome of the contest was a cause of relief. Only perhaps in Inverness did the Liberals have any real chance of adding to their meagre parliamentary tally. In the event, no seats were gained but none was lost either. For the first time since 1929 the party's position had not deteriorated compared with the previous general election. Liberal statisticians derived a crumb of comfort from a marginal increase in the average Liberal poll from 14.7 to 15.1 per cent.

Most significantly, now that the post-war electorate had had an opportunity to taste a full term of both Labour and Conservative governments, the Liberal party had begun to benefit from what would become one of its greatest assets, the protest vote. An examination of the constituency of Bristol North suggested that more than half the Liberal vote derived from dissatisfaction with the major parties rather than a genuine conversion to Liberalism.[116] For all that, whatever advance had occurred, it scarcely merited the ecstatic reaction of party headquarters. 'It is not just a "moral" victory,' insisted *Liberal News*, 'it is concrete progress on which we can begin at once to build for the full triumph at the next election.'[117]

At the end of more than twenty years of steady decline, the Liberal party was still in business, just about a national force in British politics. This is a phenomenon worthy in itself of a word of explanation. John Stevenson has wisely written that 'the party's structure as a loose grouping of largely middle-class individuals, tied together by sentiment, friendship and voluntary commitment, was one well-adapted to survival and to resisting takeover'.[118] Within this context, tribute must be paid to key figures – parliamentarians, senior party officials and dedicated constituency workers – who managed to convince at least themselves that the Liberal cause was not lost and that the flame must not be extinguished. Looking back from the more promising days of the early 1970s, Leonard Behrens recalled that one of the encouragements he had received when touring the country during his two years (1955–56) as Acting President and then President of the Liberal Party Organisation was to find 'in every town and even in little villages groups of determined Liberals who, without any expectation of success, continued to keep the Party alive in preparation for the great days which are to come'.[119] In addition, it is clear that Liberalism had survived on the strength of its own tradition, of voting Liberal from one generation to the next, all the party's remaining constituencies being ones of long-term Liberal strength. Such pockets of support continued, oblivious almost of what was happening to the party elsewhere in the country. Furthermore, no serious challenger to the Liberal party had emerged for the third place in British politics, and there remained a sizeable number of voters who were wary of the duopolistic stranglehold of Labour and the Conservatives. These were fragile bases for survival, but offered just sufficient foundation to hand over a viable party into the more promising era that now awaited.

4

TWO STEPS FORWARD AND ONE BACK, 1955–1979

At the beginning of 1956 both Clement Davies and Leonard Behrens, the party's acting president, published optimistic New Year messages, claiming that Liberalism was now on the march again. Though such optimism prompted a measure of ridicule in the press and among political opponents, there was nothing surprising in these Liberal pronouncements. At least since the 1920s, the party's unrealistic and sometimes illogical pretensions had been an important factor in keeping it alive. Objectively, however, and notwithstanding the bottoming-out of the process of Liberal decline revealed in the recent General Election, there was little hard evidence to sustain such high hopes apart from an encouraging by-election result at Torquay in December 1955, when the Liberal candidate took 23.8 per cent of the vote. Even when, the following February, with the Conservatives' post-election honeymoon rapidly receding in the face of a worsening economic climate, Liberals secured 36.4 per cent at Hereford and 21.4 per cent at Gainsborough, any triumphal flag-waving was surely premature. Yet, with the hindsight of almost half a century, it is now clear that Davies and Behrens had at least an element of truth on their side. The Liberal tide had turned and, though there would be much ebbing as well as flowing in the years ahead, the process of revival had indeed begun.

Not surprisingly, not all Liberals had yet detected this turn-around in their fortunes. Frank Byers, for example, had begun to work out a plan for the next general election which would have reduced the Liberals to the status of little more than a guerrilla force rather than a conventional political party. 'Operation Blackmail' involved putting up candidates in vulnerable Conservative seats with the aim of contesting or not contesting them as party strategy determined: 'This wld. be the only way to make terms for ourselves with the Conservatives for the next Election.' Violet Bonham Carter was sympathetic to this idea, recognising that in the future Liberals were only likely to win contests in straight fights and that the Conservatives would only concede these if the Liberal party was prepared to 'exploit real nuisance value' where the Tories themselves were in danger of defeat.[1] In practice, the threat that the Liberal party might be swallowed up by the Conservatives, which had been very real at the beginning of the decade, had largely passed, not least because the Conservatives had proved to themselves that they could comfortably defeat their Labour opponents while an independent Liberal party continued to exist. But, at the same time, this experience also suggested that there was little scope to build upon the example of Huddersfield-style co-operation. Two successive general election victories weakened the case for anti-socialist pacts. Nor did it seem likely that Liberalism would fall victim to the embrace of the Labour party, in part because the evidence suggested that the presence of a Liberal candidate did more harm to the Conservatives than it did to Labour. Indeed, when Labour won a by-election in Gloucester in October 1957, this was widely attributed to the effects of Liberal intervention. But while the risks of an overt takeover by one or other of the larger parties may have receded, Liberals in the mid-1950s still faced the likely, and equally damaging, prospect of the remorseless, attritional erosion of their support, both among the politically active and from within their now fragile electoral base. In July 1956, a significant group of defectors, including Dingle Foot and Wilfrid Roberts, went over to Labour, claiming that there was 'a great deal of common ground between Radicals and the Labour Party and that the differences between them now largely belong to the past'.[2]

One hopeful possibility was that the electorate might grow tired of a second-term Conservative government and, especially if economic problems continued to mount, turn to the Liberals rather than travelling the full distance to support the Labour party. But in 1955 there seemed little prospect of such a development. Drawing upon his long experience, Hugh Dalton described the general election of that year as the 'most tedious, apathetic, uninteresting' in which he had participated, the product of the electorate's inability to find grave fault in the way in which the country was being run.[3] In Anthony Eden, moreover, the Conservatives now had a new and comparatively young leader, a man with a long-standing 'liberal' pedigree with which to appeal to a broad spectrum of British opinion. That the Liberals would advance upon their recent marginal progress was, therefore, by no means inevitable. That they did so was the product of two important catalysts, the first within their own control, the second entirely beyond it.

By the end of 1955 Clement Attlee had retired after two decades at the head of the Labour party. His replacement was the 49-year-old Hugh Gaitskell. This left Clement Davies, until recently the youngest of the three party leaders, now by some way the most elderly. His recent record was not impressive. Illness had largely kept him out of the 1955 election campaign and he was in any case waging a personal battle against the ravages of drink. In private at least, many prominent Liberals, including Major-General Grey, the Party Treasurer, and Philip Fothergill, Party Vice-President, had concluded that it was time for a change. That change effectively took place at the 1956 Party Assembly in Folkestone, even though in strict constitutional terms the decision did not lie within its remit. The youthful chief whip, Jo Grimond, found himself acclaimed as 'the white hope' of the future, even before Davies formally announced that he was stepping down. The later vote by the parliamentary Liberal party was little more than a formality. In practice, Grimond was the only viable candidate. Among the small band of Liberal MPs, only he combined an unequivocal and full-time commitment to the Liberal cause with a reasonably secure electoral position in his constituency. The outgoing leader was warmly received, though it is clear that 'gratitude for past service and relief at his decision to step down were mixed in about equal proportions'.[4] It was clearly a wise move. As the *Economist* commented, 'pensioning off an old servant is a sad business, but when the Liberals have paid their tributes to Clement Davies, they are bound to feel relieved that their leadership, like that of the two main parties, has now moved into the next generation'.[5]

Grimond's assumption of the leadership coincided with the early stages of a crisis for the government which would transform for ever the relationship between the Liberal and Conservative parties. Opinions on what the Eden government did in the course of the Suez adventure have differed violently, both at the time and in subsequent historiography. But for the Liberal party this was a watershed, all the more poignant because of the Prime Minister's well deserved reputation until this time for commitment to the principles of liberal internationalism. Violet Bonham Carter confessed that she had 'almost persuaded [herself] during the 51–56 Government [that] Toryism was shading into Liberalism'. Now, she insisted to a Conservative Suez sceptic, 'I feel there is reversion to type'.[6] Even so, the initial Liberal response to the crisis was far more equivocal than it later appeared. As Lady Violet recorded after a 'terrible' Liberal party committee meeting:

> Jo . . . says Nasser's action is the parallel of Hitler's when he invaded the Rhineland and that unless we bring about his fall the whole Middle East will go his way – nationalize their oil, threaten to cut us off etc. I think this is true. Yet I hardly feel that we can 'go it alone' and align world opinion against us.[7]

In the House of Lords both Samuel and Sinclair supported Eden and when Labour first divided the Commons on 30 October, three Liberal MPs, Davies, Roderic Bowen and Arthur Holt – who, after all, comprised 50 per cent of the parliamentary party – voted with the government. In the country, too, many Liberal supporters found it difficult to criticise the government when the nation was effectively at war.[8] As rumours spread, however, of British collusion with France and Israel prior to the latter's attack on Egypt, it became easier for Grimond to distance his party from the

Conservative administration. For at least a generation, the image of the Conservatives as the natural repository for the best traditions of British Liberalism had been destroyed. Many former Liberals returned to the party fold. Others looked to it for the first time. Rather like the Hoare–Laval Pact of twenty years before, Suez opened up new opportunities for redefining the Liberal party in a way that clearly distinguished it from its political opponents.

The replacement of a 72–year-old leader in poor health by a vigorous 43-year-old offered obvious advantages, especially when the new leader had Grimond's freshness and imagination, combined with an ability to communicate and striking good looks which gave an impression of openness and reliability. The new man's personality would be a key factor in the Liberal party's subsequent revival, but on its own it was not enough. The party was unlikely to make much progress until it succeeded in establishing a clear and identifiable image in the British political spectrum. The most common image of Liberalism at this time among Liberal supporters was that it was a compromise party which combined the better traits of its larger opponents. Many voters could only identify it in terms of what it was not, rather than on the basis of what it was. As late as 1959, Gallup found that 59 per cent of the population did not know what Liberal policy was, a figure which included almost half of those who said they were going to vote Liberal. For too long the party had tried to define itself in terms of its two rivals, as a sort of moderating influence between the extremes of socialism and conservatism. Such a stance had every disadvantage. For those who accepted this caricature of the reality of British politics in the 1950s, Liberals offered themselves as a classless party to an electorate divided by class. For the more perceptive, who recognised that no vast chasm divided the Conservative party of Harold Macmillan from that of Labour under Hugh Gaitskell, it left the Liberal party with little political ground to call its own. As the Conservative Angus Maude pointed out:

> If anyone . . . imagines that the Liberals are providing an essential moderating influence between a lot of revolutionary Socialists

and a crowd of reactionary die-hard Tories, he should banish the idea at once. Both the big parties are chock full of people making sensible, moderate speeches to such an extent that the atmosphere often becomes positively stifling.[9]

On balance, by the time that Grimond became leader, the party had become a largely right-leaning body, an anti-socialist rather than an anti-Conservative force in British politics. Its continuing commitment to free trade and low taxation did little to hone its progressive credentials at a time when Labour and the Conservatives were competing with each other in their claims to run the managed economy. Despite numerous defections to Labour, a strand of left-wing radicalism did persist, and the Radical Reform Group had formally realigned itself with the party early in 1956. A contributor to an important volume on Liberal thought, published in 1957, insisted that 'by any strict use of language Liberals are the true Left, the real progressives', but objectively it was difficult to sustain such a contention.[10] Yet the fact that such diverse ideas could be embraced within one relatively small political grouping was still seen by many as a virtue. Writing in the month of Grimond's accession, the party president explained:

> We are a Party of individualists, with minds of our own. We do not take directions from our leaders: we combine to hammer out our policies. That is one of the reasons why it is not easy to be a Liberal, and why it is common for Liberals to disagree.[11]

To the wider public, however, Liberal diversity merely created confusion and was not conducive to building up the party's electoral appeal.

Grimond was a man of ideas. His literary output in terms of books, pamphlets and articles was considerable. In time, he came to dominate his party's thinking in a way that no leader had done since Lloyd George. Almost half of the party's manifesto for the 1959 General Election was his personal statement. His first period as leader, however, was not one in which he stamped his distinctive ideological imprint upon the party. For the time being, traditional Liberal preoccupations with high taxation and government waste continued. In what was almost an anticipation of the Conservatism of Keith Joseph and Margaret Thatcher, Grimond warned of the danger that an overweening state would create a dependency culture. The population was at risk of being lulled into the belief that it was right to transfer responsibility from individual enterprise to state activity at the cost of ever higher taxes. In similar vein, he singled out inflation as the most serious economic problem facing the country and advocated monetarist solutions to curb it.[12] At the same time, Grimond's Liberal party did adopt a distinctive position on two important policy issues. At the 1956 Folkestone Assembly the party had passed a resolution calling for Britain's active participation in the setting up of a Common Market. This came just over a year after the powers of Western Europe had gathered at Messina to plan the next stages of European integration, a process from which the British Conservative government had quickly withdrawn. Grimond seemed at first to have misgivings. An article published in *Liberal News* in February 1957, apparently with his approval, suggested that Britain should join a free-trade area, but not a customs union. Such a stance was consistent with the party's ongoing commitment to free trade. By the end of 1958, however, by which time the European Economic Community had become a reality, Grimond was ready to abandon his doubts about that body's common external tariff, won round by figures such as his mother-in-law, Violet Bonham Carter, to the view that the Community provided the best approach to further European co-operation. The other policy development related to defence. In March 1957 the parliamentary party, at Grimond's prompting, stated that it was time for Britain to abandon the manufacture of its own nuclear deterrent and concentrate instead on nuclear research, so as to continue to make a contribution to the protective shield provided by the United States. Coming in the wake of the Suez episode, the most important implication of this initiative was to confirm the party's separation from the Conservatives.

Grimond's leadership saw early evidence of progress in two areas which were to be vital to the party's recovery as a national political force – an improved performance in by-elections and a revival of its almost dormant base in local politics. Between Torquay in December 1955 and Galloway in April 1959 there were 53 by-elections. Of these, the Liberals contested just 19. But significantly only one deposit was lost and in seven contests the party came first or second. The Liberals began to understand the importance of a good by-election result, not only in the hope of increasing representation at Westminster, but also in raising the morale of party workers and focusing national attention in a way that was impossible in a general election campaign. The curtain-raiser came at Rochdale in February 1958 when the well-known media personality, Ludovic Kennedy, forced the Conservatives into third place, a sufficiently bad result to prompt an offer of resignation from the Tory chairman, Lord Hailsham. Then, the following month, Mark Bonham Carter, Violet's son and Asquith's grandson, snatched the Devon constituency of Torrington from the Conservatives. It was the first Liberal by-elections gain for almost thirty years and prompted hyperbolic if understandable elation. Lady Violet recalled 'the strange sense of being a member of an army of liberation entering occupied territory which for years had been ruled by quislings and collaborators and that their day was over once and for all'.[13] Victory was particularly sweet since the defeated Tory candidate had sought to tap into the historic traditions of West Country Liberalism by adopting the hybrid designation of 'National Liberal and Conservative'. In the wake of this triumph, Grimond began to expound the themes which would be so important for his repositioning of the party over the following years. The Liberals' task now would be to 'carve out a niche for ourselves Left of Centre . . . in the sense that we stand for personal freedom against authority . . . in the sense that we believe there is still too much poverty, too many slums and too much cruelty . . . in the sense that we want and mean to have a wide dispersal of property and power'.[14]

Though with little prompting from Grimond himself, the party also began to appreciate the importance of securing successes in local government, largely neglected by Liberals for a generation, as a first foundation in the creation of a broader party base. In organisational terms it was obviously easier to compete with the major parties on a ward basis than across an entire constituency. The process of recovery had begun before he took over the leadership, with modest gains being registered in both 1955 and 1956. The improvement continued and in 1958 the Liberals had their best results since before the war, with 54 gains notched up in the boroughs and 59 in the urban and rural district councils. In another anticipation of its later tactics, the party showed signs of varying its image and appeal to suit the demands of the particular locality being contested. In Exeter the Liberal assault was mounted against the Tories; by contrast, Bradford Liberals still tended to work in partnership with the Conservatives to breach a Labour stronghold.[15]

It was tempting for party loyalists to be carried away by what were in fact only modest advances from a very low base-line. Most new Liberal votes were coming from disgruntled Conservatives, registering a probably temporary displeasure at the apparent inability of Macmillan's succession of Chancellors to manage the managed economy. Even the victory at Torrington only cancelled out the loss of Carmarthen to Labour in February 1957 following the death of Sir Rhys Hopkin Morris. The strength of the parliamentary party remained stuck at six and it was still possible to make jokes at Liberal expense about party conferences being held in telephone boxes. Though the small band of Liberal MPs became markedly more critical of the Conservative government than it had been under Davies, it failed to make a real impact in this period. More significantly, the extra-parliamentary party, though enthused by Grimond's energy and commitment, was not necessarily moving in step with its leader. The 1958 Torquay Assembly was something of a shambles, dominated, the *Economist* suggested, by a combination of 'vacuous youth' and 'blithering old age'.[16] The passage of a resolution reaffirming the party's commitment to the idea of unilateral free trade was hard to reconcile with Grimond's wish to locate Liberalism at the heart of the modern political agenda. Some of those surviving Liberal outposts which might have been expected to provide a launch pad for future growth seemed curiously resistant to Grimond's message. 'Welsh Liberals increasingly appeared a relatively conservative party, thus driving radical thinkers disillusioned with Labour into the arms of Plaid Cymru.'[17] Most disappointingly, however, it proved difficult, if not impossible, to sustain the momentum of advance.

As the General Election approached, the majority of floating voters drifted towards their natural points of allegiance. None the less, Liberals went into the contest with some grounds for optimism. Organisational revival was reflected in the party's readiness to contest 216 seats, almost double the total of the last two elections. The party's finances were on a more stable footing than for some time. By the end of 1957 the annual accounts had been balanced at more than £24,000. Yet this was still a small sum compared with the money available to the major parties and there remained relatively few constituencies where the Liberals were in a position to conduct a comprehensive canvass or even to spend the full amount of money legally permitted. It was eloquent commentary on the progress that still needed to be made that about three-quarters of those Liberals who went to the polls in party cars reported that they had done so in non-Liberal vehicles. Overall, the Liberals were still seen as 'the largest of the minor parties, a federation of independently operating candidates rather than as a broad national movement'.[18] The manifesto *People Count* reiterated many well-worn themes, in particular that 'a Liberal vote is a protest against the British political system being divided up between two powerful Party machines, one largely financed by the employers and the other by the Trade Unions'. It called for more money to be spent on education and roads and for an increase in the old-age pension. But overall the document offered few specific policy promises, stressing instead the need for a substantial Liberal presence in the new House of Commons to 'save us from Tory or Labour reactionaries'. Such an aspiration hinted at the objective, which seemed at one point realisable, of holding the balance in the new parliament. Yet neither in the manifesto nor the campaign itself did Grimond clarify how Liberals would behave in such a situation.

In the event, the result was both a considerable encouragement and a great disappointment. Granted that the doubling of the number of seats contested meant that Liberals were fighting some less promising constituencies, the average Liberal vote still rose from 15.1 per cent to 16.9 per cent. At the same time, the number of lost deposits fell to 55. In 16 more seats compared with 1955 the Liberal candidate forced himself into second place. The overall Liberal vote went up to 1.6 million, some 5.9 per cent of the total. But on the debit side the party still returned just six MPs. To Grimond's dismay, Bonham Carter failed to hold on to Torrington, but this loss was balanced by the victory of the youthful Jeremy Thorpe in the neighbouring constituency of North Devon. But by far the most promising feature of the result from Grimond's point of view was the effect it had on the Conservative–Labour contest, even though this was far from leaving the Liberals holding the balance of power. The government had now extended its majority to 100 seats. For the third successive election Labour found itself on the losing side, defying the expectations of contemporary psephologists that the natural swing of the electoral pendulum would return it to power. Before long, commentators were ready to suggest that the Labour party was in a state of terminal decline, increasingly deprived of its perennial power base among the manual working class, as an ever-expanding proportion of the electorate, benefiting from the unprecedented affluence of 1950s Britain, took on the characteristics of a middle-class lifestyle, including a propensity to vote Conservative. Grimond was quick to see the possibilities that such a situation might afford to the Liberal party.

Grimond's aim was to secure a realignment of British politics such as would bring about a more relevant division between the parties than had come to exist by the late 1950s. The real divide, he believed, lay between progressives and conservatives and, while the Liberals might constitute the nucleus of a new progressive grouping, recruits would also have to be found inside Labour's non-socialist wing and even among moderate Tories.

Such a body could unite in support of individual freedom and responsibility and a commitment to work towards equality of opportunity and international co-operation. The present party system had had the practical effect of entrenching in power the forces of conservatism, whether of the right or left. Believing that the pattern of class voting was now likely to decline, Grimond was the first Liberal leader since Lloyd George to see his party's salvation lying not purely in its own efforts but as part of a restructuring of Britain's political left. As soon as the election was over, he spelt out his vision:

> I would like to see the radical side of politics – the Liberals and most of the Labour Party – make a new appeal to people to take a more active part in all sorts of real political issues . . . . There must be a bridge between socialism and the Liberal policy of co-ownership in industry through a type of syndicalism coupled with a non-conformist outlook such as was propounded on many issues by George Orwell.[19]

An article by Grimond in *The Times* three years later adds greater clarity: 'The divisions in politics fall in the wrong place. The natural breakdown should be into a Conservative Party – a small group of convinced Socialists in the full sense – and a broadly based progressive Party. It is the foundations of the last named that the Liberal Party seeks to provide.'[20]

In practice, the goal of realignment depended on a major split occurring within the Labour party. During the first three years of the new parliament this looked a realistic proposition. Members of the Labour party reacted in varying ways to their third successive electoral defeat, but as far as the party leader, Hugh Gaitskell, was concerned, the voters' message was clear: Labour had to modernise or perish. Influenced by the example of the German SPD, he proposed that the party should drop the famous Clause Four of its constitution which committed it to the principle of the public ownership of British industry. Though Clause Four was of largely symbolic importance, Gaitskell saw that if Labour remained stuck with its almost exclusively working-class image, it might never be elected again in a rapidly changing and increasingly affluent society. It was the beginning of a Labour civil war in which the party leader took on his own left wing at successive party conferences, losing the battle over Clause Four but emerging victorious in the struggle to resist a commitment to unilateral nuclear disarmament. At one point it looked quite possible that the party's non-socialist right wing might break away in the manner anticipated in Grimond's vision of realignment. The Campaign for Democratic Socialism, set up immediately after Labour's 1960 Scarborough Conference, where the left carried a resolution in favour of unilateralism but at which Gaitskell pledged to 'fight and fight and fight again' to save the party he loved, contained many similarities, even down to some of the personnel involved, with the breakaway of the Social Democratic Party two decades later. Quite possibly, moreover, Grimond could have worked amicably enough with many of the Gaitskellites had Labour's left emerged triumphant from the party's internecine feuds. William Rodgers, the Campaign for Democratic Socialism's full-time organiser, later recalled being matched with Mark Bonham Carter in a *Sunday Times* discussion of the common ground between the Labour and Liberal parties: 'Although it was nearly thirty years before we found ourselves in the same party as Liberal Democrats, Mark and I reached a surprising measure of agreement.'[21]

Yet these optimistic signs probably served to conceal what was really happening on the electoral ground. The continuing progress of the Liberal party among the voters was far more the product of the unpopularity of the Conservative government than it was of Labour's divisions. Macmillan's political touch rapidly deserted him after 1960. The image of 'Supermac' was quickly replaced by that of an ageing, out-of-touch and increasingly accident-prone prime minister. The introduction of Selwyn Lloyd's pay pause in 1961 was probably more important in sustaining the momentum of Liberal electoral advance than were the chasms within the Labour party publicly displayed at its Scarborough Conference the previous year. Labour's unappealing image merely encouraged disillusioned Conservatives to stop at the halfway house of Liberalism rather than travel the full distance and transfer their support to Labour.

The party was in any case ill-equipped to compete with Labour and the Conservatives on anything like equal terms. Liberal organisation remained rudimentary compared with that of its opponents. The party went into the 1964 General Election with just 60 full-time agents; its annual income stood at around £70,000. Party headquarters lacked the funds to provide a library service and even had to do without a typing pool. Too much depended on Grimond himself. 'You have taken all the strings into your own hands', declared the party's candidate at the Ebbw Vale by-election of 1960, 'and the whole success or failure of Liberalism now rests on your shoulders alone.'[22] That same candidate had recently resigned as Party Treasurer, complaining that the party organisation must become a democratic body responsible to the party as a whole 'and not remain, as it is today, the preserve of a small private coterie'.[23] Grimond was restricted, particularly in parliament, by the talent available to him. In practice, he could rely on the services of just four MPs including himself and 'the amount of work required of Donald [Wade], Arthur [Holt] and Jeremy [Thorpe] [was] preposterous'.[24] Violet Bonham Carter described the party's parlous position in the Commons in July 1961:

> Wade is ill, Jeremy is ill, Clem [Davies] is a chronic absentee and useless when present. [Grimond] wrote imploring Bowen to be with him for the Berlin debate on Monday and to *speak* – and Bowen replied that he had 'a function'. He does damn all in the House. As Jo says – why go into it? [25]

For the time being, none of this seemed to matter. The evidence of Liberal revival was there for all to see. By the end of 1959 party membership had risen to an estimated 150,000. By the winter of 1961–2 it had gone up to 250,000 and peaked at around 350,000 in 1963. The 1960 Assembly at Eastbourne was the best attended since the war and enthusiastically endorsed the leadership's policy of seeking membership of the Common Market – this at just the time when informed opinion at least was becoming aware of unflattering comparisons between Britain's recent economic performance and that of her continental neighbours. The decision to contest a by-election in Bolton East that November effectively marked the end of an era of Conservative-Liberal electoral co-operation and represented an important confirmation of Grimond's insistence that Liberalism was a party of the radical left, even though it left at least two of the party's small band of MPs dangerously exposed to a future Conservative challenge. His vision of Liberalism necessitated some adjustment in his policy stance. A continuation of the proto-Thatcherite programme of rolling back the frontiers of the state and allowing free rein to the workings of the market economy no longer made much sense, especially as the late 1950s and early 1960s witnessed the progressive departure of 'economic liberals' from the party's ranks. Instead, Grimond began to emphasise the need to modernise the British economy and shake it out of the lethargy into which it had increasingly fallen. The change was apparent when he addressed the Young Liberals in December 1961. In place of the traditional shibboleths of free trade and individual liberty, he stressed the importance of economic growth and regional development and called for a wages policy and a national plan to guide the country's development in a new technological era. Grimond himself was an obvious asset. His youth and tendency to iconoclasm chimed in well with the increasingly anti-establishment and anti-deference mood of the new decade – notwithstanding his own quintessentially establishment background.

The party made about fifty scattered gains in the local borough elections of 1960. The following year almost two hundred new seats were captured, leaving the Liberals as the largest group on such councils as Huddersfield and Darwen and in control of Bacup, Saddleworth and Fletton. But 1962, with the Conservative government becoming embroiled in a succession of sex and security scandals, was the party's *annus mirabilis*. As many as 567 gains were recorded in the May council elections – nearly 400 of them from the Conservatives – while in March the party secured what remains to this day its most celebrated single by-election victory. On 13 March the Liberal candidate in Blackpool North did better than expected in cutting the Conservative majority from nearly 16,000 to just 973. The following day it was the turn of the voters of the Kent constituency of Orpington to go to the polls. Orpington was, it seemed, a rock-solid Conservative stronghold. The Tories had enjoyed a majority of 14,760 in the 1959 General Election. Now the Liberal candidate, Eric Lubbock, took the seat with a majority of 7,855. Even allowing for changes in the electoral register, about 10,000 former Conservative voters had moved over to the Liberal party. 'We have been swept off our feet', noted Harold Macmillan in the privacy of his diary, 'by a *Liberal* revival.'[26] A few months later the Prime Minister sacked seven members of his cabinet in a desperate attempt to breathe new life into the Conservative government. Briefly, anything seemed possible. A National Opinion Poll published on 28 March suggested that, on the question 'How would you vote in a general election held tomorrow?', the Liberals were in the lead on 30 per cent of the poll, with Labour on 29.9 per cent and the Conservatives 29.2 per cent. 'Orpington Man' was conceived as the symbol of the upwardly aspiring, professional, suburban commuter to whom Grimond's classless Liberal party was uniquely well placed to appeal. The reality was somewhat more complex. The Liberals' gain was less dramatic than at first appeared, the product of a carefully tended local base developed over the previous few years. By 1961 the party had brought its representation on the local 33-member Urban District Council to 12 seats. Furthermore, 'Orpington was no archetypal prosperous middle-aged established suburb, but an area of growth, conflict and change' in which the Conservatives had failed to respond to the interests and needs of newly arrived voters.[27]

As after Torrington, however, the Liberal tide soon began to ebb. Though the party contested all but one of the 17 by-elections held during 1962, there were no further gains. By October the proportion of those intending to vote for the Liberals had fallen to 20 per cent. Three promising seats in West Derbyshire, Chippenham and Colne Valley all produced respectable second places but no new MPs. By 1963 the Liberal by-election vote was averaging at 17 per cent compared to 28 per cent the previous year. The 1963 local elections witnessed a net gain of around two hundred and fifty seats, by most criteria a satisfying outcome, yet a disappointment when set against the earlier trend.

What had gone wrong? As the next general election approached, the Labour party was again looking like a viable alternative government. This was largely Gaitskell's personal achievement and his sudden death in January 1963 was in many ways a tragedy. But his successor, Harold Wilson, succeeded in binding the party together in a way that Gaitskell, with his obvious leanings towards the social democratic right, would always have found difficult. At the same time, the Conservatives belatedly responded to the Liberal challenge. In June 1962 Iain Macleod, the Party Chairman, was given the task of snuffing out the Liberal revival before it got out of hand. Many subsequent government policy initiatives, such as the abolition of Schedule A tax, were designed to win back those disgruntled middle-class voters who had flirted with the Liberal party.

The Liberals' brief moment of policy distinctiveness also passed. Wilson quickly stole Grimond's clothes as he successfully projected himself as the youthful innovator of British politics who understood and could cope with the white heat of the technological revolution. It was now the Labour leader who epitomised the widespread desire for a classless and modernised future. Even the last years of the Conservative ascendancy saw policy initiatives which stole the Liberals' thunder. In August 1961 the Macmillan government applied for British membership of the European Community. The Tories were also converted to the virtues of indicative planning. With the setting up of the National Economic Development Council and the National Incomes Commission, and the introduction of a formal incomes policy, Conservatism moved nearer than ever before to embracing the idea of the corporate state. In February 1963 the NEDC approved the ambitious target of a 4 per cent growth rate for the British economy. As the post-war consensus between Conservatives and Labour reached its peak, notwithstanding the two parties' continuing capacity to vilify one another with apparently unrestrained fervour, little space remained into which to squeeze a third serious contender for power.

Liberal policy had in any case only played a small part in its electoral revival. As one activist recalled, 'there was not much knowledge of – still less enthusiasm for – any particular Liberal policies, either new or old'.[28] A poll taken in September 1961 revealed that under a third of declared Liberal supporters knew that their party was in favour of joining the Common Market. Two years later NOP indicated the fragility of Liberal commitment. On a range of policy issues from education to foreign affairs, Liberal voters consistently preferred the programmes of either the Conservative or Labour party to that put forward by the Liberals themselves. This was not entirely surprising. The thousands of ex-Conservatives at Orpington had not suddenly been converted to a left-of-centre radicalism. Theirs was primarily a protest vote, subject to all the potential transience which this implied. Grimond in fact had been more successful in creating the vision of Liberal salvation than in working out the means by which it would be achieved. He seems to have understood the paradox of the Liberal revival, while becoming intoxicated for a while by the sweet smell of passing electoral success:

> We cannot concentrate on certain issues and co-ordinate our work on them effectively until we find what issues Liberals really care about. This is the crux of the matter. I must confess failure here. For years Timothy Joyce supplied us with an admirable Public Opinion Poll which showed that many Liberals don't want to be Radical, they are comfortable, not very political, middle of the road people. I fear this may be true. If it is, it makes nonsense of nine-tenths of what the group at the top of the party are trying to say or do.[29]

These contradictions became more apparent in the General Election of 1964. Granted Grimond's insistence that Liberalism was now a radical party of the left, it was inevitable that the thrust of the party's manifesto and campaign should be directed against the incumbent Conservative government. The manifesto, *Think for Yourself, Vote Liberal* was full of policy initiatives, drawing upon the work of the party's new Research Department under Harry Cowie. Logically, however, the prospects of a realignment of parties would be strongest if the Conservatives were to secure their fourth successive victory. Only then would there be much likelihood of the Labour party breaking up. By a ratio of about four to one the Liberals' 365 candidates were fighting Conservative-rather than Labour-held seats. It was here in middle-class suburbia that the party had been most successful in building up its organisational base. Thus, with Liberals largely picking up the votes of former Tories, their aim of forming the nucleus of a new opposition to Conservatism could only materialise if the Labour vote declined independently of anything the Liberals did. In practice, this did not happen. Labour's share of the poll increased marginally from 1959, when it had been heavily defeated. By contrast, the Conservative share fell by 6 per cent.

In many ways the Liberal performance in 1964 gave cause for statistical satisfaction. At 11.2 per cent the Liberal share of the poll had almost doubled since 1959. Even though 149 more constituencies were being contested than in 1959, the average Liberal vote went up from 16.9 per cent to 18.4 per cent and only 53 deposits were lost. In 54 seats the party had come second and nine members were returned to Westminster, the first increase in Liberal representation at a general election since 1929. All the victories had been secured in three-cornered fights. The most marked success was in terms of votes cast, more than 3.1 million, again the highest total since 1929. Yet, at another and more profound level, 1964 represented a considerable defeat, not least for Grimond himself. Labour's narrow overall victory by just five seats showed that the party had not become unelectable. In consequence it set back any prospect of a realignment of the British political left.

The outcome of the 1964 General Election deprived the Liberal party of the clear sense of political purpose which Grimond had developed over the previous parliament. As one member of the party executive put it:

Our trouble is simply that we need a strategy and don't have one. The party's principles aren't precise enough to tell us what to do without one, and without a strategy you're bound to get muddle. Why don't we have one? Because we were deprived of our traditional strategy by Labour's winning last autumn, and because the party hasn't been able to agree on a substitute. Most Liberals really have no very clear idea of where the party should go from here.[30]

The Conservatives were the obvious alternative for those who wanted Labour back in opposition, while the new government seemed determined to carry on without making obvious concessions to the Liberals. For a time, following the death of the Speaker and a by-election defeat at Leyton, it looked as if Labour would lose its parliamentary majority, necessitating some sort of arrangement with the Liberals. But Wilson cancelled out the numerical impact of the appointment of a Labour Speaker by tempting the Liberal Roderic Bowen to accept the Deputy Chairmanship of Ways and Means. Then, by avoiding such contentious legislation as the renationalisation of steel, which would have prompted defections from his own right wing, Wilson managed to soldier on.

Adopting a stance of constructive opposition, the parliamentary Liberal party determined to treat each government measure on its merits. By the end of May 1965, by which time they had been reinforced by the election of the youthful David Steel in a by-election in Roxburgh, Selkirk and Peebles, the Liberals had voted 40 times in the government lobby, opposed Labour on 85 occasions and abstained 3 times. Some of Labour's early initiatives, such as the creation of a Department of Economic Affairs under George Brown, separate from the Treasury, were in line with declared Liberal policy.[31] In general, however, Grimond found the new government insufficiently radical. On the other hand, he had no wish to force an early general election which might have seen the return of a Conservative administration.

Grimond's heart remained in the project of realignment and in early June 1965 he put out a first feeler in an article in the *Sun*. 'If you are living on a small majority,' he suggested, 'it is common sense either to approach the Liberals . . . with proposals for active co-operation, or at least to concentrate your proposals within a range where their support is likely.'[32] Grimond spelt out his views in more detail in an interview published in the *Guardian* on 24 June under the somewhat exaggerated headline 'Coalition offer to Labour by Mr Grimond'. A few right-wing Labour MPs including Woodrow Wyatt evinced interest in Grimond's initiative but in general its impact was more apparent among the parliamentary Liberal party than within Labour's ranks. As before, Grimond had to work with those figures whom the randomness of electoral fortune had returned to the Commons rather than with soul mates of his own choosing, and two recent parliamentary recruits, Emlyn Hooson, who had succeeded Clement Davies in Montgomeryshire on the latter's death in 1962, and Peter Bessell, newly elected in Bodmin, were among Grimond's sternest critics. By early August there were reports in the press of a right-wing revolt against the leadership.

Grimond found it difficult to follow the logic of his opponents. 'There is only one course open to the Liberal Party,' insisted Hooson. 'That is to soldier on in complete independence of any arrangement with Conservatives or Labour and press for policies in which we believe.'[33] In abstract terms there may have been something admirable in this sort of commitment to party political virginity. For a practical movement, however, interested in translating its ideals into concrete action and reality, it made little sense. The transition from a parliamentary party of ten to a governing majority in the House of Commons was likely to take the Liberal party, unaided, decades to achieve. Moreover, for a party which had been committed to electoral reform for more than a generation, it was almost a contradiction in terms to insist on maintaining the purity of Liberal doctrine, uncontaminated by association with any other party. Inter-party co-operation was likely to be both a prerequisite and a consequence of the introduction of a system of proportional representation. As Grimond later explained: 'If electoral reform led to the results for which Liberals hoped and which statistics foretold, that is the fifty to seventy MPs to which our vote entitled us, then if government was to be carried on, coalitions of some sort would often be essential.'[34] Recognising, however, that any formal approach to the Labour government would produce a serious split in the Liberal ranks, Grimond was obliged to proceed with care. Through the good offices of the editor of the *Guardian*, Alastair Hetherington, Grimond held a private meeting with Wilson in early August. Though the Prime Minister was friendly and suggested that the government's planned legislative programme would be acceptable to the Liberal party, he evinced no interest in a formal agreement. At the 1965 Liberal Assembly, Grimond spoke bravely of Liberal teeth being in the real meat of power, but his words lacked substance. By the winter of 1965–6 the concept of realignment was to all intents and purposes dead. This situation left Grimond depressed and there were rumours at the beginning of the new year of his imminent resignation. In the event, with Labour's stock rising and every likelihood that Wilson would seize his chance and seek a renewed mandate from the electorate, Grimond determined to lead his party into the next election. But his creative contribution to Liberalism was effectively at an end.

Like its predecessor, the General Election of 1966 was something of a curate's egg from the Liberal point of view. The party attempted to focus its resources on carefully targeted seats and, within a reduced total of 311 candidates, 87 constituencies contested in 1964 now had no Liberal standard-bearer. That said, in 33 seats the Liberals put up a candidate where none had stood two years before. Overall, the Liberal vote was bound to decline and it did so by almost 800,000, a fall of about 2.7 per cent in its share of the national vote. More disappointingly, the Liberal share of the poll fell in 278 of the constituencies also fought in 1964 and rose in only 29. On the credit side, the vagaries of third-party politics worked for once to the Liberals' advantage and its parliamentary representation rose to 12 MPs. The victories of Michael Winstanley in Cheadle and Richard Wainwright in Colne Valley suggested that Liberalism was at least breaking out of its Celtic redoubt. Even so, 10 of the party's 12 MPs survived on majorities of under 2,500 while in only eight constituencies was a beaten Liberal within 5000 votes of victory.

But the most striking feature of the results and the one which provided a symbolic conclusion to Grimond's period as party leader was the size of Labour's majority, which now stood at just under a hundred seats. Grimond still spoke of the creation of a radical new coalition, uniting in the first instance around the issue of British membership of the European Community but, as Hooson recognised, the election had 'definitely given Lib-Labory the axe once and for all'.[35] As the last remaining prospect of Labour's disintegration apparently receded, it was not long before Harold Wilson began to proclaim that his had become the natural governing party of British politics. The position of the Liberal party, by contrast, seemed altogether less secure. Grimond's decade at its head had served to reveal a yawning gap between the Liberal voter and the vision with which the leader had enthused at least some of the party hierarchy. 'That we do better when a Tory government is in office', Grimond later admitted, 'indicates that to some extent we are a haven for loosely attached Tories, disappointed in their government.'[36] Though written shortly after the events described, the verdict of the Nuffield historians merits repetition:

> Labour's comfortable victory in 1966 meant that the Liberals, although both their voting strength and their parliamentary representation had increased since Mr. Grimond became leader, had made no real strategic advance. In the weeks after polling day in 1966 it was no clearer than it had been ten years before how the Liberals were going either to form a new radical coalition with elements from both the Conservative and Labour parties, or to supplant Labour as the chief opposition to the Conservatives . . . to the extent that an opportunity existed [between 1964 and 1966], the Liberals failed to seize it.[37]

In January 1967 Grimond resigned as Liberal leader. He was still only 53 years of age and it is difficult to escape the conclusion that, after just over a decade in the post, he felt that he had achieved all that he could. Though his electoral strategy had disintegrated in the face of Labour's victories in 1964 and 1966, his legacy remained important and would be revived at a later date. Grimond had forced his party at least to consider its relations with other parties not, as in the immediate post-war era, as a means of political survival, but in terms of bringing Liberals closer to government. In this sense he 'paved the way for inter-party co-operation that ultimately led to the formation of the Liberal Democrats in 1988'.[38] Two months after Grimond's resignation, Lord Rea, the Liberal leader in the Lords, also stood down, in his case on grounds of ill health. Rea's career had paralleled Grimond's, having taken over from Lord Samuel in 1955. His replacement was Frank Byers, ennobled in 1964. The latter's appointment offered some prospect that Liberal peers would be organised into a professional political force for the first time for several decades. When Violet Bonham Carter had been belatedly elevated to the upper house in 1964, she had asked Rea how regularly the contingent of Liberal peers met, only to be told that they never did. By December 1968 *The Times* diary columnist offered a cautious tribute to what Byers had managed to achieve: 'Starved of new creations by the Conservatives, the Liberal Lords were an ill-organised band before Byers arrived. By common consent he does a good job leading what is still an awkward crew.'[39] Meanwhile, in the Commons no obvious successor to Grimond stood out, but in a vote of the 12 MPs Jeremy Thorpe secured the support of half the parliamentary party, after which his two rivals, Emlyn Hooson and Eric Lubbock, withdrew. Though some senior figures doubted whether Thorpe possessed the necessary attributes of intellect and judgement, the general consensus was that the party had made the best choice from the available talent.

Thorpe's career is now so coloured by the way in which it ultimately collapsed and by the charges and allegations from which his reputation has never fully recovered, that it remains difficult to assess his nine years at the head of the Liberal party with appropriate objectivity. Most of the writing about him ranges from the realm of 'investigative journalism' to that of the merely sensational and salacious. His own volume of dilettante reminiscences offers few insights. With hindsight his leadership, sandwiched as it was between the clearer, more creative, visions of Jo Grimond and David Steel, emerges as a period in which, notwithstanding some considerable electoral successes, the party drifted without a sense of conviction or underlying purpose. Instead, new Liberal revivals fed off Thorpe's very real but somewhat superficial qualities – his 'enormous flair, charisma, showmanship and boundless energy'.[40] He was effective as a communicator, an organiser and a fund-raiser. Interviewed by the *Observer* in 1973 he claimed that, Grimond having given the party *intellectual* credibility, his task was to give it *political* credibility. More cynically, it might be suggested that the Thorpe era would be dominated by tactics rather than ideas.

In the late 1960s the party seemed to be unsure how to present itself. Its projected image ranged from that of the radical alternative to two essentially conservative parties – 'which twin is the Tory?' asked one effective piece of Liberal propaganda – to that of a moderate force between two ideological extremes. In the public mind it was the latter image which predominated. Liberals were seen as pleasant, middle-of-the-road and reasonable, but without the radical cutting edge for which Grimond had striven. One opinion poll taken in 1968 suggested that as many as 52 per cent of the population might vote Liberal if they believed that the party had a genuine prospect of success. Such statistics fostered a simplistic belief that only a modest hurdle of electoral credibility lay between the Liberal party and the prospect of government. In practice, Liberalism had become a temporary port of call for the increasing number of those who wished to register a protest vote against the governmental failures of Conservatives and Labour alike.

The early years of Thorpe's leadership were dominated by financial crisis. Once the high tide of the Grimond revival had passed, the party found itself dangerously overstretched. It was a problem to which Thorpe, who had partly established his reputation though his success as Party Treasurer, responded with energy and imagination. A number of fund-raising schemes were mounted, of which the most famous was the 'Liberal Million

Fund' campaign launched in 1967. A number of economies were also necessary and in 1968 party headquarters were transferred from Smith Square in Westminster to a cheaper but less convenient location off the Strand with a resulting 50 per cent saving in rent. Even so, Liberal finances were still in a parlous state on the eve of the 1970 General Election. One consequence of this was a decline in the number of constituencies able to afford a full-time agent. The figure fell to just 17 in April 1969. Yet in seats which the Liberals held, their organisation and the size of their local party membership stood comparison with the best of those of their opponents. Liberals had, of necessity, learnt the importance of nursing their constituencies

Public opinion polls suggested that the level of Liberal support remained reasonably steady at between 7 and 11 per cent, but the electoral history of these years offered little cause for optimism. The local government revival of the early 1960s was not sustained. It was the Conservatives who were the major beneficiaries of an unpopular Labour government. But one particularly worrying feature of this period was the growth of Welsh and particularly Scottish nationalism. The long-standing Liberal policy of Welsh and Scottish assemblies was in danger of being outflanked by the more strident demands of Plaid Cymru and the SNP. At the 1967 Liberal Assembly, Ludovic Kennedy and Michael Starforth pressed the case for an electoral pact with the Scottish Nationalists. However, other leading Scottish Liberals, including Russell Johnston, the MP for Inverness, were opposed, and in any case informal approaches to the SNP by the remaining MPs with Scottish seats, Grimond, Steel, James Davidson and Alasdair Mackenzie, proved unsuccessful. Liberal deposits were lost in 12 of the 28 by-elections contested during the 1966 parliament. Only the surprise victory of Councillor Wallace Lawler in June 1969 in Birmingham, Ladywood bucked the trend. In some ways this was an astonishing victory. The swing from Labour to Liberal was a staggering 32 per cent. There was, after all, no real Liberal tradition in the city. Even in the Liberal landslide of 1906 Birmingham had remained solidly Conservative/Unionist. Lawler's victory in this small and much depopulated constituency was in fact the product of grass-roots politics, with local activists led by Lawler himself patiently building up a well-cultivated local base. At one level the result seemed to suggest that no area was closed to the party, providing its workers were prepared to roll up their sleeves and engage with the local community. At the same time, the new MP was recognised as being unique, a Lawlerite rather than a Liberal, and the views attributed to him on some issues, including immigration, threatened to embarrass his colleagues at Westminster. Arguably, the capture of the Ladywood seat had little to do with the fortunes of the national party.

Thorpe, who never enjoyed the sort of whole-hearted commitment offered to Grimond by the party hierarchy, survived a serious effort to remove him from the leadership in June 1968, launched while he himself was absent on his honeymoon. Only months after he became leader, a series of articles in *New Outlook* had criticised his failure to confront those issues which would win support for the Liberals at the next election. Thorpe was overwhelmingly re-endorsed by a meeting of the party executive but, as a sop to his critics, he accepted a call for an element of 'collective leadership' to shape decisions. A commission was set up to convert the party's principles into a coherent programme for the next general election. But the timing of that election was inevitably a function of the fortunes of the Labour government. After three years of carefully and often painfully rebuilding the national economy following the devaluation of 1967, Labour finally saw the opinion polls beginning to move in its favour and Wilson sought to capitalise on this recovery by going to the country in June 1970.

The Liberals seemed to have little new to offer. Their policies on immigration, the powers of the police and government secrecy were distinctive, but not necessarily vote winners on any significant scale. The traditional appeal for Welsh and Scottish self-government was now being articulated with greater vigour by the Nationalists. Likewise, both Labour and the Conservatives had become converted to the virtues of British membership of the European Community. The election was focused on the state of the economy and here the choice seemed to lie between a continuation of Chancellor Roy Jenkins's Keynesian-style stewardship and the apparent return of the Conservatives, particularly following a celebrated meeting of the shadow cabinet at Selsdon Park in January, to a more market-orientated alternative. For the first time for several elections the Liberals seemed less 'relevant' and, as a consequence, the party attracted less notice from either its opponents or the media. As even the Chief Whip later conceded, 'we had no very clear message, except the assumption of innate virtue and superiority in a host of Liberal policies'.[41]

Finance remained a serious problem. By mid-May only 286 prospective candidates were in place. Only when Thorpe announced a sudden windfall of donations to party funds, later attributed by *The Times* largely to the beneficence of the multimillionaire businessman Jack Hayward, did this rise to 332. Within this total, about three dozen seats were designated as 'winnable' and benefited from extra injections of cash and effort. The majority of candidates, however, lacked the funds needed to carry out a comprehensive canvass of their constituencies or to hold large, indoor meetings.

Thorpe himself emerged as an accomplished electioneer. With television playing a greater role in the campaign than ever before, his flair for showmanship and his ability to take advantage of any available 'photo-opportunity' won much praise. He was able to criticise both of the main parties for the way in which they had ruined the British economy and, like so many of his predecessors, insisted that a Liberal revival was just over the horizon. In reality, the party entertained few serious hopes of an improvement in its electoral fortunes. Even so, the actual result was worse than expected. Seven of the thirteen Liberal seats were lost, including Lawler's recent gain in Ladywood. A few hundred votes had saved the seats of three further MPs, including Thorpe himself. Only Grimond in Orkney and Shetland, and Hooson in Montgomery enjoyed anything approaching comfortable majorities. For the first time in the party's history there was no Liberal representation outside Scotland, Wales and the West Country. The party's share of the total vote declined from 8.5 per cent in 1966 to 7.5 per cent.

The average constituency vote fell from 16.1 per cent to 13.5 per cent. In Scotland and Wales it was clear that the Nationalists had been particularly successful in attracting former Liberal voters. As many as 182 deposits were lost. The one redeeming feature was the way in which the national trend had been bucked in a handful of seats such as Rochdale, Southport and Liverpool, Wavertree where a well-regarded, incumbent Liberal councillor had secured an increased Liberal vote, testimony it seemed to the readiness of the electorate to repay patient hard work carried out at a municipal level. Otherwise, there were eerie parallels to be drawn between the 1970 result and those of the early 1950s. It was as if the progress made under Grimond had been entirely in vain.

This disappointing outcome inevitably stirred active Liberals at all levels into an agonising reappraisal of the party's strategy and organisation. Fleetingly, some again questioned whether any purpose remained in trying to sustain an independent Liberal identity. It was in such an atmosphere of gloomy introspection that, at the autumn Assembly, the party accepted a resolution put forward by the Young Liberals that it should now focus its campaigning at a community level. The party became committed 'to help organise people in their communities to take and use power . . . to build a Liberal power-base in the major cities of the country . . . to capture people's imagination as a credible political movement, with local roots and local successes'. This proved to be an important movement in the evolution of modern Liberalism and both the new strategy and its proposers merit closer attention.

At one level the adoption of the community politics resolution was the logical culmination of a strategy initiated by the party hierarchy during the Grimond era. Back in 1960 the Local Government Department had been set up under the direction of Richard Wainwright with the purpose, after a generation of neglect, of encouraging Liberals to participate in local government elections. The reasoning was simple enough. As Mark Bonham Carter put it, 'it is easier to change voting habits at local elections than at by-elections and at by-elections than at general elections'.[42] Significant gains at the parliamentary level would be more likely to occur once the party had established a solid foundation in local politics. Thus, suggested Grimond, 'every time a local Liberal councillor gets a bus stop moved to a better place he strikes a blow for the Liberal party'.[43] It was, in other words, a simple technique to strengthen the party's power base and the following decade had afforded some evidence of its success. Figures such as Lawler in Birmingham, and Cyril Carr and Trevor Jones in Liverpool had begun the process of cutting into rock-solid Labour heartlands on the basis of associating the Liberal party with a practical concern for the everyday needs and interests of the working-class voter. For the most part these advances seemed to be at odds with the party's scattered successes in by-elections and general elections over the same period, where it was in comfortable suburbia and at the expense of the Conservatives that victories such as that in Orpington had been achieved. But Lawler's triumph in Ladywood in 1969, though not repeated in the general election a year later, appeared to open new doors. Party workers in Ladywood were struck by the way in which voters pledged their support to the Liberal candidate on the basis of services he had already rendered to them as their local councillor. Within a few years the new approach achieved its most spectacular success in Liverpool, like Birmingham a city with no significant Liberal tradition over the previous half century. As late as May 1968, when the anti-Labour tide was at its height, the Liberals held just one council seat as against 34 Labour and 79 Conservatives. Yet by 1973 the Liberals had become the largest single party on the Liverpool City Council.

The community politics strategy was not without its problems. Though it offered genuine and active representation to the benefit of the local community, its links with Liberalism as a national political force were often tenuous. Recognising that a Liberal councillor could be helpful in solving a domestic problem did not necessarily convince a voter that the national party was an equally appropriate body for resolving an altogether different set of problems. While the planned scenario was clear enough – that a strong cohort of local councillors would form the basis for a later advance at a general election – the danger existed that electors would develop the habit of differential voting, supporting Liberals for the local council, but reverting to traditional Labour or Conservative loyalties when it was a question of choosing a new government for the country. To an extent, this clearly happened. In Liverpool, for example, the Liberal party never achieved a breakthrough in parliamentary seats comparable to its strength in the city's municipal politics even when, as in 1979, local and national elections were held on the same day. Furthermore, the peculiarities of local situations inevitably encouraged a tendency for Liberals to adjust their politics to suit the requirements of a given area, a trend which enabled critics to claim that, while the party might have a 'policy for every street corner', it lacked a consistent attitude to the great issues of national politics.

Most seriously, by 1970 the concept of community politics was no longer the preserve of the mainstream party but had been appropriated, some might have said hijacked, by the party's youth movement, the National League of Young Liberals and the Union of Liberal Students. Indeed, the actual term 'community politics' appears to have been coined by two prominent Young Liberals, Gordon Lishman and Lawrie Freedman, at a strategy meeting early in 1969. The entry of enthusiastic and committed students and other young people into the Liberal ranks, first noted by Clement Davies in the early 1950s, had been an important factor in the party's subsequent revival. Many had been attracted by the campaigning style and patent integrity of Jo Grimond. But wider forces were at work. For others, in the context of the rapid social changes of the 1960s, the Liberals offered the most appropriate political vehicle for the expression and achievement of their aims, whether or not these were in line with official party policy. The Young Liberals became particularly prominent when disillusionment set in over the failure of Wilson's Labour government to satisfy those radical and idealistic aspirations which many had entrusted to it. They became closely associated with a series of international issues of which opposition to the Vietnam War and condemnation of the apartheid regime in South Africa enjoyed the highest public profile.

The concept of 'direct action' was put forward to compensate for the failures of conventional politics. Though the levels of disorder in Britain never reached the scale seen in the university campuses of continental Europe and the United States, the Young Liberals were widely regarded, particularly in sections of the press, as part of a wider youth movement challenging the existing assumptions of British society. As such, they posed rather more problems to the Liberal leadership than they offered advantages, for while the label 'radical' was one which, whatever their understanding of it, most prominent Liberals were happy to wear, that of 'revolutionary' was a different matter. At the 1966 Brighton Assembly, the Youth Movement's so-called 'Red Guards' did little to enhance the party's broader appeal. They pressed the case for the withdrawal of American troops from Vietnam, for British withdrawal from NATO, for a stance of non-alignment in the Cold War and for active support to be given to the anti-apartheid movement. In 1969–70 the activities of Young Liberals led by Peter Hain in trying to stop a tour by the all-white South African cricket team were not likely to enthuse the sort of 'respectable' ex-Conservative voter whom the party had been particularly successful in attracting to its cause. Not surprisingly, much effort was expended in the late 1960s in trying to curb the excesses of the Young Liberals, a process which culminated in January 1970 in a formal request to them by the party's National Executive to dismiss their chairman, Louis Eaks. In such hands the concept of community politics became much more than just a means of winning local elections or even a longer-term political strategy to increase the Liberal party's representation at Westminster. It was seen as a form of participatory politics which, freed from the stultifying embrace of centralised bureaucracies, could begin a process of social transformation at the grass-roots of British political life. In these differing conceptions an important conflict was introduced into Liberal politics. 'Jeremy Thorpe always equated [community politics] with being a good constituency MP,' recalled one activist, 'rather than with a radical platform for change.'[44]

That, however, was for the future. In the shorter term Thorpe's Liberal party had to cope with the obvious setback occasioned by the General Election of 1970. For the first two years of the new parliament the Liberals performed indifferently in by-elections, most local elections and in national opinion polls. In the background lay disturbing rumours about the party leader's private life, although an internal enquiry chaired by Lord Byers in 1971 dismissed as without foundation the accusations made by the stable-hand and male model, Norman Scott, of a homosexual affair in the early 1960s. Yet, as before, events over which the Liberals had little control conspired to work in their favour. The 1970 election had, against the expectations and predictions of most commentators and opinion polls, seen the return of a Conservative government and, as recent history had confirmed, the Liberals were more likely to benefit from protest votes registered against an unpopular Tory administration than would be the case with an equally unpopular Labour one. With clear evidence that Labour in opposition was moving distinctly leftwards, the propensity of disgruntled Conservatives to switch to the Liberals rather than the main opposition party was likely to be particularly marked.

The government's unpopularity was not long in coming. Considerable controversy has developed over the extent to which Edward Heath's Conservative party set out consciously to break away from the post-war consensus. Certainly, Heath himself entered Downing Street pledged to 'change the course of history of this nation, nothing less' and, in its rhetoric at least, the new government seemed determined to give the country policies that were fundamentally different from any seen since 1945. Whatever the intention, the outcome was disappointing. Notwithstanding apparently careful preparation during the years of opposition, most of Heath's policies went badly wrong. All the key economic indicators continued to move in an unfavourable direction. Despite the attempt to introduce a new legal framework through the Industrial Relations Act of 1971, industrial relations had never been worse in the whole post-war era and the government suffered a humiliating defeat at the hands of the miners in 1972. Heath was particularly shaken when unemployment reached the politically sensitive total of one million early that year. By that stage, however, a massive U-turn was already under way, a process which led to the nationalisation of ailing industries such as Rolls-Royce and Upper Clyde Shipbuilders, the passing of a highly interventionist Industry Bill and the adoption, in direct contravention of the party's 1970 manifesto, of a formal incomes policy.

It was not long before the Liberal party began to feel the benefits of the government's travails. By good fortune in October 1972 a by-election arose in the Lancashire town of Rochdale, one of the few seats in the country where Liberals stood as the main challenger to the Labour party. Benefiting from a popular local candidate in Cyril Smith, and squeezing the third-placed Conservative vote, the Liberals secured a striking victory with a majority of more than 5000. Six weeks later the solid Conservative seat of Sutton and Cheam fell to the Liberals on a turnover of votes greater even than that at Orpington a decade before. The victor, Graham Tope, had entered Liberal politics inspired by the radicalism of the Young Liberals and as an advocate of community politics. The campaign was dominated by local issues such as concessionary travel for the elderly and plans for comprehensive schooling, and for much of the time it was the Liverpudlian Trevor Jones, bringing with him his celebrated *Focus* newsletter, rather than national party headquarters, who made the running. Strikingly, a later opinion poll showed that the majority of defecting Tories opposed the successful Liberal candidate on issues such as Europe and immigration. None the less, the fact that the Liberal party lost its deposit in the not dissimilar and neighbouring constituency of Uxbridge in a by-election held on the same day forced even the most reluctant of traditional Liberals to take the new style of campaigning seriously.

The party's national rating now began to rise and, by August of the following year, had reached 20 per cent. In the meantime there were spectacular advances in the 1973 local elections where Liberals won over 900 seats, easily their best performance since before the Second World War. Victories in parliamentary by-elections in the Isle of Ely and Ripon that July seemed to place a question mark over the safety of every Conservative seat in the land. Dick Taverne's resignation as Labour MP for Lincoln, after a lengthy dispute with his constituency party, and his subsequent victory as a Democratic Labour candidate at a by-election in March 1973 at which Liberals offered unofficial support, seemed to confirm that the electorate was anxious to vote for a new party of the moderate centre ground. Elsewhere the Liberals successfully presented themselves in this guise. In all the by-elections held during 1973 the Liberals won a larger total number of votes than either Labour or the Conservatives. This was an upsurge in the party's fortunes which far outstripped those which had surrounded Torrington or Orpington. It was in fact the best Liberal performance since the Lloyd George-inspired revival of the late 1920s.

By now, and despite on-going financial worries, the party was becoming a more professional campaigning force than ever before. Its ability to mobilise its resources in by-elections offered the most convincing evidence of the transformation. But it was also a wiser party, less inclined to be carried away by its own successes than in the heady days of the earlier false dawns of the Grimond era. As a result, many believed that the tide of Liberal advance would follow a now-established pattern and ebb once again with the approach of the next general election. Indeed, though the party recaptured Beveridge's old seat of Berwick-upon-Tweed in November 1973, the swing against the government was less marked than of late, while the Liberals' national poll ratings were again drifting downwards. On the other hand, other factors suggested that the improvement in the party's fortunes might prove more durable. The most important long-term trend in the electoral history of the 1960s and 1970s was a clear process of dealignment. At the General Election of 1951 as many as 96.8 per cent of all votes cast had gone to the Conservative and Labour parties. By 1964 this figure had gone down to 87.5 per cent and at the General Election of October 1974 it would fall again to just 75.1 per cent. Put another way, back in 1951 just one voter in thirty had supported the minor parties, but by October 1974 it was as many as one in four.[45] This movement was in part the result of the beginnings of a breakdown in the pattern of class voting which had dominated British politics since the First World

War. In a more fluid social structure than had ever existed before, the working-class voter was becoming a less reliable adherent of the Labour party, while the support of his middle-class counterpart could no longer be counted upon by the Conservatives. By the mid-1970s, moreover, the mood of post-war optimism was at an end. As Britain's economic and social problems mounted and as solutions to them appeared ever more illusory, it was even said that Britain was becoming ungovernable. The faith of the electorate in party politics in general inevitably waned and the Liberals, as the least party-like of the three main parties and the only one without a sullied record in government to explain or defend, were an inevitable beneficiary. Ironically, the most optimistic of political creeds picked up support in a mood of mounting pessimism. While Liberals continued to attract votes despite, as much as because of, what they stood for, issues of constitutional reform and a new British identity inside Europe did strike a chord among those who saw the only salvation for a declining Britain lying in radical departures in public policy.

In the event, the general election came earlier than expected. Confronted by a second major strike in the coalmines and tempted into an appeal around the theme of 'Who Governs Britain?', Heath went to the country in February 1974. With as many as 517 candidates in the field, the Liberals posed a serious national challenge for the first time in half a century. The key features in the party manifesto were decentralisation and devolution, industrial partnership, a guaranteed minimum income and a fairer distribution of national wealth. *Change the Face of Britain* stressed that the immediate crisis over the miners' strike was only the culmination of a long process of decline in Britain's ability to manage its affairs 'efficiently and with tolerable sanity'. It was now time to set aside sterile class-conflict and to question any new initiative on the basis of whether or not it would narrow the gulf between classes and reduce conflict. Overall, image was far more important than detailed policy. Though it conflicted with on-going aspirations to 'radicalism', Thorpe successfully presented the party as one of the moderate centre, a ground that had been deserted by the increasingly extremist Labour and Conservatives.

The adversarial circumstances of the election might, in an earlier era, have sent voters scurrying back to traditional patterns of class loyalty, but with a growing number of voters reaching the conclusion that both the main parties had now been tried and found wanting, support for the Liberal stance of sweet reasonableness grew as the campaign progressed. One poll suggested that 40 per cent of voters would back the Liberals if the party had a chance of holding the balance of power and a massive 48 per cent if it was believed capable of forming the next government.

Thorpe himself ran an effective campaign even though, aware of the fragility of his 1970 majority, he hardly moved out of his own constituency. There was a freshness about him in contrast with the rather shop-soiled image of both Heath and Wilson, upon which he capitalised as he sought photographic attention – leaping over fences in his tours of his constituency. A television link between Thorpe's Barnstaple headquarters and the National Liberal Club in London enabled him to conduct the party's daily press conference. Because of the number of candidates fielded the party enjoyed a greater television exposure than ever before. In contrast to what had happened in both 1966 and 1970 the level of Liberal support held up remarkably well, at least until the final days of the campaign. On 25 February Thorpe declared that the party's primary intention was to form a government. If this proved not to be possible, he was ready to work with 'any person of moderate and progressive views to get this country back on the rails'. At last, Liberals seemed to have buried the bogey that a vote for them was a wasted vote and, with apparent justification, the closing stages of the campaign saw the adoption of the slogan 'If you want a Liberal Government you can have one'. More soberly, Liberal headquarters were confidently thinking in terms of winning 50 seats.

The election results showed that the expected breakthrough had still not been secured. With a poll in excess of 6 million, more than 19 per cent of the total votes cast, the party had only 14 MPs elected. Territorially, no new ground had been taken, apart from a gain in the Isle of Wight, largely attributable to local circumstances. Liberal strategists had greatly underestimated the extent to which the first-past-the-post electoral system worked against them. With no Liberal heartlands comparable to those enjoyed by its rivals, the party needed to poll well over 30 per cent nationally before it would see a significant difference in the number of seats won. If any Liberals had not understood the merits of proportional representation hitherto, the case was vividly made for them in February 1974. It had taken 432,000 votes to elect each Liberal MP, but just 40,000 and 39,000 respectively for each Conservative and Labour counterpart.

On the credit side the party had polled respectably throughout the country. In England only four deposits were lost. Though the party appeared to have taken votes from both its opponents, the Liberal challenge was slanted overwhelmingly against the Conservatives. Of the hundred losing Liberals with the highest percentage votes, only two had been defeated by a Labour opponent. But there were disappointing features too. The failure to win target seats in places such as Liverpool, where the party had been successfully building up its council base, raised question-marks over the appropriateness of community politics as a strategy for a national political party. And the nationalist challenge had not been contained. The SNP was now the third party in Scotland while Plaid Cymru's total of two seats matched that of the Welsh Liberals.

But if the overall result offered both comfort and disappointment to the Liberal party, neither Labour nor the Conservatives had real cause for satisfaction. With 200,000 more votes than Labour, the Conservatives had four fewer MPs; with only 301 MPs, Labour was 17 short of an overall majority. In this situation Heath did not immediately tender his resignation but, arguing that over Europe and the key question of an incomes policy the Conservatives and Liberals were in fundamental agreement, sought talks with Thorpe to see whether any basis existed for a deal. Despite the outcry which came from within the Liberal ranks, Thorpe's readiness at least to explore the situation was reasonable enough. As a minority of the parliamentary party pointed out, it made no sense for a party which espoused the cause of proportional representation not to be willing, in principle, to work with others. Moreover, Thorpe had already declared that, in the event of the Liberals holding the balance, he would be ready to co-operate with the forces of moderation in other parties. On the other hand, Thorpe's willingness to respond to Heath's overture was almost bound to excite a hostile reaction. Over the weekend following the election, complaints poured into party headquarters from activists throughout the country. The former chairman of the Young Liberals, Peter Hain, warned of mass resignations from the party in the event of any deal with the Conservatives. The Liberals did not in fact hold the balance in the new parliament and it would have needed an additional agreement with another minority group such as the Ulster Unionists to provide Heath with a Commons majority. More importantly, most Liberal activists interpreted their party's huge vote as one directed primarily against the failure of the Heath government to cope with the country's deteriorating economic and industrial condition and were not now keen to be seen propping up Heath's efforts to stay in office. Thorpe aggravated the situation by accepting the Prime Minister's invitation to talk without first seeking the views of his senior colleagues. As David Steel recalled, 'Neither I as Chief Whip, number two in the parliamentary hierarchy, or anyone else had been consulted. I was confused and irritated.'[46]

It seems that Heath was willing to offer Thorpe a seat in his cabinet together with junior office for some of his colleagues, but the issue of proportional representation proved to be the sticking point. Though Thorpe was clearly interested in Heath's suggestions, and hopeful that he could secure the Home Office for himself, electoral reform was understandably a *sine qua non*, especially in the light of the recent electoral outcome. Heath was ready to concede a Speaker's Conference on the subject, but remained personally uncommitted and would not pledge the government to abide by the outcome of such an investigation. In this way the negotiations were brought to a speedy end and Harold Wilson took office at the head of a minority Labour administration.

With hindsight, it is clear that Thorpe's career as Liberal leader had now peaked. The impression that he had been keen on a deal with the Conservatives undermined his position and opened up a rift with the majority of party activists. It was inevitable that another general election would be held before long with Wilson, as in 1966, seizing the first perceived opportunity to try to secure a working parliamentary majority. Liberals spent the intervening months arguing about whether their aim should be to boost their parliamentary representation and then strive for electoral reform within a coalition government or stick to the long haul of working towards a Liberal government. Thorpe himself stressed that the Liberals needed to project themselves as a national party if they were to secure a national following. His campaign received a boost when the Labour MP and former minister, Christopher Mayhew, defected to the party in July. Against accusations of treachery from Young Liberals, Thorpe succeeded in persuading the party assembly in September that the option of Liberal participation in a coalition, after proper consultation with the party, should not be closed off.

The anticipated election duly came in October. The party made great efforts to put 619 candidates into the field. Every seat in England and Wales, except Lincoln, was contested, as were all but a handful north of the border. In policy terms the Liberals offered the country much of what they had put forward in February, but the emphasis now was on transforming the nature of the party political conflict by increasing the number of Liberal MPs. A strong Liberal representation would 'break up the confrontation of the two class parties and create the conditions for a broad based radical alliance led by Liberals'. By adopting the phrase 'one more heave', the party tried to encourage the belief that its ambitions were eminently realisable. In practice, however, the task of retaining the fickle support which had been attracted in February, while at the same time persuading another substantial tranche of voters to desert their traditional homes, was enormous. Even an extra five per cent of the total vote, evenly distributed across the country, would only have produced six extra MPs. As it was, something of the Thorpe electoral magic seemed to have disappeared. He had always straddled an uncomfortable divide between the accomplished professional politician and the amiable clown. Now he appeared to get the balance wrong. A hovercraft tour of the West Country was noted more for its attendant mishaps than for any political message which the leader conveyed. A second tour by helicopter of Conservative marginals again smacked of gimmickry. Liberals were unable to make further inroads, despite ample evidence of continuing dissatisfaction with both the major parties. Opinion polls suggested that about half the electorate judged Labour's performance in government to be poor, while less than a third were sure that the Conservatives could do better. The election was, as the Nuffield historians described it, something of an 'unpopularity contest'.[47]

The result made only a marginal difference to the national political scene. Labour secured its overall parliamentary majority, but it was a majority of just three seats. The Liberals made one gain in Truro, but both Hazel Grove and Bodmin fell to the Conservatives. Since February, the total Liberal vote had fallen from over six million (19.3 per cent) to 5.3 million (18.3 per cent). In fact, the party's decline was more marked than these figures implied. With 102 more candidates in the field than in February, the average vote per candidate had dropped quite sharply. In those seats fought on both occasions, the total Liberal vote fell by more than a million. The results in Scotland, where the SNP captured 11 seats, were particularly disappointing, despite the fact that the Liberals had promised a Scottish parliament elected by proportional representation which would have enjoyed control over 50 per cent of the revenue derived from North Sea oil. With Labour holding on to office with just 39.2 per cent of the vote on a low turn-out of 72.8 per cent, Liberals could not be other than disheartened. The party still lacked a political identity, apart from simply being neither Labour nor Conservative. Surveys showed that the party's policies were the least known or understood and that the proportion of Liberal voters feeling a commitment to the party was much lower than in the other parties.[48]

After seven years in office these failures were in part an indictment of the leader, Jeremy Thorpe. His enemies tended to blame the party's relatively poor performance on discussions before the election of the possibility of a coalition. More seriously, Thorpe had subordinated the creation of a clear sense of direction to the chimera of short-term political advantage. It was striking that polling evidence suggested that Liberal voters were fairly evenly divided as to whether the Labour or Conservative party would be their second choice in the event that no Liberal candidate was available to them. The party spent the following year campaigning for devolution and electoral reform, a natural reaction to the enormous disparity between the Liberals' popular vote in 1974 and their meagre return of MPs. Despite murmurings among Young Liberals and other activists, Thorpe secured the unanimous backing of his parliamentary colleagues at the 1975 Assembly. He appeared confident that he could ride out this storm as he had others in the past. Criticism of his handling of the 1970 campaign had been stifled amidst the welter of sympathy which surrounded him following his first wife's death in a road accident. Over the following 18 months he had been involved in an increasingly acrimonious and sometimes public wrangle with the Liberal Treasurer, Sir Frank Medlicott, when the latter had the temerity to question his autocratic and sometimes bizarre handling of the party's funds. In 1973 more general doubts emerged about Thorpe's financial judgement as a result of his involvement as a non-executive director of the ill-fated London and County Securities.

At the back of everything, however, lay the ticking bomb of Norman Scott, whom Thorpe had befriended in the early 1960s and to whom Peter Bessell, Liberal MP for Bodmin from 1964 to 1970, had made a number of payments since 1966. By the mid-1970s it was becoming increasingly difficult to keep the lid on Scott's allegations and, it was later alleged, in 1975 figures close to Thorpe went to the length of staging a bungled attempt to kill the leader's troublesome tormentor. Appearing in court in January 1976, charged with defrauding the DHSS, Scott used the privilege of the courtroom to publicise his accusations against Thorpe. The following month Richard Wainwright, MP for Colne Valley, learnt from Bessell the story of the latter's involvement in the Scott affair and began a discreet campaign for Thorpe's resignation. In a desperate attempt to pre-empt any sensational disclosures by Bessell, Thorpe allowed letters he had sent to Scott to be published in the *Sunday Times*. Though these contained no conclusive confirmation of a homosexual affair, they did open Thorpe up to ridicule and their publication ended any last hope he may have had of clinging on to the party leadership. On 9 May 1976 he resigned. Notwithstanding widespread regret that Thorpe's career should end in such an ignominious fashion, most Liberals breathed a sigh of relief. By-elections in March and local government elections in May suggested a significant fall in the party's support. It was time for a fresh beginning.

At a moment of evident crisis, Liberals turned, understandably enough, to the reassuring figure of Jo Grimond, who agreed to resume the leadership on a temporary basis. Such was his standing across the party spectrum that he could, almost certainly, have taken charge in the longer term had he so wished. He was, after all, only 63 years old. But a second sustained period with Grimond at the helm might have taken the party in an altogether different direction from that explored in the early 1960s. As he watched the economic mismanagement of the Labour government, Grimond was now coming to question his earlier confidence in the beneficent effects of state intervention and to toy once more with classical economic liberalism at just the time that this doctrine was making inroads into the Conservative party of Margaret Thatcher and Sir Keith Joseph. As it was, Grimond stayed in charge long enough to restore the party's self-confidence and to hand over to David Steel, a comfortable victor over John Pardoe in the first leadership contest, of the Liberals or for that matter any major British party, determined by the wishes of the wider party membership.

Though only 38 at his assumption of the leadership, Steel had already been an MP for 11 years. That period had been critical in shaping his political vision of the future of the Liberal party. An unequivocal disciple of Grimond, he believed like his mentor that the way forward lay in a realignment of the left in British politics. By now, moreover, the internal tensions within the Labour party, particularly following Wilson's decision to hold a referendum on Britain's continuing membership of the European Community, had become far more acute than had been the case when

Grimond had waited in vain for Labour to fragment. 'Many of the self-styled social democrats', Steel wrote towards the end of 1975, 'would be in happier company in combination with Liberals than Socialists.' If the opportunity for realignment arose, it was important that Liberals should be ready to join with others for the more effective promotion of liberalism and not behave 'like a more rigid sect of the exclusive brethren'.[49] Strikingly, he once confessed that, if Gaitskell had succeeded in shaping the Labour party entirely in his own image, the need for and relevance of a separate Liberal party would largely have disappeared.[50] This near equation of Gaitskellite social democracy with his own conception of Liberalism deserved to be more closely noted than it was.

Steel's experience in parliament had shown that positive achievements were not the preserve of action on strictly party lines. He had risen to national prominence in sponsoring a reform of the law on abortion and, in guiding his private member's bill towards the statute book in 1967, had relied heavily on the support of like-minded members in other parties, not least Labour's Home Secretary, Roy Jenkins. Similarly, over Kenyan Asian immigration, opposition to apartheid, campaigning for the homeless and, most recently, arguing for a 'yes' vote in the European referendum, Steel had operated 'more as a Liberal working with others outside the Liberal Party than within it to advance Liberal causes'.[51] In 1968 he and a group of like-minded Liberals had formed the Radical Action Movement, designed to bring together the progressive forces in British public life, whether or not they were individually members of the Liberal party. Though short-lived, it was indicative of his thinking at the time. The electoral setback of 1970 had convinced Steel of the pitfalls, the futility indeed, of the long-haul approach to Liberal revival. It was impossible for the party to 'plod on as before, spending the next ten years building back up to a dozen MPs only to face near annihilation again on a sudden swing of the pendulum'.[52] He regarded the hung parliament of 1974 as a missed opportunity and, though he did not believe that a Conservative–Liberal coalition could or should have been formed that February, the ferocity of the party's reaction to the mere exploration of a possible agreement with

Heath convinced him that the issue of coalition government had got to be addressed head-on: by 'simply pretending to be an alternative government in exile we would continue to fail'.[53] While Thorpe negotiated with Heath, Steel made tentative contacts with Roy Jenkins to see whether there might be any possibility of a Lib–Lab agreement.

In seeking the Liberal leadership in 1976, Steel made no effort to conceal his thoughts as to the direction in which, if elected, he intended to take the party. Announcing his candidacy in an address in Hampstead on 18 May, he declared:

> The role of the Liberal Party is not that of a shadow third government with a detailed policy on every single issue of the day, ready and waiting in the wings for a shift in electoral opinion to sweep us into power . . . . We must concentrate less on giving day-to-day commentary on the policies of others, and far more on setting out our own programme. And we should combine our long-term programme with a readiness to work with others wherever we see what Jo Grimond has called the break in the clouds – the chance to implement any of [our] Liberal policies.[54]

In an interview in the *Guardian* within weeks of becoming leader, Steel confirmed that Liberals had to 'start by getting a toe-hold on power which *must* mean some form of coalition'. Then, at the end of a long speech to the September Assembly in Llandudno, he sought the backing of the wider party:

> I want the Liberal Party to be the fulcrum and centre of the next election argument – not something peripheral to it. If that is to happen we must not give the impression of being afraid to soil our hands with the responsibilities of sharing power. We must be bold enough to deploy the coalition case positively.[55]

The protests of a number of Young Liberals, concerned at the possible loss of their ideological purity, were drowned out in the rapturous reception which Steel received at the end of his speech, convincing him that he had captured the minds as well as the hearts of Liberal activists and that he had a mandate to pursue his chosen course should the opportunity arise.

That opportunity was not long in coming. By the end of 1976 the Labour government, now headed by James Callaghan, was enveloped in Britain's most serious economic crisis for decades. Forced into the humiliating position of having to seek the aid of the International Monetary Fund, it had also lost its parliamentary majority as a result of by-election defeats and defections. By the following spring it faced the prospect of defeat in the House of Commons as the Conservative party announced its intention of tabling a motion of no confidence. After soundings by intermediaries, Steel accepted an invitation to talks with the Prime Minister. On the basis of a modest set of demands from the Liberal leader, a pact was concluded and the government's parliamentary defeat averted. Steel wanted an on-going consultative committee to scrutinise government business; an immediate meeting between Chancellor Denis Healey and the Liberal economics spokesman, John Pardoe, to confirm that a basis did exist for agreement on economic policy; a government bill to allow for direct elections to the European parliament; a fresh attempt to bring devolution to Scotland and Wales; a halt to any further nationalisation; and an agreement to drop the government's proposed Local Government Direct Labour Bill. The pact was very much Steel's personal creation. There was no discussion with the parliamentary party about the precise terms and no vote on those terms. Still less was there consultation with the wider party in the country. The parliamentary party accepted what Steel had negotiated with varying degrees of enthusiasm and in some cases a complete absence of it. Interestingly, the Mark II Jo Grimond was the most critical, doubting whether Callaghan's government intrinsically merited Liberal support. For the time being, at least, most Liberals were prepared to acquiesce in what Steel had done, not least because the general election which would otherwise have resulted would probably have produced an overwhelming victory for Thatcherite Conservatism.

It could not be claimed that Steel had driven a hard bargain. The bill for direct elections to the European parliament, for example, would not necessarily involve proportional representation, although the government agreed to 'take account' of the Liberals' wish for this to be the system adopted. Critics argued that this revealed Steel's weakness as a negotiator and that he had fallen an easy victim to Callaghan's greater experience and avuncular charm. In fact, Steel was more concerned with the concept of a pact and the idea of consultation – the toe-hold on power of which he had earlier spoken – than with specific policy commitments. It would, he hoped, be the first step in a process which, by getting the Liberal party locked into the governmental machine, would one day lead it, via formal coalition and proportional representation, to real power.

The Lib–Lab pact lasted for 18 months. Its achievements were limited and its impact upon the Liberal party of questionable value. It certainly enabled the government to continue in office without the ever-present threat of parliamentary defeat and, during this time, progress was made in stabilising the economy and bringing down, at least temporarily, the rate of inflation. Relations between Healey and Pardoe were often strained: 'More than once Joel Barnett [Healey's deputy] had to pick up the pieces after we had sent the crockery flying.'[56] But it is difficult to sustain Steel's contention that the pact had the effect of blocking further left-wing legislation. A Labour government headed by Callaghan and Healey, and constrained by the watchful eye of the IMF, was never likely to lurch too far in the direction of socialism. The onward march of Labour's Left had, in fact, been arrested at the time of the European referendum and in the very fact of IMF intervention. Furthermore, as Grimond pointed out, it was difficult to point to anything conspicuously 'Liberal' which could be attributed to the pact, apart from some limited measures of profit-sharing in the 1978 Finance Bill. Perhaps it was wrong to expect much more. After all, the Liberal bargaining position was never strong in numerical terms – 13 MPs against Labour's 310.

More seriously, the Liberal party associated itself in the public mind, and even more in the criticisms of the Conservative opposition, with what remained an unpopular government. Tories argued that the pact was a cynical device to save Liberal MPs from electoral defeat. There seemed to be some substance in the claim. In the May local elections, held just two months after the pact was concluded, the party lost three-quarters of its county councillors. In ten by-elections held before the announcement in May 1978 of the pact's termination, the Liberal share of the poll dropped on average by 9.5 per cent. As even Steel conceded, 'We were lambasted for simply keeping in office a government which had outstayed its welcome.'[57] Steel resisted calls at the Brighton Assembly in September 1977 for the renegotiation of the pact, declaring that he had 'never thought that there could be a secure or expandable future for the Liberal party as a kind of convenient temporary wastepaper basket for the ballot papers of discontented Tories'.[58] But when in December Labour MPs declined to back proportional representation for the European elections, many Liberals, who had regarded this as the one tangible prize within their grasp, felt bitterly let down. There was now no prospect of continuing the pact into a third session of parliament in the autumn of 1978.

Against most expectations, Callaghan did not go to the country in the autumn of 1978, but soldiered on through the so-called Winter of Discontent of widespread industrial unrest to the following spring. A by-election victory in March 1979 in the Edge Hill division of Liverpool provided the Liberals with a welcome boost, but when the General Election finally came in May the party was inevitably on the defensive, easily castigated for the country's problems because of its earlier role in the Lib–Lab Pact. Steel, however, fought an effective campaign, focusing his attention on existing Liberal seats and Tory-held marginals, and had the pleasure of seeing his party's poll rating climb steadily during the course of the hustings. His message dropped the charade of so many earlier elections that a Liberal government was a realistic goal. Instead, he spoke of the need for a 'powerful wedge' of Liberal MPs in the next parliament as the best means of ending the politics of two-party confrontation. Realignment still underlay his thinking. 'There are good people and good ideas in both the other parties,' Steel insisted, 'but the party system prevents them ever co-operating. And the good people and good ideas have to give way to the extremists on both sides.'[59] The issue of Jeremy Thorpe proved to be an unwanted distraction as it had been at the party's autumn assembly in Southport. Most of the former leader's parliamentary colleagues had urged him not to contest his North Devon seat, but Thorpe, with the strong backing of his local constituency party, had put himself forward once again. As by this stage he was awaiting trial on charges of incitement and conspiracy to murder Norman Scott, his chances of electoral success were slim.

In the event, the party did less badly than might have been expected and than many had feared. The Liberals held on to 11 of their 14 seats, many with increased majorities. Though the party's share of the vote dropped from 18.3 per cent to 13.8 per cent, it tended to perform better in those seats where it was already a strong contender. On the debit side, the fact that the party performed markedly better in the local elections which were held on the same day underlined that a voter might value a Liberal councillor while still seeing national politics as a choice between Labour and the Conservatives: 'It would seem that something in the order of a million people may have voted Liberal locally whilst on the same day choosing between a Callaghan and a Thatcher government.'[60] Above all, for the first time since 1970 a government, in this case Margaret Thatcher's Conservatives, had been returned with a comfortable parliamentary majority. The Liberal party seemed as far away from 'power', however defined, as it had ever been.

Almost a quarter of a century had elapsed since Jo Grimond had taken over the leadership of a party which was then near to extinction. At first sight it is difficult to make much sense of the bewildering series of ups and downs which had characterised the fortunes of British Liberalism in the succeeding years. But some sense of pattern does exist. In the first place, the seemingly remorseless process of electoral decline had been arrested and reversed. In a remarkable comeback, the party had, against the odds, confirmed its permanent position on the British political landscape. Furthermore, though the peaks of revival had been followed by troughs of setback and disappointment, each low point had tended to be at a higher level than its predecessor, leaving the long-term trend pointing firmly up. Typically, the Liberals had done best during periods of Conservative government, which often coincided with internal dissension within the Labour party, though there was a tendency for disillusioned voters to return to their traditional loyalties with the approach of a general election. Over the period as a whole, the party had benefited from a gradual weakening of the class associations of the major parties, but at the same time the 'classlessness' of the Liberals worked to their disadvantage to the extent that it prevented the development of solid Liberal heartlands and thus accentuated the disadvantages inherent in the existing electoral system.

But the most worrying feature of the Liberal revival was the nature of its vote. While a party capable of attracting the support of more than six million electors was clearly a major player on the political scene, too much of that vote was a purely negative response to one or both of the two leading parties, a retrospective judgement on the governmental failings of Labour and the Conservatives. Psephologists have identified a relatively small 'core' Liberal vote, espousing traditional Liberal values and ideas, and a far larger 'sympathy' vote with a much weaker commitment to the merits of the Liberal party. While this second group was crucial to the Liberals' further advance, its loyalty was never reliable. It has been shown that, in the General Elections from 1959 to 1979, on average less than 50 per cent of those who voted Liberal at one election did so at the following contest. This may be set against a figure of around 75 per cent in the case of the Labour and Conservative parties.[61] Staggeringly, just 2 per cent of the electorate offered consistent support to the Liberal party in each of the four elections of the 1970s.

It is, then, at least arguable that the Liberal revival owed little to the efforts of the party leadership, except to the extent that Grimond, Thorpe and Steel all succeeded in conveying the image of a positive and dynamic alternative to the Labour–Conservative duopoly. All three were on the left of the Liberal party, anxious to assert their 'radical' credentials. Grimond and Steel championed the goal of realignment which in practice meant partnership with at least a part of the Labour party. Though Conservative defectors would be welcomed, neither called for a realignment of the 'centre right'. Yet each proved most successful in attracting erstwhile Conservative supporters to the Liberal cause.

The volatility of the Liberal vote was matched by a continuing difficulty in identifying Liberal policies and values. Protest voters frequently turned to the party in spite rather than because of its views. Nowhere was this more the case than in relation to Europe: 'A disproportionate number of those voting against British membership [in the 1975 referendum] appeared from electoral and opinion-survey evidence to be drawn from Liberal ranks, suggesting that Liberal leaders and activists were out of line with over 50 per cent of the party's voters.'[62] Rather than sharing Liberal values, many transient Liberal voters attempted to project on to the party their own concerns and preoccupations as part of their dissatisfaction with the performance of the other two parties. Whatever recovery Liberalism had made, these problems remained unresolved as British politics entered the most decisive period of transformation experienced since the Second World War.

5

A CRACKED MOULD AND A NEW BEGINNING, 1979–2001

For most of the period since 1945 one of the most difficult problems facing the Liberal party was that of identity. Committed Liberal activists believed they knew where they stood – though they often disagreed on this issue amongst themselves – but the voting public was altogether less certain. In part this reflected the way in which the post-war Conservative and Labour parties, dominated by their left and right wings respectively, had competed for the centre ground of British politics. That convergence was often disputed and denied. The two main parties had a vested interest in maintaining the outward appearance of confrontation, stressing the extremism of their opponents – that Labour threatened full-blown socialism and that the Conservatives would unleash the unbridled forces of the free market. The Liberals too saw considerable advantage in projecting their opponents on to the extremes of the political spectrum. In 1980 David Steel suggested that post-war British politics had seen relatively small changes in public opinion result in alternating periods of Conservative and Labour government, which were accompanied by 'violent switches in public policy'. Thus 'each swing of the political pendulum threatens to take the country on yet more violently diverse directions to left and right'.[1] But as regards the key areas of policy, the first post-war decades witnessed far more consistency and continuity than the rhetoric of political debate implied. In practical terms this left very little empty space within the congested centre ground of British politics for Liberals to occupy. Of course, Liberals themselves could claim that their own politics did not fit into a simple left–right linear pattern. Liberal 'radicalism' placed the party on a different plane, uncontested by its larger rivals. The average voter, however, was never comfortable with this proposition and, in so far as he had any clear view of the Liberal stance, tended to locate it in the comfortable centre, an area where one or other of the major parties had generally succeeded in satisfying the majority of the electorate.

By 1979 this situation was clearly changing. The General Election of that year brought to power a government, and more particularly a Prime Minister, who made something of a virtue of their determination to break the post-war consensus. To an audience in Cardiff in April 1979, Mrs Thatcher declared: 'I am a conviction politician. The Old Testament prophets did not say "Brothers, I want a consensus". They said "this is my faith. This is what I passionately believe. If you believe it too, then come with me." '[2]

The destruction of the consensus would, she hoped, one day become one of the lasting achievements for which she would be remembered. In her belief, consensus could be equated with the appeasement of socialism and the progressive advance of collectivism since 1945. Once in government, Mrs Thatcher began the process of dismantling many of the key aspects of the post-war settlement, upon which the Labour and Conservative parties had hitherto been in broad agreement, and building instead a very different socio-economic structure, dominated by ideas about initiative and enterprise. At the same time, the emergence of a New Right within the Conservative party was matched by the renaissance of the Left in Labour's ranks. So traumatic was the experience of the last months of Callaghan's government that the Left found it relatively easy to argue that socialism and the class struggle had been betrayed while a Labour government had sought to prop up the failing edifice of capitalism. Freed from the constraints of office, the party moved rapidly to the left, with the annual conference and the National Executive Committee achieving unprecedented power over the direction of policy. In January 1980 an opinion poll found that 60 per cent of the population believed that the Labour party had moved too far to the left, while 46 per cent agreed with the proposition that the Conservatives had moved too far to the right. This perception of party polarisation – and for the first time since 1945 there was significant evidence that it was also the reality – clearly opened up promising possibilities for the third force in British politics and, as it turned out, for a fourth force too: 'The political seas had parted as if by magic, leaving the centre ground of British politics free for the first time in recent history.' [3]

The history of the Social Democratic Party is quite distinct from that of the Liberal party, but its origins must at least be outlined if its future troubled relationship with the Liberals is to be understood. Throughout its history, the Labour party had existed as a somewhat uneasy coalition of ideas and beliefs which, but for the accident of its birth, might easily have developed into separate political movements. Generally speaking, the forces of non-doctrinaire moderation had managed to hold on to the reins of power, notwithstanding the party's theoretical commitment to the creation of a socialist state, as embodied in its constitution of 1918. Modern social democracy can be traced back to the very beginnings of the Labour movement. It flourished in the context of the Progressive Alliance and owed much to the infusion of social liberalism during and after the First World War. But its more recent manifestations are most usefully dated to the development of the Keynesian–Beveridgite welfare state and the reformulation of Labour thinking carried out in the mid-1950s by such figures as Anthony Crosland, Hugh Gaitskell and Douglas Jay. Gaitskell's leadership of the party opened up the possibility of the complete triumph of social democratic revisionism but, at the time of his death in 1963, Labour had proved strikingly resistant to some of Gaitskell's efforts at modernisation. Harold Wilson's priorities as Labour leader were focused on holding the party's competing factions together and, while the social democratic right remained dominant within his cabinets, the clear sense of vision and direction offered by Gaitskell was largely lost.

During the later years of Wilson's leadership, and particularly after 1970, there was unmistakable evidence of a significant advance by Labour's Left, especially within the extra-parliamentary party. The issue of British membership of the European community emerged as the acid test within the increasingly warring factions of the Labour party and in 1971 the votes of the parliamentary right offered crucial support to the Heath government's efforts to pilot British membership through the House of Commons. A few months later, Harold Lever, George Thomson and Roy Jenkins resigned from Labour's shadow cabinet rather than accept their party's decision to commit a future Labour government to submit the issue of British membership to another general election or referendum. Thus began a process by which Jenkins, a former Labour Home Secretary, Chancellor and Deputy Leader, started to drift away from a party in whose interest he had first been elected to parliament in 1948. Though he served again as Home Secretary in Wilson's 1974 government, he failed to secure the succession to the party leadership – as had at one time seemed probable – and left the cabinet in 1976 to take up the post of President of the European Commission. From his voluntary exile in Brussels, he watched the fortunes of the Callaghan government with some dismay, while quietly allowing his Labour party membership to lapse.

By 1979, with the end of his presidency coming into view, Jenkins began to give thought to his own future and to the future shape of British politics. Invited to give the annual Dimbleby lecture that November, Jenkins chose the theme of 'Home Thoughts from Abroad'. Condemning the paralysing rigidity of the existing party system, he called for the creation of a new political force and spoke of the need for a 'strengthening of the radical centre', a somewhat confusing phrase included at the prompting of the academic and former Labour MP, David Marquand. Jenkins criticised Britain's excessive changes of policy direction which, he claimed, were an inevitable consequence of the existing electoral system and called for the introduction of proportional representation. The address was generally well received and invited intense speculation that Jenkins intended, on his return to Britain, to launch a new political party.

How such a party would relate to the existing Liberal party and whether there was room in the British political spectrum for a new fourth force was, of course, a matter of acute interest, not least to Liberals themselves. Jenkins later described his own thinking in characteristically relaxed terms:

> If I came quietly back from Brussels to a not very political semi-retirement, I thought that I would become a nominal Liberal, for that party was now much closer to my outlook than was either the Labour Party or the Conservatives. But if a combination of circumstances and my strength of purpose made it possible for me to mount a major political initiative then I was convinced that it ought to start separate from but in partnership with the Liberals.[4]

Perhaps more important were the views of David Steel, who was convinced that his duty as Liberal party leader was 'to assess how most speedily we can reach [the] objective' of forming a government.[5] Steel, who had exchanged thoughts with Jenkins over a period of time, made it clear that the best way to break the two-party stranglehold was to challenge it with strong, but separate, Liberal and Social Democratic parties. The experience of Christopher Mayhew, who had lost his seat at the October 1974 General Election, offered little support for encouraging a handful of further defections from Labour to the Liberals. By January 1980 Jenkins recorded that Steel

> perfectly understands that there is no question of me or anybody else joining the Liberal Party. He equally is anxious to work very closely, and possibly, if things went well, to consider an amalgamation after a general election. He would like the closeness at the time of the election itself to take the form not merely of a non-aggression pact, but of working together on policy and indeed sharing broadcasts etc.[6]

At this same time those leading social democrats still within the Labour party, who would eventually be associated with Jenkins in the so-called 'Gang of Four', were thinking in rather different terms, though the possibility of their being forced to leave the Labour movement had no doubt crossed their minds. Unlike Jenkins, who had enjoyed the luxury of a gradual separation from his Labour roots over a number of years, David Owen, Shirley Williams and Bill Rodgers had all fought the 1979 election in support of Labour's manifesto and remained committed to it. Owen and Rodgers were still members of Labour's shadow cabinet and Williams of the National Executive Committee, expressions of the hope which all three felt that their cause was not lost and that the social democratic tradition could yet be saved from inside the Labour movement. Owen, in particular, believed that the centre party envisaged in Jenkins's Dimbleby lecture had little in common with the sort of ideals in which he believed. It would be 'rootless, brought together out of frustration' and 'would soon split apart when faced with the real choices and could easily reflect the attitudes of a London-based liberalism that had neither a base in the provinces nor a bedrock of principles'.[7] 'For the three of us,' he recalled, 'rightly or wrongly, the Liberal Party was low on our agenda. There were other priorities.'[8]

Over the course of 1980, however, the 'gang of three' were obliged to reconsider their position. In June the Labour party's own Commission of Inquiry endorsed the idea of the mandatory reselection of MPs, together with the setting up of an electoral college to choose the party leader. Social Democrats interpreted these moves, fairly enough, as an attempt to place Labour MPs at the mercy of left-wing constituency and union activists. The election later that year, but still under the old rules, of the veteran left-winger, Michael Foot, to succeed Callaghan as party leader was a sign of how far the balance of power had shifted, even within the parliamentary party. 'I cannot pretend that I was other than elated,' noted Roy Jenkins, 'as it clearly opened up a much greater prospect of political realignment.'[9] At the annual conference, commitments were made to an 'alternative economic strategy', including more public ownership, a massive reflation of the economy, selective import controls and a 35-hour working week with no reduction in pay. Then, in January 1981, a special party conference agreed to the creation of an electoral college for subsequent leadership elections in which the largest vote would be given to the trade unions (40 per cent), with the parliamentary party and the constituency parties receiving 30 per cent each. By the end of 1980 the Gang of Three, by now in close contact with Roy Jenkins, were, with varying degrees of conviction, agreed that the game was up as far as their continued membership of the Labour party was concerned. The outcome of the special conference provided an appropriate backdrop against which to issue the Limehouse Declaration on 25 January 1981 and launch the Council for Social Democracy. This, as everyone now realised, would soon be transformed into a new party and the SDP came formally into existence on 26 March.

The new party found itself running before it had even attempted to walk. It immediately secured the support of 14 sitting MPs, taking it above the Liberal total of 11, while opinion polls between the end of January and the end of March projected support in the country at between 23 and 31 per cent. Significantly, those same polls revealed that this figure would rise to between 38 and 48 per cent for a Liberal–Social-Democratic alliance. For many years the polls had suggested that a marked differential existed between the support actually offered to the Liberal party and that which might be offered if electors believed that the Liberals had a chance of winning. In a survey taken at the end of 1980, this difference was between 13 and 42 per cent. In this respect the new party offered clear opportunities. In combination, the Liberals and the SDP enjoyed the image of an alternative government which the former, standing alone, did not. The Gang of Four had all held cabinet office and presented the electorate with the gravitas which even the most able of contemporary Liberals appeared to lack. Shirley Williams, in particular, enjoyed a standing with the general public which might hold enormous electoral potential. Furthermore, as the SDP was essentially a breakaway from the Labour party – only one Conservative MP ever joined its ranks – the hope clearly existed that the new party could appeal to former Labour voters in a way that the Liberals, even at the peak of their recent revivals, had never fully succeeded in doing. David Owen was very clear on this point:

If we are to realign British politics, it is vital that the Social Democrats cut into the Labour vote, and particularly cut into the Labour vote in the northern part of the country so that, in combination with disillusioned Tories and Liberals in seats that have hitherto been considered 'safe Labour', a Social Democrat can be returned.[10]

In tandem, therefore, could Liberals and Social Democrats achieve that elusive realignment of the centre-left of British politics for which Liberals since Jo Grimond had striven so earnestly, but as yet so unsuccessfully?

The question of whether Liberalism and Social Democracy were in effect the same thing exercised many minds. Traditionally, Liberalism gave priority to the rights of individuals and of minorities in society whereas social democracy seemed to be guided by a Benthamite attachment to the search for the greatest happiness of the greatest number. For a Liberal, the pursuit of liberty was more important than that for equality. In the post-war era, moreover, social democrats had become enveloped in a cocoon of bureaucratic centralism which was anathema to Liberal traditions of devolution and decentralisation. That said, there was a pattern of co-operation between the two traditions going back to the Progressive Alliance of the Edwardian age and, in practice, relations between the Liberal and Social Democratic parties would be determined more by the gut reactions of individuals on the ground than by any perceived philosophical affinities or differences. What did complicate those relations, however, was a lack of clarity, only half concealed in the euphoria surrounding the new party's creation and early success, about what the SDP really represented. Many had difficulties with Jenkins's concept of a radical centre, not least in the context of a political environment in which the Bennite Left and the Thatcherite Right were also offering their versions of 'radicalism'. More generally, a fundamental division existed between those who saw the SDP as an entirely new force in British politics and those for whom it was essentially a Mark II Labour party, seeking to rebuild the Butskellite consensus from which the other parties had now departed. Did it offer the British electorate an exciting and novel future or, in Ralf Dahrendorf's telling words, and as some of the phraseology of the Limehouse Declaration implied, 'no more than a better yesterday'? Labour defectors such as Owen saw in the SDP an opportunity for creative political innovation: 'I wanted to take the ethic of redistribution into our new Party, but to lose all the trappings of state socialism; to break the institutional links with but not the respect for the trade unions.'[11] For other former Labour MPs, however, it was little more than a port of refuge from an increasingly predatory left-wing constituency party.

David Steel who, in consultation with Roy Jenkins, had already worked out a clear picture of how he wished to proceed, welcomed the Limehouse Declaration with enthusiasm. Other Liberals were altogether less certain. Jo Grimond, far from seeing an SDP–Liberal alliance as the missing link in his vision of realignment, was concerned by the inherent conservatism of the new party, its nascent Butskellism and firm location in the safe centre of consensual politics. Cyril Smith, the flamboyant MP for Rochdale, famously declared that the new creation should be strangled at birth. More soberly, he had already suggested that, if Jenkins wished to join the Liberal party, 'I for one would welcome him, but I think any electoral arrangement with Mr Jenkins and any new party that he envisages would be wholly undesirable and I would have thought that history proves that point.'[12] Similarly, the social democratic embrace offered few attractions for those Liberals committed to the notion of community politics. Their strategy was 'a direct reaction to the corporatism and ineffectiveness of the old-style social democracy. Was the nature of this new beast any different?'[13] As Michael Meadowcroft, writing in 1982, explained, 'For better or worse, witting or unwittingly, the vast expanse of soulless council estates, the confusion of mobility with roads, and above all the wanton destruction of urban neighbourliness, are the products of the social democratic consensus of the post-war years.'[14]

Nor were the Social Democrats of one mind about their relationship with the Liberals. In personal terms Bill Rodgers and Shirley Williams were far closer to Jenkins than was David Owen. But both were more tied to their Labour party roots than was Jenkins. Furthermore, Rodgers, Williams and Owen still spoke the language of democratic 'socialism', something which Jenkins had for some time excluded from his vocabulary. The first edition, at least, of Owen's *Face the Future*, published early in 1981, suggested that there was 'a yearning for a fresh and valid socialist alternative' and argued for a 'socialist philosophy'. Neither Rodgers nor Williams excluded the possibility of an eventual merger with the Liberals but, unlike Jenkins, they did not yet see this as the desired outcome of their present actions. Owen, by contrast, was clear that the new Social Democratic Party should be a permanent feature of his and the nation's political landscape, an end in itself rather than the means to an end. He rapidly developed a commitment to the new party and its values, as he understood them, which was unmatched by the other members of the Gang of Four. These differences, particularly between Jenkins and Owen and their respective followers, were never fully confronted, still less resolved, and translated into very different attitudes towards the Liberal party. These in turn lay at the root of the troubled history of the Liberal–SDP Alliance.

When they came to write their respective memoirs, Jenkins and Owen sought to parody each other's position, while each capturing an element of the truth. According to Jenkins, Owen 'essentially regarded the Liberal Party as a disorderly group of bearded vegetarian pacifists, and his treatment of them as such not unnaturally brought out such of these tendencies as existed. I treated them as the statesmanlike heirs of Gladstone and Asquith.'[15] By contrast, Owen judged that

> having sniffed the two parties as if they were bottles of claret, his nose, he kept telling us, was unable to detect a Liberal from a Social Democrat. This Olympian assessment owed too much to dining with Mark Bonham Carter and the type of old Asquithian Liberal who had little in common with the new community politicians and pavement politics.[16]

In reality Jenkins, the biographer of Asquith and later of Gladstone, was himself an instinctive Liberal, never fully at home in the working-class fraternity of the Labour movement and always more interested in the achievement of specific political goals than in playing the party political game for its own sake. He had enjoyed working on a cross-party basis during the European referendum campaign – 'it made some of the divisions in politics seem a little artificial'[17] – and now felt perfectly at ease with the Liberal party of David Steel, while appreciating the tactical advantages of maintaining a degree of separate identity for the time being. By contrast, Owen had not been impressed by the Liberals' performance in the Lib–Lab Pact and was much influenced by his personal experience as a West Country MP, where it was the legacy of Jeremy Thorpe and Peter Bessell which had left a lasting impression. He doubted whether the Liberals as a whole were tough enough to confront the problems facing British society in the 1980s: 'They constantly showed their lack of moorings in their indiscipline'; 'when the going gets rough on a political issue they back off.' As a result he was convinced that 'joining a Centre party based on the Liberals would be jumping out of the frying pan into the cotton wool'.[18]

For a time, relations between the two parties developed informally. In April 1981 Steel, Rodgers and Mrs Williams had the opportunity to consult at the annual meeting of the Anglo–German Society at Königswinter. Agreement was reached on the need for a minimum degree of policy co-ordination and a share-out of by-election and parliamentary seats between the two parties. The SDP was not ready to fight the May local elections, but the Liberals alone secured 250 net gains, profiting from Labour's continuing disarray and the unpopular economic policies of the Conservative government. This was followed by the issuing of a joint statement of principles on 16 June entitled *A Fresh Start for Britain*. The words 'socialist' and 'socialism' were conspicuous by their absence and the emphasis on such issues as devolution, industrial partnership and above all proportional representation (notably missing from the Limehouse Declaration) emphasised a strong Liberal input. David Owen remained wary, 'increasingly worried about the way we are merging into an amorphous amalgam with the Liberal Party. I cannot put my finger on how to stop it.'[19] His instinct told him 'that it could only harm our new party if we were too identified with the Liberals'.[20] No one, however, could ignore the new party's performance at its first by-election test in Warrington in July. After some hesitation on the part of Shirley Williams, Roy Jenkins decided to throw his hat into the ring. The seat was not, on paper, promising territory for the SDP. Solidly Labour, it had no tradition of residual Liberal strength. But taking more easily to a North of England constituency campaign than might have been expected, Jenkins, with generous Liberal support, came within 1700 votes of a dramatic victory.

A computer projection extrapolated from the Warrington result by the BBC suggested that, at a general election, an SDP–Liberal alliance could win 501 seats in the House of Commons, leaving Labour with 113 and the Conservatives just one. This was, of course, exaggerated nonsense but there seemed reasonable grounds for believing that, for the first time in half a century, the mould of British politics shaped around the Labour–Conservative duopoly was about to be broken. Liberal or SDP candidates were successful in almost half the local government by-elections held between Warrington and the end of 1981. Recognising that what had been achieved at Warrington could not have been done by the Liberals acting alone, Steel renewed his efforts to confirm the alliance of the two parties. After Warrington the Liberal leader took advantage of every media opportunity to stress the benefits of a close and formalised working relationship. At the Liberals' Llandudno assembly in September the proposal for an alliance was over-whelmingly endorsed, while Steel planted in the minds of dele-gates the prospect of genuine political power which had eluded them for so long:

> Now at last we have the reality in our grasp. We must have the nerve and courage not to let it slip. I have the good fortune to be the first Liberal leader for over half a century who is able to say to you at the end of our annual assembly: go back to your constituencies and prepare for government.[21]

For the time being, the Alliance bandwagon continued to roll. A new wave of defections from Labour brought the SDP's tally of MPs to over twenty. In October the Liberals, fielding a relatively undistinguished candidate, captured Croydon North-West from the Conservatives. The following month Mrs Williams scaled a seemingly impregnable 18,000 Conservative majority to take the seat of Crosby by more than 5000 votes. Scarcely a constituency in the land seemed invulnerable to the Alliance's advance, as Gallup in December put the two parties' combined support at 50 per cent. But the balloon was bound to burst or at the very least to deflate. Alliance performances in such differing constituencies as Warrington and Crosby might suggest to optimists that the SDP had succeeded in broadening the existing third party's appeal into areas hitherto outside the Liberals' grasp. In reality, it revealed that Alliance support was as transient and rootless as had been the Liberals' at earlier peaks of revival. The SDP had succeeded, even more effectively than earlier Liberals, in mobilising the protest vote at a time of unprecedented unpopularity for the two major parties. Many had been enthused by the new party to get involved in political activity for the first time, but what attracted the typical Alliance voter was the reassuring familiarity of its message. In place of the disturbing doctrines of socialism and monetarism were comfortable reaffirmations of the advantages of the mixed economy. The SDP had 'sold itself at its launch as a party of common sense, moderation and good men and true who were against sin and in favour of virtue' and thus 'it was easy for many voters to regard the Social Democrats as their sort of people'.[22] In an unguarded but revealing comment, Shirley Williams herself admitted that the new party had attracted 'broad and frothy support at Crosby, without much organisation or intellectual underpinning'.[23]

The downturn in the Alliance's fortunes became apparent in the New Year. Though Roy Jenkins got back to Westminster following victory at a by-election at Glasgow, Hillhead, the swing to the Alliance was less dramatic than at Croydon or Crosby. Then, Conservative fortunes started to recover with the first signs that their unorthodox economic strategy might be beginning to bear fruit, a process that was rapidly accelerated by the outbreak and successful conclusion of the Falklands War. By July 1982 Conservative poll support was running at 46 per cent, while that of the Alliance had gone down to a respectable, but not earth-shattering, 24 per cent. Votes in the May local elections were nowhere near to being translated into a comparable proportion of seats won, clear evidence that the Alliance would need to poll at a significantly higher level if it were to make a real breakthrough at the expense of Labour and the Conservatives. It was also striking that Liberals managed to win five times as many seats as did the SDP. David Owen was inclined to blame the loss of support on the Alliance itself. Earlier levels of public backing had been 'dissipated by constantly talking about an Alliance and giving the impression that the SDP and Liberals are in the process of merging'.[24] But it seems unlikely that voters were deserting the Alliance because of a loss of identity on the part of the SDP.

That said, clear damage was done by the public exposure of strains within and between the two parties which made up the Alliance. Much had been made of a style of politics in which individuals could work constructively with others whose views were not identitical to their own. But, as an earlier generation of Liberals had quickly discovered, the doctrine of agreeing to differ had strict limitations. Roy Jenkins attributed the worsening of personal relations to the decline in the Alliance's standing in the polls: 'With the change of mood there came . . . a shrinkage of generosity between the two parties.'[25] But the reverse was also true as electors recoiled from the spectacle of Alliance politicians squabbling with a relish equal to that of Labour and the Conservatives. Attentive observers may have noticed that Dr Owen dropped references to 'socialism' from the second edition of his book, *Face the Future*, published in the autumn of 1981. But this owed more to the beginnings of the political odyssey which would eventually take him to a distinctive position on the centre right of British politics than it did to any warming of feelings towards the Liberal party. Indeed, in an interview in the *Alliance* magazine the following year, Owen spelt out publicly what would be his consistent and defining attitude towards the relationship between the two parties throughout the lifetime of the SDP and beyond:

> I'm in business to fashion a new Social Democratic party, a totally new force in British politics. If we blur our identities too much and the Liberals and the Social Democrats look as if they are 'an Alliance party', nothing would please the Conservative and Labour party more: they would narrow us to what they would brand as a centralist band of opinion.[26]

But the issue, which brought the strains within the Alliance fully into the public domain, was the attempt to negotiate a deal between the two parties on the division of seats at the next general election. Deciding who should stand where in the handful of by-elections which had been held since the launch of the SDP had been no easy matter, as the experience of Croydon had shown. Reaching a decision on the six hundred or so seats on the British mainland was a task of monumental proportions. At the start of the negotiations both sides believed they were in a strong position. The SDP felt that it was they who had transformed the prospects of third-party politics in a way that the Liberals alone could not have done. Furthermore, the leading figures of the SDP enjoyed a higher public profile than, with the exception of David Steel, did their Liberal counterparts. For Owen, indeed, and those SDP MPs who thought like him, the negotiation of any electoral pact ought to involve a trial of strength with the Liberals to demonstrate that the new party could not be treated as a junior partner within the Alliance. On the other hand, the Liberals were far more firmly entrenched on the ground than were their new allies. In many cases they had been nursing constituencies for a number of years, watching their strength grow to the point where electoral victory was apparently within their grasp. In such situations they were understandably loath to step down in favour of a 'Johnny come lately' put forward by the SDP. So while the principle of an approximate 50–50 overall split of constituencies was easy enough to agree, deciding precisely which seats would be entrusted to each party in a way that offered any chance of an equality of successful electoral outcomes was an entirely different matter. In particular, the SDP demand that Liberals should stand aside in many of their most promising seats was bound to cause enormous resentment.

As the negotiations proceeded in the autumn of 1981, the Owenite MP, Mike Thomas, warned that 'the likely outcome of the next election is that the Liberals will win more seats (possibly twice as many as us), even though we stand at 30 per cent in the opinion polls and they stand at 8 per cent'.[27] Only if the Alliance were to win well in excess of two hundred seats, an increasingly remote prospect, was the division between Liberal and SDP successes likely to come more into balance. Thomas, who often spoke for Owen, tried to convince Jenkins of the seriousness of the situation from an SDP point of view:

> What I want to communicate to you is that you are not here deal-ing with a little political awkwardness that has to be circum-vented or overcome, you are approaching a fundamental sticking point . . . for many in our Party. I don't want an Alliance party. I don't want to be a part of parachuting a few people into the upper echelons of what is essentially the Liberal Party. I want a true partnership between two distinct forces – each of which brings the Alliance its own strengths and convictions. That is why, for me, the outcome of the negotiations with the Liberals is actually about preserving the capacity of our own party to survive and develop, and thus contribute to a genuine alliance.[28]

But what brought these internal disputes to public attention was the decision, during the 1981 Christmas recess, of Bill Rodgers, leading the SDP team, to announce the suspension of the negotiations, claiming that the Liberals were being far too greedy in their demands. The quarrel was eventually patched up on the basis of the Liberals retaining their 50 most winnable seats, in return for the SDP standing in two-thirds of the next 100 most promising constituencies, but many believed that lasting damage had been done to the Alliance's public image. When a final deal, still very much to the Liberals' advantage, was put in place in time for the Liberal party's annual assembly in 1982, Owen recorded his belief that a decisive moment had been reached:

> When eventually the history of the SDP is written historians may have to decide at what point it became inevitable that it merged into the Liberal Party and of all the thresholds and of all the turning points it may be that they will conclude that it was this week that the final determination was made.[29]

By the beginning of 1983, minds were turning to the prospect of a general election, with Mrs Thatcher, whose government was presiding over record levels of unemployment, under some pressure to go to the polls before the electoral effects of the 'Falklands factor' finally disappeared. In January a Joint Policy Resolution Group was set up, headed by Richard Wainwright for the Liberals and John Horam for the SDP, to iron out points of policy difference between the two parties. The resulting manifesto was inevitably something of a compromise and as such lacked the cutting edge that the concept of the 'radical centre' had once seemed to promise. It was, judged one critic, 'little more than a rehash of that cosy, corporatist, social democracy which nearly sank this country in the 1960s and 1970s'.[30] The manifesto contained a clear commitment to constitutional reform and a thorough overhaul of the welfare state, but in economic policy – one of the key dividing issues between Labour and the Conservatives – seemed to hark back to the Butskellite consensus of earlier years. Those who read it, suggested the *Financial Times*, were likely to 'suffer something very like nostalgia'. Owen bemoaned the dominant influence of Jenkins's views, 'rooted in the 1960s', and regretted that he had failed to attract him to the concept of a social market economy.[31] The manifesto carried the subtitle *Programme for Government*, however unlikely that outcome now appeared. A more realistic possibility was that the Liberals and SDP might together hold the balance of power in the new parliament. In such a situation, electors would wish, reasonably enough, to know to which side Alliance support would be given to form a government. But the decision was taken to show no leaning either to the left or right.

Thus the Alliance went into the election campaign in May as two parties united under a single manifesto, and with two leaders, David Steel in charge of the campaign and Roy Jenkins projected as Prime Minister designate in the event of an Alliance victory. This last decision seemed to make sense in terms of Jenkins's standing and experience and, in any case, Steel, as the much younger man, could reasonably calculate that the leadership of any joint party could be expected to fall to himself some time in the future. But opinion polls revealed that, both among Alliance supporters and the electorate at large, Steel enjoyed a far higher approval rating than Jenkins, who had never recovered his earlier parliamentary ascendancy since returning to Westminster. On 29 May, over an informal lunch meeting of Alliance leaders at Steel's home in the Borders, the Liberal leader attempted unsuccessfully to dethrone a startled Jenkins from his position, arguing that the Alliance itself would benefit if Jenkins played a less prominent role. In general, the two parties campaigned together effectively, although there was some tension in Liverpool, Leeds and the West Country, with a few Liberal candidates refusing to stand on the Alliance ticket.

As had been the Liberals' experience at several polls since the 1950s, the General Election of 1983 combined both achievement and disappointment for the Alliance. In securing 25.4 per cent of the popular vote, the Alliance did better than any third party since 1923. With 7.75 million votes, it was only 0.75 million behind Labour. Under a strict system of proportional representation, this level of public endorsement would have translated into about 160 seats, almost certainly enough to force entry into a coalition government. As it was, the Alliance secured just 23 seats in the new parliament against Labour's 209, introducing, as the *Sunday Times* put it, 'a new order of unfairness'. In terms of the strategic goal of replacing the Labour party, little had been achieved. It was true that the left of centre vote had been split, but the practical effect of this was to hand Mrs. Thatcher a massive 144-seat majority over all other parties combined on just 42.4 per cent of the poll. Just one seat, Leeds West, had been captured by the Liberals from the Labour party. The Alliance had apparently reached a plateau of support which was not enough to make real inroads into the seats of its opponents. Meanwhile Labour, though suffering its worst defeat since 1931, continued to pile up votes in its electoral heartlands sufficient to maintain a sizeable parliamentary presence. A further worrying feature was the shallowness of Alliance support. Polls showed that only slightly over half its voters identified firmly with it. 'The centre vote in 1983, like the Liberal vote in 1974, was a protest vote; it did not represent a fundamental shift in voters' loyalties.'[32] Liberals could draw one small crumb of comfort from a clear shift in the balance of power within the Alliance. The respective Liberal and SDP tallies of MPs had changed from 13 and 29 at the dissolution to 17 and just 6 in the new House of Commons.

This change of relative strength was qualified by post-election developments in the leadership of the two parties. Steel was taken aback by the critical tone displayed at a meeting of Liberal MPs on 15 June, which called for the election by the parliamentary party of a deputy leader and of the Chief Whip, clear attempts to curtail his own authority. Tired out by the recent campaign and disappointed at the failure to secure an electoral breakthrough, Steel wrote out a letter of resignation as Liberal leader a fortnight later. Though he was eventually dissuaded from this course, Steel insisted on taking a three-month sabbatical break during which time the acting leadership of the party passed to the Chief Whip, Alan Beith. Steel's authority had been badly bruised and his temporary withdrawal enabled the initiative within the Alliance to pass to the SDP. Here Roy Jenkins had rapidly given up the party leadership to be replaced, without a great deal of discussion, by David Owen. Within the depleted ranks of the SDP's parliamentary party, and with both Shirley Williams and Bill Rodgers numbered among the electoral casualties, there was no serious alternative to his appointment. During his time within the party, Owen had greatly enhanced his public standing. After a 'good' Falklands War, he had emerged as a reasoned but trenchant critic of the Conservative government and as a formidable parliamentary and television performer whose views carried considerable authority beyond the confines of his own party.

But Owen's elevation to the leadership was a significant moment in the history of the Alliance. Until the General Election of 1983, Alliance politics had been as much a partnership between David Steel and Roy Jenkins as between two parties. The two men understood and liked one another, shared a common vision of where they were going and had succeeded in carrying – and occasionally dragging – their followers along with them, while papering over the divisions and contradictions which had been inherent since the birth of the SDP. Owen, as his memoirs reveal, had travelled reluctantly along this path, while nurturing a clear and coherent alternative view of what the new party was all about. Known for his somewhat abrasive style, Owen never succeeded in establishing a relationship of warmth and trust with Steel comparable to that already developed by Jenkins. 'I never underestimated David Steel's manipulative skills,' Owen once conceded. 'If they had been matched by an interest in the policies best suited to our country, he would have been a formidable politician.'[33] But, even as leader of a diminished parliamentary band, Owen now had far more scope than hitherto to influence the future shape of the Alliance.

Thus, while Steel continued to believe that fusion was the logical destiny of the Alliance parties, Owen drew and promulgated a very different conclusion from the outcome of the recent election. Though in public he did not rule out the possibility of an eventual merger, Owen remained determined to preserve the SDP's independence. Its goal was the achievement, in co-operation with the Liberals, of proportional representation, after which it could look forward to a separate existence within the very different political structure which electoral reform would create. For Owen, moreover, the 1983 results showed the limited attractions of an appeal to moderation and the comfortable middle ground. 'If we could simultaneously break right on the market and left on social policy,' he later explained, 'I believed we could find an electorally attractive political mix', an approach which perhaps explains his later sympathy for John Major's recipe of 'Thatcherism with a human face'.[34] Influenced by the American political philosopher, John Rawls, Owen differentiated between a belief in the equality of a citizen's rights and liberties and the sort of social and economic equality still espoused by the political left. He wanted to couple a high degree of social concern and responsibility with an emphasis on the primacy of the market and the importance of competition and free enterprise. Under Owen's influence the SDP endorsed the concept of the 'social market' at its Buxton conference in 1984, though it was one about which most Liberals remained sceptical. This approach meant a readiness to apply market forces to the public services – the SDP spoke of an internal market within the Health Service before the Conservatives did – in a way that finally distanced Owen from his Labour past, while encouraging the belief among many Liberals that his agenda was sub-Thatcherite. Such thinking was intellectually defensible, but it probably did little to clarify for the electorate precisely where the Alliance stood within the political spectrum. Equally seriously, it did not suggest that relations within the Alliance would run as smoothly as in the years 1981–83.

The electoral history of the 1983 parliament revealed little that was not already known. The Alliance's average opinion-poll rating stood at 26.9 per cent. In March 1987 Marplan put the level of support at 31 per cent, while Gallup suggested 31.5 per cent, two points ahead of Labour. The now-established pattern of spectacular by-election gains (and several near misses), largely at the expense of an unpopular Conservative government, was maintained. In a June 1984 by-election, held on the same day that elections to the European parliament failed to produce a single Alliance victory, the SDP snatched Portsmouth South from the Conservatives. Brecon and Radnor was captured by the Liberals a year later, while the apparently safe Conservative seat of Ryedale fell to the Liberals with a 5000 majority in May 1986. Only at Greenwich in February 1987 was this pattern challenged, with Rosie Barnes for the SDP taking the seat from Labour. Even here, however, it was the collapse of the Conservative vote, as electors polled tactically to defeat a left-wing Labour candidate, which largely determined the outcome. Each of these victories usefully contributed to the Alliance's parliamentary strength, while adding to the oxygen of publicity, so often denied to a third party. At the same time, they also suggested that the declared goal of replacing Labour as the main non-Conservative force was an unrealisable aspiration. Indeed, as Labour began, under Michael Foot's successor, Neil Kinnock, to tread the long path back to the political centre ground, a clear blow was struck in favour of the traditional two-party mould of British politics. As David Owen looked back, he saw Kinnock's attack on the Militant Tendency at Labour's 1985 party conference as a clear turning-point. As far as local politics were concerned, it was possible to discern a pattern of steady progress on the part of the Alliance. By the time of the 1987 council elections, the Liberal party had made gains for nine consecutive years and the SDP for four. But even the 400 net Alliance gains in 1987 still left it in control of only 15 district and borough councils, and the flagship Liverpool council was lost to Labour.

Owen proved far less reluctant than Jenkins had been to confront the SDP's policy differences with the Liberals. He was also keen to redress the imbalance of parliamentary strength between the parties. As negotiations began to allocate seats for the next general election, Owen expressed the hope that these would 'take as their objective to restore a balance to equality of seats with a view to not only having parity of numbers of seats fought but also some attempt to redress the imbalance of votes cast between Liberals and SDP'.[35] But the Liberals had been quick off the mark and 'most of the very best Liberal seats readopted their previous P[rospective] P[arliamentary] C[andidate]s soon after the 1983 General Election and we didn't get a look in'.[36] What particularly worried Owen was that SDP candidates, seeking selection by joint local constituency committees, would find it expedient to compromise their views on precisely those issues – 'a continuation of a British nuclear deterrent after Polaris . . . promising more expenditure [on social services] and generally ducking out of some of the hard edges of SDP policy' – where key differences with the Liberal party existed. As a result, 'we would have an Alliance policy that would look very like the Liberal policies over the years which have never been able to win sufficient support to break through'.[37] In the event, the SDP managed to secure rough parity in the allocation of seats, including those deemed to be most winnable.

Owen's reference to the issue of Britain's nuclear deterrent reflected the priority he gave to defence policy, an area in which he had developed a deep and detailed expertise. It had become, moreover, the issue upon which he felt most profoundly separated from the now unilateralist Labour party, the issue in fact which, he believed, disqualified Labour from a fitness to govern. The issue had also always had the potential to create discord within the Alliance. The Liberals had a strong unilateralist tradition, while several leading figures in the SDP, in particular Owen and Bill Rodgers, were strong supporters of the notion of an independent British deterrent. A serious split had been averted prior to the General Election of 1983 and in the summer of 1984 a Joint Commission on Defence and Disarmament was set up to prepare proposals for an agreed defence policy. The key question was what would be done when the existing Polaris nuclear submarines, dating from the 1960s, reached the end of their useful life. Both parties opposed the Trident missile option adopted by the Conservative government, the Liberals on principle and the SDP on grounds of cost, but the latter admitted that by the time an Alliance government came to power the costs of cancellation might outweigh those of continuing with the project and that, in such circumstances, it would be foolish to abandon what was already or almost in place. By the spring of 1986 it was becoming known that the Commission was likely to suggest that the decision on what happened after Polaris could be deferred since Polaris itself might well remain in service until the mid- or late 1990s.

For Owen this was precisely the sort of fudge which he regarded as constitutionally characteristic of the Liberal party, but for the time being he kept his counsel on the matter. The crisis which now arose could easily have been avoided, but reflected the lack of mutual confidence and trust existing at the highest levels of the Alliance. In mid-May David Steel briefed the lobby correspondent of the *Scotsman* and confirmed that the Commission's report would not commit Liberals to replacing the Polaris system. By the time this accurate, if unwise, admission reached the pages of the newspaper, it had been translated into the headline 'Alliance report rejects UK deterrent: Owen's nuclear hopes dashed'. Owen, convinced that Steel had been party to a deliberate and humiliating snub, now made no attempt to resolve the matter through private investigation and discussion but instead used his speech on 17 May to the meeting of the Council for Social Democracy in Southport to reaffirm his conviction that Britain should remain a nuclear power and to state that, if the Alliance was going to campaign for the cancellation of Trident, it must be ready to find a replacement. To confirm his position he then told a meeting of the Anglo–German society in Bonn that Britain's contribution to Nato must include, at least for the time being, a minimum nuclear deterrent.

Owen's démarche sent shock waves through the Alliance and through the SDP itself. Referring to Owen's speech to the Council for Social Democracy, Roy Jenkins later suggested 'that the alliance began to die on that wet Southport Saturday morning'.[38] For Shirley Williams, the maintenance of the Alliance seemed more important than the detail of policy:

> I hope . . . that you might welcome what [the Commission] has achieved, while making clear that your own position remains unchanged. That would strengthen cooperation between our two parties. I do hope you will not repudiate the Commission's conclusions, for the alliance between the SDP and Liberal parties offers the country the one sane alternative to the policies of the old parties, and demands all our efforts to sustain and strengthen it.[39]

Owen, his position endorsed by the SDP's parliamentary party, felt let down by Rodgers, a member of the joint Commission, whose position had changed 'from being one of the foremost supporters . . . of a British nuclear deterrent to now, I gather, being "agnostic" . . . Your position is both unexpected and makes me in personal terms very sad.'[40] Rodgers, in turn, 'had every reason at Southport to be angry that you were undermining the Commission's report in advance of publication'. Owen had been understandably provoked by the leak in the *Scotsman*, but 'after five years' experience, we all know how difficult Liberals can often be'.[41]

Once the Commission's report had been published on 11 June, Owen and Steel set about trying to repair the damage caused by their respective actions. They came to the conclusion that there might be some mileage in Owen's idea of Anglo–French co-operation over nuclear weapons and agreed to explore this possibility in a series of meetings with European and NATO leaders. But these efforts at reconciliation were undermined by events at the Liberals' annual assembly at Eastbourne in September. With the party leadership misjudging the mood of the meeting and after passionate contributions to the debate from Simon Hughes and Michael Meadowcroft, MPs for Bermondsey and Leeds West respectively, a motion opposing a nuclear element in any European defence co-operation was carried by the narrow margin of 652 votes to 625. Many of those in the majority, believing that Steel had been consistently outmanoeuvred in his partnership with the SDP leader so far, felt that they would be strengthening Steel's hand in his negotiations with Owen; others, without serious expectation of winning the vote, felt that they were delivering a rebuke to the SDP leader. Steel criticised his party in his closing speech to the assembly and he and Owen then redoubled their efforts to find an acceptable compromise. When it came, it represented a substantial triumph for David Owen. By mid-December a new defence statement was ready which committed an Alliance government to maintaining, with whatever necessary modernisation, a minimum British nuclear deterrent until it could be safely negotiated away as part of a global agreement involving substantial concessions on the part of the Soviet Union.

In this way, the nominal unity of the Alliance was maintained, but at a significant long-term cost. The damage was immediately apparent in the opinion polls. Alliance support which had stood as high as 35 per cent in January was back down to 23.5 per cent in December, having been even lower immediately after Eastbourne. More profoundly, questions had been posed about the viability of the Alliance itself. Paddy Ashdown, a Liberal representative on the joint Commission, gave vent to his feelings:

> I will not be party to an attempt to railroad the Alliance into a position where its freedom of action after the next election is pre-empted now; or participate in a conspiracy to extract one-sided concessions which are not reciprocated; or proselytise for political partnership unless we can show rather more of it between ourselves; or make more sacrifices, or call for them from others, without some evidence that this is a two-way street.[42]

More generally, Liberal doubts about David Owen were confirmed. By now, many would have concurred with Roy Jenkins's later assessment that it was 'the especial misfortune of the Alliance to be a political grouping which stood for consensus but which contained one of the two most abrasive figures in British politics'.[43] For some, the difficulties of working with Owen stemmed from his own abandonment of the progressive left in British politics. Others believed that Owen had not wanted agreement on the defence issue as the continuation of separate SDP and Liberal policies would strengthen his resolve to resist any future merger of the two parties.

It was against this background that the Alliance prepared for the General Election of June 1987. A successful rally at the Barbican Centre in January, victory in the Greenwich by-election and the comfortable retention of the seat of Truro, made vacant by the tragic death of David Penhaligon in a car crash, boosted morale. But underlying tensions remained. This time no attempt was made to nominate a Prime Minister designate. Despite their recent differences, Owen and Steel put themselves forward as separate party leaders and as examples of the sort of inter-party co-operation which they sought to substitute for the confrontational politics which, they believed, alienated an increasing percentage of the electorate. Negotiated by teams from the two parties, the joint manifesto, *Britain United: The Time has Come*, was inevitably something of a compromise. In a jointly signed foreword, Owen and Steel insisted that Britain could only be drawn together by 'political, economic and social reform on a scale not contemplated in our country for over forty years'. Yet in its detail, apart from constitutional issues, it was a less radical document than these words implied. As Owen later explained:

> We could not openly endorse the social market for Liberals felt that positioned us too close to the Conservatives; we could not wholeheartedly support the British nuclear deterrent for the Liberals were still deeply divided on the issue. Nor could we present Labour as totally unfit to govern because that meant closing the option of being able to form a coalition with them.[44]

The manifesto was described as a 'programme for government' but, as everyone recognised, the most to which the Alliance could realistically aspire was to hold the balance of power in the new parliament. Inevitably, this raised the question of which way the balance was likely to be tipped in the event that the Alliance got hold of it. It was a question which Steel and Owen were reluctant to answer, recognising that a clearly stated preference either way would inevitably chase away the votes of some potential supporters. In a joint letter to Alliance candidates some months before the election, the two leaders put forward the agreed line: 'We shall not allow ourselves, nor should you, to express a preference between working with Labour or Tory MPs.' Only in a general sense, however, was this position maintained. It was fairly obvious to the attentive observer that Steel's Liberal party was more of an anti-Conservative force than an anti-Labour one. Equally, Owen's SDP seemed more sympathetic to the Conservative party, especially if that party were no longer led by Mrs Thatcher. Once again, it was the issue of defence which divided the two parties. As Owen later explained, 'for me [Labour's defence policy] was the disqualifying factor for being the government, for David [Steel] it was one very good issue to measure Labour by, no more and no less'.[45] Yet it was Owen himself who did most to open the rift to public inspection when, in the course of a joint television interview of himself and Steel by Robin Day, he declared:

> In the last analysis, the one issue on which I will always judge anyone – and that is somebody who would put at jeopardy the defences and security of this country – unless the Labour Party changes its defence policy, in my judgement they are not fit to govern the country.[46]

Despite these apparent divisions, the Alliance waged a reasonably effective campaign. Both leaders came over well and impressed the electorate as committed and serious politicians. Some argued, particularly once the electoral outcome was known, that the joint leadership was a disadvantage, confusing the electorate and contrasting unfavourably with the way in which both Labour and the Conservatives sought to present their respective leaders in quasi-presidential terms. But later detailed studies failed to produce hard evidence that large numbers of voters had been alienated by the fact that the Alliance consisted of two parties with two leaders. In practice, the Alliance's fortunes were largely determined, as had so often been the case for the Liberals in the past, by the performance of the two leading parties. It was widely agreed that Labour waged a highly competent campaign. But the electorate was not convinced that Neil Kinnock had yet gone far enough to pull Labour back from socialist extremism and it had profound doubts about his personal fitness for the premiership. By contrast, the Conservatives were rewarded for low inflation, falling unemployment and widespread prosperity. Mrs. Thatcher, if not always liked, was admired for her leadership qualities. This was not a situation in which the Alliance was likely to improve upon its performance of 1983. In the event, the Alliance secured 22 seats, one fewer than four years before, on 22.7 per cent of the vote. Three seats were gained, all by the Liberals, but these were more than offset by losses which included that of Roy Jenkins at Glasgow, Hillhead. Overall, a net loss of five seats was recorded compared with the Alliance's standing at the dissolution.

The mould, then, had not been broken. It had perhaps been cracked to the extent that, in tandem with the SDP, the Liberals had performed better in two successive general elections than at any time since the 1920s. But the goal of replacing Labour as the main non-Conservative party in British politics, which had seemed not beyond the bounds of possibility in 1981–3, was now fading from view. Indeed, throughout its history the Alliance was more of a threat in Conservative seats than in those held by Labour, especially in the heartlands of industrial Britain. In the 1987 General Election, only six of the twenty seats in which Alliance candidates came closest to victory were Labour-held. Labour had proved remarkably resilient for precisely the same reasons that the Alliance had failed to break through. The concentration of Labour's vote, class-based if on a diminishing foundation, meant that, however badly it performed, it was never likely in the existing electoral system to secure fewer than 150 seats in the House of Commons. By contrast, the even spread of the Alliance vote meant that even an impressive share of the popular vote of anything up to 30 per cent was unlikely to be matched by a comparable representation in parliament. Only in the event of a freak result, with a relatively small number of Alliance MPs holding the balance between equally matched Labour and Conservative parties, would the Liberals and SDP have had the chance – but by no means the certainty – of forcing through the introduction of proportional representation and thereby transforming the pattern of British politics. Ironically, therefore, the Alliance needed Labour to perform better and not worse than it did in the 1980s.

Thus the Alliance had failed to remedy the weaknesses from which the Liberal party, standing alone, had long suffered. The Alliance, like the Liberals, enjoyed no solid ideological or geographical base. Its vote came 'from everywhere in general and nowhere in particular'.[47] As a result, and again in common with the Liberals, the Alliance enjoyed its greatest success – and sometimes that success was quite spectacular – as a repository for protest votes in individual by-elections, rather than as a serious aspirant for power in national contests. By 1987, moreover, the scope for attracting disillusioned Tory and Labour supporters was narrowing. Many of the Conservatives' reforms and innovations now seemed less radical than when Mrs. Thatcher had first advocated them, while Labour was beginning to move back to the middle ground, its new programme in the words of *The Times* 'Gaitskellism from the left of centre'. On policy and image too, the Alliance showed little advance over the performance of the Liberals. Individual policies appear to have played only a small part in generating Alliance support. Polls showed that the electorate had only a hazy notion of what the Alliance stood for. It was little more than 'a safe and decent alternative to the two established parties . . . a moderate force in an increasingly immoderate age'.[48] Ironically, as Labour under Kinnock was becoming reconciled to staying in Europe, the policy issue which had been most important for the Gang of Four in their original decision to jump ship and on which the Liberals had a long and consistent record, it appeared that the majority of Alliance voters actually supported Britain's withdrawal.

With the Conservative government comfortably re-elected, the period immediately after the 1987 General Election was, from an Alliance point of view, an appropriate one for reflection and re-evaluation. It was not to be. The question of the merger of the two parties was bound to come on to the agenda. Steel had taken the opportunity in July 1986 on the tenth anniversary of his assumption of the Liberal leadership to make clear his own belief that a formal union of the two parties was, in the long term, inevitable. Jenkins told a meeting of the Tawney Society that summer that the Alliance was, in ideological terms, 'about as cohesive as any decent democratic grouping ought ever to be'. Even Owen himself had suggested at the fifth anniversary of the founding of the SDP that merger might one day be the natural destiny of the two parties. On the ground, local Liberal and SDP activists were often acting as if they were now part of a united party and, in constituencies such as Cambridge and Saffron Walden, fusion had already taken place.

But merger was by no means an inevitable outcome. Whatever he had said in public, it was not what Owen wanted and the majority of the diminished SDP parliamentary party agreed with him. Indeed, as his own views had evolved, he felt, if anything, less comfortable in Liberal company and more distant from his erstwhile colleagues in the Gang of Four. The party's Owenite trustees no doubt spoke for their leader:

> From the beginning the SDP was seen by some members of the Gang of Four as simply a device to get people out of the Labour Party. They thought, therefore, that as soon as possible it should be merged with the Liberal Party. This view, which was no doubt a careful political decision at the beginning, has become an article of faith, if not an obsession.[49]

With Owen included, the strains within a united party would not have gone away. Indeed, they would have become more acute in the event of that party ever entering government. Differences over defence and the market economy had already surfaced and would one day have been joined by the issue of a federal Europe, to which Owen had always been opposed. It was perhaps his understanding of this position that persuaded David Steel that nothing would be gained by delay or waiting for a process of organic merger to occur of its own accord. Over the weekend following the General Election, he called for a 'democratic fusion' of the two parties. Owen responded by declaring his opposition and calling for a ballot of SDP members. That ballot was cleverly worded to maximise the numbers of those opposing total fusion, for the conciliatory alternative was to negotiate for a closer constitutional framework for the existing Alliance which still preserved the separate existence of the SDP. In the event, the proposal to begin merger negotiations with the Liberals was carried by 25,897 votes (57.4 per cent) to 19,228 (42.6 per cent). This result prompted Owen's resignation as party leader and a clear indication that he intended to work for the creation of a new fourth party in British politics based on those who had voted to retain an independent SDP. His decision, though consistent with the views he had held since the party's foundation, seemed to defy the democratic decision of the membership and earned Owen the lasting animosity of the majority of Liberals and of many members of the SDP. Meanwhile, on the Liberal side, the path to union seemed at this stage altogether more smooth. At Harrogate in September the party's annual assembly voted overwhelmingly to begin negotiations for merger. Preliminary talks between the two sides got under way on 29 September.

The prospective loss of David Owen, the most high-profile figure within the Alliance, was a considerable blow, but this was as nothing compared with the way in which negotiations towards union now proceeded. It was not just that many obstacles remained to be overcome before the marriage of the two parties could be consummated. In the words of the historians of the SDP, the negotiations themselves 'resembled a cross between the Twilight of the Gods and a Feydeau farce, with the farcical element increasingly to the fore as time went on'.[50] The chances of agreement were not improved by the inclusion within the Liberal negotiating team of figures such as Tony Greaves, head of Liberal publications, Michael Meadowcroft, the former MP for Leeds West, and Rachael Pitchford, Chair of the Young Liberals, who were most suspicious of the SDP, of its policies, its structure and its decision-making processes. Such figures represented a strong strand of opinion that the Liberals had tended to concede too much in earlier negotiations between the two parties. When a draft constitution for a new joint party was published on 18 December, it was clear either that David Steel, in the wake of Harrogate, was taking the Liberals too much for granted or else that Robert Maclennan, the new, often diffident and sometimes patently nervous, leader of the Social Democrats, was proving a more formidable negotiator than had been anticipated. The new party was to have a federal structure and, as in the SDP, responsibility for policy would be divided between the annual conference and a special policy committee. The inclusion in the preamble to the constitution of a commitment that Britain should play a full and constructive role in NATO was curious. This was something which many Liberals were more inclined to accept as an item of current policy rather than as part of a declaration of abiding principles. Nomenclature had also proved controversial. 'Liberal and

Social Democrats' might have been fair to both sides, but produced an unfortunate acronym. In the event, the proposed name of the new party – 'The New Liberal and Social Democratic Party' – was cumbersome; the proposed shorthand – 'the Alliance' – insensitive to those who wanted to build something new rather than be reminded of the tensions of the past.

Despite clear warnings from the meeting of the Liberal Party Council in December, Steel compounded his difficulties by pressing ahead apparently regardless of the mounting unease among party activists. Matters came to a head with the conclusion of the merger negotiations in the early hours of 13 January 1988. By the end of the night, four of the Liberal negotiating team had resigned, either over the question of the new party's name or the commitment to NATO. A joint policy document, *Voices and Choices for All,* supposedly the work of the two leaders but in practice largely the creation of Maclennan, proved even more contentious. For Maclennan this was a key element in the merger negotiations, necessary in order to pin down the Liberals' 'softness' on policy issues, of which Owen had so often complained, and to have any chance of attracting Owenites, if not Owen himself, to the new party. When the details of the Steel–Maclennan package emerged, it appeared that the Liberal leader had put his name to an astonishing list of unpopular and potentially damaging policies. These included the extension of VAT to food, children's clothing, newspapers, financial services and domestic fuel; the phasing out of tax relief on mortgage interest payments; the end of universal child benefit; and a commitment to retain the Trident missile system. Steel had failed to foresee that this package would be completely unacceptable to his colleagues. For a man who had enjoyed an impressive record of political dexterity and surefootedness, combining for more than a decade understated persuasiveness with resolute determination, it was an untypical aberration and one which probably ended any chance that he would lead the new party. But Steel had always enjoyed a closer rapport with the electorate than with his own party. Before the day was out, the Liberal party *en masse* seemed ready to disown him and, to the embarrassment of all concerned, a press conference, intended to proclaim agreement on the new party, had to be postponed. Borrowing a phrase from the well-known Monty Python sketch, Des Wilson soon dubbed the Steel–Maclennan document a 'dead parrot'.

For a moment it seemed possible that the entire merger process might unravel. But enough goodwill existed on either side to save the situation. A new six-man team was set up to draft a replacement policy document which took as its basis the 1987 Alliance manifesto. The earlier controversial proposals were dropped and the new document quickly gained the leaders' acceptance. 'It was a third of the length of the dead parrot; it was hardly uplifting, but it was unexciting and anodyne; it was largely uncontroversial within the parties; it served its purpose and was soon forgotten by most.'[51] Only Maclennan's dramatic but unsuccessful attempt, at the eleventh hour and in a blaze of publicity, to secure David Owen's adherence to the agreement provided one final twist to what had been an unedifying tale. Special Liberal and SDP conferences at the end of January then endorsed the deal. That of the Liberals at Blackpool, carefully controlled by the party leadership, produced an overwhelming victory for the advocates of merger – by 2099 votes to 385 with 23 abstentions. In this way the historic Liberal party formally came to an end. Liberal opponents of fusion, seeing themselves as the heirs of a north of England radical tradition which was in danger of being watered down in any new party, eventually organised themselves under the leadership of Michael Meadowcroft into the Continuing Liberal Party. This body put up 73 candidates in the 1992 General Election and polled 100,000 votes in the 1994 European elections, before fading into insignificance. Divisions within the SDP were more serious and more damaging to the prospects of the new party. Though a motion for merger was passed overwhelmingly, Owen's supporters tried to show their strength by taking no part in the proceedings. A subsequent ballot of SDP members revealed 65 per cent support for merger, but the size of the minority and the low overall poll were sufficient to encourage Owen to announce that a rump SDP would fight on. Against, then, a background of division and recrimination, the new Social and Liberal Democratic

Party (the Democrats for short), formally came into existence in March 1988.

Founded more on the ruins of its predecessors than as the beneficiary of their respective political traditions, the new party got off to a bad start. The public divisions and disputes since the General Election of 1987 had had an inevitable impact upon its standing in the opinion polls, shattering the image of co-operation and consensus which had been the most potent appeal of the old Alliance at its height. Now, the continuation of the Owenite SDP threatened to split the centre vote to the electoral detriment of both parties. Grass-roots morale had been badly shaken and, by the summer, resignations were reaching party headquarters at an alarming rate. The local elections in May offered meagre comfort. The Social and Liberal Democratic Party (SLD) suffered a net loss of over sixty seats, but its vote held up better than opinion polls had predicted. The SDP, by contrast, was all but wiped out. With Steel declining to stand for the leadership of the new party, the membership was offered a straight choice between two former Liberals, Alan Beith and Paddy Ashdown. The former committed himself to protecting the values of the old Liberal party within its successor, but few genuine policy differences emerged. In the event, the party opted by a decisive margin for Ashdown's more exciting personality and style but, with only five years' parliamentary experience under his belt, an element of risk attached to its choice.

The new leader faced, by any criteria, a daunting challenge. When Ashdown took over, the SLD was 'confused, demoralised, starved of money and in the grip of a deep identity crisis'.[52] By the autumn the party was technically bankrupt and drastic economies had to be effected. Only gradually did the position improve, though for a time it must have seemed that, for each dragon slain, a fresh one was waiting in the wings to take its place. A by-election in Kensington in July offered no evidence of revival. In December the Conservatives were able to hold on in Epping Forest even though the SLD and SDP candidates combined secured 38 per cent of the vote, which was more than the victorious Tory.

Two months later, in the Yorkshire constituency of Richmond, the Owenites forced the SLD into third place, prompting Ashdown to make a final but unsuccessful gesture of reconciliation to Owen: 'otherwise I can see only protracted trench warfare which will destroy both our parties and give Labour the chance it needs'.[53] In the 1989 council elections the SLD suffered a further net loss of more than a hundred seats, though its vote again held up reasonably well. North of the border the Scottish Nationalists were racing ahead of the Democrats in the opinion polls. Worse, however, was to come. In the third set of direct elections to the European parliament in June 1989, the party was pushed into a humiliating fourth place on just 6.4 per cent of the popular vote, behind a sudden, unexpected and spectacular advance by the Green Party. This was a particular blow in view of the efforts which the Liberals had made since the 1970s to focus upon environmental issues. The upsurge of the Greens, reflective of mounting concern about global warming and the depletion of the ozone layer, would fade as quickly as it had arrived. Yet this was precisely the voice of passing protest which the Liberals and the Alliance had been so adept at attracting. Now, as one leading Democrat quipped, 'we are no longer the cop-out vote'.[54] Even the party's name proved to be contentious and divisive, and it was changed to the 'Liberal Democrats' following a postal ballot of members in October 1989. That membership had now fallen to around 75,000. Ashdown confessed to being haunted by the nightmare that the party which had started with Gladstone would end with himself. 'A very, very black week', he recorded at the end of June, 'which may well mark the end of the Party altogether. It's down to me and a few others to try and keep the thing together.'[55] As late as September 1990 the party's Gallup rating stood at just 9.3 per cent. Changes of name appeared only to have exacerbated long-standing problems over image and identity. Nearly three-quarters of those questioned could not give the party its proper name, while 80 per cent were unable to say with any accuracy what the Liberal Democrats stood for. Inevitably, questions were being asked as to whether the price of merger had been too high.

Salvation arrived in a familiar fashion. By the end of 1988 the

Conservatives were trailing Labour in the polls. The government's reputation for economic competence was badly dented as the boom engineered by Chancellor Nigel Lawson turned sour and inflation began once more to rise. In introducing the Community Charge (or poll tax), Mrs Thatcher appeared to have lost her acute and instinctive sensitivity to the public mood, which had been a key feature in her earlier ascendancy. With the government shaken by a succession of ministerial resignations and the Conservative party increasingly divided by the Prime Minister's strident opposition to further European integration, the Liberal Democrats had their chance to profit once again at the expense of an unpopular Tory government. At a by-election in October 1990 in Eastbourne, solidly Conservative throughout the century, the Liberal Democrat candidate, David Bellotti, captured the seat on an anti-Conservative swing of more than 20 per cent. By this time too, the threat from the Greens and the Owenite SDP had passed. Owen had abandoned any pretensions to be leading a national party following the 1989 local elections and his group was effectively wound up after its candidate at the May 1990 Bootle by-election came in behind Screaming Lord Sutch of the Monster Raving Loony Party. It was the one consequence of any political importance secured during the latter body's overlong and undistinguished lifetime. Further by-election successes followed at Ribble Valley (March 1991) and Kincardine and Deeside (November 1991) on swings of 25 and 11.4 per cent respectively. But it was the 1991 local elections which gave most cause for celebration. Despite defending a high base-line secured by the Alliance in 1987, the Liberal Democrats registered a further 520 net gains through effective targeting, winning control of 19 councils.

With the party enjoying a stronger base in the country, Ashdown had more opportunity to mould the Liberal Democrats in his own image. He personally had emerged as a politician of stature – though there were always those who found him sanctimonious. His particularly forthright views on issues of foreign policy including Yugoslavia and the Gulf, though they often aroused resentment among some of his parliamentary followers, ensured him a high public profile and an approval rating which always ran ahead of his party's. As chairman of the Liberal Democrats' Policy Committee, Ashdown removed the last vestiges of what he once called 'soggy corporatism', the old-style Liberal commitment to the managed economy of incomes policies and governmental control. In their place he encouraged a whole-hearted espousal of the free market, competition and enterprise. With Labour and the Conservatives showing renewed signs of convergence, Ashdown also sought to broaden the agenda of political debate with a new emphasis on constitutional reform, the rights of women and the family, environmental issues and improved public services. Above all, he succeeded in making Britain's third party look a more serious political force than at any time for 60 years. It was at this time that the party finally shook off the 'beards and sandals' image which had dogged its predecessor for so long. As Ashdown later explained:

> the thing which drove me through my leadership of the Liberal Democrats was getting the Party into power. I have never been at all attracted by the notion that it was sufficient for us to be the unpaid think tank for new ideas in British politics; or the repository for community politics without a purpose.[56]

It was, then, a very different and rejuvenated party which faced the General Election of 1992 from that which had emerged from the botched process of merger four years before. The political landscape too was showing a distinct change from the pattern of the 1980s. After the General Election of 1987, its third successive defeat, the Labour party had begun its first major policy review since the 1950s. Seven policy groups were set up to rethink its approach to domestic and international affairs with the clear aim of throwing out those policies which had made Labour unelectable. In practice this meant coming 'to terms with the irreversibility of many Thatcherite reforms by recognising that the market economy should be regarded as innocent until found guilty, rather than vice versa'.[57] The results were startling. Any residual commitments to extend public ownership soon disappeared. The 1989 policy statement, *Meet the Challenge, Make the Change*, bound a future Labour government to work through a successful market economy. It was perhaps the least socialist policy statement in the party's history to date. State intervention would now be limited to specific areas such as industrial training where the market was perceived to be failing. In 1990, Labour's *Looking to the Future* declared that only the water industry among those enterprises privatised by the Conservative governments since 1979 was to be returned to the public sector. Two years later, even this commitment had been dropped, with the party settling now merely for 'public control'. Similarly, in the area of industrial relations Labour had by 1990 moved towards an acceptance of much of the legal framework constructed by the Conservatives. The party also swung back to support for British membership of the European community, its path eased by the perception that, under the Commission presidency of Jacques Delors, that body was now more sympathetic to Labour's aspirations than had once been the case. Perhaps most strikingly of all in view of Neil Kinnock's well-known personal views, the 1989 Labour conference abandoned the policy of unilateral nuclear disarmament.

These dramatic changes opened up both opportunities and dangers for the Liberal Democrats. At the time of his campaign for the party leadership in 1988, Ashdown had declared that his strategic aim remained that of the Alliance throughout its history – to replace Labour as the main opposition to the Conservatives. Yet if the 1987 General Election had already shown that this ambition was unlikely to be achieved, by the early 1990s it had become totally unrealistic. Most commentators agreed that Labour looked electable for the first time in a decade, and opinion polls indicated that this perception was shared by the wider electorate. Ashdown was not blind to this evolving situation and began to think in terms of a political realignment not unlike that which had attracted Jo Grimond a generation earlier. Though he was unimpressed by Kinnock and, in his own mind, ruled out any formal relationship with Labour before the next election, he believed that a fourth Conservative electoral victory would place realignment firmly on the political agenda. Such a possibility had become more likely following Margaret Thatcher's replacement by John Major in November 1990. The new Prime Minister's easy-going and moderate image registered an immediate appeal with the electorate. On the other hand, it was also possible that the next General Election would leave the Liberal Democrats holding the balance of power in the House of Commons and able to negotiate their way into a coalition government.

Major delayed holding an election until April 1992 and most observers predicted a close outcome. The Liberal Democrats' manifesto, *Changing Britain for Good*, pledged wide-ranging constitutional reform and a more constructive role for Britain within the European Community. It stressed the need to invest in the public services and, defying conventional wisdom that electors will not vote for higher taxation, promised to raise income tax by a penny in the pound in order to fund investment in education. In addition, the Liberal Democrats would repeal some of the Conservative government's recent innovations in health and education, in particular GP fundholding schemes, hospital trusts and City Technology Colleges. In its editorial the *Guardian* enthused that the Liberal Democrats, unlike the Liberals of old, were a 'proper party' which had produced a 'proper manifesto', one which 'far out-distances its competitors with a fizz of ideas and an absence of fudge'. It was an appropriate tribute to the party's recovery under Ashdown's leadership and to the importance of its inheritance from the SDP of an efficient party structure and an effective policy-making process. Ashdown himself waged an impressive campaign, his personal standing unharmed, perhaps even enhanced, by the recent newspaper disclosure of an earlier affair with his secretary. Though a hung parliament seemed an increasing possibility, he resolutely refused to express a preference as between supporting a minority Labour or a minority Conservative administration. In practice this was an unrealistic stance. On several key issues, including devolution for Scotland and investment in education, Labour was clearly closer to the Liberal Democrat position. In the course of the campaign, moreover, Major ruled out the possibility of proportional representation – which would have been the Liberal Democrats' bottom line in any coalition negotiations – while Labour was at least prepared to examine the pros and cons of electoral reform. But Ashdown was wary about making any statement which might alienate potential supporters and had long believed that, by at least holding out the possibility of a Liberal Democrat–Tory coalition, he would make Labour more inclined to concede proportional representation for Westminster.

The outcome was among the more intriguing of post-war election results. The Conservatives finished 8 percentage points ahead of Labour in the popular vote but their overall parliamentary majority was cut to just 21 seats. At long last the electoral system had begun to work against them. The Liberal Democrats' performance was in many ways disappointing – just 20 seats on 18.3 per cent of the vote, with a million fewer supporters than had rallied to the Alliance in 1987. Nor did the party's challenge appear to be growing as the number of second places dropped from 261 to 154. In a number of promising constituencies, Labour's partial recovery had thwarted Liberal Democrat hopes. There was some comfort to be had when comparisons were made with the 6 per cent rating which the party had enjoyed when Ashdown assumed its leadership and even with the 15 per cent recorded at the start of the campaign. But most activists found it hard to sustain the inveterate optimism which had seen the party and its predecessors through so many past setbacks. In particular, the tantalising prospect of a hung parliament, predicted even in the BBC's supposedly reliable exit polls, had quickly faded from view as the results came in. Yet beyond these disappointments lay some interesting features. The first was evidence of an increasingly sophisticated electorate. The Liberal Democrats had hoped to boost their parliamentary representation as a result of anti-Conservative tactical voting. In most seats in which the Alliance had come second in 1987 – and by definition these were overwhelmingly Conservative seats – the party had sought to emphasise the opportunities for tactical voting, attempting to squeeze Labour support by stressing the impossibility of a local Labour victory. This strategy had enjoyed only limited success. Tactical voting clearly had occurred, reducing Major's prospective majority by about a half, but Labour rather than the Liberal Democrats had been the main beneficiary. Even so, two and possibly three of the four seats gained by the Liberal Democrats could be attributed to tactical voting. The hope had to be that, if this apparent desire to remove the Conservatives from office were to grow, increasing numbers of voters would see the need to support the Liberal Democrats where they were the main challenger. In the second place the party's vote was less evenly, and therefore more effectively, distributed across the country than at any election since the Liberals had resumed standing on a fully national basis. The South-West in particular was beginning to look like a Liberal Democrat stronghold where further success might be anticipated.

At least Ashdown seemed well satisfied with the outcome:

> There is a real opportunity now for us to drive a wedge in Labour on PR. Despite the disappointment, this is the result I always said I wanted, with the Tories ahead and Labour going down to a fourth defeat and into an internal battle. We must make use of this opportunity to realign the left.[58]

It was his belief that if, after 13 years in power and with the country at the bottom of a recession, the Conservatives could secure a fourth successive victory, then Labour would have to realise that they could no longer win a general election on their own. Forthcoming boundary changes were likely still further to entrench the Conservative position before the next general election was held. If nothing was done to change this pattern, then Britain faced the very real prospect of one-party government. As the century neared its close, Ashdown increasingly viewed the current situation within the historical context of the twentieth century as a whole. The breakdown of the Progressive Alliance in the century's second decade had, he believed, opened the way to a long era of Conservative domination sustained on a minority of the popular vote. The restored unity of the forces of progressivism was to be his mission. Events would show that Ashdown's calculations were, in key respects, wide of the mark. But they formed the starting point of the strategy which would guide and inform his leadership of the party, sometimes obsessively so, from then on.

Ashdown moved quickly to prepare his party for a major strategic review. The speech which he delivered to a tiny audience of his constituents in Chard on 9 May 1992 was probably the most important of his whole career. Ashdown declared that his purpose was to initiate a wide-ranging discussion about the Liberal Democrats' strategic options in the wake of the recent general election. But he left few doubts as to the direction in which he personally hoped the party would travel. Its purpose, he insisted, should be to 'create the force powerful enough to remove the Tories; to assemble policies capable of sustaining a different government; and to draw together the forces in Britain which will bring change and reform'. Labour had become a 'drag factor' on those others who wished to fight the Conservatives and had lost its historic role as the only left-of-centre party capable of holding power: 'The Tory–Labour duopoly is finished.' It was time for Liberal Democrats to seize the initiative, but they could not do so on their own. They must 'reach out beyond the limits of [their] own party' and 'be the catalyst, the gathering point for a broader movement dedicated to winning the battle of ideas which will give Britain an electable alternative to Conservative government'. That alternative would have a reformed voting system at its heart. The notion of equidistance, tenuously sustained during the election campaign, was not mentioned, but the implication of Ashdown's words was clear. Like Grimond and Steel before him, he saw the Liberal Democrats' future lying primarily in partnership with the non-socialist wing of the Labour party.[59]

Also like his predecessors, however, and for all his brave words about the end of the Tory–Labour duopoly, Ashdown would find that the fortunes of the Liberal Democrats were largely determined by events inside the two main parties. The Conservative government's honeymoon was short-lived. The events of 'Black Wednesday', 16 September 1992, when Britain was forced ignominiously to withdraw from the European Exchange Rate Mechanism, hitherto trumpeted as a vital component of the government's anti-inflation strategy, destroyed for years to come the Conservative party's reputation for economic competence. Gallup revealed a halving in public satisfaction with John Major and his government's record, and in optimism about the British economy. It was a slump from which the government never recovered. Despite a steady improvement in economic indicators achieved *outside* the ERM, ministers waited in vain for the much-vaunted 'feel-good' factor to translate into signs of electoral approval. The government's difficulties were exacerbated by increasingly open divisions within the party and inside the cabinet itself on the question of Europe, particularly during and after the passage through parliament of the Maastricht Treaty, paving the way for a further tranche of measures of European integration. The government also became associated in the public mind with the idea of 'sleaze', as a succession of ministers and MPs got embroiled in personal and financial scandals. With Major seemingly lacking the strength of purpose to hold his party together, all these misfortunes were skilfully manipulated by their opponents, especially by a rejuvenated Labour party.

Liberal Democrats prospered as they and their predecessors had been doing now for over thirty years whenever there was an unpopular Tory administration. The party enjoyed four by-election gains during the course of the parliament. That at Christchurch in July 1993 witnessed an astonishing 35 per cent swing. With a couple of defections added in, Liberal Democrat strength in the House of Commons at the 1997 dissolution stood at 26. The picture in local government was even more gratifying. Building upon the unexpected successes of 1991, the party made a further 308 net gains in 1992, 341 in 1993, and 388 in 1994. Following the 1996 council elections, the Liberals held approximately 5100 council seats as against the Conservatives' 4700. To emerge as the second party in local government was no small achievement for a party whose standing in the opinion polls at the time of Ashdown's accession to power had been 'within the statistical margin of error of zero'.[60]

But the fortunes of the Labour party were probably of greater long-term significance from a Liberal Democrat point of view than were those of an unprecedentedly unpopular Conservative government. Contrary to Ashdown's expectations, Labour responded in a disciplined and businesslike manner to the renewed tasks of opposition. It was a sign of the times that, in the contest between John Smith and Bryan Gould to succeed Neil Kinnock as party leader, Gould – who might, in another era, have been described as an unrepentant Keynesian – was now seen as the candidate of the Left. But it was also a sign of the times that Smith emerged the comfortable victor. A cautious Scottish lawyer, Smith's leadership did not witness any significant change of direction from that already mapped out by his predecessor. But he won the respect and support of a united party, less disheartened than it might have been by the 1992 result. In general terms, the decline of Labour's Left continued, with Smith's close allies, Gordon Brown and Tony Blair, securing election to the National Executive Committee. Smith was not interested in formal co-operation with the Liberal Democrats at Westminster, but an encouraging development was the way in which he placed constitutional reform firmly on Labour's agenda and the two parties worked well together on the Scottish Constitutional Convention which had held its first meeting in 1989. Labour and the Liberal Democrats agreed on a joint programme which centred on the creation of a Scottish parliament. Ashdown, however, was disappointed by what he regarded as Labour's opportunistic opposition to the Maastricht Treaty, an issue which for him was one of principle and not of party politics. European integration was, after all, an issue upon which the Liberal party, unlike its opponents, could point to a long, honourable and consistent record of support. Liberal votes in the Commons helped the government to survive the opposition of its own Eurosceptic backbenchers. Smith was committed to a patient, long-term strategy to return Labour to government, but he died suddenly in May 1994. It was his successor, Tony Blair, who transformed the prospects not only of the Labour party but of the Liberal Democrats as well.

Blair soon made it clear that he intended to take Labour even further towards the centre ground of British politics. One of his first major initiatives as party leader was to propose to the 1994 Labour conference the replacement of the much-venerated Clause

IV of the party's constitution, one of the last remaining symbols of its commitment to traditional socialism. He got his way with surprising ease. A special conference in April 1995 approved his proposed change with just over two-thirds of the total vote. Labour was now pledged 'to work for a dynamic economy, serving the public interest, in which the enterprise of the market and the rigour of competition are joined with the forces of partnership and cooperation . . . with a thriving public sector and high quality public services'.[61] Before long, Labour was explicitly endorsing the market economy and proclaiming a 'Third Way' in which a stake-holding society would develop policies of social inclusion for all its citizens. So dramatic was the transformation which had occurred since Labour had offered itself to the electorate under Michael Foot's leadership a little over a decade earlier that the assumption of a changed name, albeit an unofficial one – New Labour – seemed entirely appropriate. Liberal Democrats could not ignore these developments. On the one hand, it could now be asked whether any space remained within the political spectrum for the Liberal Democrats to occupy. David Marquand, whose shifting political allegiance left him well-placed to judge, concluded that New Labour and the Liberal Democrats both 'belong to the same broad-based progressive tradition that goes back, by way of Beveridge, Keynes and the Attlee government, to the ethical socialists and the New Liberals of the early century'.[62] On the other hand, New Labour reopened the genuine possibility of that realignment of the left, of which Liberal leaders had dreamed for almost four decades, or at the very least presented itself as a viable partner for Liberal Democrats in coalition government.

Paddy Ashdown's published diaries describe in voluminous, agonised and sometimes repetitive detail the way in which he wrestled with this dilemma. Though as yet largely uncorroborated, they provide the historian of this period with his most important primary source. While Smith remained at Labour's helm, Ashdown continued to think in terms of Labour's fragmentation. The Liberal Democrats' covert aim was to promote debate within the Labour party between its modernisers and its traditionalists in order to drive a wedge between the two groups. By April 1994, shortly before John Smith's death, Ashdown had privately decided to abandon the policy of equidistance, to declare publicly that the Liberal Democrats could not support a Conservative government after the next election, and then to set tough conditions for a relationship with Labour. But Blair's arrival – 'the deepest and most desperate point of depression in my whole leadership of the party'[63] – forced a rethink:

> I have been building the Party to fill a certain gap in politics, which I know is there and which would give us real electoral appeal. But then along comes Blair with all the power of Labour behind him, and fills exactly the space I have been aiming at for the last seven years![64]

Ashdown had started meeting Blair some months before the latter succeeded John Smith. He found him congenial and, unlike Smith, ready to consider co-operation between the two parties, and he quickly realised that Blair's political vision was very like his own: 'There is very little difference between his thinking and mine. We have come to the same analysis from different directions.'[65]

Blair's leadership forced the abandonment of any lingering belief that the Liberal Democrats could replace Labour as the major left-of-centre force in British politics. Instead, Ashdown came to the conclusion that the best option was to forge a new relationship between the two parties based on a common progressive agenda in which the introduction of a system of proportional representation would form an indispensable element. In a series of usually clandestine meetings with Blair over the next three years, concealed from the majority of the Liberal Democrat parliamentary party, Ashdown explored this 'Project'. His preferred option was the so-called 'Big Thing' – that the two parties should go into the next election as separate entities but offering the electorate a joint heads of agreement document. The two men began with the assumption that Labour would not be able to win the next election on its own but, as the Conservative government's fortunes failed to show any significant signs of recovery despite an improving economic climate, the possibility of a majority Labour government had to be admitted. In such a situation the question would be whether Labour–Liberal Democrat co-operation would prove to be more than a matter of electoral convenience. Ashdown recorded a conversation with Blair in October 1994:

> Ashdown: If you got a majority, do you still see us working together in government?
> Blair: Yes.
> Ashdown: In which case I think we have the opportunity to do something really historic in politics.[66]

On this basis the policy of equidistance was formally renounced in May 1995 and the Liberal Democrats became an overtly anti-Conservative party.

It was a high-risk strategy and at times Ashdown seemed to lose confidence in it, not least because of his failure to extract from Blair a formal promise to reform the Westminster electoral system. The Labour leader repeatedly declared himself unconvinced by the arguments, while making it clear that he faced strong opposition to the 'Project' in the upper echelons of his party. The popularity of New Labour, as registered in the opinion polls, was part of the problem. 'I am becoming really worried', Ashdown wrote in June 1995:

> I can't see a role for us. If the Tories collapse completely I suppose we could become HM Opposition. But then what? Our policies are too close to Labour's for us to be a genuine Opposition and the Tories would simply recover again. Meanwhile, Labour has stolen our ground comprehensively.[67]

But Ashdown received repeated assurances, not least from Roy Jenkins, by now the Leader of the Liberal Democrat peers but also a confidant and advisor of the Labour leader and hopeful that New Labour offered the prospect of resurrecting his failed mission to break the mould of British politics, that Blair would prefer to head a government which contained Liberal Democrats than one that was made up entirely from the ranks of the Labour party, irrespective of whether Labour won an overall majority. Increasingly, indeed, he believed that, despite the disparity of resources and parliamentary strength between the two parties, it was essentially a Liberal agenda around which realignment could take place. 'If, as it appears, I have more in common with Blair than he has with his left wing,' reasoned Ashdown, 'surely the logical thing is for us to create a new, powerful alternative force which would be unified around a broadly liberal agenda.'[68] Even Gordon Brown, Labour's shadow chancellor, assured Ashdown that he was in practice adopting a classical Liberal programme, based on competition, enterprise and equality of opportunity. Blair and Ashdown repeatedly reflected upon the historical context of their plans. 'The real shame', noted Blair, was that 'our two parties weren't able to stay together in the early part of the century . . . Lloyd George was incomparably the most radical figure in the second and third decades of the twentieth century, but he wasn't in a party that could deliver. We have to bring these two streams back together again.'[69] In 1996 the two leaders asked two of their senior parliamentary colleagues, Robert Maclennan and Robin Cook, to lay the groundwork for a stable relationship between the two parties by exploring the possibilities of co-operation on questions of constitutional reform. The outcome was the Cook–Maclennan agreement of March 1997, outlining the areas in which Labour and the Liberal Democrats could work together in the next parliament.

It was, then, with a more realistic prospect of being in government than at any time since the 1920s that the Liberal Democrats went into the general election of April 1997, delayed by John Major for almost as long as the constitution permitted in the ultimately forlorn hope of a Conservative revival. They had hardly put a foot wrong throughout the parliament. Only at the 1994 annual assembly, at a time when Ashdown was trying to convince Blair that the Liberal Democrats were a responsible party which could be trusted with power, had they come near to scoring an own goal. Then, an exasperated Ashdown had walked off the platform after a badly organised debate on the possible legalisation of soft drugs. Otherwise, both the party and its leader had developed a gravitas that had been lacking hitherto. Most observers believed that the Liberal Democrats were better prepared for an election than a third party had ever been. Even their demand for electoral reform seemed to be making ground as Ashdown, with scant recognition of what many regarded as a finely balanced argument, repeatedly and insistently equated proportional representation with 'fair votes'. With a modernising agenda, the party also called for a written constitution, a bill of rights and sweeping changes to the institution of parliament.

Both Blair and Ashdown understood the importance of tactical voting. The Labour-supporting *Daily Mirror* was given and subsequently published a list of seats where Liberal Democrats could beat the Conservatives if Labour supporters voted tactically. Targeting was therefore central to the Liberal Democrats' campaign and Ashdown covered more than 17,000 miles in visiting 75 seats where he believed his party had a realistic prospect of victory. Once again, the party campaigned on its unashamed readiness to increase taxes to invest in the public services. Despite the now well-established links with Labour, Liberal Democrats sought to claim the high moral ground, dismissing the 'Punch and Judy' spats of the two larger parties. None the less, voters were left in no doubt that support for the Liberal Democrats would in the first instance help secure the defeat and removal of an unpopular Conservative government.

The outcome revealed both how much progress the Liberal Democrats had made and why Ashdown had been right to view Blair's arrival on the scene as a mixed blessing. The Liberal Democrats secured 46 seats, by far the best third-party performance for almost seventy years and twice as many as won by the Alliance in 1983. But they did so on just 17 per cent of the popular vote, the party's second worst performance since it had resumed contesting general elections on a truly national basis. The election had been a huge triumph for New Labour (with 419 seats), which had taken votes and seats from the Conservatives, including protest votes which might normally have been expected to benefit the Liberal Democrats. The latter's success in terms of seats reflected the fact that anti-Conservative tactical voting had been more prevalent than ever before. Had the movement of votes been consistent across the country, the Liberal Democrats would have won just 28 seats. As it was, they prospered in constituencies where they were already well-placed, with tactical support from Labour voters, to unseat a Conservative incumbent, and in areas where their credibility had been enhanced by their record in local government. These tended also to be constituencies which the Liberal Democrats had been targeting for at least the previous four years. Such seats were overwhelmingly in the South and South-West.

Where did this result leave the Project? Ashdown's first reaction was that the scale of Labour's victory made co-operation between the parties more difficult. It would, he thought, be 'somehow unseemly' to join forces and deprive the country of an effective opposition: 'I am plagued by the idea that it would be seen as an undemocratic, self-serving act.'[70] When, however, he met the new Prime Minister on 2 May, Blair discussed the prospect of Liberal Democrat representation on two cabinet committees. More significantly, he stressed that the 'end position' remained Liberal Democrat participation in the government and even held out the possibility of an eventual merger between the two parties 'some way down the track'.[71] But Ashdown was struck by a change in Blair's demeanour. In what must strike the outsider as a curiously naïve passage, he later reflected:

> Was Blair 'got at' by some of the 'anti-project' people on the night of 1 May? I am unable to say, but there was certainly a curious change in tone between the telephone call I took from him . . . on the morning of 1 May and our conversation the following morning.[72]

What had surely changed was that the electorate had undermined the assumption with which the Project itself had begun, that Labour could not on its own unseat the Conservative government. Though the opinion polls had long predicted a Labour landslide, even the most sanguine inhabitant of Millbank Tower had nurtured a sneaking suspicion that, on the day, the gap between Labour and the Conservatives would be much narrower, with many voters concealing their Conservative inclinations until they reached the privacy of the polling booth, as was believed to have happened in 1992. In the event, Labour secured an overall majority of 177 seats. To proceed now with the Project would mean depriving a number of expectant Labour politicians of office, depriving a considerable number of Labour MPs of their seats at the next general election and, with the introduction of proportional representation, depriving the Labour party itself of any realistic prospect of forming a majority government in the future. All this would in all probability be accompanied by a major split in the Labour movement. The Deputy Prime Minister, John Prescott, was reported to have warned that 'the day that man [Ashdown] walks through the door is the day that I walk out of it'.[73] If Blair now hesitated, his caution was entirely understandable. Had the result of the election been a hung parliament or even a narrow Labour victory, his room for manoeuvre would have been altogether greater.

Being outside the government, at least for the moment, yet broadly sympathetic to much of its programme, created a difficult situation for the Liberal Democrats. Ashdown feared that the inevitable pressures of Britain's confrontational political structure could easily destroy his hopes of long-term realignment if his party remained on the opposition benches for too long. He therefore determined to adopt a stance of 'constructive opposition', which involved criticising the government where the two parties differed but working with it where agreement existed, especially on the programme of constitutional reform worked out by Robin Cook and Robert Maclennan. In the months which followed, the public saw clear manifestations of a new style of politics emerging. Five Liberal Democrats took seats on the cabinet committee on constitutional change; a Liberal Democrat MP became chairman of the Commons Social Security Select Committee; and two junior ministers in the Labour government spoke to fringe meetings at the Liberal Democrats' conference in Eastbourne. In the meantime Blair continued to suggest that he would bring Liberal

Democrats inside his government 'within a matter of months'.[74] But not all of the party were comfortable with these new arrangements. Bill Rodgers argued that the presence of Liberal Democrats on the new consultative committee could create a situation of responsibility without power, 'inhibiting the Liberal Democrats with nothing in exchange except the symbol of closeness'.[75] Peter Mandelson, one of the principal architects of New Labour and a committed supporter of the Project, seemed to confirm this point when he publicly warned Ashdown that the evolving relationship between their parties required him to ensure that the Liberal Democrats behaved responsibly and did not revert to a stance of 'oppositionitis', 'making invalid criticisms and promising pointless profligacy'.[76] But there was much in the government's conduct which the party felt obliged to criticise, not least Chancellor Gordon Brown's determination not to raise direct taxation and to stick for two years to the public-spending plans of the outgoing Conservative government. Such policies, argued the Liberal Democrats' Treasury spokesman Malcolm Bruce, would delay much-needed investment in education and the health service. Concern was also expressed at Labour's failure to give a clear commitment to take Britain into the Single European Currency.

In the meantime Ashdown found it impossible to convince Blair of the centrality of proportional representation to any further progress on realignment. The former argued that electoral reform would guarantee Blair a two-term government, with no possibility of the Conservatives regaining power, and thus the opportunity to transform and modernise the country. But the Prime Minister, worried about the long-term implications, remained sceptical and suggested that the formal merger of the two parties might be a necessary consequence of a change to the electoral system: 'Look, I must tell you that if I give you guys PR, without getting from you a guarantee of merger, or at least some bottom-line assurance that you won't break away later, my party will think I have lost my marbles.'[77]

Blair needed to be sure that, once a change in the voting system had been made, Liberal Democrats would not abandon the Project, leaving Labour stranded in a permanent minority position:

> I think the basic question is: Are our two parties in fact both modern social democratic parties? The answer is, substantially, yes. At the moment I am being asked to sacrifice a large part of my party and accept permanent coalition politics with no guarantee that our coalition partner remains constant.[78]

Ashdown's response was to accept that there was a broad identity between New Labour and the Liberal Democrats but to remind Blair that much of the Labour party, particularly in local government, had still to be converted to the new variant. Merger might well come some time in the future, but it was 'not an option in the short term' and in any case not something to which Ashdown could commit his party.[79]

On this basis the dialogue continued throughout 1998, though the prospect of a formal coalition was repeatedly postponed and ultimately abandoned. Blair continued to make encouraging noises, telling the post-election Labour party conference that he numbered Keynes, Beveridge and Lloyd George as well as Bevin, Bevan and Attlee among his heroes. From a Liberal Democrat point of view there were some positive achievements of which the introduction of proportional representation for elections to the European parliament and to the newly created Scottish Parliament and Welsh Assembly were the most notable. For a time it seemed that even 'the citadel of Westminster [was] surrounded by PR forests – creeping like Birnam Wood, in the last act of Macbeth, ever closer to the walls'.[80] In September 1998 Blair proposed to strengthen existing links by broadening out the joint cabinet committee to include issues beyond constitutional ones. But there were also disappointments. Ashdown reached the reluctant conclusion that constitutional reform was not 'the iron in Blair's soul' that he had hoped.[81] New Labour seemed keener on the theory of devolution than on its practical consequences and, in key respects, showed itself as inclined to centralisation as its Conservative predecessor had been. Government proposals for a

Freedom of Information Act were quietly watered down and their leading champion dropped from the cabinet. The first stage in the reform of the House of Lords, which allowed for the temporary survival of 92 hereditary peers resulted from a backstairs pact between the government and the Conservative leader in the upper chamber for which the latter was summarily dismissed. 'The deal was done without reference to the Liberal Democrats and a thoroughly unsatisfactory dog's breakfast of a deal it turned out to be.'[82] Ashdown found the pace of change disappointingly slow and his diaries reveal an increasing exasperation with Blair's failure to deliver:

> It's always us who put the propositions to you. Then you and I agree how to go forward. Then, at the last moment, it's discovered you can't. Then we – never you – go off and find a different way to keep the project on track and the whole depressing cycle starts over again. Frankly, I don't know how long we can keep doing this. [83]

But the decisive moment probably came in October 1998 with the publication of the report of a commission headed by Lord Jenkins into the reform of the Westminster electoral system. Jenkins proposed to replace the existing first-past-the-post system with a scheme which was christened 'AV plus'. It involved the majority of MPs being elected by single-member constituencies using the system of the Alternative Vote. This would retain the widely-valued link between the voter and his local MP. But the remaining hundred or so MPs would be elected by a list system within broad geographical areas in order to create a broadly proportional overall outcome. These proposals, as might be expected from a commission headed by Jenkins, were warmly welcomed by Liberal Democrats but were met with a luke-warm response in the Commons from the Home Secretary, Jack Straw, apparently endorsed by the Prime Minister. At the time of writing, four years on, no attempt has been made to implement them or even to submit them to a referendum of the British people.

On the ground the Liberal Democrats experienced some difficulty in differentiating themselves from the Labour government, especially when that government was carrying out many of the key Liberal Democrat policies. It might now have been appropriate to project the party's appeal somewhat to the left of Labour. On public expenditure, in particular, its approach seemed closer to that espoused by an earlier incarnation of the Labour movement. 'My concern', wrote William Rodgers, who became Liberal Democrat Leader in the Lords in 1998, 'is that the Blair government is not facing up to the question of inequality which, for me, is central to any party of the centre-left.'[84] Ashdown, however, was wary of any overt move to the left, especially as the party's most promising prospects of further electoral advance remained in Conservative-held constituencies. In the circumstances, the party's electoral record during the 1997 parliament was surprisingly impressive. In line with the experience of earlier periods of Labour government, there were some signs of a Conservative recovery at Liberal Democrat expense at a local level. The 1998 council elections witnessed substantial Tory gains in places such as Tunbridge Wells, Richmond-upon-Thames and the Isle of Wight. That said, the Liberal Democrats recaptured Liverpool from Labour in 1998 and took control of Sheffield in 1999. On the other hand, the country showed no enthusiasm for the return of a Conservative government and the Liberal Democrats took the usually safe Tory seat of Romsey in a by-election in May 2000. A proportional system of voting helped the party take ten seats in the European elections of 1999, though the national turn-out was as low as 24 per cent. In elections that year to the Scottish Parliament and Welsh Assembly, the same reform allowed for some recovery of the Conservative position, leaving the Liberal Democrats in fourth place in terms of seats in both countries. As, however, proportional representation deprived any one party of an outright majority, the Liberal Democrats joined Labour in a coalition administration in Scotland and eventually in Wales too.

In August 1999 Ashdown stood down from the party leadership after 11 years in the post. Arguably, he had been the most significant leader since Grimond. 'He created, out of the wreckage of the Liberal–SDP Alliance, a professional, modernised and effective Liberal Party. He took the party . . . to a new respectability, stunning local election and by-election victories and – finally overcoming the barriers of the first-past-the-post electoral system – a higher number of Commons seats than at any time since 1929.'[85] Judgements on the Project must remain more tentative, especially until we have Blair's version of the story to set alongside Ashdown's own. As the latter always recognised, one interpretation of what happened is likely to be that Ashdown, the dupe, was led by the nose by the charlatan Blair. More charitably, it remains questionable whether even a fully committed Blair could have taken his party with him. Bill Rodgers heard from one senior minister that, apart from the Prime Minister and Peter Mandelson, there was no real support for the Project inside the cabinet.[86] Events since Ashdown's departure – continuing Labour reticence over Lords reform and the euro, and the effective disappearance of proportional representation from the Westminster agenda – do not suggest that the path to realignment would have been an easy one. The problem perhaps lay in what Ashdown once described as 'the compromises of power', something with which Liberals have not had to grapple for 80 years. Even selling the abandonment of a specifically Liberal identity to the Liberal Democrat party would have been a task of Herculean proportions. 'Liberal Democrats loved their leader', commented Tony Greaves, 'but, insofar as they sensed his strategy, most wanted none of it.'[87] Despite an abiding sense of history and a belief that the twentieth century might end as it had begun with a Progressive Alliance of the centre-left, Ashdown seemed curiously unaware of the historical fate of the junior partners of peacetime coalitions. As earlier groups of Liberals had discovered, it was the lot of such as the Liberal Unionists and the Liberal Nationals to be absorbed within the embrace of their more powerful ally and to disappear without trace from the political stage. Though New Labour had unashamedly appropriated many of the policies first espoused by the Liberals, there was always something fanciful, granted the disparity of strength between the two parties, about Ashdown's perception that realignment might take place around a *Liberal* agenda, 'a sort of reverse takeover process'.[88]

In the contest to determine Ashdown's successor, the party opted for Charles Kennedy over Simon Hughes. The choice of the former Social Democratic MP for Ross, Cromarty and Skye was evidence that the scars left from the process of merger had finally faded from view. In terms of his relaxed style and personality, the new leader was very different from his predecessor, but the party's strategy in the period before the 2001 General Election remained largely unchanged. Liberal Democrats were still ready to criticise New Labour's shortcomings in the field of social and educational reform, but they also left no doubt about their overwhelming preference for Labour compared with the Conservative party of William Hague. Moreover, the party went into the General Election with the advantage that the main opposition party was showing few signs of recovery from its 1997 nadir. Once again, the Liberal Democrats presented themselves as the only party ready to increase taxes to invest in the underfunded public services. They were now fully established as a national party. They could point to their achievements in government in Scotland, where their effective opposition to student tuition fees in Scottish universities demonstrated the practical consequences of devolution; they could draw attention to a positive record in local government. But they had also learnt the advantages of ruthlessly targeting their resources on their most promising seats. Broadly speaking, this meant trying to attract tactical Labour votes in the South of England and Conservative ones in the North. The party and its leader waged an effective campaign. Mounting confidence led in the final week to the claim that the Liberal Democrats were the party most likely to provide an effective opposition to a re-elected Labour government. It was a striking (albeit somewhat exaggerated) commentary on reversing party fortunes that the Liberal Democrats were now able to turn on its head the old Conservative slogan of earlier campaigns and warn the electorate not to waste its votes on the Tories. Yet there was something of a contradiction in the suggestion that the Liberal Democrats could replace the Conservatives as the main party of opposition when on issues such as taxation, public expenditure, crime and asylum the party seemed to be positioning itself somewhere to the left of Labour. That said, there was good cause to be pleased with the outcome. The party polled 4.8 million votes, 18.3 per cent of the total and captured 52 seats, its best parliamentary tally since 1929, and the first time ever that the party had increased its vote after a full-term Labour government. The decline in the share of the vote, apparent since the Alliance's high point in 1983, had finally been arrested. As in 1997, the party was a clear beneficiary of tactical voting with the electorate displaying a continuing determination to resist the return of a Conservative government. By most standards of judgement it was a heartening performance, though critics suggested that, in the context of a deeply unpopular opposition and a government for which, judging by the turnout of just 59.4 per cent, the electorate lacked real enthusiasm, it should have been even better. Large numbers seemed to prefer to stay at home rather than register a protest vote in favour of the Liberal Democrats.

CONCLUSION

A survey of 100 years of the history of the Liberal party and its successor, the Liberal Democrats, demands that some tentative conclusions be drawn. The most intriguing question concerns the relationship between the party as it stood in 1900 and that which exists at the opening of the twenty-first century. The name on the bottle has certainly changed, but are its contents essentially the same? All parties must develop and adapt if they are to survive, but all need also to ensure that their core beliefs and values are retained. The balance of importance between political and economic Liberalism has inevitably varied greatly over the period under review but, arguably, a continuity of Liberal principles has been upheld. Liberalism remains committed to the rights of the individual and to personal liberty; it retains its faith in the market and the need to restrict the intrusions of government; it continues to proclaim the need for social justice and a fairer society; it upholds the ideal of internationalism above that of the nation state; and it has given a new lease of life to the quest for political Liberalism by championing such issues as devolution and freedom of information. Indeed, the history of the twentieth century is not just about the survival of the Liberal party; it is also in part the story of the triumph of liberalism. Britain has become a more 'liberal' society, one which is more permeated with 'liberal' values than it was 100 years ago.

Yet herein lies one of the party's most formidable problems. The Liberal party has survived within an increasingly 'liberal' democratic polity. Liberals have looked on while their rivals have appropriated many of their most characteristic aims and policies. To this extent such aims and policies have ceased to be distinctively 'Liberal' even if they remain essentially 'liberal'. Over the last 25 years first the Conservatives and then New Labour have discovered the virtues of the liberal market economy. At the same time, Labour has become, not always convincingly, the champion of constitutional reform including devolution. Thus, as during much of the period covered by this book, the contemporary Liberal Democratic party struggles to lay claim to a distinctive identity. Ironically, the one policy area over which the Liberal Democrats may assert their greatest claim to a unique ownership is the party's consistent espousal of the ideal of a united Europe, including acceptance of a federal dimension. This separates them from both Labour and the Conservatives which have both changed course and significantly divided on this issue. But it also probably separates Liberal Democrats from the majority of the British electorate which remains at best unenthusiastic about this goal.

Uncertainty over Liberal identity and the appropriation of its policies and ideas by its rivals would matter less to the Liberal party if it had ever succeeded in regaining the position, which it had lost by the end of the second decade of the twentieth century, as one of the two contenders for power operating within an electoral system which disadvantages the prospects of any third force. As it is, Liberals have had to grapple with the central dilemma of their continuing third-party status – whether their best advantage lies in preserving a fully independent identity or whether, notwithstanding the ultimate fate of earlier schismatics such as the Liberal Unionists and the Liberal Nationals, the best course is to co-operate with one or other of the two leading parties. To date, though both paths have been explored, neither has produced a clear and unambiguous way forward, still less a route to the recovery of political power.

The proper province of the historian lies in the past – its elucidation and its explanation. But when history is brought to the present, the historian may be permitted a few speculative observations about the future. In the early 1950s it would have been a matter of little surprise had the Liberal party ceased to exist. The achievement of its successor half a century later in holding more than fifty seats in the House of Commons cannot be gainsaid. Yet in 2001 the Liberal Democrats secured a percentage of the popular vote comparable to that gained in October 1974 when the

Liberals won just 13 seats. There have been few signs of reaching that level of popular support where the party, on its own, would become a serious contender for power or even, for that matter, of matching the Alliance performances of 1983 and 1987. What the party has managed to do is to surmount some of the obstacles placed in its path by the first-past-the-post electoral system, through the development of tactical voting and a somewhat more effective geographical concentration of its support. But Liberal Democrat votes, no more than Liberal ones in the past, are not solidly entrenched. Only 55 per cent of those who voted for the Alliance in 1987 and who voted again in 1992, supported the Liberal Democrats in the latter year. Between 1992 and 1997 the Liberal Democrats held on to just 59 per cent of their support.[1] Such statistics suggest that the new party remains overdependent upon the 'protest' voter, unable to rely on the support of a sufficient number committed to its own cause on its intrinsic merits. Another old problem that remains is the electorate's greater readiness to support the party as a force in local government than as a contender for national power. Liberal Democrats did better in the local elections held on the same day as the 1997 General Election than in the national contest.

The party's dilemmas are well encapsulated in changes which have taken place since the 2001 General Election. Charles Kennedy has effectively ended the Lib–Lab co-operation which was at the heart of his predecessor's strategy, while declaring that it is now the Liberal Democrats' goal to replace the Conservative party as the main alternative to Labour. Both developments make some sense. The Blair government in its second term has drawn back from its earlier enthusiasm for radical constitutional change, especially electoral reform. Meanwhile, the path to European Economic and Monetary Union seems beset with ever increasing political and economic obstacles. Yet it is doubtful whether much electoral benefit lies in the voters' perception of a difference between Labour and the Liberal Democrats on such matters. In the key area of public expenditure on health and education Labour has now closed the gap between its own commitments and Liberal Democrat demands. With independent commentators warning of a 'black hole' of deficit at the end of the Chancellor's medium-term plans, it would be unwise for the Liberal Democrats to argue for an even higher level of public expenditure. The danger must exist that voters, seeking a clear alternative to Labour, will not find it in the Liberal Democrats and will instead transfer their allegiance to the Tories.

Where does this leave Kennedy's stated ambition of replacing the Conservative party? Again, the logic of the situation is only partially compelling. The Conservatives have failed to show any significant signs of recovery since their debacle of 1997. In Labour's second term, amid evidence of mounting economic difficulties and with the electorate increasingly dissatisfied with the government's performance and doubtful of its probity, Her Majesty's Opposition under Iain Duncan Smith continues, at the time of writing, to record a level of voter support of only around 30 per cent. Furthermore, it remains the case at constituency level that the Liberal Democrats are a more potent threat to the Conservatives than to Labour. In only a handful of seats are they well-placed to overtake a sitting Labour MP. To this extent Kennedy recognises the weakness which has undermined successive Liberal, Alliance and Liberal Democrat electoral strategies since Grimond first spoke of a realignment of the left – that the Liberals and their successors have been singularly unsuccessful in making inroads into the heartlands of Labour support. But the replacement of the Conservatives as even the leading party of opposition would require a more considerable improvement on the party's current standing than the simple statistics might suggest. Such is the distribution of the party's votes that, according to one recent calculation, even drawing level with the Conservatives on something like 30 per cent of the popular vote at the next general election might leave the Liberal Democrats with just 90 seats and the Conservatives around 170. Not until *both* the Conservatives and Labour drop to about a 30 per cent standing in public support can the Liberal Democrats expect to secure more than a hundred Commons seats.[2] Furthermore, Kennedy's Liberal Democrats seek to displace the Conservatives while remaining a party of the radical centre-left. Thus they 'might be described as a party with a preponderance of left-of-centre policies supported preponderantly by centre and right-of-centre voters'.[3] Whether such a strategy can be sustained in the long term remains questionable, particularly if Conservative fortunes begin to recover of their own accord, possibly under a new leader. There is always likely to remain a strong right-of-centre constituency among the British electorate. Paddy Ashdown's scepticism seems well founded: 'Some believe that we can somehow replace the Tories. I have never shared this view . . . We will not be able to hold perpetually on to the bulk of this 'borrowed' vote, because we are not a centre right party, we are a centre left party.'[4]

If, therefore, the new century opens up an intriguing range of possibilities, by no means all appear entirely positive from a Liberal Democrat point of view.

NOTES

INTRODUCTION

1 M. Bentley, *The Climax of Liberal Politics: British Liberalism in Theory and Practice 1868–1918* (London, 1987), p. 123.
2 M. Pottle (ed.), *Daring to Hope: The Diaries and Letters of Violet Bonham Carter* (London, 2000), p. 178.
3 R. Muir, *The Liberal Way* (London, 1934), p. 169.
4 Cited in M. Pugh, *The Making of Modern British Politics 1867–1939* (Oxford, 1982), p. 22.
5 S. Koss, *Asquith* (London, 1976), p. 30.
6 A. Sykes, *The Rise and Fall of British Liberalism 1776–1988* (London, 1997), p. 269.
7 H. C. G. Matthew (ed.), *The Gladstone Diaries* vol. XI (Oxford, 1990), p. 341.
8 Bentley, *Climax*, p. 106.
9 J. Spender, *Sir Robert Hudson: A Memoir* (London, 1930), p. 53.
10 Cited in D. Tanner, *Political Change and the Labour Party 1900–1918* (Cambridge, 1990), p. 60.
11 John Rylands University of Manchester Library, MacDonald MSS, RMD/1/1/10, MacDonald to W. Allard, Secretary Home Counties Division, National Liberal Federation 9 Dec. 1893.
12 Ibid., RMD/1/1/27, J Randolph to E. Pease 10 May 1894.
13 University of Liverpool Library, Bruce Glasier MSS, GP/1/1/569, Glasier to K. Hardie 21 Oct. 1902.
14 L. T. Hobhouse, *Democracy and Reaction* (London, 1904), pp. 209–10.
15 M. Rathbone, 'The Rainbow Circle and the New Liberalism', *Journal of Liberal History* 38 (2003), p. 26.
16 R. Barker, 'Socialism and Progressivism in the Political Thought of Ramsay MacDonald' in A. J. A. Morris (ed.), *Edwardian Radicalism 1900–1914* (London, 1974), p. 116.
17 Koss, *Asquith,* p. 77.
18 P. Clarke, *Liberals and Social Democrats* (Cambridge, 1978), p. 63.

1 STRANGE DEATH OR EDWARDIAN SUMMER, 1902–1916

1 L. S. Amery, *My Political Life*, vol. 1 (London, 1953), p. 235.
2 H. W. McCready, 'The Revolt of the Unionist Free Traders', *Parliamentary Affairs*, 16 (1963), p. 188.
3 A. K. Russell, *Liberal Landslide: The General Election of 1906* (Newton Abbot, 1973), p. 145.
4 Bodleian Library, Oxford, Selborne MSS 2/118, St John Brodrick to Selborne 24 Nov. 1905; W. A. S. Hewins, *The Apologia of an Imperialist*, vol. 1 (London, 1929), p. 155.
5 P. F. Clarke, *Lancashire and the New Liberalism* (Cambridge, 1971), p. 375.
6 *Northern Daily Telegraph* 22 Dec. 1905, cited Clarke, *Lancashire*, pp. 355–6.
7 Russell, *Landslide*, p. 71.
8 Clarke, *Lancashire*, p. 234.
9 A. Sykes, *The rise and fall of British Liberalism 1776–1988* (London, 1997), p. 270.
10 Clarke, *Lancashire*, p. 398.
11 Crewe to Campbell-Bannerman 14 Nov. 1905, cited Russell, *Landslide*, p. 33.
12 Campbell-Bannerman to Asquith 17 Jan. 1906, cited ibid., p. 210.
13 J. F. Harris and C. Hazlehurst, 'Campbell-Bannerman as Prime Minister', *History* 55 (1970), p. 376.
14 Ibid., pp. 382–3.
15 University of Liverpool Library, Bruce Glasier MSS, GP/1/1/812, Glasier to Elizabeth Glasier-Foster 5 July 1907.
16 C. Hazlehurst, 'Asquith as Prime Minister, 1908–1916', *English Historical Review* 85 (1970), p. 514.
17 J. M. McEwen (ed.), *The Riddell Diaries: A Selection* (London, 1986), p. 39.
18 Ibid., p. 43.
19 E. David (ed.), *Inside Asquith's Cabinet: From the Diaries of Charles Hobhouse* (London, 1977), p. 74.
20 B. K. Murray, 'The Politics of the "People's Budget" ', *Historical Journal* 16 (1973), pp. 555–70; J. Grigg, *Lloyd George: The People's Champion 1902–1911* (London, 1978), p. 180.
21 S. Koss, *Asquith* (London, 1976), p. 103.
22 N. Blewett, *The Peers, the Parties and the People: The General Elections of 1910* (London, 1972), p. 407.

23 N. and J. MacKenzie (eds), *The Diary of Beatrice Webb*, vol. 3 (London, 1984), p. 149.

24 Ibid., p. 134.

25 McEwen (ed.), *Riddell Diaries*, p. 46.

26 B. K. Murray, *The People's Budget: Lloyd George and Liberal Politics* (Oxford, 1980), p. 54.

27 G. Dangerfield, *The Damnable Question* (London, 1979), p. 53.

28 David (ed.), *Asquith's Cabinet*, p. 171.

29 W. S. Churchill, *The World Crisis*, vol. 1 (pb. edn, 1968), p. 114.

30 McEwen (ed.), *Riddell Diaries*, p. 64.

31 T. Morgan, *Churchill: Young Man in a Hurry 1874–1915* (New York, 1982), p. 315.

32 McEwen (ed.), *Riddell Diaries*, p. 76.

33 T. Wilson (ed.), *The Political Diaries of C. P. Scott 1911–1928* (London, 1970), p. 70.

34 I. Packer, *Lloyd George, Liberalism and the Land: The Land Issue and Party Politics in England, 1906–1914* (Woodbridge, 2001), p. 194.

35 House of Lords Record Office, Bonar Law MSS 39/4/40, Steel-Maitland to Law 23 June 1914.

36 B. K. Murray, ' "Battered and Shattered": Lloyd George and the 1914 Budget Fiasco', *Albion* 23, 3 (1991), p. 503.

37 Carrington diary 8 July 1914, cited ibid., p. 505.

38 M. and E. Brock (eds), *H. H. Asquith: Letters to Venetia Stanley* (pb. edn, Oxford, 1985), p. 89.

39 B. B. Gilbert, 'David Lloyd Geroge: The Reform of British Land-Holding and the Budget of 1914', *Historical Journal* 21, 1 (1978), p. 141.

40 I. Packer, 'The Liberal Cave and the 1914 Budget', *English Historical Review* 442 (1996), pp. 621, 628.

41 Liverpool Record Office, Holt-Durning MSS, Holt diary 19 July 1914.

42 David (ed.), *Asquith's Cabinet*, p. 125.

43 P. Stansky cited in C. W. White, ' "The Strange Death of Liberal England" in its Time', *Albion* 17 (1985), p. 446.

44 T. Wilson, *The Downfall of the Liberal Party 1914–1935* (London, 1966), p. 17.

45 G. Dangerfield, *The Strange Death of Liberal England* (London, 1936), p. 10.

46 The 'franchise factor' is discussed below, pp. 76–8.

47 H. Pelling, 'Labour and the Downfall of Liberalism' in Pelling, *Popular Politics and Society in Late Victorian Britain* (London, 1968), p. 120.

48 Ibid., p. 118.

49 R. McKibbin, *The Evolution of the Labour Party 1910–1924* (pb. edn, Oxford, 1983), pp. xiv, 244.

50 Wilson, *Downfall*; Clarke, *Lancashire*.

51 Clarke, *Lancashire*, p. 406.

52 Ibid., p. 6.

53 Samuel Storey, Chairman of the Northern Liberal Federation, cited G. R. Searle, *The Liberal Party: Triumph and Disintegration, 1886–1929* (Houndmills, 1992), p. 72.

54 Memorandum by J. Herbert for H. Gladstone 6 March 1903, cited F. Bealey, 'Negotiations between the Liberal Party and the Labour Representation Committee before the General Election of 1906', *Bulletin of the Institute of Historial Research* 29 (1956), p. 266.

55 Gladstone memorandum 6 March 1903, cited Clarke, *Lancashire*, p. 314.

56 Gladstone memorandum 13 March 1903, cited D. Powell, 'The New Liberalism and the Rise of Labour, 1886–1906', *Historical Journal* 29 (1986), p. 383.

57 F. Bealey and H. Pelling, *Labour and Politics 1900–1906*, (London, 1958), p. 155.

58 Bryce to Goldwin Smith 16 June 1906, cited M. Petter, 'The Progressive Alliance' *History* 58 (1973), p. 45.

59 Clarke, *Lancashire*, p. 376; J. A. Spender, *Sir Robert Hudson: A Memoir* (London, 1930), p. 198.

60 J. Herbert to H. Gladstone 6 Feb 1906, cited Bealey, 'Negotiations', p. 273.

61 Powell, 'New Liberalism', p. 383.

62 C. Hazlehurst and C. Woodland (eds), *A Liberal Chronicle: Journals and Papers of J. A. Pease, 1908 to 1910* (London, 1994), p. 141.

63 Petter, 'Progressive Alliance', p. 48.

64 Cited A. Hetherington, *The Guardian Years* (London, 1981), p. 326.

65 R. Douglas, 'Labour in Decline 1910–14' in K. D. Brown (ed.), *Essays in Anti-Labour History* (London, 1974), p. 125.

66 *The Nation* 31 Jan. 1914, cited Petter, 'Progressive Alliance', p. 49.

67 Douglas, 'Labour in Decline', p. 124.

68 McKibbin, *Evolution*, p. 71.

69 Petter, 'Progressive Alliance', p. 60; G. L. Bernstein, 'Liberalism and the Progressive Alliance in the Constituencies, 1900–1914: Three Case Studies', *Historical Journal* 26 (1983), p. 637.

70 K. Laybourn and J. Reynolds, *Liberalism and the Rise of Labour 1890–1918* (London, 1984), p. 154.

71 A. W. Purdue, 'The Liberal and Labour Parties in North-East Politics, 1900–14: The Struggle for Supremacy', *International Review of Social History* 26 (1981), p. 15.

72 P. Thompson, *Socialists, Liberals and Labour: The Struggle for London 1885–1914* (London, 1967), pp. 295–6. It should be noted that both Peter Clarke and Neal Blewett have questioned Thompson's conclusions and believe that his findings are compatible with growing working-class support for the Liberal party.

73 C. Cook, 'Labour and the Downfall of the Liberal Party, 1906–14' in A. Sked and C. Cook (eds), *Crisis and Controversy: Essays in Honour of A. J. P. Taylor* (London, 1976), pp. 55, 58, 62.

74 D. Tanner, *Political Change and the Labour Party 1900–1918* (Cambridge, 1990), p. 317.

75 Ibid., p. 332.

76 Ibid., p. 337.

77 B. B. Gilbert, *David Lloyd George: The Architect of Change 1863–1912* (London, 1987), p. 290.

78 McEwen, *Riddell Diaries*, p. 44.

79 Tanner, *Political Change*, p. 44.

80 Searle, *Triumph and Disintegration*, p. 85.

81 M. Bentley, *The Climax of Liberal Politics: British Liberalism in Theory and Practice 1868–1918* (London, 1987), p. 144.

82 Powell, 'New Liberalism', p. 383.

83 G. L. Bernstein, *Liberalism and Liberal Politics in Edwardian England* (London, 1986), p. 200.

84 Hazlehurst and Woodland (eds), *Liberal Chronicle*, p. 74.

85 Wilson (ed.), *Political Diaries of C. P. Scott*, pp. 100–1.

86 Bernstein, 'Three Case Studies', pp. 617–40.

87 Laybourn and Reynolds, *Liberalism and Rise of Labour*, pp. 168, 173.

88 M. D. Pugh, 'Yorkshire and the New Liberalism', *Journal of Modern History*, 50, 3 (1978), p. D1155.

89 Purdue, 'Liberal and Labour Parties', pp. 1–24; K. O. Morgan, 'The New Liberalism and the Challenge of Labour: The Welsh Experience, 1885–1929' in Brown (ed.), *Essays in Anti-Labour History*, pp. 163–4.

90 K. Laybourn, *The Rise of Labour: The British Labour Party 1890–1979* (London, 1988), p. 26.

91 Glasier MSS, GP/1/1/944, Glasier to Hardie 17 Dec. 1908.

92 C. Wrigley, 'Labour and the Trade Unions', in K. D. Brown (ed.), *The First Labour Party 1906–1914* (London, 1985), p. 151.

93 Bentley, *Climax*, p. 124.

94 Searle, *Triumph and Disintegration*, p. 122.

95 K. O. Morgan, *The Age of Lloyd George: The Liberal Party and British Politics, 1890–1929* (London, 1978), p. 58.

96 Wilson, *Downfall*, p. 18.

97 R. Rouglas, *The History of the Liberal Party 1895–1970* (London, 1971), p. 91.

98 C. Addison, *Politics from Within*, vol. 1 (London, 1924), p. 38.

99 Holt diary 2 Aug. 1914.

100 Ibid., 9 Aug. 1914.

101 John Rylands Library, Manchester, MacDonald MSS, RMD/1/3/1, Trevelyan to MacDonald 7 Aug. 1914 and MacDonald's later annotation.

102 I. Packer (ed.), *The Letters of Arnold Stephen Rowntree to May Katherine Rowntree 1910–1918* (London, 2002), pp. 159–60.

103 R. E. Dowse, 'The Entry of the Liberals into the Labour Party, 1910–1920', *Yorkshire Bulletin of Economic and Social Research* 13 (1961), p. 86.

104 MacDonald MSS, Trevelyan to MacDonald 6 Jan. 1924.

105 William Llewelyn Williams, MP for Carmarthen District 5 July 1915, cited E. David, 'The Liberal Party Divided 1916–1918', *Historical Journal* 13 (1970), p. 511.

106 MacDonald MSS, RMD/1/3/41, Trevelyan to Simon 22 Aug. 1915.

107 McEwen (ed), *Riddell Diaries*, p. 95.

108 McKibbin, *Evolution*, p. 238.

109 G. Bernstein, 'Yorkshire Liberalism During the First World War', *Historical Journal* 32 (1989), pp. 107–29.

110 M. D. Pugh, 'Asquith, Bonar Law and the First Coalition', *Historical Journal* 17 (1974), p. 813.

111 V. Bonham Carter, *Winston Churchill as I Knew Him* (London, 1965), p. 404.

112 Holt diary 30 May 1915.

113 University of Newcastle-upon-Tyne, Runciman MSS 136, Hobhouse to Runciman 28 May 1915.

114 C. Hazlehurst, *Politicians at War July 1914 to May 1915* (London, 1971), pp. 286–7.

115 Holt diary 20 June 1915.

116 *Nation* 22 May 1915, cited Wilson, *Downfall*, p. 80.

117 R. Jenkins, *Asquith* (London, 1964), p. 371.

118 Bodleian Library, Oxford, Simon MSS, SP52, fols 26–7, Asquith to Simon, McKenna and Runciman 28 Dec. 1915.

119 *Nation* 1 Jan. 1916, cited Wilson, *Downfall*, p. 82.

120 McEwen (ed.), *Riddell Diaries*, p. 138.

121 P. F. Clarke, *Liberals and Social Democrats* (Cambridge, 1978), p. 181.

122 Packer (ed.), *Letters of Arnold Stephen Rowntree*, p. 198.

123 Hazlehurst, 'Asquith as Prime Minister', p. 530.

124 Wilson (ed.), *Political Diaries of C. P. Scott*, p. 216.

125 Jenkins, *Asquith*, p. 410.

126 D. Lloyd George, *War Memoirs*, vol. 2 (London, 1933), p. 997.

127 Clarke, *Lancashire*, p. 394.

128 Wilson (ed.), *Political Diaries of C. P. Scott*, p. 242.

2   THE LIBERAL CIVIL WAR

1 Liverpool Record Office, Richard Holt MSS, diary 10 Dec. 1916.

2 A. J. P Taylor, 'Politics in the First World War' in Taylor (ed.), *Politics in Wartime* (London, 1964), p. 32; E. David, 'The Liberal Party Divided 1916–1918', *Historical Journal* 13 (1970), pp. 527, 529, 531.

3 B. McGill, 'Asquith's Predicament, 1914–1918', *Journal of Modern History* 39 (1967), p. 297.

4 T. Wilson, *The Downfall of the Liberal Party 1914–1935* (London, 1966), p. 123.

5 Ibid., p. 125.

6 D. Tanner, *Political Change and the Labour Party 1900–1918* (Cambridge, 1990), p. 382.

7 House of Lords Record Office, Lloyd George MSS F/21/2/30, Guest to Lloyd George 3 Aug. 1918.

8 Holt diary 18 Dec. 1917.

9 R. Douglas, 'The Background to the "Coupon" Election Arrangements', *English Historical Review* 86 (1971), p. 322.

10 D. Dutton (ed.), *Paris 1918: The War Diary of the British Ambassador, the 17th Earl of Derby* (Liverpool, 2001), p. 316.

11 Douglas, 'Background', p. 329.

12 Asquith to Spender 6 Oct. 1926, cited S. Ball, 'Asquith's Decline and the General Election of 1918', *Scottish Historical Review* LXI, 171 (1982), p. 61.

13 Memorandum by Gladstone 18 Nov. 1924, cited M. Hart, 'The Decline of the Liberal Party in Parliament and in the Constituencies', Oxford D. Phil. (1982), p. 145.

14 Crewe to Grey 12 June 1928, cited ibid., p. 93.

15 Manchester Central Library, E. D. Simon MSS, M11/11/5 addnl, diary 16 Nov. 1918.

16 P. Harris, *Forty Years in and out of Parliament* (London, n.d.), p. 76.

17 G. Bernstein, 'Yorkshire Liberalism During the First World War', *Historical Journal* 32 (1989), p. 129.

18 E. D. Simon MSS, M11/11/5 addnl, diary 27 Apr. and 15 Dec. 1918.

19 Ibid., 15 Dec. 1918.

20 M. Pugh, *The Making of Modern British Politics* (Oxford, 1982), p. 201.

21 H. C. G. Matthew, R. I. McKibbin and J. A. Kay, 'The Franchise Factor in the Rise of the Labour Party', *English Historical Review* 91 (1976), pp. 723–52.

22 Ibid., p. 740.

23 D. Tanner, 'The Parliamentary Electoral System, the "Fourth" Reform Act and the Rise of Labour in England and Wales', *Bulletin of the Institute of Historical Research* 56 (1983), pp. 205–19.

24 M. Childs, 'Labour Grows Up: The Electoral System, Political Generations, and British Politics 1890–1929', *Twentieth Century British History* 6, 2 (1995), p. 142.

25 Holt diary, 15 and 23 Dec. 1918.

26 E. D. Simon MSS, M 11/11/5 addnl, diary 15 Dec. 1918.

27 Viscount Simon, *Retrospect* (London, 1952), p. 121.

28 Lloyd George MSS F/40/2/24, Montagu to Lloyd George 16 Nov. 1918.

29 University of Liverpool Library, Veitch MSS D40/15, Muir to G. Veitch 25 Oct. 1928.

30 R. Jenkins, *Asquith* (London, 1986), p. 517.

31 A. C. Murray's diary 12 May 1920, cited Wilson, *Downfall*, p. 212.

32 M. Bentley, *The Liberal Mind 1914–1929* (Cambridge, 1977), p. 66.

33 St Deiniol's Library, Hawarden, Glynne-Gladstone MSS 965, Henry Gladstone to Herbert Gladstone 10 Mar. 1921.

34 University of Newcastle-upon-Tyne, Runciman MSS 177, McKenna to Runciman 4 Jan. 1919.

35 Cecil to Runciman 24 Jan. 1920, cited M. Bentley, 'Liberal Politics and the Grey Conspiracy of 1921', *Historical Journal* 20 (1977), p. 465.

36 Herbert Gladstone to Henry Gladstone 27 Feb. 1921, cited ibid., p. 467.

37 E. D. Simon MSS, M/11/11/5 addnl, diary 7 Feb. 1920.

38 R. Muir, *An Autobiography and Some Essays* (London, 1943), p. 181.

39 Wilson, *Downfall*, p. 216.

40 Glynne-Gladstone MSS 964, Henry Gladstone to Herbert Gladstone 3 Apr. 1919.

41 M. Bentley, 'The Liberal Response to Socialism 1918–29' in K. D. Brown (ed.), *Essays in Anti-Labour History: Responses to the Rise of Labour in Britain* (London, 1974), p. 47.

42 Glynne-Gladstone MSS 964–5, Henry Gladstone to Herbert Gladstone 30 Aug. 1919 and 26 Feb. 1922.

43 P. F. Clarke in V. Bogdanor (ed.), *Liberal Party Politics* (Oxford, 1983), p. 36.

44 E. D. Simon MSS, M/11/11/5 addnl, diary 2 June 1920.

45 Ibid., diary 2 Oct. 1921.

46 D. Cregier, *Chiefs Without Indians* (Washington, 1982), pp. 149–63.

47 Glynne-Gladstone MSS 965, Henry Gladstone to Herbert Gladstone 18 Nov. 1921.

48 Lord Riddell, *Intimate Diary of the Peace Conference and After 1918–1923* (London, 1933), p. 139.

49 K. Morgan, 'Lloyd George's Stage Army: The Coalition Liberals 1918–22' in A. J. P. Taylor (ed.), *Lloyd George: Twelve Essays* (London, 1971), p. 246.

50 J. Ramsden (ed.), *Real Old Tory Politics* (London, 1984), p. 131.

51 *Nation* 11 Nov. 1922, cited M. Kinnear, *The Fall of Lloyd George: The Political Crisis of 1922* (London, 1973), p. 135.

52 T. Wilson (ed.), *The Political Diaries of C. P. Scott 1911–1928* (London, 1970), p. 434.

53 S. Koss, *Asquith* (London, 1976), p. 255.

54 M. Pottle (ed.), *Champion Redoubtable: The Diaries and Letters of Violet Bonham Carter 1914–1945* (London, 1998), p. 137.

55 Bodleian Library, Oxford, J. Simon MSS, SP 5, diary 18 Nov. 1922.

56 Wilson (ed.), *Political Diaries of C. P. Scott*, p. 433.

57 J. Campbell, *Lloyd George: The Goat in the Wilderness 1922–1931* (London, 1977), p. 58.

58 Hart, 'Decline of the Liberal Party', p. 205.

59 C. Cook, *The Age of Alignment: Electoral Politics in Britain 1922–1929* (London, 1975), p. 92.

60 Jenkins, *Asquith*, p. 498.

61 E. D. Simon MSS, M 11/11, diary 21 Jan. 1924.

62 *The Times* 19 Dec. 1923.

63 E. D. Simon MSS, M 11/11, diary 21 Jan. 1924.

64 Ibid., note by Simon 22 Feb. 1924.

65 Ibid., note by Simon Mar. 1925.

66 MacDonald to G. Murray 10 Oct. 1924, cited Bentley, 'Liberal Response', p. 57.

67 Speech at Llanfairfechan 22 Apr. 1924, cited Campbell, *Goat*, pp. 94–5.

68 Wilson (ed.), *Political Diaries of C. P. Scott*, p. 462.

69 Harris, *Forty Years*, p. 97.

70 E. D. Simon MSS, M/11/11, parliamentary diary for 1924, Mar. 1925.

71 House of Lords Record Office, Stansgate MSS, ST/66, diary 20 Feb. 1924.

72 Glynne-Gladstone MSS 966, Henry Gladstone to Herbert Gladstone 14 Jan. 1924.

73 House of Commons Debates, 5th Series, vol. 169, col. 601.

74 University of Birmingham, Chamberlain MSS, AC 35/4/19, Chamberlain to S. Hoare 28 Jan. 1924.

75 Amery to Baldwin 21 Dec. 1923, cited Campbell, *Goat*, p. 87.

76 Stansgate MSS, ST/66, diary 8 Oct. 1924.

77 Hudson to Herbert Gladstone 4 July 1924, cited S. Koss, 'Asquith versus Lloyd George: The Last Phase and Beyond' in A. Sked and C. Cook (eds), *Crisis and Controversy: Essays in Honour of A. J. P. Taylor* (London, 1976), p. 80.

78 J. A. Spender, *Sir Robert Hudson: A Memoir* (London, 1930), p. 199.

79 V. Phillipps, *My Days and Ways* (London, c.1943), p. 113.

80 Lloyd George to Viscount Inchcape 5 Nov. 1924, cited R. Douglas, *History of the Liberal Party 1895–1970* (London, 1971), p. 184.

81 M. Cole (ed.), *Beatrice Webb's Diaries, 1924–1932* (London, 1956), p. 48.

82 G. Searle, *The Liberal Party: Triumph and Disintegration, 1886–1929* (Houndmills, 1992), p. 154.

83 C. Cook, 'Liberals, Labour and Local Elections' in G. Peele and C. Cook (eds), *The Politics of Reappraisal 1918–1939* (London, 1975), pp. 166–88.

84 Stansgate MSS, ST/66, diary 10 Nov. 1924.

85 Glynne-Gladstone MSS 966, Henry Gladstone to Herbert Gladstone 30 Oct. 1924.

86 British Library Add. MS 46477, Gladstone MSS, Runciman to Herbert Gladstone 21 Nov. 1924.

87 J. M. Keynes, *Essays in Persuasion* (London, 1931), p. 343.

88 E. D. Simon, *The Inheritance of Riches* (London, 1925), p. 12.

89 Gladstone to Samuel 30 Apr. 1927, cited Campbell, *Goat*, p. 159.

90 E. D. Simon MSS, M/11/11/5, diary 27 Feb. 1925.

91 *Daily Chronicle* 1 Nov. 1924, cited Campbell, *Goat*, p. 108.

92 A. J. P. Taylor (ed.), *Lloyd George: A Diary by Frances Stevenson* (London, 1971), p. 246.

93 Wilson (ed.), *Political Diaries of C. P. Scott*, p. 472.
94 Lady Kennet's diary Jan. 1925, cited Koss, 'Asquith versus Lloyd George', p. 82.
95 A. J. P. Taylor (ed.), *My Darling Pussy: The Letters of Lloyd George and Frances Stevenson 1913–41* (London, 1975), p. 101.
96 Hart, 'Decline of the Liberal Party', p. 225.
97 J. Simon MSS, SP 60, Simon and others to Asquith 31 May 1926.
98 Ibid., memorandum by J. Rowland Evans 20 June 1926.
99 Holt diary 24 Oct. 1926.
100 *Manchester Guardian* 19 Oct. 1926.
101 Pottle (ed.), *Champion Redoubtable*, p. 171.
102 Holt diary 25 Nov. 1926.
103 Pottle (ed.), *Champion Redoubtable*, p. 171.
104 J. Wallace, 'The Political Career of Walter Runciman, First Viscount Runciman of Doxford', University of Newcastle Ph.D., 1995, p. 291
105 E. D. Simon MSS, M/11/11/5, diary 1929–1935.
106 Taylor (ed.), *Darling Pussy*, p. 108.
107 Ibid., p. 121.
108 Glynne-Gladstone MSS 968–9, Henry Gladstone to Herbert Gladstone 15 Oct. 1928 and 19 Apr. 1929.
109 Holt diary 29 Mar. 1929.
110 Campbell, *Goat*, p. 230; *Manchester Guardian* 16 May 1929.
111 British Library, Simon MSS Eur F77/5/56, Simon to Irwin 6 June 1929.
112 Runciman MSS 221, note by D. Maclean 14 June 1929.
113 E. D. Simon MSS, M/11/11/5, diary 18 June 1929.
114 Ibid., diary 27 July 1929.
115 Ibid., Simon to R. Hutchison July 1930 (not sent).
116 O. Mosley, *My Life* (London, 1968), p. 249.
117 J. Simon MSS 249, Simon to Lloyd George 25 Oct. 1930.
118 E. D. Simon MSS, M/11/11/5, Simon to R. Hutchison July 1930 (not sent).
119 J. Campbell, 'The Renewal of Liberalism: Liberalism without Liberals' in Peele and Cook (eds), *Politics of Reappraisal*, p. 94.
120 *Sunday News* 1 Mar. 1931.
121 E. D. Simon MSS, M/11/11/5, diary 27 Nov. 1930.
122 J. Simon MSS, SP 249, diary 27 Nov. 1930.
123 Churchill College, Cambridge, Thurso MSS I/17/4, Sinclair to V. Finney 19 Mar. 1931.
124 Lloyd George to Lansbury 16 Feb. 1931, cited Campbell, *Goat*, p. 283.
125 J. Simon MSS, SP68, Simon to Sinclair 26 June 1931.

126 T. Clarke, *My Lloyd George Diary* (London, 1939), p. 121; Beatrice Webb unpublished diary 15 Mar. 1931.

127 B. Wasserstein, *Herbert Samuel: A Political Life* (Oxford, 1992), p. 326.

128 Glynne-Gladstone MSS 945, report by Maclean 19 Sept. 1931.

129 Wasserstein, *Samuel*, p. 327.

130 K. Morgan, *The Age of Lloyd George: The Liberal Party and British Politics, 1890–1929* (London, 1978), p. 104.

131 Lloyd George to R. Muir 13 Apr. 1932, cited T. Stannage, *Baldwin Thwarts the Opposition* (London, 1980), p. 88.

132 Flintshire Record Office, Henry Morris Jones MSS 12, diary 2 Oct. 1931.

133 Taylor (ed.), *Darling Pussy*, p. 192.

134 Morris Jones MSS 12, diary 2 Nov. 1931.

135 Glynne-Gladstone MSS 945, Maclean to Herbert Gladstone 29 Jan. 1932.

136 National Library of Wales, Clement Davies MSS C1/16, Davies to S. Clement-Davies 3 Nov. 1943.

137 J. Simon MSS, SP71, Simon to I. Macpherson 5 Feb. 1932.

138 *The Times* 27 May 1932.

139 House of Lords Record Office, Samuel MSS A/89/26, MacDonald to Samuel 10 Sept. 1932.

140 University of Birmingham, Chamberlain MSS, NC 7/11/25/35, Runciman to N. Chamberlain 21 Sept. 1932.

141 Runciman MSS 254, Shakespeare to Simon 23 Sept. 1932.

142 Cambridge University Library, Baldwin MSS 46, Simon to Baldwin 28 Sept. 1932.

143 Wasserstein, *Samuel*, pp. 360–1.

144 Simon MSS, SP73, Baldwin to Simon 26 Oct. 1932.

145 E. Granville, 'The Liberal Resignations', *Contemporary Review*, Nov. 1932, p. 539.

146 Thurso MSS, III/1/3, Sinclair to Samuel 14 Oct. 1933.

147 Ibid., II/1934/37, Samuel to Sinclair 30 Oct. 1933.

148 Morris Jones MSS, diary 28 Nov. 1932.

149 M. Baines, 'The Survival of the British Liberal Party 1932–1959', University of Oxford D.Phil., 1991, p. 30.

150 D. Rees, 'The Disintegration of the Liberal Party 1931–33', University of Wales MA, 1980, p. 191.

151 Lloyd George MSS G/19/7/6, notes on the political situation 26 Nov. 1933.

152 A. Sinclair, 'Crossing the Floor', *Contemporary Review*, Dec. 1933, p. 9.

153 G. De Groot, *Liberal Crusader: The Life of Sir Archibald Sinclair* (London, 1993), p. 98.

154 Memorandum by Lord Lothian 16 Nov. 1932, cited M. Baines, 'The Samuelites and the National Government: A Study in Liberal Survival, August 1931 – November 1933', University of Lancaster MA, 1983, p. 73.

155 *West Briton* 26 Mar. 1931, cited G. Tregidga, *The Liberal Party in South-West Britain Since 1918: Political Decline, Dormancy and Rebirth* (Exeter, 2000), p. 58.

156 De Groot, *Liberal Crusader*, p. 84.

157 R. Muir, *The Liberal Way* (London, 1934), p. 120.

158 Muir to Lothian 29 Oct. 1934, cited De Groot, *Crusader*, p. 105.

159 Sinclair to Samuel 21 Jan. 1935, cited De Groot, *Crusader*, p. 105.

160 Cook, 'Liberals, Labour and Local Elections', pp. 178–9.

161 Wilson, *Downfall*, p. 377.

162 Glynne-Gladstone MSS 945, Johnstone to Herbert Gladstone n.d. (but 1932).

163 Tregidga, *Liberal Party in South-West Britain*, p. 83.

164 Johnstone to Lothian 19 Nov. 1934, cited Stannage, *Baldwin Thwarts Opposition*, p. 104.

165 Stannage, *Baldwin Thwarts Opposition*, p. 207.

3   SO FEW AND SO FUTILE, 1935–1955

1 C. Cook, *A Short History of the Liberal Party 1900–1976* (London, 1976), p. 124.

2 M. Steed, 'The Liberal Party' in H. M. Drucker (ed.), *Multi-Party Britain* (London, 1979), p. 76.

3 Churchill College, Cambridge, Thurso MSS II, 71/2, Sinclair to Scott 19 Nov. 1935.

4 T. Wilson, *The Downfall of the Liberal Party 1914–1935* (London, 1966), pp. 377–8.

5 House of Lords Record Office, Lloyd George MSS G/141/28/28, Lothian to Lloyd George 25 Nov. 1935.

6 Flintshire Record Office, Henry Morris Jones MSS 13, diary 10 Nov. 1932.

7 Sinclair to General Secretary, Scottish Liberal Federation 4 Feb. 1937, cited M. Baines, 'The Survival of the British Liberal Party 1932–1959', Oxford, D.Phil., 1991, p. 29.

8   Hammond to Crewe 13 Jan. 1939, cited M. Hart, 'The Decline of the Liberal Party in Parliament and in the Constituencies', Oxford, D.Phil., 1982, p. 91.

9   Baines, 'Survival of the British Liberal Party', p. 138.

10 D. Johnson, *Bars and Barricades* (London, 1952), pp. 73–4.

11 R. Grayson, *Liberals, International Relations and Appeasement: The Liberal Party, 1919–1939* (London, 2001), p. 75.

12 G. De Groot, *Liberal Crusader: The Life of Sir Archibald Sinclair* (London, 1993), p. 114.

13 Horabin to G. White 7 June 1939, cited Baines, 'Survival of the British Liberal Party', p. 46.

14 *Oxford Guardian* 21 Feb. 1939, cited G. Sell, 'Liberal Revival: Jo Grimond and the Politics of British Liberalism 1956–1967', University of London, Ph.D., 1996, p. 16.

15 Baines, 'Survival of the British Liberal Party', p. 40.

16 P. Harris, *Forty Years in and out of Parliament* (London, n.d.), p. 127.

17 M. Pottle (ed.), *Champion Redoubtable: The Diaries and Letters of Violet Bonham Carter 1914–1945* (London, 1998), p. 308.

18 W. Beveridge, *Power and Influence* (London, 1953), p. 350.

19 Baines, 'Survival of the British Liberal Party', pp. 51, 62.

20 Ibid., p. 51; A. Watkins, *The Liberal Dilemma* (London, 1966), p. 42.

21 De Groot, *Liberal Crusader*, p. 206.

22 Morris Jones MSS 24, diary 13 and 28 July 1943.

23 *The Times* 19 July 1943.

24 National Library of Wales, Megan Lloyd George MSS, 20475, C3173, Foot to M. Lloyd George 7 Aug. 1943.

25 National Library of Wales, Clement Davies MSS C/1/16, C. Davies to S. Clement-Davies 3 Nov. 1943.

26 Harris, *Forty Years*, p. 184.

27 Pottle (ed.), *Champion Redoubtable*, p. 312.

28 De Groot, *Liberal Crusader*, p. 215.

29 R. McCallum and A. Readman, *The British General Election of 1945* (Oxford, 1947), p. 61.

30 M. Baines, 'The Liberal Party and the 1945 General Election', *Contemporary Record* 9, 1 (1995), p. 54.

31 McCallum and Readman, *General Election of 1945*, p. 166.

32 De Groot, *Liberal Crusader*, p. 224.

33 Baines, 'Liberal Party and 1945', p. 59.

34 J. Rasmussen, *The Liberal Party: A Study of Retrenchment and Revival* (London, 1965), p. 12.

35 *Liberal Magazine*, Aug. 1945.

36 Baines, 'Liberal Party and 1945', p. 60.

37 J. G. Jones, 'Churchill, Clement Davies and the Ministry of Education', *Journal of Liberal Democrat History* 27 (2000), p. 7.

38 *Liberal Magazine*, Aug. 1946, cited ibid., p. 8.

39 *Montgomeryshire Express* 11 Oct. 1947, cited ibid., p. 8.

40 J. Grimond, *Memoirs* (London, 1979), p. 148.

41 J. Stevenson, *Third Party Politics since 1945: Liberals, Alliance and Liberal Democrats* (Oxford, 1993), p. 33.

42 Davies MSS J/3/26i, Davies to G. Murray 11 May 1950.

43 John Rylands University Library of Manchester, Leonard Behrens MSS 4, V. Bonham Carter to Behrens 4 Apr. 1949.

44 D. Roberts, 'The Strange Death of Liberal Wales' in J. Osmond (ed.), *The National Question Again: Welsh Political Identity in the 1980s* (Llandysul, 1985), p. 80.

45 J. G. Jones, 'The Clement Davies Papers: A Review', *The National Library of Wales Journal*, xxiii, 4 (1984), p. 413.

46 M. Young, *The Chipped White Cups of Dover* (London, 1960), p. 2.

47 Grimond, *Memoirs*, p. 148.

48 R. Garner and R. Kelly, *British Political Parties Today* (Manchester, 1993), p. 204.

49 Johnson, *Bars and Barricades*, p. 285.

50 McCallum and Readman, *General Election of 1945*, pp. 141, 185.

51 R. Douglas, *The History of the Liberal Party, 1895–1970* (London, 1971), p. 253.

52 *The Times* 18 Nov. 1946.

53 Douglas, *Liberal Party*, p. 253.

54 H. Macmillan, *Tides of Fortune* (London, 1969), p. 288.

55 A. Horne, *Macmillan 1894–1956* (London, 1988), p. 298.

56 I. Hunter, 'The Final Quest for Liberal Reunion 1943–46', *Journal of Liberal Democrat History* 32 (2001), pp. 14–16.

57 Macmillan, *Tides of Fortune*, p. 310.

58 *The Times* 27 Nov. 1947.

59 M. Pottle (ed.), *Daring to Hope: The Diaries and Letters of Violet Bonham Carter 1946–1969* (London, 2000), p. 36.

60 Megan Lloyd George MSS 20475, C3168, V. Bonham Carter to M. Lloyd George 17 Nov. 1947.

61 N. Nicolson (ed.), *Harold Nicolson: Diaries and Letters 1945–62* (London, 1968), pp. 111–12.

62 Pottle (ed.), *Daring to Hope*, p. 28.

63 *Western Morning News* 12 Jan. 1949.
64 Megan Lloyd George MSS 20475, C3174, Foot to Lloyd George 15 Aug. 1949.
65 Davies MSS J/3/4 and 6, V. Bonham Carter to Davies 2 and 9 May 1949.
66 The Liberal Nationals were renamed National Liberals in 1948.
67 H. G. Nicholas, *The British General Election of 1950* (London, 1951), pp. 83–4.
68 Watkins, *Liberal Dilemma*, p. 50.
69 Nicholas, *General Election of 1950*, pp. 83–4.
70 Davies MSS J/3/12, Davies to Sinclair 17 Jan. 1950.
71 Ibid., J/3/10, Davies to Sinclair 6 Jan. 1950.
72 Pottle (ed.), *Daring to Hope*, p. 75.
73 Lord Kilmuir, *Political Adventure* (London, 1964), p. 170.
74 Davies MSS J/3/25i, G. Murray to Davies 10 May 1950.
75 Nicholas, *General Election of 1950*, p. 299.
76 J. Thorpe, *In My Own Time: Reminiscences of a Liberal Leader* (London, 1999), p. 94.
77 Pottle (ed.), *Daring to Hope*, p. 84.
78 Nicolson (ed.), *Harold Nicolson: Diaries and Letters*, p. 188.
79 S. Ball (ed.), *Parliament and Politics in the Age of Churchill and Attlee: The Headlam Diaries 1935–1951* (London, 1999), p. 615.
80 M. Gilbert, *Winston S. Churchill*, vol. 8 (London, 1988), p. 529.
81 House of Commons Debates, 5th Series, vol. 472, col. 592.
82 *The Times* 1 and 3 May 1950.
83 Ibid., 17 Apr. 1950.
84 Davies MSS J/3/23, Sinclair to Davies 3 May 1950.
85 Pottle (ed.), *Daring to Hope*, p. 83.
86 Macmillan, *Tides of Fortune*, p. 318.
87 N. Fisher, *Harold Macmillan* (London, 1982), p. 132.
88 A. Howard, *RAB: The Life of R. A. Butler* (London, 1987), p. 170.
89 Ibid., pp. 168–71.
90 Davies MSS C/1/54, 'Liberal position as put by me to Mr Winston Churchill and Lord Woolton', n.d.
91 Ibid., J/3/45, Davies to V. Bonham Carter 15 Nov. 1950.
92 Ibid., J/4/17, Davies to Churchill 4 May 1950.
93 Ibid., J/3/43, V. Bonham Carter to Davies 27 Oct. 1950.
94 D. Butler, *The British General Election of 1951* (London, 1952), pp. 94–95.
95 Ibid., pp. 146–47.

96 M. McManus, *Jo Grimond: Towards the Sound of Gunfire* (Edinburgh, 2001), p. 92.
97 Davies MSS J/3/58, Teviot to Davies 4 Oct. 1951.
98 Gilbert, *Churchill*, vol. 8, p. 646.
99 *The Times* 27 Oct. 1951.
100 *Manchester Guardian* 27 Oct. 1951.
101 Butler, *General Election of 1951*, pp. 242, 266–7.
102 Macmillan, *Tides of Fortune*, pp. 360–1.
103 Jones, 'Churchill, Davies and Education', pp. 6–14.
104 *News Chronicle* 29 Oct. 1951.
105 *The Times* 19 May 1952.
106 Davies MSS J/3/67i, Davies to G. Murray 15 Nov. 1951.
107 Ibid., J/3/65, Davies to Murray 9 Nov. 1951.
108 House of Lords Record Office, Samuel MSS, A/155(xiii)161, M. Lloyd George to Samuel 9 Nov. 1951.
109 R. Cockett (ed.), *My Dear Max: The Letters of Brendan Bracken to Lord Beaverbrook 1925–1958* (London, 1990), p. 128.
110 Davies MSS C/1/76.
111 J. Bowle, *Viscount Samuel* (London, 1957), p. 357.
112 Davies MSS J/3/66, Murray to Davies 12 Nov. 1951.
113 D. Wilson, *Gilbert Murray OM 1866–1957* (Oxford, 1987), p. 391.
114 Sell, 'Liberal Revival', p. 51.
115 R.S. Milne and H. C. Mackenzie, *Marginal Seat, 1955: A Study of Voting Behaviour in the Constituency of Bristol North East at the General Election of 1955* (London, 1958), p. 19.
116 Ibid., p. 50.
117 Rasmussen, *Liberal Party*, p. 24.
118 Stevenson, *Third Party Politics*, p. 41.
119 Behrens MSS 4, Behrens to President, Liberal Party Organisation 4 Sept. 1973.

4   TWO STEPS FORWARD AND ONE BACK, 1955–1979

1 M. Pottle (ed.), *Daring to Hope: The Diaries and Letters of Violet Bonham Carter 1946–1969* (London, 2000), pp. 148–51.
2 *The Times* 10 July 1956.
3 B. Pimlott (ed.), *The Political Diary of Hugh Dalton 1918–40, 1945–60* (London, 1986), p. 671.
4 A. Watkins, *The Liberal Dilemma* (London, 1966), p. 82.

5 G. Sell, ' "A Sad Business": The Resignation of Clement Davies', *Journal of Liberal Democrat History* 24 (1999), p. 16.

6 K. Morgan, *The People's Peace* (Oxford, pb. edn., 1992), p. 155.

7 Pottle (ed.), *Daring to Hope,* p. 170.

8 See, for example, John Rylands University Library of Manchester, Leonard Behrens MSS 4, J. MacCullum Scott to Editor, *Liberal News* 9 Nov. 1956.

9 *The Spectator* 29 November 1957, cited G. Sell, 'Liberal Revival: Jo Grimond and the Politics of British Liberalism 1956–1967', University of London Ph.D. (1996), p. 180.

10 Elliot Dodds, 'Liberty and Welfare' in G. Watson (ed.), *The Unservile State* (London, 1957), p. 25.

11 L. Behrens, 'Why Do We Do It?', *The Liberal Forward* 266 (Sept. 1956).

12 M. McManus, *Jo Grimond: Towards the Sound of Gunfire* (Edinburgh, 2001), pp. 107, 119.

13 A. Cyr, *Liberal Party Politics in Britain* (London, 1977), p. 101.

14 *News Chronicle* 29 Mar. 1958, cited McManus, *Grimond,* p. 129.

15 Sell, 'Liberal Revival', p. 95.

16 Cyr, *Liberal Party Politics,* p. 179.

17 J. G. Jones, 'The Liberal Party and Wales, 1945–79', *Welsh History Review* 16, 3 (1993), p. 354.

18 D. Butler and R. Rose, *The British General Election of 1959* (London, 1960), p. 51.

19 R. Douglas, *History of the Liberal Party 1895–1970* (London, 1971), pp. 271–2.

20 *The Times* 17 Mar. 1962.

21 W. Rodgers, *Fourth Among Equals* (London, 2000), p. 40.

22 Jones, 'Liberal Party and Wales', p. 342.

23 Behrens MSS 4, Patrick Lort-Phillips to Harold Granville 6 Apr. 1960.

24 Ibid., memorandum by Grimond 13 Apr. 1961.

25 Pottle (ed.), *Daring to Hope,* p. 242.

26 H. Macmillan, *At the End of the Day* (London, 1973), p. 58.

27 C. Cook and J. Ramsden (eds), *By-Elections in British Politics* (London, 1973), p. 213.

28 Douglas, *Liberal Party,* p. 278.

29 Behrens MSS 4, memorandum by Grimond 13 Apr. 1961.

30 D. Butler and A. King, *The British General Election of 1966* (London, 1966), pp. 74–5.

31 H. Cowie, *Why Liberal* (Harmondsworth, 1964), p. 40.

32 Butler and King, *Election of 1966,* p. 36.

33 Jones, 'Liberal Party and Wales', p. 345.

34 J. Grimond, *Memoirs* (London, 1979), p. 212.

35 Jones, 'Liberal Party and Wales', pp. 346–7.

36 Grimond, *Memoirs*, p. 254.

37 Butler and King, *Election of 1966*, p. 269.

38 Sell, 'Liberal Revival', p. 247.

39 *The Times* 30 Dec. 1968.

40 D. Steel, *Against Goliath: David Steel's Story* (London, 1989), p. 109.

41 D. Steel, *A House Divided: The Lib–Lab Pact and the Future of British Politics* (London, 1980), p. 10.

42 Watkins, *Liberal Dilemma*, p. 109.

43 Ibid., p. 108.

44 J. Tankard, 'The Sutton and Cheam By-election', *Liberal Democrat History Group Newsletter* 14 (Mar. 1997), p. 13.

45 C. Cook, 'The Challengers to the Two-Party System' in C. Cook and J. Ramsden (eds), *Trends in British Politics since 1945* (London, 1978), p. 132.

46 Steel, *Against Goliath*, p. 79.

47 D. Butler and D. Kavanagh, *The British General Election of October 1974* (London, 1975), p. 272.

48 Ibid., p. 285.

49 Steel, *Against Goliath*, pp. 87–8.

50 Steel, *House Divided*, p. 2.

51 Steel, *Against Goliath*, p. 65.

52 *Liberal News*, July 1970, quoted ibid., p. 70.

53 Steel, *House Divided*, p. 16.

54 Ibid., p. 22.

55 Ibid., p. 25.

56 D. Healey, *The Time of My Life* (pb. edn., London, 1990), p. 403.

57 Steel, *House Divided*, p. 153.

58 P. Bartram, *David Steel: His Life and Politics* (London, 1981), p. 161.

59 Ibid., p. 177.

60 M. Steed, 'The Liberal Party', in H. M. Drucker (ed.), *Multi-Party Britain* (London, 1979), p. 106.

61 J. Curtice in V. Bogdanor (ed.), *Liberal Party Politics* (Oxford, 1983), p. 102.

62 A. Butt Philip in ibid., p. 224.

5   A CRACKED MOULD AND A NEW BEGINNING

1 D. Steel, *A House Divided: The Lib–Lab Pact and the Future of British Politics* (London, 1980), p. 160.

2 R. Rose, *Do Parties Make a Difference?* (London, 1980), p. 4.

3 P. Zentner, *Social Democracy in Britain: Must Labour Lose?* (London, 1982), p. 8.

4 R. Jenkins, *A Life at the Centre* (London, 1991), p. 514.

5 Speech at Llandudno Assembly, Sept. 1976.

6 R. Jenkins, *European Diary 1977–1981* (London, 1989), p. 553.

7 D. Owen, *Time to Declare* (London, 1991), p. 428.

8 Ibid., p. 448.

9 Jenkins, *European Diary*, p. 645.

10 Owen, *Time to Declare*, p. 489.

11 Ibid., p. 500.

12 H. Stephenson, *Claret and Chips: The Rise of the SDP* (London, 1982), p. 26.

13 D. Thomson, *The Shocktroops of Pavement Politics? An Assessment of the Influence of Community Politics in the Liberal Party* (Hebden Bridge, 1985), p. 22.

14 J. Josephs, *Inside the Alliance: An Inside Account of the Development and Prospects of the Liberal–SDP Alliance* (London, 1983), p. 86.

15 Jenkins, *Life at the Centre*, p. 587.

16 Owen, *Time to Declare*, p. 653.

17 I. Bradley, *Breaking the Mould? The Birth and Prospects of the Social Democratic Party* (Oxford, 1981), p. 35.

18 Owen, *Time to Declare*, pp. 441, 614, 446.

19 Ibid., p. 522.

20 Ibid., p. 485.

21 Stephenson, *Claret and Chips*, p. 84.

22 Bradley, *Breaking the Mould?* p. 149.

23 Josephs, *Inside the Alliance*, p. 73.

24 University of Liverpool Library, Owen MSS, D709 3/11/1/1, Owen to Geoff White 23 Sept. 1982.

25 Jenkins, *Life at the Centre*, p. 569.

26 I. Crewe and A. King, *SDP: The Birth, Life and Death of the Social Democratic Party* (Oxford, 1995), p. 160.

27 Owen MSS, D709 3/11/1/1, Thomas to Owen 19 Oct. 1981.

28 Ibid., D709 3/11/1/1, Thomas to Jenkins 7 Sept. 1982.

29 Owen, *Time to Declare*, p. 559.

30 I. Bradley, *The Strange Rebirth of Liberal Britain* (London, 1985), p. 4.

31 Owen, *Time to Declare*, pp. 496–7. Critics have argued that Owen's idea of a 'social market economy' was little more than a slogan, designed to differentiate himself from his opponents, whoever they were at any

particular time. See D. Brack, *The Myth of the Social Market: David Owen's Economic Policy* (London, 1989).

32 Crewe and King, *SDP*, p. 289.

33 Owen, *Time to Declare*, p. 507.

34 Ibid., p. 599.

35 Owen MSS, D709 3/11/1/1, Owen to M. Thomas 5 Mar. 1984.

36 Ibid., D709 3/11/1/1, W. Rodgers to Owen 31 Oct. 1985.

37 Ibid., D709 3/11/1/1, Owen to G. Saltmarsh 30 Oct. 1984.

38 Jenkins, *Life at the Centre*, p. 590.

39 Owen MSS, D709 3/11/2/8, Williams to Owen 9 June 1986.

40 Ibid., D709 3/11/2/8, Owen to Rodgers 9 June 1986.

41 Ibid., D709 3/11/2/8, Rodgers to Owen 12 June 1986.

42 Ibid., D709 3/11/2/8, Ashdown to Constituency Party Chairman, copied to Owen 25 June 1986.

43 Jenkins, *Life at the Centre*, p. 603.

44 Owen, *Time to Declare*, p. 682.

45 Ibid., p. 694.

46 D. Steel, *Against Goliath: David Steel's Story* (London, 1989), p. 279.

47 Crewe and King, *SDP*, p. 292.

48 Ibid., p. 298.

49 Owen, *Time to Declare*, p. 724.

50 Crewe and King, *SDP*, p. 416.

51 R. Pitchford and T. Greaves, *Merger: The Inside Story* (London, 1989), p. 134.

52 *The Independent* 7 Sept. 1991, cited S. Ingle, 'Britain's Third Party' in L. Robins, H. Blackmore and R. Pyper (eds), *Britain's Changing Party System* (London, 1994), p. 104.

53 P. Ashdown, *The Ashdown Diaries 1988–1997* (London, 2000), p. 30.

54 D. Butler and D. Kavanagh, *The British General Election of 1992* (Houndmills, 1992), p. 69.

55 Ashdown, *Diaries 1988–1997*, p. 56.

56 P. Ashdown, *The Ashdown Diaries 1997–1999* (London, 2001), p. 493.

57 K. Jefferys, *The Labour Party since 1945* (London, 1993), p. 122.

58 Ashdown, *Diaries 1988–1997*, p. 159.

59 D. Brack and T. Little (eds), *Great Liberal Speeches* (London, 2001), pp. 423–8.

60 Ibid., p. 421.

61 E. Shaw, *The Labour Party since 1945* (Oxford, 1996), p. 199.

62 P. Joyce, *Towards the Sound of Gunfire: A History of the Liberal Democrats* (Dorchester, 1994), p. 62.

63 A. Rawnsley, D. Brack and H. Smith, 'Ashdown as Leader', *Journal of Liberal Democrat History* 30 (2001), p. 7.

64 Ashdown, *Diaries 1988–1997*, p. 273.

65 Ibid., p. 244.

66 Ibid., p. 287.

67 Ibid., p. 324.

68 Ibid., p. 419.

69 Ibid., p. 456.

70 Ibid., pp. 557–8.

71 Ibid., p. 560.

72 Ashdown, *Diaries 1997–1999*, p. 498.

73 A. Rawnsley, *Servants of the People: The Inside Story of New Labour* (London, 2000), p. 199.

74 Ashdown, *Diaries 1997–1999*, p. 3.

75 W. Rodgers, *Fourth Among Equals* (London, 2000), p. 287.

76 P. Joyce, *Realignment of the Left? A History of the Relationship between the Liberal Democrat and Labour Parties* (Houndmills, 1999), p. 297.

77 Ashdown, *Diaries 1997–1999*, p. 30.

78 Ibid., p. 36.

79 Ibid., p. 15.

80 *The Times* 25 July 1997.

81 Rawnsley, Brack and Smith, 'Ashdown as Leader', p. 9.

82 Rodgers, *Fourth Among Equals*, p. 288.

83 Ashdown, *Diaries 1997–1999*, p. 319.

84 Rodgers, *Fourth Among Equals*, p. 293.

85 Brack and Little (eds), *Great Liberal Speeches*, p. 421.

86 Rodgers, *Fourth Among Equals*, p. 289.

87 Brack and Little (eds), *Great Liberal Speeches*, p. 421.

88 Ashdown, *Diaries 1997–1999*, p. 153.

CONCLUSION

1 P. Joyce, *Realignment of the Left? A History of the Relationship between the Liberal Democrat and Labour Parties* (Houndmills, 1999), p. 286.

2 'Lib Dems' New Dawn', *Sunday Times*, 21 Sept. 2003.

3 S. Ingle, 'Britain's Third Party' in L. Robins, H. Blackmore and R. Pyper (eds), *Britain's Changing Party System* (London, 1994), p. 106.

4 P. Ashdown, *The Ashdown Diaries 1997–1999* (London, 2001), p. 504.

GUIDE TO FURTHER READING

The history of the Liberal party over the last hundred years has been covered in a vast array of books and articles and no attempt has been made below to list more than some of the most important works. Readers who wish to keep up to date with an on-going historiography are urged to consult the *Journal of Liberal History*, published by the Liberal Democrat History Group. The same body has produced three valuable works of reference: Duncan Brack (ed.), *Dictionary of Liberal Biography* (1998); Duncan Brack and Robert Ingham (eds), *Dictionary of Liberal Quotations* (1999); and Duncan Brack and Tony Little (eds), *Great Liberal Speeches* (2001). It maintains a website at www.liberalhistory.org.uk

Each work is listed only under the heading where it has been found most useful. Many, however, are relevant to more than one chapter of the book. The place of publication is London unless otherwise indicated.

GENERAL AND INTRODUCTION

Chris Cook, *A Short History of the Liberal Party* was first published in 1976 but successive editions have now taken the story up to 2001. It provides a readable introductory narrative, particularly useful for the party's electoral history. Roy Douglas, *History of the Liberal Party 1895–1970* (1971) contains much of value, but is now somewhat dated and was clearly written from a position of commitment. Alan Sykes, *The Rise and Fall of British Liberalism 1776–1988* (1997) has the advantage of a wide chronological framework. Iain Dale (ed.), *Liberal Party General Election Manifestos, 1900–1997* (2000) provides easy access into important electoral material, while Peter Joyce, *Realignment of the Left? A History of the Relationship between the Liberal Democrat and Labour Parties*

(Houndmills, 1999) usefully considers Liberal–Labour relations over the entire twentieth century. Anthony Howe, *Free Trade and Liberal England, 1846–1946* (Oxford, 1997) expertly charts a key theme. For the origins of the party, John Vincent, *The Formation of the Liberal Party 1857–1868* (1966) remains indispensable. Michael Bentley, *The Climax of Liberal Politics: British Liberalism in Theory and Practice, 1868–1918* (1987) offers much food for thought. The history of nineteenth-century Liberalism falls largely outside the scope of the present work, but readers may be directed to Jonathan Parry, *The Rise and Fall of Liberal Governments in Victorian Britain* (New Haven, CT, 1993), T. A. Jenkins, *The Liberal Ascendancy 1830–1886* (1994), D. A. Hamer, *Liberal Politics in the Age of Gladstone and Rosebery* (Oxford, 1972), Colin Matthew, *The Liberal Imperialists* (Oxford, 1973), Stephen Koss, *Non-conformity in Modern British Politics* (1975) and Peter Stansky, *Ambitions and Strategies: The Struggle for the Leadership of the Liberal Party in the 1890s* (Oxford, 1964).

STRANGE DEATH OR EDWARDIAN SUMMER

George Dangerfield, *The Strange Death of Liberal England* (1935) may be enjoyed as literature, but should also be read – with caution – as history because of the huge impact it has had on later writing. The General Elections of Edwardian England have been well covered by A. K. Russell, *Liberal Landslide: The General Election of 1906* (Newton Abbot, 1973), and Neal Blewett, *The Peers, the Parties and the People: The General Elections of 1910* (1972), while Peter Rowland, *The Last Liberal Governments* (2 vols, 1968 and 1971) offers a solid narrative account of the Liberals in office. For early relations with the embryonic Labour party, reference should still be made to two articles by Frank Bealey: 'The Electoral Arrangements between the LRC and the Liberal Party', *Journal of Modern History* (1956) and 'Negotiations between the Liberals and the LRC before the 1906 Election', *Bulletin of the Institute of Historical Research* (1956). Martin Petter, 'The Progressive Alliance', *History* (1973) offers a broader perspective. For the impact of the New Liberalism, the seminal work is Peter

Clarke's *Lancashire and the New Liberalism* (Cambridge, 1971). Important additional material may be found in the same author's *Liberals and Social Democrats* (Cambridge, 1978) and in Michael Freeden, *The New Liberalism: An Ideology of Social Reform* (Oxford, 1978). George Bernstein, *Liberalism and Liberal Politics in Edwardian England* (1986), Keith Laybourn and Jack Reynolds, *Liberalism and the Rise of Labour 1890–1918* (1984) and David Powell, 'The New Liberalism and the Rise of Labour, 1886–1906', *Historical Journal* (1986) offer much less optimistic interpretations of Liberalism's fortunes in the face of the rise of a new political party. Though their primary focus is not the Liberal party, Ross McKibbin, *The Evolution of the Labour Party 1910–1924* (Oxford, 1974) and Duncan Tanner, *Political Change and the Labour Party 1900–1918* (Cambridge, 1990) are key works within the historiographical debate.

Among significant monographs relating to the Edwardian era, mention should be made of Bruce Murray, *The People's Budget 1909–10* (Oxford 1980), H. V. Emy, *Liberals, Radicals and Social Politics, 1892–1914* (Cambridge, 1973), and Ian Packer, *Lloyd George, Liberalism and the Land: The Land Issue and Party Politics in England, 1906–1914* (Woodbridge, 2001). K. D. Brown (ed.), *Essays in Anti-Labour History* (1974), Alan O'Day (ed.), *The Edwardian Age: Conflict and Stability 1900–1914* (1979), Henry Pelling, *Popular Politics and Society in Late Victorian Britain* (1968) and Alan Sked and Chris Cook (eds), *Crisis and Controversy: Essays in Honour of A. J. P. Taylor* (1976) all contain important essays. If the reader remains confused by the diversity of interpretations of the Liberal party's fortunes, reference may profitably be made to G. R. Searle, *The Liberal Party: Triumph and Disintegration, 1886–1929* (Houndmills, 1992). Searle writes lucidly, carries his learning lightly and offers a balanced and persuasive account. Keith Laybourn, 'The Rise of Labour and the Decline of Liberalism: The State of the Debate', *History* (1995) is also helpful.

Among the biographies of Liberal leaders, John Wilson, *C. B. – A Life of Sir Henry Campbell-Bannerman* (1973) should be supplemented by José Harris and Cameron Hazlehurst, 'Campbell-Bannerman as Prime Minister', *History* (1970). Roy Jenkins,

Asquith (1964) and Stephen Koss, *Asquith* (1976) paint rather different pictures from one another. See also Cameron Hazlehurst, 'Asquith as Prime Minister, 1908–1916', *English Historical Review* (1970). Lloyd George has been undergoing multi-volume biographical treatment à la Churchill. That by John Grigg (4 vols, 1973–2002) has reached 1918 but will not now be completed, unless by another hand, because of the author's untimely death. Bentley Gilbert's two volumes have reached 1916: *David Lloyd George: The Architect of Change 1863–1912* (1987) and *David Lloyd George: Organizer of Victory 1912–1916* (1992). Pending completion, the best, if somewhat plodding, single-volume life is probably Peter Rowland, *Lloyd George* (1975), although both Martin Pugh, *Lloyd George* (1988) and Chris Wrigley, *Lloyd George* (1992) managed to say a lot within a small compass. Kenneth Morgan, *The Age of Lloyd George: The Liberal Party and British Politics, 1890–1929* (1971) also deserves to be mentioned.

Historians of this period are fortunate in the number of important diaries and collections of letters that have been published. These include: Mark Bonham Carter and Mark Pottle (eds), *Lantern Slides: The Diaries and Letters of Violet Bonham Carter 1904–1914* (1996); Michael and Eleanor Brock (eds), *H. H. Asquith: Letters to Venetia Stanley* (Oxford, 1982); Edward David (ed.), *Inside Asquith's Cabinet: From the Diaries of Charles Hobhouse* (1977); David Dutton (ed.), *Odyssey of an Edwardian Liberal: The Political Diary of Richard Durning Holt* (Gloucester, 1989); Cameron Hazlehurst and Christine Woodland (eds), *A Liberal Chronicle: Journals and Papers of J. A. Pease, 1908 to 1910* (1994); John McEwen (ed.), *The Riddell Diaries: A Selection* (1986); Kenneth Morgan (ed.), *Lloyd George: Family Letters 1885–1936* (Cardiff, 1973); and Trevor Wilson (ed.), *The Political Diaries of C. P. Scott 1911–1928* (1970).

Trevor Wilson, *The Downfall of the Liberal Party 1914–1935* (1966) remains the best starting point for an examination of the impact of the First World War on Liberal politics. But its argument is now somewhat dated and some of its analysis should be treated with care. Cameron Hazlehurst, *Politicians at War: July 1914 to May 1915* (1971) offers a microscopic study of Liberal high politics in the early months of the war, while Martin Pugh, 'Asquith,

Bonar Law and the First Coalition', *Historical Journal* (1974) presents a convincing explanation of the end of Britain's last Liberal government. Michael Fry, 'Political Change in Britain, August 1914 to December 1916: Lloyd George Replaces Asquith: The Issues Underlying the Drama', *Historical Journal* (1988) and John McEwen, 'The Struggle for Mastery in Britain: Lloyd George Versus Asquith, December 1916', *Journal of British Studies* (1978) seek to explain Lloyd George's rise to the premiership.

THE LIBERAL CIVIL WAR

The most useful works on the second half of the First World War are John Turner, *British Politics and the Great War: Coalition and Conflict 1915–1918* (New Haven, CT, 1992), Edward David, 'The Liberal Party Divided 1916–1918', *Historical Journal* (1970) and Barry McGill, 'Asquith's Predicament, 1914–1918', *Journal of Modern History* (1967). Michael Hart's unpublished Oxford D.Phil. thesis, 'The Decline of the Liberal Party in Parliament and in the Constituencies' (1982) is indispensable and carries the story beyond the end of hostilities. The controversy over the 'franchise factor' may be followed in H. C. G. Matthew, R. I. McKibbin and J. A. Kay, 'The Franchise Factor in the Rise of the Labour Party', *English Historical Review* (1976), Duncan Tanner, 'The Parliamentary Electoral System, the "Fourth" Reform Act and the Rise of Labour in England and Wales', *Bulletin of the Institute of Historical Research* (1983) and Michael Hart, 'The Liberals, the War and the Franchise', *English Historical Review* (1982). Michael Childs, 'Labour Grows Up: The Electoral System, Political Generations and British Politics 1890–1929', *Twentieth Century British History* (1995) adds usefully to the debate. Roy Douglas, 'The Background to the "Coupon" Election Arrangements', *English Historical Review* (1971) clarifies arrangements surrounding the 1918 General Election. Kenneth Morgan, *Consensus and Disunity: The Lloyd George Coalition Government 1918–1922* (Oxford, 1979) is likely to remain the standard work on the postwar coalition, but see also Chris Wrigley, *David Lloyd George and the British Labour Movement* (Hassocks, 1976) and the same author's *Lloyd George and the Challenge of Labour: The Post War Coalition 1918–1922* (Hemel Hempstead, 1990). Lloyd George's loss of office is dealt with in Michael Kinnear, *The Fall of Lloyd George: The Political Crisis of 1922* (1973).

For Liberal thought in the interwar years, see Michael Bentley, *The Liberal Mind 1914–1929* (Cambridge, 1977) and Michael Freeden, *Liberalism Divided: A Study in British Political Thought* (Oxford, 1986). Chris Cook, *The Age of Alignment: Electoral Politics in Britain 1922–1929* (1975) explores the Liberal party's decline at the ballot box and there is much useful material in John Campbell, *Lloyd George: The Goat in the Wilderness 1922–1931* (1977), though not all will find his argument totally convincing. There are important essays in A. J. P. Taylor (ed.), *Lloyd George: Twelve Essays* (1971), Gillian Peele and Chris Cook (eds), *The Politics of Reappraisal 1918–1939* (1975) and Don Cregier, *Chiefs without Indians* (Washington, 1982). The Liberal role in the formation of the National Government may be traced in Philip Williamson, *National Crisis and National Government: British Politics, the Economy and Empire 1926–32* (Cambridge, 1992), while the General Elections of 1931 and 1935 are well covered by Andrew Thorpe, *The British General Election of 1931* (Oxford, 1991) and Tom Stannage, *Baldwin Thwarts the Opposition* (1980) respectively. David Dutton, '1932: A Neglected Date in the History of the Decline of the British Liberal Party', *Twentieth Century British History* (2003) argues for the importance of the split with the Liberal Nationals. Revealing light is thrown on Lloyd George's continuing role in Liberal politics by A. J. P. Taylor (ed.), *Lloyd George: A Diary by Frances Stevenson* (1971) and *My Darling Pussy: The Letters of Lloyd George and Frances Stevenson 1913–41* (1975). The privately published Vivian Phillipps, *My Days and Ways* (c. 1943) sees matters from a different perspective.

SO FEW AND SO FUTILE, 1935–1955

The period of Liberal impotence is inevitably less well covered but some important works have been written. Malcolm Baines, 'The Survival of the British Liberal Party 1932–1959', Oxford D.Phil.

(1991) remains unfortunately unpublished, but is indispensable. His argument is summarised in a chapter of the same title in A. Gorst, L. Johnman and W. S. Lucas (eds), *Contemporary British History, 1931–61: Politics and the Limits of Policy* (1991). Two recent works have illuminated different aspects of the 1930s: Richard Grayson, *Liberals, International Relations and Appeasement: The Liberal Party, 1919–1939* (2001) and Garry Tregidga, *The Liberal Party in South West Britain since 1918: Political Decline, Dormancy and Rebirth* (Exeter, 2000). Successive Liberal leaders of this period have been well served by their biographers: Bernard Wasserstein, *Herbert Samuel: A Political Life* (Oxford, 1992); Gerard De Groot, *Liberal Crusader: The Life of Sir Archibald Sinclair* (1993); and David Roberts, 'Clement Davies and the Liberal Party, 1929–56', University of Wales M. A. thesis (1975), supplemented by several articles by J. Graham Jones listed in the notes of this book. Alun Wyburn-Powell, *Clement Davies: Liberal Leader* (2003) appeared after the present work was completed. For relations with the Liberal Nationals see David Dutton, *Simon: A Political Biography of Sir John Simon* (1992) and, by the same author, 'John Simon and the Post-War National Liberal Party: An Historical Postscript', *Historical Journal* (1989). John Vincent has found interesting information about the outbreak of the Second World War: 'Chamberlain, the Liberals and the Outbreak of War, 1939', *English Historical Review* (1998). John Stevenson provides an accessible introduction to the postwar era in *Third Party Politics since 1945: Liberals, Alliance and Liberal Democrats* (Oxford, 1993), but this does not entirely replace Jorgen Rasmussen, *The Liberal Party: A Study of Retrenchment and Revival* (1965) which remains of value. David Dutton, 'On the Brink of Oblivion: The Post-War Crisis of British Liberalism', *Canadian Journal of History* (1992) analyses the threat to Liberal independence in the years after 1945. For the whole of the period since the war, the Nuffield General Election studies are invaluable. The memoirs of Percy Harris, *Forty Years in and out of Parliament* (*c.* 1947), the biography of Megan Lloyd George, Mervyn Jones, *A Radical Life* (1991) and the published diaries of Violet Bonham Carter, Mark Pottle (ed.), *Champion Redoubtable: The Diaries and Letters of Violet Bonham Carter*

1914–1945 (1998) and *Daring to Hope: The Diaries and Letters of Violet Bonham Carter 1946–1969* (2000) may all be used with profit.

TWO STEPS FORWARD AND ONE BACK, 1955–1979

Vernon Bogdanor (ed.), *Liberal Party Politics* (Oxford, 1983) contains an important collection of essays. Michael Steed, 'The Liberal Party' in H. M. Drucker (ed.), *Multi-Party Britain* (1979) is also worth reading. Two significant studies have appeared recently on the Grimond era. Michael McManus, *Jo Grimond: Towards the Sound of Gunfire* (Edinburgh, 2001) and Geoffrey Sell, 'Liberal Revival: Jo Grimond and the Politics of British Liberalism 1956–1967', University of London Ph.D. (1996) are both scholarly and perceptive. Grimond's own *Memoirs* (1979) offer only occasional insights. The leadership of Jeremy Thorpe is, as yet, less well served. Lewis Chester, Magnus Linklater and David May, *Jeremy Thorpe: A Secret Life* (1979) is journalistic, but contains some useful information. The same is true of Simon Freeman and Barrie Penrose, *Rinkagate: The Rise and Fall of Jeremy Thorpe* (1996). Thorpe's reminiscences, *In My Own Time: Reminiscences of a Liberal Leader* (1999) are largely inconsequential. David Thomson considers the rise of community politics in *The Shocktroops of Pavement Politics? An Assessment of the Influence of Community Politics in the Liberal Party* (Hebden Bridge, 1985). Alan Watkins, *The Liberal Dilemma* (1966) is now interesting largely as a period piece. Very much in that mould and helpful therefore for the evolution of Liberal thought are Harry Cowie, *Why Liberal?* (Harmondsworth, 1964) and George Watson (ed.), *The Unservile State: Essays in Liberty and Welfare* (1957). David Steel has, so far, largely been his own historian. *Against Goliath: David Steel's Story* (1989) surveys his career as a whole, while *A House Divided: The Lib–Lab Pact and the Future of British Politics* (1980) is important for the period of co-operation with the Callaghan government. For this, see also Alistair Michie and Simon Hoggart, *The Pact: The Inside Story of the Lib–Lab Government, 1977–8* (1978). Peter Bartram, *David Steel: His Life and Politics* (1981) adds little.

A CRACKED MOULD AND A NEW BEGINNING, 1979–2001

Not surprisingly, there is a dearth of quality monographs relating to the last quarter-century. A shining exception is Ivor Crewe and Anthony King, *SDP: The Birth, Life and Death of the Social Democratic Party* (Oxford, 1995) in which the authors combine scholarship with much inside information. Earlier works such as Ian Bradley, *Breaking the Mould? The Birth and Prospects of the Social Democratic Party* (Oxford, 1981), Jeremy Josephs, *Inside the Alliance: An Inside Account of the Development and Prospects of the Liberal–SDP Alliance* (1983) and Hugh Stephenson, *Claret and Chips: The Rise of the SDP* (1982) remain valuable. The fusion of the Liberals and the SDP is chronicled from an admittedly hostile standpoint in Rachael Pitchford and Tony Greaves, *Merger: The Inside Story* (Hebden Bridge, 1989). The best work so far on the Liberal Democrats is Don MacIver (ed.), *The Liberal Democrats* (1996). But see also Peter Joyce, *Towards the Sound of Gunfire: A History of the Liberal Democrats* (Dorchester, 1994). Fortunately, while further academic analysis is awaited, the historian has at his disposal several important memoirs and diaries. Among these are David Owen, *Time to Declare* (1991), Roy Jenkins, *A Life at the Centre* (1991), Bill Rodgers, *Fourth Among Equals* (2000), Roy Jenkins, *European Diary 1977–1981* (1989) and Paddy Ashdown, *The Ashdown Diaries* (2 vols, 2000–1).This material is bound to grow considerably in the years to come, not least once the 'project' is chronicled from a New Labour perspective.

Appendix: The Liberal Performance at General Elections in the Twentieth Century

Year	A	B	C	D
1900	670	406	184	44.6
1906	670	539	400	49.0
Jan. 1910	670	516	275	43.2
Dec. 1910	670	467	272	43.9
1918a	707	411	161	25.6
1922a	615	490	116	29.1
1923	615	453	159	29.6
1924	615	340	40	17.6
1929	615	513	59	23.4
1931b	615	119	37	7.0
1935b	615	161	21	6.4
1945	640	306	12	9.0
1950	625	475	9	9.1
1951	625	109	6	2.6
1955	630	110	6	2.7
1959	630	216	6	5.9
1964	630	365	9	11.2
1966	630	311	12	8.5
1970	630	332	6	7.5
Feb. 1974	635	517	14	19.3
Oct. 1974	635	619	13	18.3
1979	635	577	11	13.8
1983c	650	633	23	25.4
1987c	650	633	22	22.6
1992d	651	632	20	17.8
1997d	659	639	46	17
2001d	659	639	52	18.3

Key:
A   Number of seats in the House of Commons
B   Number of Liberal candidates
C   Number of Liberal MPs elected
D   Liberal percentage of the total vote
Notes:
aFigures for supporters of Lloyd George and Asquith are combined.
bExcludes Liberal Nationals but includes followers of Lloyd George.
cIncludes figures for Social Democrat wing of the Alliance.
dThe Liberal Democrats.

INDEX